Shaping the Great City

Modern Architecture in Central Europe, 1890–1937

Edited by
Eve Blau and Monika Platzer

In association with
the Bundesministerium für Unterricht und Kulturelle Angelegenheiten, Vienna,
the Canadian Centre for Architecture, Montréal,
and the Getty Research Institute, Los Angeles

With contributions by
Friedrich Achleitner, Renate Banik-Schweitzer, Eve Blau,
Iain Boyd Whyte, Moritz Csáky, András Ferkai, János Gerle, Andrew Herscher,
Petr Krajči, Aleksander Laslo, Charles S. Maier, Breda Mihelič, Ileana Pintilie,
Monika Platzer, Jacek Purchla, Rostislav Švácha, Ihor Žuk

Prestel
Munich · London · New York

Editors: Eve Blau, Monika Platzer
Project coordination: Lesley Johnstone
Editing: Klaus Spechtenhauser
Coordination: Isabella Marte

Translations:
Elisabeth Frank-Großebner (Hungarian-German)
Waltraud Göschl (Russian-German)
Klaus Spechtenhauser (Czech-German)
Irena Steiner (Croatian-German)
Annette Wiethüchter (English-German)
Christiane Court (English-German)
John W. Gabriel (German-English)
Rosemarie Baines (German-English)
John Tingley (German-English)

Photographs:
Friedrich Achleitner
Gábor Barka
Miroslav Beneš
Herman Czech
Istvá Füzi
Karel Šabata
Zoltán Seidner
Judit Szalatnyay
Petru Teleaga

Published by Prestel in association with the Bundesministerium für Unterricht
und Kulturelle Angelegenheiten, Vienna, The Canadian Centre for Architecture,
Montréal, and The Getty Research Institute, Los Angeles.

Jacket images: Otto Wagner, Die Großstadt, 1911 (see p. 79)
Slavko Löwy, Radovan Residential and Business Premises, Zagreb,
1933–34 (see p. 194)

Library of Congress Card Number: 99-067782

Die Deutsche Bibliothek – CIP Cataloguing in Publication Data
A catalogue credit for this publication is available from Die Deutsche Bibliothek

Prestel-Verlag, Mandlstraße 26, D-80802 Munich, Germany
Tel.: (89) 38-17-09-0, Fax: (89) 38-17-09-35
4 Bloomsbury Place, London, WC1A 2QA
Tel.: (171) 323 5004, Fax: (171) 636 8004
16 West 22 Street, New York, NY 10010
Tel.: (212) 627 8199, Fax: (212) 627 9866
Prestel books are available worldwide. Please contact your nearest bookseller or
any of the above addresses for information concerning your local distributor.

Edited by Kate Ferry-Swainson; Karina Horitz; Balázs Kicsiny

Designed by Rainald Schwarz, Munich
Typesetting by Setzerei Vornehm, Munich
Color separations by eurocrom 4, Villorba
Printed by Pera Druck, Gräfelfing
Bound by Almesberger, Salzburg
Printed on chlorine-free bleached paper

Printed in Germany

ISBN 3-7913-2151-X (English hardback edition)
ISBN 3-7913-2185-4 (German hardback edition)
ISBN 3-7913-2358-X (English paperback edition)
ISBN 3-7913-2357-1 (German paperback edition)

Contents

FOREWORD

This publication appears in conjunction with an exhibition jointly organized by the Bundesministerium für Unterricht und Kulturelle Angelegenheiten, Vienna, the Canadian Centre for Architecture, Montréal, and the Getty Research Institute, Los Angeles, in association with the Kunstforum Wien. It looks at modern architecture and the city in a vast geographical area over nearly fifty years of tumultuous social and political change; at regional trends which are only now beginning to be researched; and at local developments upon which transnational discussion and inquiry is only now emerging.

From the start, we have seen *Shaping the Great City: Modern Architecture in Central Europe, 1890–1937* less as a definitive study than as a way to suggest avenues for research and to open discussion of the central issues it raises: How did modern architecture construct "meaning" in relation to the complex cultural traditions, conflicting political agendas, and historical narratives of modernizing urban society in the cities of Central Europe? What role did the cities themselves—as the principal arenas of public culture in the multinational empire and successor republics—play in the evolution of modern architectural culture? These questions remain pertinent to the current relationship between cities and the increasingly diverse cultures within them, and to the role of the great city today in the age of globalization.

A steering committee from the participating institutions, Dieter Bogner for the Bundesministerium für Unterricht und Kulturelle Angelegenheiten, Wim de Wit of the Getty Research Institute, Eve Blau and Nicholas Olsberg for the Canadian Centre for Architecture, has guided the project from its inception in 1992. The project began with an intensive research phase, completed in April 1996, directed by Anthony Alofsin and organized in collaboration with the Internationale Forschungszentrum für Kulturwissenschaft, Vienna. During the three years of this exploratory work, critical lines of inquiry, archives, and scholarly resources were identified. This first research phase benefited from the counsel of an advisory panel consisting of Eduard F. Sekler, Otto Antonia Graf, Paul Asenbaum, Ákos Moravánsky, and August Sarnitz, and from an extensive research team, which included Matúš Dulla, Rudolf Klein, Petr Krajči, Aleksander Laslo, Christopher Long, Henrieta H. Moravčíková, Marco Pozzetto, Damjan Prelovšek, Monika Platzer, Jacek Purchla, Rostislav Švácha, Ilona Sármány-Parsons, and Ihor Žuk. Late in 1996, the steering committee widened the scope and structure of the project and invited Eve Blau, Dieter Bogner, and Monika Platzer to develop and curate an exhibition which, under their direction, would focus on the city and urban architecture. Eve Blau and Monika Platzer also developed the scope and framework of this publication and served as its editors.

In preparing the final exhibition and publication, the curatorial team has worked with a number of scholars in Central Europe, who have generously shared information and expertise and directed the curators to source material. For their essential collaboration during this development phase we thank András Ferkai, János Gerle, Andras Hadik, Andrew Herscher, Andrej Hrausky, Rudolf Klein, Petr Krajči, Aleksander Laslo, Christopher Long, Breda Mihelič, Ileana Pintilie, Jacek Purchla, Rostislav Švácha, and Ihor Žuk—many of whose investigations appear here in published form. The other contributors to this volume—Friedrich Achleitner, Renate Banik-Schweitzer, Moritz Csáky, and Charles S. Maier—have also been involved in helping to formulate the concept and ideas of both book and exhibition.

The exhibition would have been impossible without the help of Elisabeth Gehrer of the Bundesministerium, the generosity of its many lenders, and the support of governments at all levels in the twelve countries involved. Silvia Burner has coordinated the unusually complex production of the exhibition on behalf of the Kunstforum Wien. Thanks are also due to Irene Martin and Quincy Houghton of the J. Paul Getty Museum, Wim de Wit, Julia Bloomfield, and Barbara Anderson of the Getty Research Institute, Helen Malkin, Lesley Johnstone, and Anne Troise of the Canadian Centre for Architecture, and Christine Hopf of the Bundesministerium.

For serving as hosts to the exhibition we are very grateful to František Laudát and Dušan Seidl of the Municipal House, Prague, Klaus Albrecht Schröder and Evelyn Benesch of the Kunstforum Wien, and John Walsh and Deborah Gribbon of the J. Paul Getty Museum, Los Angeles—who have helped guide this project to its final form.

Finally we would like to extend our thanks to the curators of *Shaping the Great City*, Eve Blau, Dieter Bogner, and Monika Platzer, for their dedication to a project of daunting proportions. This book is evidence of their great success in making a subject so complex more comprehensible.

Phyllis Lambert
Kurt W. Forster
Canadian Centre for Architecture, Montréal

Deborah Marrow
Getty Research Institute, Los Angeles

Rudolf Wran
Bundesministerium für Unterricht und Kulturelle Angelegenheiten, Vienna

THE CULTURAL SPACE
OF CENTRAL EUROPE

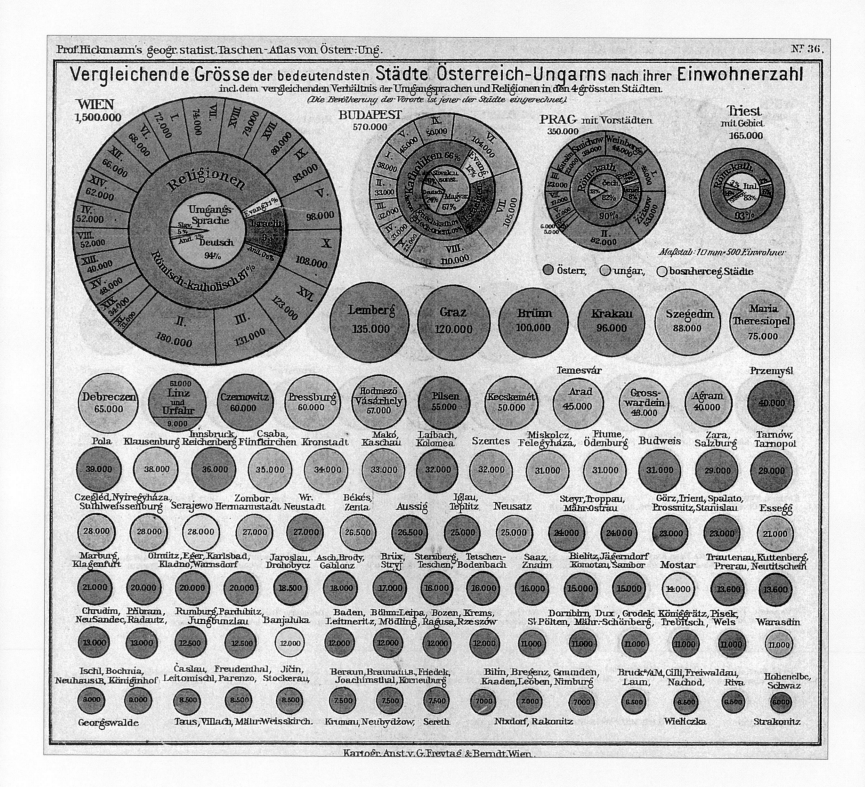

Vergleichende Grösse der bedeutendsten Städte Österreich-Ungarns nach ihrer Einwohnerzahl
incl. dem vergleichenden Verhältnis der Umgangsprachen und Religionen in den 4 grössten Städten.
(Die Bevölkerung der Vororte ist jener der Städte eingerechnet.)

THE CITY AS PROTAGONIST: ARCHITECTURE AND THE CULTURES OF CENTRAL EUROPE

Eve Blau

...We must take the search for a Hungarian language of form seriously. Rapid developments in technology, new feats in engineering...have created a great stir in architecture. This new shift in evolution gives us an excellent opportunity to incorporate our national character in a new language of form and in architecture.

Ödön Lechner, 1906[1]

...The artistic expression of architectural works must be similar in every center of culture, since the way of life and the system of government are similar. If we accept this argument, we should realize that a national style cannot exist.

Otto Wagner, 1915[2]

For architects in Central Europe seeking to shape a modern architecture in the last decades of the Habsburg Empire and first years of the new republics that succeeded it, it was necessary to stake out a position not only in relation to the historical moment, that is, to time, but also in relation to place. For the Hungarian architect Ödön Lechner, charting a new direction for contemporary architecture necessitated a break not only with the past and the historicism of late nineteenth-century academic practice, but also with the center: with Vienna and the dominant German culture of the capital, of which the heavy neo-Baroque and neo-Renaissance forms of the empire's public architecture were the official architectural expression. The creative locus of the new architecture that Lechner discovered was Hungarian national culture, for which Magyar folk art, with imagined pre-Christian Asian origins in Persia and India, was considered an authentic source. For the Viennese architect Otto Wagner, by contrast, the locus of the new architecture was not the nation but the *Großstadt*—the great city—and the cosmopolitan culture of the modern metropolis. In the context of late Habsburg central Europe, both Lechner's "nation" and Wagner's deracinated "cosmopolis" were utopias that existed principally in the ideological force-field defined by the opposing claims of supranational empire and self-determining peoples which polarized Austro-Hungarian political life in the period preceding World War I.

This book and the exhibition it documents propose that it was in the lived cities of the region that the conflicting aspirations of empire and people, and the intersecting trajectories of urban modernization and national autonomy gave shape to a modern architectural culture, one that was deeply rooted in place and in a conception of the great city as a protagonist in the making of history. In the late nineteenth century, the cities of Habsburg central Europe were the sites of modernization where industry and finance were concentrated. But they were also its places of history, accretions of the accumulated knowledges, memories, and skills of the empire's multinational, polyethnic, and pluricultural urban societies. As administrative and cultural centers of the multinational empire, they had translocal—even transnational—identities and significance. To build in them, therefore, was not only to shape the spaces of modern urban life but to engage the history of their imbricated fabric; it was to enter into debate with, and question the authority of the forces that had shaped them. Architecture, during the nearly fifty-year period of intensifying political conflict and radical social transformation covered by this volume, was therefore charged not only with producing the spaces of the emerging culture of the modern city, but also with constructing meaning in relation to its complex multinational history, diverse cultural traditions, conflicting political agendas and identities. By taking the city and urban architecture as its subject, the exhibition attempts to re-engage the debates of that moment, both to show the extraordinary diversity and richness of architectural responses to the lived experience of modernizing urban society in central Europe, and because the metropoles, as the principal arenas of public culture in the multinational empire and successor republics, provide a framework for addressing questions regarding the complex interrelation of architecture, ideology, and urban history central to an understanding of the emerging architectural culture of this region.[3]

The Habsburg-ruled cities of central Europe, as Charles Maier points out in this volume, had a special role as the places where the imperial met the local. They also fulfilled specific local and central functions. In 1908 the empire covered some 676,000 square kilometers and encompassed almost all of eastern Central Europe. By the end of 1910 it had 51.4 million inhabitants representing eleven major linguistically defined nationalities—Germans, Magyars, Czechs, Poles, Ukrainians, Serbs, Croats, Romanians, Slovaks, Slovenes, Italians—and several times as many minor nationalities. This was the second largest land area in Europe and the third largest population (after Russia and Germany). Administratively the Habsburg lands were divided by the terms of the *Ausgleich* or Compromise Agreement of 1867 into two associated states: the Austrian Monarchy (Cisleithania, which included the German-speaking Austrian lands, Bohemia, Moravia, Silesia, Galicia, Bukovina, Istria, Dalmatia, and Slovenia-Carniola represented in the Vienna Reichsrat) and the Kingdom of Hungary (Transleithania, including Croatia-Slavonia, Transylvania, and all other "historic" lands of the Holy Crown of St. Stephen).[4]

By the dawn of the twentieth century, Vienna, the economic and administrative center of Austria-Hungary with more than two million inhabitants, had become one of the world's largest cities. Metropolitan Budapest, the administrative, financial, and cultural center in which trade, industry, and transport were concentrated in the Hungarian lands, had a population of almost one million.[5] These capital cities were physically linked to each other and to the capitals of the provincial crown lands: Prague (Bohemia), Brünn/Brno (Moravia), Lemberg/Ľviv (Galicia), Agram/Zagreb (Croatia-Slavonia), Laibach/Ljubljana (Carniola), Czernowitz/Černivci (Bukovina), and Hermannstadt/Nagyszeben (Transylvania), among others, by a dense network of railway lines, the major ones built in 1836–75.[6] They were also bound by a large and intricately interwoven imperial bureaucracy that performed essential administrative functions and constituted the core of the German-speaking *Bildungsbürgertum*, the educated middle classes of the crown land capitals, peripheral urban centers, and garrison towns of the empire.[7] Many of these provincial capitals, in particular Kraków, Prague, Ljubljana, and Zagreb, were also important "national" cultural capitals, vested with the history and memory of the (non-German) Polish, Czech, Slovene, and Croatian subject peoples of those crown lands. In the nineteenth century Ľviv, Černivci, Ljubljana, and Zagreb also became important university towns.[8]

Through much of the nineteenth century the crown was the principal client for major cultural initiatives, including large-scale modernization and urban architectural projects. In Austria-Hungary official buildings were approved by the imperial government and in many cases designed by "official" architects in the building departments of various ministries responsible for public building and planning projects. The network of railway stations, administrative buildings, cultural institutions, and broad new ring-boulevards with attendant parks, built (often on the foundations of razed city walls) in the 1870s and 1880s in cities across the empire—from Ľviv and Černivci to Kraków and Zagreb—attest to the imperial effort to meld the peripheral urban centers of the ethnically diverse state into a homogeneous civilization. Theaters, concert halls, and opera houses, courthouses, museums, and universities, often designed by architects with empire-wide practices, also served to imprint these far flung "centers" with the distinctive spatial hierarchies, patterns of building, repertory of public institutional buildings, and historicist styles of the center. The Viennese firm of Fellner and Helmer, for example, built theaters, concert halls, and opera houses in almost every major town in both parts of the monarchy.[9] Until well after 1850 cities in Bohemia, Moravia, Slovenia-Carniola, Hungary, Transylvania, Galicia, and Bukovina were not only oriented toward Vienna but were also almost all German in language as well as culture.[10] They were thus enclaves, separated by their urban culture as well as by language from the surrounding Magyar, Czech, Slovak, Ukrainian, or Romanian rural peasantry. By the 1890s, however, both their physical aspect and their ethnic composition had radically changed.

Economic modernization began late in Austria-Hungary, considerably later than in Germany and France. It was held back by several factors. One was a lack of liquid capital for industrial development, resulting in part from the fact that banks preferred to lend to the state and the aristocracy whose wealth was tied up in land and who tended to be suspicious of industrial development. Another was the relatively late construction of railway lines connecting the empire's coal-producing with its steel-producing regions and shipping ports, which slowed the growth and continued to hamper the development of the steel industry, which remained burdened by high transportation costs. Last was a shortage of skilled workers caused by regressive educational policies.[11] Indeed, throughout the nineteenth century, the principal industry in Austria-Hungary was agriculture. This was especially true in the Hungarian territories, where, in 1910, 68.4 percent of the working population was involved in agricultural production, although even in the Austrian territories the figure was as high as 53 percent. Nevertheless, once started, industrial development was both intense and rapid.[12]

In Vienna, construction of the railways brought heavy industry to the capital. At first these industries (metal-producing and machine-building for the most part) were directly related to the production of materials and equipment for the railway itself. Subsequently, as the demand for heavy machinery expanded, new engineering and electrical industries also located on the outskirts of the capital. In 1848 the passing of a bill known as the *Grundentlastung* freed peasants from feudal dues and other obligations and gave every individual the right to move freely within the Habsburg Empire, a concession to the revolutionary fervor of that year intended to prevent the spread of discontent to the countryside. The result was a flood of migration into Vienna from rural areas. Population in the inner city and suburbs grew from 431,000 in 1850 to 810,000 in 1890; in the outer, most rapidly urbanizing industrial districts it grew from 67,000 in 1850 to 600,000 in 1890.[13] Budapest, the commercial center of Hungary, grew even faster than Vienna. Its manufacturing capacity expanded in the second half of the nineteenth century to include the largest steam flour-milling industry in Europe, as well as engineering, chemical, and electrical plants. The expanding labor market likewise attracted mass immigration from the countryside, and Budapest became one of the fastest growing cities in Europe, its population increasing from 270,000 in 1859 to almost one million in 1913.[14]

The growth of industry in Vienna and Budapest had consequences for provincial cities in both parts of the empire. As heavy industry settled in Vienna in the 1840s and 1850s, the textile industry, centered in the capital since the eighteenth century, mechanized and moved to less expensive locations in northern Bohemia. There, towns such as Reichenberg/Liberec burgeoned into small industrial cities. Bohemia and Moravia, with their concentration of coal mines and steel mills (around Ostrau/Ostrava), textile weaving and chemical industries (Brno and Aussig/Ústi nad Labem), and machine building, weapons factories, and breweries (Pilsen/Plzeň), developed into the industrial center of the empire.[15] In Hungary the industrial expansion of Budapest was accompanied by the growth of a number of small agrarian villages in the Alföld plain into large market centers; at the end of the nineteenth century Szegedin/Szeged, Debrecen, Subotica, Kecskemét, each at around 100,000 in population, were among the largest cities of the empire.[16] In Galicia, the oil fields of Drohobyč and Boryslav led to the rapid expansion of L'viv into a manufacturing and financial center with well over 150,000 inhabitants at the start of the new century.[17]

These demographic shifts changed the ethnic composition as well as the density of urban populations in the latter part of the nineteenth century. The majority of immigrants to the larger industrial, administrative, and cultural centers of the empire—particularly Vienna, Budapest, and Prague—tended to come from within a 300-500 kilometer radius of the metropolitan area. In Vienna, this localized immigration, mostly Czechs and Jews from parts of Moravia that were no longer purely agrarian, increased the heterogeneity of the capital, but in other cities of the empire, including Budapest and Prague, it had the opposite effect of homogenizing their populations.[18] In Budapest, the new urban immigrants included Jews, Germans, Slovaks, and Czechs, but the mass of new arrivals who came to work in Budapest's mills, factories, and electrical plants were Magyars from the surrounding countryside. Whereas Germans had accounted for 56 percent and Magyars for 33 percent of the population of Budapest in 1850, by 1890 the Magyar population had far outstripped the German to account for 90 percent of the inhabitants of the metropolitan area (it is important to note that no separate count is given for the Jewish population, which was for the most part counted as Magyar). Prague, which had been almost purely German in the early 1800s, had only a residual German and German-Jewish population (8.5 percent) at the end of the century.[19]

In middle- and smaller-sized provincial cities, the new immigrant population was also (as it had always been) "local," drawn from the Slav, Magyar, or Romanian peasantry of the surrounding countryside. But whereas in earlier periods the process of urbanization had involved assimilation into the predominantly German urban society of these towns and the purposeful "forgetting" of ethnic origins, this late nineteenth-century migration from rural areas was so massive and occurred so rapidly that the newly arrived peasant population made the transition to an urban lifestyle without shedding ethnic identities or assimilating into the more established urban society. As Dennison Rusinow notes, "The peasant became urban without losing his (peasant) national identity, and the German . . . islands in a Slav or Romanian sea were overwhelmed one by one."[20] The consequences of this development were far reaching. As historians of the "nationalities question" in the last decades of the Habsburg Empire have shown, ethnic peasant identities (rather than being shed) were shaped and hardened into politicized national identities in the cities. Thus late nineteenth-century central European nationalism, unlike Western nationalism, from which it drew inspiration, was an urban phenomenon. Its origins, as Istvan Deak has argued, were complex and multifaceted; it derived from "denominational and cultural divisions . . . from the painful memory of foreign rule, from nostalgic longing for the often mythical greatness of a distant past, from the alien ethnic composition of the city and sometimes of the entire ruling elite, from the dread of being overwhelmed by more powerful neighbors, and from the humiliation of relative backwardness and poverty . . . ."[21] But, as Deak states, it was in the cities rather than the rural villages that most of the different national groups first encountered the idea of nationalism:

> This was the type of nationalism, at once fearful and triumphant, elegiac and truculent, with which the urban immigrant had to contend. Himself, unpolitical and barely conscious of his own nationality, the immigrant Jew or peasant suffered a steady bombardment of assimilationist propaganda and coercion, often by fellow immigrants who had preceded him into the city.[22]

Because of the division between urban and rural national cultures in the Habsburg Empire, the demographic shifts and sociospatial transformations associated with industrialization and capitalist development translated in the modernizing cities of the empire into national/ethnic conflicts. The newly arrived peasant population constituting not only what Otto Bauer (following Marx and Engels) identified as "nations without history," but also a disenfranchised urban proletariat, was doubly alienated as members of a social underclass and an alien nationality from the established urban middle classes who controlled local business, the bureaucracy, and the professions, and who constituted the empire's privileged "nations with history."[23] Thus class conflicts frequently transmuted into national or ethnic conflicts. In fact at every level of society, the social, economic, and political problems of modernizing society were recast, or at least in some way refracted or inflected, by the "nationalities question."

Frustrated desires for personal social mobility, an entrepreneur's, lawyer's, or bureaucrat's fear of competition for business or jobs, a capitalist's fear of organized labor and labor's resentment of the boss's power and prerogatives, the peasant's hatred of the great landowner and the landowner's fear of the peasantry, value clashes between old and newly urbanized, between secularist and clericalist and among Catholic, Protestant, and Orthodox worldviews—all were projected as clashes among nationalities, largely because in any locality the role players in each category could usually be identified with a particular ethnic group.[24]

Rusinow makes the further observation that the conflict of nationalities was so bitter and so pervasive in the lands of the Dual Monarchy because the empire itself was constituted entirely of ethnic minorities. Indeed, as Robert Kann has shown, in a number of Austrian crown lands there was no identifiable national majority.[25]

There was another, spatial, dimension to the nationalities issue that had a special bearing on the emerging modern architectural culture of the region. The cities, whose urban bourgeoisie constituted the region's "nations with history," became highly contested space. For the ethnic groups who were cultural nations with no independent politico-national history of their own (the so-called "nations without history") and who aspired to national self-determination, the city was not only formed by history, but was the privileged *place* of history—the place where history had been and could be made. Consequently, in the last decade of the nineteenth century and early years of the twentieth, urbanized subject peoples—particularly in Bohemia and Moravia, where the Czech-German language conflict escalated to near revolutionary intensity in the late 1890s—founded rival cultural institutions (and created tasks for architects): Czech theaters, universities, libraries, museums (of applied arts) in Prague and Brno, for example, that existed in parallel with the old, long-established German institutions in those cities.[26]

With the dissolution of the Dual Monarchy in 1918, this process of cultural appropriation continued as many of the modernizing cities of the empire became the new capitals of the sovereign states of post-World War I central Europe. But even in these new nation states, founded on principles of national self-determination and ethnolinguistic unity, geopolitical boundaries did not in fact correspond to national boundaries, and the interterritoriality of national groups persisted. In fact only two of the new states, the residual Republic of German-Austria and the considerably reduced Republic of Hungary, could be considered nations on the Western European model. Poland (which acquired the Ukrainian, German, and Jewish "minorities" of Galicia) and Romania (which acquired a large Hungarian minority with the acquisition of Bukovina and much of Transylvania) perpetuated the power imbalance of the Hungarian part of the empire. Czechoslovakia and Yugoslavia were officially multinational, but had dominant minorities (Czechs and Serbs respectively). Thus rather than resolving the nationalities question, "national liberation" after World War I perpetuated and in some cases even compounded it.[27]

How then did modern architecture construct meaning in relation to these complex and changing conditions? That is the central question posed by the exhibition and this book. It is of course impossible to characterize, much less to generalize in any meaningful way, about the extraordinary range of architectural responses to the lived experience of modernizing urban society in the cities of central Europe. The cultures, economic structures, and political life of Vienna, Budapest, Prague, Kraków, L'viv, Zagreb, Ljubljana, and the other cities examined in the exhibition, were as different from each other as were their urban histories.[28]

But it is possible to identify broad cross-cultural currents and, especially in terms of ideas about the city, to trace lines of development and persistent widely circulating concepts and models. These then provide a backdrop for considering the diverse built and unbuilt projects and discourses of the architects and planners who imagined the modern worlds of Central Europe, in relation to the particular codes, building practices, and urban histories of those cities where they staked their claims.

To reflect this interrelation between the local and translocal—between the overarching concerns and common threads of development that bound the region together, and the specificities of place that divided it—the exhibition and this volume are organized in two parts:

"The City as Form and Idea" and "Modernity and Place." To these, this volume adds a preamble, two essays concerned with the historical matrix—political, cultural, social—within which the modern architectural culture examined in the exhibition developed. They are speculative rather than conclusive; their purpose is to pose questions and propose broad themes for research. In the first Charles Maier suggests that "rather than continuing to examine urban values and their representation in terms of a retreat from public disappointment and rebuff, whether from an authoritarian, capricious imperial government or demagogic antisemitic populism," the historian of modern central Europe might ask the more fruitful question: "How was the modernist project for ordering urban space and designing its representational structures compatible with a political framework . . . which, as an empire, must insist on tradition, impose spatial hierarchy, and limit strivings for autonomy?" On one level economic modernization had its own momentum (in the cities of the Habsburg Empire as elsewhere) and municipal officials in Vienna, Budapest, and a number of the smaller industrializing cities, most notably Kraków, Timișoara, and Ľviv, responded with large-scale urban infrastructural projects: the construction of municipal gas, electricity, drinking water, sewage systems, electrified tram lines, municipal railway services, new paved streets.[29] On another level, however, Maier points out, the empire fostered cultural innovation and experiment, as it also respected the local and promoted the vernacular, because it had to in order to survive. "It was the multiethnic strains and diverse centers of vitality that ensured that this deeply conservative empire could and had to remain tolerant of innovation. Given the desire to preserve, one had to allow a framework for pluralism, intellectual and stylistic."

Moritz Csáky takes up the claims of postmodern philosophy, and of Jean-François Lyotard in particular, that turn-of-the-century Central European multicultural and multilingual society contained within it the seeds of delegitimation and fragmentation of grand narratives. Is it possible, he asks, to establish this claim historically? If so, what implications can be drawn from it? Late nineteenth-century urban society in the empire, he suggests, was in fact more heterogeneous than elsewhere (exhibiting both endogenous and exogenous plurality). Not only did most inhabitants of the empire speak two or more languages, but certain cultural codes were understood and assimilated by all. The constant presence of difference, of opposition, and contrast, Csáky argues, shaped national identities; even rural peasant identities were permeated by other cultures. Cultural identity in the region is thus best understood as "multipolar." If we rethink the concept of multiculturalism as the presence of difference within culture, rather than as the happy coexistence of different cultures, Csáky concludes, the early twentieth-century experience of central Europe holds great significance for the age of globalization at century's end.

The City as Form and Idea

The first part of the exhibition takes up the patterns of city-building and the conceptual models that dominated planning practice at the turn of the century. These are documented in drawings, photographs, books, and models, a selection of which are presented here in a portfolio of images from the exhibition. The section begins with early manifestations of the new science of town planning in the 1890s. The nineteenth-century model for modernizing the old city (employed by Baron Haussmann in Paris, for example) created a form that was fixed and static, not a model for change that could accommodate growth. In the 1890s, the concern of architects and city officials engaged with questions of town planning was to develop a method of planning for expansion and a conceptual model that could deal comprehensively with the whole urban terrain.[30]

Two ideas dominated expansion planning at the turn of the century. The first was the notion that the problem of planning for growth itself was essentially an engineering problem, not an architectural one. The emphasis in expansion plans of the 1890s was correspondingly on technical infrastructure: circulation, sanitation, hygiene. Fundamental to this conception of "engineer's planning" (exemplified by the work of Reinhard Baumeister[31]) was the new German invention of zoning, a concept derived from industrial culture, according to which the city is analyzed rationally and functionally in terms of its operations. The second idea, related to this, was that of the city as biological organism with systems that need to function together to keep it healthy. The planning tool that emerged from these considerations in the German-speaking world was the *Regulierungsplan* [regulatory plan], which for the first time considered the city in its entirety, put in place various infrastructural systems (municipal railway, tram, sewage, gas, electricity, drinking water, etc.), analyzed the city in terms of its constituent parts (streets, building blocks, public spaces, green spaces), and, finally, reassembled those parts rationally into a (theoretically) infinitely extendable urban grid.

In Vienna planning of this kind was introduced in 1892/93 with the *Generalregulierungsplan* [general regulatory plan] competition, the most significant outcome of which was the (unexecuted) prize-winning scheme of Otto Wagner. Wagner translated the two dimensions of the *Regulierungsplan* grid into a volumetric *Bebauungsplan* [building mass plan] that conceived the city as a complex three-dimensional mechanism. His plan comprehended Greater Vienna in its totality as an economic and cultural entity, but also as an architectonic unity, conceived in terms of three-dimensional spatial relationships.[32] Wagner's volumetric conception of the city has much in common with the space-positive approach to urban design of his contemporary, Camillo Sitte, a vociferous critic of late nineteenth-century two-dimensional engineer's planning and, especially through his book, *Der Städtebau nach seinen künstlerischen Grundsätzen* (1889), one of the most influential urban architectural thinkers of his time.

Most often portrayed as antagonists who espoused radically different principles of urban architectural form ("nostalgic" and tradition-bound versus positivist and future-oriented), Sitte and Wagner were in fact proponents of a shared conception of the city as a cultural artifact that had evolved out of custom, use, and habit and that must be considered as a three-dimensional architectonic unity. For both Sitte and Wagner an underlying objective of urban design was to reconcile the new with the old, to bring the facts of modern urban life into harmony with traditional concepts of place making. Where they differed most emphatically was in their conception of the urban architectonic unit itself. Sitte focused his attention on the definition of public space and composition of discrete squares, views, and prospects within the containable dimensions of civic center or medium-sized town. That is also where he left his mark, on the cities he planned throughout the Habsburg territories: Marienberg/Ostrava-Mariánské Hory, Ljubljana, Bielitz/Bielsko-Biała, Olmütz/Olomouc, Teschen/Český Těšín, Ostrau/Ostrava among others, and those throughout the Western world whose plans were inspired by his enormously influential book.[33] For Wagner the urban architectonic unit was the expanding metropolis, taken whole. Wagner was to develop the ideas contained in the *Generalregulierungsplan* into one of the most important Central European conceptions of the modern metropolis. *Die Großstadt, eine Studie über diese* [the metropolis, a study of the same] published in 1911, conceived the city as a cluster of interrelated organisms (boroughs), each with its own civic structure and amenities; a system that enabled unbounded growth at the same time as assuring continued multifunctional density and urbanity.[34]

Wagner's *Großstadt* is a powerful argument in favor of the metropolis, and can be understood as a critical "counterproject" to both the North American "City Beautiful" and to Ebenezer Howard's Garden City proposal (first published in 1898), which had such tremendous impact on early twentieth-century planning and thinking about the city. It was against the static formalism of the first and the decentralization and disurbanization of the second that Wagner directed his *Großstadt* proposal and presented the visually compelling drawings of the "future twenty-second district of Vienna" as an example of how the urban morphology of the historical city could be adapted to the new mass scale and technological social character of the modern metropolis.[35] Developed in plan, Wagner's *Großstadt* is visualized in perspective. So too are the building typologies Wagner projected for the new metropolis; rendered in elaborate perspectives that not only convey their three-dimensional form but also carefully situate each building within the physical as well as historical context of its urban site. Wagner's intensely visual, perceptual understanding of urban composition, which accommodates both the increased scale of spaces in the metropolis and the constantly shifting vantage point of the urban viewer, is clearly informed by turn-of-the-century German aesthetic theories (in particular those of Adolf von Hildebrand and August Schmarsow) regarding the way in which objects are perceived from near and distant, stationary and moving viewpoints; simultaneously as wholes and as fragments, as figure and ground, or to use Wagner's words, in terms of "point" and "counterpoint." Despite the traditional urban morphology of its plan, the *Groß-stadt* thus participates in a modernist kinesthetic urban sensibility, and manifests the dynamic, fragmentary, indeterminate spatial experience of the metropolis famously described by Georg Simmel some years earlier.[36]

By the 1920s the political and economic imperatives of the post-war period had made the traditional architectural conception of Wagner's *Großstadt* obsolete. The dissolution of the empire opened the region to experimentation, new architectural ideas, and theoretical models of the city, including Le Corbusier's Ville Contemporaine (1922) and Ludwig Hilberseimer's Hochhausstadt (1924–27), which addressed what were perceived to be new problems of scale, density, and urban economic organization.[37] The planning projects of this period—whether purely theoretical, such as Farkas Molnár's modular, anticapitalist KURI City (standing for Konstruktiv, Utilitär, Rationell, International [Constructive, Utilitarian, Rational, International] of 1925, or designed to be implemented, as Josef Gočár's *Regulierungsplan* for Hradec Králové (1925–28) or the *Gemeindebauten* of "Red Vienna" (1923–34)—show the evolution of a new scale of urban building and architectonic form—the superblock and megastructure—commensurate with the scale of post-war industrial culture and the aspirations of newly enfranchised peoples whose municipal and federal governments strove to reshape the spaces of production, public life, and cultural representation in the cities they had inherited.

In her contribution to this part of the volume, Renate Banik-Schweitzer suggests that the urban models and projects originating in this part of Central Europe—from Sitte's "artistic principles" to Wagner's unbounded *Großstadt*, Molnár's KURI City, and the Social Democratic project of Red Vienna—were all host to an ideal of multifunctional urbanity. The persistence of this ideal, she argues, attests to the relative backwardness of economic and urban development in this region, but also to the fact that the densely urban, vertically stratified, multifunctional matrix of the *Großstadt* had not yet run its course in Central Europe, and was considered to be not only viable but to have a future—to be a model capable of development, technological as well as social, in order to meet the needs of modern urban society in the new century.

Indeed, the idea that the city, or its urban morphology, constituted a sociospatial model of society and therefore held within it the potential for social transformation, runs through these projects. For Sitte the late nineteenth-century city was the material representation of bourgeois society, its spaces and fabric charged with the aesthetic-didactic task of encoding the sociocultural values of that class and establishing its ascendancy over the absolutist planning system of the past. Wagner's *Großstadt*, by contrast, was conceived to serve the purposes of turn-of-the-century monopoly capitalism; it insisted on efficient communication, hygiene, and strong centralized control over urban land development. Molnár's KURI—proposed as a corrective to Le Corbusier's capitalist Ville Contemporaine (1922) and with close affinities to Ludwig Hilberseimer's Hochhausstadt (highrise city) of 1924—was a modular, decentralized, yet vertically stratified socialist city of work, much indebted (as was Hilberseimer's project) to Wagner's *Großstadt*. Red Vienna (1923–34), the Social Democratic project to reshape the former imperial capital along socialist lines, likewise took the metropolis as its model, inter-weaving the multiform, multipurpose spaces of the "new" Vienna with those of the old, to recast it as a "*Großstadt* of the proletariat." The students of Otto Wagner who gave the Viennese program its distinctive architectural character (particularly Hubert Gessner, Karl Ehn, Heinrich Schmid, and Hermann Aichinger), translated Wagner's *Großstadt* vision and the formal dialectic between point and counterpoint it encoded, into an architecture of social relations between collective and individual, insider and outsider dwelling, public and private use as well as ownership. It was really only in the 1930s, with the embrace of CIAM's (Congrès Internationaux d'Architecture Moderne) Taylorist concept of the "functional city" and the founding of "CIAM-Ost" in 1937, that the *Großstadt* and the ideal of multifunctional urbanity it embodied were abandoned in Central Europe in favor of regional economic development.

Modernity and Place

The second part of the book and exhibition shifts the focus from common threads of development and patterns of city-building to points of difference and singularities of place. The contributions, each conceived as an "episode," focus on individual cities at particular moments of distinctive architectural innovation and vitality. The first seven essays and portfolios of images from the exhibition cover Budapest (János Gerle), Prague (Petr Krajči and Rotislav Švácha), Vienna (Iain Boyd Whyte), Zagreb (Aleksander Laslo), Ľviv (Ihor Žuk), Kraków (Jacek Purchla), and Timoșoara (Ileana Pintilie). Each is an episode in the growth and urban transformation preceding World War I.

The fact that many of the cities in Habsburg Central Europe urbanized and industrialized late (some at the very end of the nineteenth century) meant that in many cases extensive modernization of social and technological infrastructure coincided with a period of intense nationalist agitation, when national groups were asserting cultural, and seeking political, independence from Vienna. Shaped by these forces, the modern architectures that emerged in the early years of the twentieth century were heterodox, politically charged, and characterized by a complex historically rooted dialectic in which advanced building techniques and innovative spatial planning were often combined with local reference and historical allusion.

Thus in turn-of-the-century Budapest, for example, the search for a Hungarian national architectural language and indigenous expression of modernity, by Ödön Lechner and his followers, Béla Lajta, Marcell Komor, Dezső Jakob among others, as well as Otto Wagner's student, István Medgyaszay, was rooted in Hungarian folk traditions (and the Moorish, Islamic, and Hindu forms which they claimed as the sources of those traditions). But it was also cognizant of the reformist programs for the arts and crafts of John Ruskin and William Morris as well as the theories regarding ornament and abstraction of Alois Riegl (especially his concept of *Kunstwollen*[38]), and was furthermore open to the possibilities of the new technology: making use of exposed steel beams to create a free flow of interior space, experimenting with new industrially produced surfacing tiles, and, in the case of Medgyaszay, developing innovative reinforced concrete construction and even experimenting with curtain wall glazing.

Similarly, the Prague-based Czech cubists, Pavel Janák, Josef Chochol, Josef Gočár, and Vlatislav Hofman, who likewise strove to distance themselves from Vienna and Wagner school "rationalist" modernism, drew inspiration from advanced aesthetic theory (in particular, from Adolf von Hildebrandt, Riegl's *Stilfragen*, and Theodor Lipps's *Einfühlungstheorie*) and the experiments of the international avant-garde, and fused these with indigenous traditions of Bohemian late Baroque architecture.[39] The result was an architecture of formal invention and vibrant surfaces charged with energy and spatial ambiguity, but conventional from a typological and technological point of view—and, though deeply rooted in the imbricated fabric of Prague, little engaged with the larger spatial possibilities of the city.

Zagreb, where a horseshoe-shaped Ringstrasse boulevard with parks and public buildings had been built in the late 1880s, was shaped in the early years of the twentieth century by internationalist ideals and persistent efforts to connect with progressive architectural movements beyond its borders. In a politically motivated turn from Budapest, architects trained in Vienna, Munich, and Karlsruhe, as well as the Hungarian capital, cultivated a cosmopolitan Art Nouveau in the urban blocks that soon flanked the public spaces of the "Green Horseshoe." At the instigation of Otto Wagner's students Viktor Kovačić and Vjekoslav Bastl, among others, the Club of Croatian Architects determined in 1905 that all future commissions for public projects in Zagreb would be distributed by open competition with juries composed of acknowledged European experts.

L'viv, the capital of Galicia, and Timişoara, in the Hungarian-ruled Banat, also looked to Vienna, assimilating the spatial models and *Großstadt* scale of the capital as architect-builder-developers laid out new residential and commercial districts and extensive urban infrastructure to accommodate their expanding urban populations. In Timişoara the architects who designed the city-block-sized new buildings along the main boulevards were mostly Budapest-trained, and drew on local Transylvanian forms and Magyar-derived motifs in the articulation of those monumental "Viennese" blocks. In L'viv, where a Polytechnical Institute had been founded in the 1870s, locally trained architect-builders—the most important of which were the firms of Levyns'kyj and Sosnowski-Zachariewicz—shaped a local Jugendstil, closely modeled on Vienna, but also infused with Ukrainian elements and (through the Polytechnic) knowledge of French innovations in structural engineering. Folk-style Polish national architecture was cultivated (in a famous incident) by the central government, which in 1913 shipped to L'viv plans for an administrative building designed (in Vienna) in the "indigenous" style of the region, which met with violent opposition from the local architectural community.[40] In Kraków, the cultural capital of Polish Galicia, architects affiliated with the irredentist "Young Poland" movement, most notably Stanisław Wyspianski, cultivated a "Polish" Art Nouveau that incorporated folk art forms, but was also aligned with developments in northern Europe: the work of Charles Rennie Mackintosh and the Glasgow School and the brick modernism of Hendrik Petrus Berlage in the Netherlands in particular.

The pluralism of this pre-World War I modern architecture attests not only to the wide range of reference points—from the folk art of the Hungarian rural village, to international Art Nouveau, German aesthetic theory, French avant-garde painting, and ferroconcrete engineering, by which architects and their clients set their course as they charted new directions for modern architecture—but also to the all-important communicative function of the work itself. Modern architecture in this period of urban expansion and political unrest was charged with articulating not only the material purposes of the institutions and functions it shaped, but also the ideas that engendered them, and the relationship of those ideas to the larger history and cultural fabric of the cities in which they were built. In this context, the façade took on special significance with respect to the city, as the expressive field for architecture, conveying the specific (as opposed to typological) meaning of the building and mediating between it and the world. It is not without significance that this notion of a communicative, mediating façade had been theorized in nineteenth-century Central European architectural culture within the *Bekleidungstheorie* of Gottfried Semper.[41] In connection with this, Friedrich Achleitner, in his discussion in this volume of the architectonic "language problem" of Central Europe, makes the telling observation that the largely illiterate population of the multilingual empire was not only accustomed to hearing and speaking more than one language, but also (perhaps as a result) to reading non-verbal codes—to decoding complex visual imagery—and was thus visually highly literate.

In inter-war architectural culture, visual literacy took on greater complexity. After World War I the new "succession states," which were generally hostile to Vienna, often looked outside their borders and beyond the region itself to forge connections to cultural movements in Western and Eastern Europe and beyond. The breadth of new reference points is evident in the post-war episodes, covered in essays and portfolios on manifesto architecture (Monika Platzer), Budapest (András Ferkai), Zagreb (Aleksander Laslo), Ljubljana (Breda Mihelič), Vienna (Eve Blau), Prague, Zlín, and Brno (Rotislav Švácha), and CIAM and Central Europe (Monika Platzer).

In Budapest, for example, a group of architects trained at the Bauhaus and organized around avant-garde periodicals, including *MA* [Today] and *Tér és forma* [Space and Form], carried forward the elementarist formal experiments of the Bauhaus in the limited field afforded progressive architecture in post-war Hungary. In Zagreb city officials and architects looked beyond the borders of Croatia, to Germany in particular, for planning models and architectural ideas to solve the problems of Zagreb's post-war industrial and urban expansion. A number of Zagreb architects, including Zlatko Neumann, Drago Ibler, and Juraj Neidhardt, studied with Adof Loos, Le Corbusier, Peter Behrens, and Hans Poelzig (in Vienna, Paris, and Berlin), and brought back with them a sophisticated understanding of the major tenets of the new movements. City officials participated in this embrace of radical architectural ideas, sponsoring international competitions for the planned expansion of the city in the 1930s.

Elsewhere historical reference points were revalidated and appropriated to serve new social and political purposes. Thus, for example, Jože Plečnik's (re)discovery of Roman memory in a series of idiosyncratic urban interventions in Ljubljana can be understood, as Friedrich Achleitner suggests, as "using the vocabulary of the old to think new thoughts" as part of an effort to develop a universal language "from below." In Red Vienna, the Social Democratic city council appropriated the spaces and cultural markers of the imperial capital on behalf of the newly enfranchised urban proletariat in some 400 new buildings (in which workers' dwellings were incorporated with socialist institutions) that were inserted into the existing fabric of the historical city. In the new democratic Czechoslovak Republic, which had inherited many of the empire's modern industrial plants, captains of industry, including the shoe manufacturer Tomas Bat'a, fostered the development of advanced modern architecture aligned with Berlin, Paris, and Moscow, in the capital and the industrial cities of Brno and Zlín. At the same time, leftist architects in the circle of the theorist Karel Teige, who were associated with the periodical *Stavba* [Building], forged connections to the Soviet avant-garde and Russian Constructivism in their theoretical work and designs for collectivist utopias in Prague. Indeed, as Andrew Herscher discusses in his contribution to this part of the volume, magazines played an important role in the emergence of an architectural avant-garde in post-war Central Europe. The main public venue for advanced architectural thinking and design, progressive periodicals flourished in the early 1920s in Budapest and Zagreb, and until the late 1920s in Prague and Brno. At first concerned to identify and document progressive tendencies in contemporary architectural culture outside the region, they later shifted focus to local developments and the emergence of a new universal language: that of "international" Modernism.

Yet the past remained a constant reference point. Both before and after the dissolution of the Habsburg Empire, the heterodox, pluralistic modernism that emerged in the cities of Central Europe in the first decades of the twentieth century was marked by an intense engagement with the cultural topography of those cities. Charged with history and conflict, their contested spaces cast architecture itself in an active, instrumental role. To build in any one of them was to enter into debate with "what is present," with the palimpsest of cultural identities and political forces that had shaped them.[42] Modern architecture in this period of political and cultural dislocation thus generated a discursive space in the city that was public, palpable, and unavoidably present in the lives of those who inhabited them. Even as they lost their multinational character and became more culturally distinct from each other, Vienna, Prague, Budapest, and the other cities in what was Habsburg central Europe retained their supranational metropolitan identity, to a large extent because of the persistent presence of *difference* in their cultural fabric, the mark of their great-city urbanism.

1 Ödön Lechner, "Magyar formanyelv nem volt, hanem lesz" (So far there has not been a Hungarian language of form, but there will be), *Művészet* [Art] (Budapest), V, (1906), pp. 1–18. English translation from *Ödön Lechner 1845–1914*, exh. cat., The Hungarian Museum of Architecture, Budapest, 1988, p. 20.
2 Otto Wagner in a lecture delivered in Budapest in 1915, (published as Otto Wagner, "Üdvözlet a magyar építőművészeknek," *Vállalkozók Lapja* 51 [22 December 1915]), cited in Ákos Moravánszky, *Competing Visions: Aesthetic Invention and Social Imagination in Central European Architecture, 1867–1918*, Cambridge, Mass., 1998, pp. 239–40.

3 For a discussion of the models of explanation that have dominated scholarship on Austrian culture in the last 35 years, see Allan Janik, "Vienna 1900 Revisited: Paradigms and Problems," in *Austrian History Yearbook* (Minneapolis), vol. XXVIII (1997), pp. 1–27.

4 For population statistics, see Robert A. Kann, *A History of the Habsburg Empire 1526–1918*, Berkeley, Los Angeles, London, 1974, p. 605; for the distribution of national groups, Kann, *The Multinational Empire: Nationalism and National Reform in the Habsburg Monarchy 1848–1918* , 2 vols., New York, 1950; and further István Deak, *Assimilation and Nationalism in East Central Europe During the Last Century of Habsburg Rule*. The Carl Beck Papers in Russian and East European Studies, Pittsburgh, 1985, pp. 1–4; Dennison Rusinow, "Ethnic Politics in the Habsburg Monarchy and Successor States: Three Answers to the National Question," in Richard L. Rudolph and David F. Good, eds. *Nationalism and Empire: The Habsburg Empire and the Soviet Union*, New York, 1992, pp. 243–67.

5 Vera Bácskai, "The Historic Metropolis in Hungary in the 19th and 20th Centuries," in Jacek Purchla, (ed.), *The Historical Metropolis: A Hidden Potential*, Kraków, 1996, pp. 133–36.

6 For the railways see, David F. Good, *The Economic Rise of the Habsburg Empire, 1750–1914*, Berkeley, Los Angeles, London, 1984, pp. 99–104.

7 Garrison towns included Kraków, Olmütz/Olomouc, Przemyśl, Pola/Pula.

8 See Gary B. Cohen, "Neither Absolutism nor Anarchy: New Narratives on Society and Government in Late Imperial Austria," *Austrian History Yearbook* XXIX, part 1 (1998), pp. 37–61; Ernst Bruckmüller, "Bildungsbürgertum und Intellektuelle in Wien und in den Kronländern," and Waltraud Heindl, "Bildungsbürgertum zwischen Metropole und Provinz: die kaiserliche Bürokratie," in Andrei Corbea-Hoisie and Jacques Le Rider (eds.), *Metropole und Provinzen in Altösterreich (1880–1918)*, Vienna, Cologne, Weimar, 1996, pp. 17–29, 81–93.

9 See Moravánszky, *Competing Visions*, chapter 2: "The City as Political Monument." See also Ilona Sármány-Parsons, "Die Rahmenbedingungen für 'die Moderne' in den ungarischen Provinzstädten um die Jahrhundertwende," in Corbea-Hoisie and Le Rider, *Metropole und Provinzen*, pp. 180–217; Vladimir Bedenko, "The Role of History in the Creation of Zagreb as a Historical Metropolis in the 19th and 20th Centuries" in Purchla, (ed.), *The Historical Metropolis*, pp. 166–68, and in the same volume, Thomas DaCosta Kaufmann, "The Problem of Artistic Metopolises in East Central Europe from the Fifteenth to the Twentieth Century," p. 119.

10 Deak, *Assimilation and Nationalism*, pp. 10–11. Deak also notes that "Jews, who were not identified as a separate ethnic group, but were usually counted as German, were a majority in Galicia and Bukowina; Greeks and Serbs along the Danube in Hungary; Italians in Croatian inhabited Dalmatia and Istria." See also Adam Wandruszka and Peter Urbanitsch, (eds.), *Die Völker des Reichs*, Vienna, 1980. Recent research has shown that state centralism was combined with considerable regional and especially municipal political autonomy, which increased over the course of the nineteenth century and was a significant factor in the successful implementation of large-scale urban infrastructural modernization schemes and housing construction in many of these cities at the turn of the century and in the post-war republics. See, Cohen, " Neither Absolutism nor Anarchy," pp. 45–61.

11 Good, *Economic Rise*, pp. 96–124.

12 By 1913 economic modernization in the Austrian territories had reached the same level as in other major European countries. Ibid., pp. 139, 241. See also Iván T. Berend and György Ránki, *The Hungarian Economy in the Twentieth Century*, Beckenham, 1985, pp. 13–23.

13 Renate Banik-Schweitzer, *Zur sozialräumlichen Gliederung Wiens 1869–1934*, Publikationen des Instituts für Stadtforschung, vol. 63, Vienna, 1982; Banik-Schweitzer, "Vienna," in M.J. Daunton (ed.), *Housing the Workers, 1850–1914*, London 1990, p. 112.

14 Bácskai, "The Historic Metropolis," p. 135.

15 Good, *The Economic Rise*, pp. 133–35.

16 In the meantime a number of the old royal free cities [*königliche Freistädte*] in Upper Hungary (Slovakia) and Transylvania stagnated. See, Sármány-Parsons, "Die Rahmenbedingungen," p. 184.

17 Good, *The Economic Rise*, pp. 146–48.

18 Gerhard Melinz and Susan Zimmermann, "Großstadtgeschichte und Modernisierung in der Habsburgermonarchie" and Renate Banik-Schweitzer, "Die Großstädte im gesellschaftlichen Entwicklungsprozess in der zweiten Hälfte des 19. Jahrhunderts," in Gerhard Melinz and Susan Zimmermann (eds.), *Wien-Prag-Budapest: Blütezeit der Habsburgermetropolen: Urbanisierung, Kommunalpolitik, gesellschaftliche Konflikte (1867–1918)*, Vienna, 1996, pp. 15–33, 34–45 (especially 41–2).

19 Deak, *Assimilation and Nationalism*, p. 11; C.A. Macartney, *The Habsburg Empire, 1790–1918*, New York, 1969, p. 726–27.

20 Rusinow, "Ethnic Politics," p. 247.

21 Deak, *Assimilation and Nationalism*, p. 13.

22 Ibid., pp. 13–14.

23 Otto Bauer, *Die Nationalitätenfrage und die Sozialdemokratie*, Vienna, 1907, 1924. For Marx's and Engels' concept see Kann, *Multinational Empire*, p. 43.

24 Rusinow, "Ethnic Politics," p. 248.

25 Kann, *Multinational Empire*, p. 32.

26 Ibid., pp. 203–04.

27 Deak, *Assimilation and Nationalism*, pp. 1–2; Rusinow, "Ethnic Politics," p. 256.

28 These differences have been insufficiently researched because of the neglect of institutional histories in Habsburg Central Europe, see Gerald Stourzh, "The Multinational Empire Revisited: Reflections on Late Imperial Austria," *Austrian History Yearbook*, XXIII (1992), pp. 1–22.

29 For summaries of these infrastructural projects, see Melinz and Zimmermann, *Wien-Prag-Budapest*, *passim*, and Moravánszky, *Competing Visions*, chapter 10.

30 For general discussion of turn of the century planning concepts and models in German-speaking countries, see Brian Ladd, *Urban Planning and Civic Order in Germany, 1860–1914*, Cambridge, Mass., 1990; and George R. Collins and Christiane Crasemann Collins, *Camillo Sitte: The Birth of Modern City Planning*, New York, 1986, pp. 35–51.

31 Collins and Collins, *Camillo Sitte*, pp. 44–46, 422–23.

32 See Otto Antonia Graf, "Generalregulierungsplan für Wien," in *Otto Wagner: Das Werk Des Architekten 1860–1902*, Vienna, Cologne, Graz, 1985, pp. 87–121.

33 Collins and Collins, *Camillo Sitte*.

34 Otto Wagner, *Die Großstadt: eine Studie über Diese*, Vienna, 1911. Part of Wagner's text was published in English as "'The Development of a Great City,' by Otto Wagner: Together with an Appreciation of the Author by A.D. Hamlin," in *Architectural Record* 31 (1912), pp. 485–500.

35 It was also significantly different from the urban conceptions of the Deutscher Werkbund in which the central business district was to be surrounded by residential garden suburbs, see Karl Scheffler, *Die Architektur der Großstadt* (Berlin, 1913). Wagner disliked suburban developments which he called "villa cemeteries" in *Die Großstadt*.

36 Adolf von Hildebrandt, *Das Problem der Form in der bildenden Kunst*, Strasbourg, 1893; August Schmarsow, *Das Wesen der architektonischen Schöpfung*, Leipzig, 1894; Georg Simmel, "Die Großstädte und das Geistesleben," *Jahrbuch der Gehe-Stiftung zu Dresden*, 9 (1903), pp. 27–71. For a brief discussion of the impact of these theories on Wagner's ideas of urban composition, see Eve Blau, *The Architecture of Red Vienna, 1919–1934*, Cambridge, Mass., 1999, pp. 248–49.

37 For Le Corbusier's and Hilberseimer's projects in the context of European modernism and interwar urbanism, see Manfredo Tafuri and Francesco Dal Co, *Modern Architecture*, New York, 1979.

38 Alois Riegl, *Stilfragen: Grundlegungen zu einer Geschichte der Ornamentik*, Berlin, 1893.

39 Theodor Lipps, *Raumästhetik und geometrisch-optische Täuschungen*, Leipzig, 1893–97. For an insightful discussion of these and other German aesthetic theories in the last quarter of the 19th century, see Harry Francis Mallgrave and Eleftherios Ikonomou, "Introduction," in *Empathy, Form, and Space: Problems in German Aesthetics, 1873–1893*, Santa Monica, 1994, pp. 1–85.

40 Jacek Purchla, "Die Einflüsse Wiens auf die Architektur Lembergs 1772–1918," in *Die Architektur Lembergs im 19. Jahrhundert*, Kraków, 1997, p. 45.

41 Semper referred to the theory of *Bekleidung* throughout his theoretical work, but developed it most fully in: Gottfried Semper, *Der Stil in den technischen und tektonischen Künsten oder praktische Ästhetik*, 2 vols., Frankfurt, 1860–63. Further regarding Semper, see Harry Francis Mallgrave, *Gottfried Semper, Architect of the Nineteenth Century*, New Haven and London, 1996.

42 The quoted phrase is from Walter Benjamin, "The Author as Producer," in *Reflections: Essays, Aphorisms, Autobiographical Writings*, translated by Edmund Jephcott, New York, 1978, p. 235.

CITY, EMPIRE, AND IMPERIAL AFTERMATH: CONTENDING CONTEXTS FOR THE URBAN VISION

Charles S. Maier

For the inhabitant of a country has at least nine characters: a professional one, a national one, a civic one, a class one, a geographical one, a sex one, a conscious, an unconscious and perhaps even too a private one; he combines them all in himself, but they dissolve him, and he is really nothing but a little channel washed out by all these trickling streams, which flow into it and drain out of it again in order to join other little streams filling another channel. Hence every dweller on earth also has a tenth character, which is nothing more or less than the passive illusion of spaces unfilled.... This interior space—which is, it must be admitted, difficult to describe—is of a different shade and shape in Italy from what it is in England, because everything that stands out in relief against it is of a different shade and shape; and yet both here and there it is the same, merely an empty, invisible space with reality standing in the middle of it like a little toy brick town, abandoned by the imagination.

Robert Musil[1]

I

At least in the space that was Central Europe, Musil's toy city was never really abandoned by the imagination. It remained designed by some brilliantly innovative architects and planners: Otto Wagner, Joseph Olbrich, and Josef Hoffmann; Ödön Lechner, Béla Lajta, and István Medgyaszay; Adolf Loos, Maks Fabiani, Jože Plečnik, and others. Together they envisaged the structures of an imagined imperium, an empire that encompassed cities aspiring to modernity and peoples that preserved folklore and tradition. These were not easy elements to reconcile. Moreover, they were hardly the only contradictions that planners and designers had to confront in the geographical and historical context of Central Europe. How was the modernist project for ordering urban space and designing its representational structures compatible with a political framework, the Habsburg realms, which, as an empire, must insist on tradition, impose spatial hierarchy, and limit strivings for autonomy? Whence the imaginative space for innovation and experiment in a world of rank and stratification, soldiers and ceremony, of deference to the Center or of preoccupation with escaping its claims? This is the puzzle that the development of Vienna, Budapest, Prague, and the lesser cities of Austria-Hungary from Kraków to Ľviv to Černivci, Szeged, and Timişoara, Zagreb, Trieste, and Ljubljana pose for the historian of modern Europe.

To live in any one of these centers was never to dwell just in that city alone. Of course every city dweller is also resident in a wider country. But layered loyalties were particularly acute so long as Austria-Hungary survived. Its urban denizens occupied crowded and changing nodes in a transnational web of power and trade, linguistic and social layering. The Monarchy's cities grew in response to imperial policy and inspiration from the center. They also evolved in terms of size and politics as a consequence of demographic and economic pressures emanating from the imperial hinterlands. And in many ways their experiments in urban planning and architecture transcended the nation-state (including the Austro-Hungarian imperial state). Perhaps not since the diffusion of the Baroque did self-conscious international borrowing make such an impact as at the turn of the twentieth century. Architects of Central Europe looked to C.F.A. Voysey in Britain and Antoní Gaudí in Barcelona. The great expositions were international; plans for green space were a common response to urban crowding in many countries;

the great representational programs—Beaux Arts, historicist, Art Nouveau/Secession, and later Art Deco—greeted the beholder from Mexico City to Central Europe.

What, then, distinguished the Central European variant in the spectrum of responses and programs to the needs of the modern metropolis? How do we discern the elements that were a response to Central Europe from the needs of the industrial city or the representative capital elsewhere? And, to look ahead, what particular urban agendas might emerge once the Empire dissolved at the end of World War I? With reference to what loyalties must the city be created anew? National peoples given the chance to renew their own lived cities were vulnerable to conflict, poverty, the need to give form to new orientations that looked . . . where? To Paris, Dessau, Berlin, and to their "people" (but which people)? After decades of asserting the modernist adventure corsetted by Empire, now its champions had to carry it forward, thrown on their own daring and resources amidst conflict and economic adversity.

But the exhibition and the present book attempt to demonstrate how the discourses and artifacts of urbanism confronted these successive challenges. But this particular author is not a historian of architecture or planning, and this contribution addresses less architecture and urban design than the political and cultural milieu of Central Europe and the contradictory pressures to which it subjected modernist projects. These were not just the contradictions between modernity and tradition, which have been analyzed many times by cultural historians and critics. Just as compelling for planners and architects were the contradictions inherent in imperial governance and nation building in a region of ethnic layering and conflict, international rivalry, and social conflict—of centrifugal impulses within an empire and fratricidal hostilities after empire.

What were the implications of the Empire for urban life?[2] A generation of cultural and intellectual historians have pointed out the paradoxes of Austro-Hungarian civilization, above all the contrast between its innovative cultural achievements and its stunted political life. Twenty years ago, Carl Schorske argued that many of the brilliant contributions, whether Freudian psychoanalysis or Klimtian portraiture, followed the disappointment of ambitions in more public projects.[3] Healing the psyche replaced mending the body politic; the innovative painter of the university aula turned toward the society portrait. Ákos Moravánsky, in his recent study of architectural tropes throughout the Empire, has also suggested that "the Central European utopia was therefore not a modernist proposal. . . . It was a recollection, not the creation of a new order . . . [but] built of fragments of the past that were carefully selected, interpreted, and densely assembled according to a universalist vision."[4] No matter how we come down on the issue of modernist and traditionalist elements in urban design and architecture, does this recurrent effort to define a Left and a Right really advance our understanding of what was at stake?

Cultural historians can get only so far if they continue to examine urban values and their representation in terms of a retreat from public disappointment and rebuff, whether from an authoritarian, capricious imperial government or demagogic antisemitic populism. After all, the urban boulevard—the outdoor counterpart to the grand staircase of the opera as a theater for bourgeois display—was advanced decisively under authoritarian, not liberal, auspices, whether in Haussmann's Paris or the early clearing of the old city walls for the Ringstrasse at the behest of the then young emperor, Franz Josef. Just as during the mid-eighteenth century when monarchs and aristocracies, who had struggled against each other's political and fiscal pretensions, arrived at an ephemeral political equilibrium reflected in the grace of the Rococo, so briefly during the second third of the nineteenth century, monarchies and empires negotiated a civic settlement with the new forces of finance, railroads, and business as well as the old dignitaries of the land, the Church, and learning. The expansion of the city, the clearing of its old walls and rookeries, the laying down of grand boulevards, were the product of that equilibrium we often term Victorian.

II

Liberalism, too, prospered with that equilibrium—and retreated as the equilibrium came unravelled. By the last decade of the nineteenth century the Victorian compromises between the forces of tradition and those of development were fraying under the impact of mass politics, including working-class parties and unions, new nationalist and imperialist pressure groups, or, in Vienna, Christian-social politics. Nineteenth-century European liberalism was all the more vulnerable insofar as it itself incorporated contradictory impulses. It was not a general thrust to expand democratic rights, but a specific body of doctrine that set clear lines to its Left as well as to its Right. Liberals stood for freedom of expression, religious toleration, and legal protection—the culture of "rights" encompassed by the so-called *Rechtsstaat*. They stood for the power of parliament to retain the authority to pass the national budget and limit the power of the monarchy. They fundamentally opposed the Catholic Church's role in public life and public education—a hostility that mid-century Catholics returned in kind. On the other hand, as the political doctrine of the cultivated middle classes, liberalism generally advocated limitation of the suffrage to the educated or the propertied. Liberals tended to eschew mobilization and appeals to the propertyless; they feared the "masses," and watched ineffectively as populist leaders mobilized these new constituencies around issues of economic protection, and increasingly nationalism and antisemitism.

In the Austrian half of the Habsburg realms, so-called Cisleithania, liberalism was identified not just with the professional middle classes in general, but increasingly with the German-speaking bourgeoisie in particular, who watched warily the demands for linguistic equality of Slovene, Polish, and Czech aristocrats and peasants. These liberals enjoyed an ephemeral decade of political leadership between the 1867 dualist "Compromise" with the Hungarians and Count Eduard Taaffe's ministry of 1879, the same historical moment in which the German National Liberals achieved their greatest influence in tandem with Bismarck on behalf of unification and a confirmation of limited parliamentary government.[5] But the progress of Central European liberalism was never unalloyed. The constitutional ground rules they secured—whether in Prussia or the Bismarckian Empire, in the Kingdom of Hungary or in Cisleithania)—assured them no parliamentary supremacy over the executive. The Habsburg ministers resorted to rule without parliament, however, less because of autocratic leanings than because national quarrels tended to paralyze the institution: Bohemians and Germans at first, later Poles as well, bickered increasingly over language rights in administration and education. Since the Magyars pursued more consistent policies of ethnic supremacy in their half of the monarchy, their subject nationalities never even attained significant parliamentary representation. (A special Settlement with the Croatians allowed that border people their own limited autonomy and group representation in the Hungarian parliament, but Slovaks, Romanians, and Ruthenians, i.e., Ukrainians, enjoyed no such privileges).[6]

By the late 1870s the liberals, who had so enthusiastically endorsed either German unification or the collaborative regime with the Emperor within dualist Austria-Hungary, were pressed into opposition. The business boom that had given the bourgeoisie such influence from the late 1860s dissipated with the mid 1870s and the clamor for protection by agrarian landlords and industrialists brought together new coalitions, such as Bismarck's protectionist majority of "rye and iron," that is the conservative and pro-tariff representatives of industry and East Elbian agriculture, or Taaffe's "Iron Ring," which relied on Bohemian conservative delegates to outnumber the German liberals. The ranks of liberalism also thinned as bourgeois elites grew more preoccupied about the "social" threat, that is the challenge from working-class parties and trade unions.

Mass suffrage hurt the liberals more than it helped them (in contrast to Britain where Liberals and Tories together accepted the coming of mass male suffrage to compete vigorously for the new, largely working-class electorate). Bismarck's Germany granted universal male suffrage for the lower house of the transitional North German economic parliament of 1867 and then for the new Reichstag of 1871; Austrian and Hungarian parliaments attained it only in the complicated crisis of 1905–06. The Austrian provincial diets and the Viennese city government were chosen by complicated skewed voting in electoral colleges or curias established according to tax liability, but the resulting bias in favor of the wealthy did not preclude a vigorous rivalry between liberals and emerging antisemitic populists. By the 1890s, Catholic and Conservative politicians had discovered the resources of peasant or urban mass populism, and learned how to mobilize the electorate against parties or bourgeois elites and — as they resorted increasingly to antisemitic demagogy — Jews, who in Central Europe were emerging as a major social component of the urban world of journalism and finance and the liberal professions.[7]

But the eclipse of bourgeois liberalism in Central Europe had no strict correlation with the success or setbacks of "modernism" such as we understand it in art or culture. Even if one accepts Schorske's suggestion that in response to the attrition of liberalism, intellectuals retreated from the public realm,[8] urban planning and architecture could not simply look backward. Economic modernization continued its relentless progress. Despite the fall in agricultural prices during the so-called "great depression" of 1873–96, industrial transformation and general economic growth continued at a dizzying pace. No planners of urban space could simply deny the evolution of the city in an era of urban electrification, street cars and (by the end of the century) early subway lines in Budapest, Milan, Boston, etc., the coming of the automobile, the vast annexation of overseas imperial territories (Austria excepted here), and the huge migration of poor peasants to the cities of Central Europe and to North America. The question was how the city should adapt to the industrial transformation of the Western world. As Moravánsky points out, even the noted contrast between Camillo Sitte, who celebrated the organic nature of the pre-industrial city, and Otto Wagner, who hoped to construct a functional equivalent for the new city, is hardly a neat one. Romantic and utopian ideas infused both concepts, even if Sitte's remained the more "organic" or historicist utopia, while Wagner's depended upon vast linear alternations of monumental and residential structures. Nor did the effort to preserve green space in the city — whether Boston's Emerald Necklace, New York's Central Park, the areas for urban recreation on the Ringstrasse, the Green Horseshoe of Zagreb — constitute a neo-romantic project. The Garden City inspiration clearly wished to offset the growth of mass urbanization, but should not be typed from the outset as a reactionary response to industrialism. The issue was not whether to accept modernity, but how to shape it. In thinking about their mission, moreover, all urban planners sought such supposedly apolitical and technocratic objectives as hygiene, social harmony, and the moralizing of labor and recreation.

Despite some large-scale projects, pre-1914 regimes, both democratic and imperial were reluctant to intervene in the nexus of capitalism and land — once, at least, they had completed the vast expropriations of church lands earlier in the century. No legislation attempted to staunch the flow of a new working class into the cities of the West, although Prussian conservatives delayed east-west canals in part to limit rural migration. No legislation succeeded very well before 1914 in suspending the workings of the real estate market. World War I and its inflationary impact, however, would bring widespread efforts at rent control and the provision of social housing. *La politique des loyers* became a vexing issue in Paris. The Vienna Social Democrats would freeze tenant payments to cover landlord costs to facilitate both low real wages and municipal acquisition of depressed real property.[9] Before the war, however, most governments were reluctant to intervene in a continually appreciating source of private wealth; even less did they envisage limiting movement. (What they did sanction was enlargement of the urban frontier — ironically enough the recourse denied to Vienna after the war.) With respect to the inhibitions on intervention in the market, the imperial regimes of Central Europe were not "feudal" enough: for all their pomp and circumstance, for all the ministers' dislike of fractious parliaments, for all the insistence on reserve rights over foreign and military policy — the empires never abolished capitalism. Their own aristocratic élites were up to their elbows in urban land speculation and building societies, mineral extraction, railroad projects, and the general creation of riches. Feudalism never had a chance. But capitalism and speculation did, and the late nineteenth century became an epoch of unparalleled financial accumulation and wealth creation.

Urban planning aspired both to acknowledge the city as the economic artifact of the industrial era and to offset its chaotic expansion under market forces. In this sense the cities of democratic North America and imperial Central Europe shared projects, whether the devotion to green land (would an island park be placed in the Charles River to emulate that of Margaret Island between Buda and Pest?), or the search for more professional city management. This was no accident in the Progressive era, as American students of good government, such as Charles Beard, traveled to Germany to learn how professional city government might be used to offset machine politics. The well-governed city seemed to be the lesson to absorb from German and Austrian politics in a period when urban planning in the most raw capitalistic and party-political society of the West emerged precisely as a way of protecting society from domination by either unbridled capitalism or demagogic electoral machines such as Tammany Hall who could virtually buy the votes of the immigrant working class.[10]

So much of the evidence that historians use to evaluate the intentionality of urban design does not come from the urban capitalist cockpit. It is based on project drafts and project spaces—including the world fairs and expositions that flourished so exuberantly in the era from the 1870s until World War II. Only a transnational industrial society of significant wealth could devote so much effort to short-lived and often daring experimental structures, most of which were designed with the knowledge that they could impress for only a few years. No matter in which country—assuming it shared in economic development—the wealth of railroad companies, municipalities, and national governments allowed enclaves of representative architecture continually to emerge and claim significant urban space. The buildings of Central Europe and the Habsburg domains were exquisitely representational and historicist—the neo-Gothic town hall of Vienna and the Hungarian parliament designed a decade and a half later; the Neoclassic parliament building in Vienna—but no more historicist or syncretic than counterparts in other European and North American cities. The form of regime was largely irrelevant to the monuments of the industrial era. Stylistic aspirations did not turn on how democratic or monarchical government was. Nonetheless, the multinational dimensions of the Habsburg imperial construction did impose particular consequences.

III

The critical tension for aesthetic design in Habsburg Central Europe can be located metaphorically not just along one axis (from traditionalist to modernist visions), which in fact characterizes industrial societies everywhere, but simultaneously along a second axis (imperial program versus ethnic autonomy) that is peculiar to the aspirations of empire. Urban visions reflected the spatial layering of the Habsburg realms, "imperial-and-royal," central and local, multinational but gradated, with some peoples "historic" and others merely subject. Architecture and urban projects reflected these conflict-laden hierarchies, not in any facile one-to-one correspondence or inspiration, but in their responsiveness to the contending constituencies that lived, uneasily, in the Habsburg domains. Otto Wagner told the Hungarian architects in 1915 that "the artistic expression of architectural works must be in every center of culture similar, since the way of life and the government system is similar. If we accept this argument, we should realize that a national style cannot exist."[11] Wagner was trying to impose limits on nativist inspirations that increasingly subverted imperial control. Subverted but did not abolish: the overarching Central European inspiration never vanished even if it evolved from a rather one-sided emulation on the periphery of the boulevards or massive government buildings of the center in the mid nineteenth century to a more problematic dialectic of replication and autonomy by 1900.

For the Empire to preserve its legitimacy, it had to respect the local. The emperor was the protector of the diverse peoples under his rule; he could not ride roughshod over their ethnic heritages. From the center came the awareness of the larger political construct, the consciousness of being part of a broader system, vast and complex. From the local came the sense of vitality, myth, the *élan vital* that turn-of-the century intellectuals attributed to *Volk*. Building in their style, moreover, involved more than mere decorative gestures to the heritage of subject peoples. Hungarian and Polish, Slovak and Czech architects who sought out the folk models of the Székely regions, the Tatra, or other farmsteads had a growing sense of retrieving their own heritage. The Habsburg project and the architecture that might legitimate it could never renounce the vernacular, or what was more often the case, the pseudo-vernacular. The city, moreover, had a particular role in Habsburg Central Europe. For it represented the site where the imperial met the local, and the architect or urban designer had to do justice simultaneously to both sources of inspiration.

Thus, on the one hand, there was a remarkable replication of elements across the Empire: the Ringstrasse adapted to each significant city, whether Zagreb or Szeged; the massive rusticated stones for banks and public buildings, reminiscent of Alberti's Renaissance palaces; the ochre colorings. Factories in Austria could ship street lamps and other decorative elements to the provinces: being part of the Empire was adapting the imperial program. No other extensive political unit cultivated a series of key urban elements that so emulated the concepts of the capital. In France the capital was without imitators; in Germany there was no alignment on Berlin, which was itself too new. But at the same time the city and its buildings, at least in Hungary, had to reflect that the Hungarians were the other historic nation. Hence the need to celebrate the founding myths of Magyardom, whether in the Millennial Park and Heroes Square or the glazed Turkic tiles that Lechner used for his Postal Savings Bank and Museum of Applied Art. In Prague, the design of the grand promenade down Wenceslaus "Square," soon to be flanked by the successive buildings of modern design from Art Nouveau (the Europa Hotel) to the Bat'a shoe salon of the 1920s, was counterposed by restorationist projects. Designers from the smaller units of imperial structures had to make their own modest statements of partial autonomy: even before Plečnik, Ljubljana took pride in its earlier role as capital of a Carniola that nurtured its affiliations to Italy, and, when inside the new Yugoslavia after 1919, to Vienna, and erected a monumental column to commemorate its brief role as capital of the Illyrian provinces under Napoleon.

Is it possible—so we might pose a more general and speculative inquiry—to identify an architecture responsive to what the European Union today calls subsidiarity? Were there, in effect, stylistic commonalities for those cities reduced to a secondary administrative or political level, that is, inspirations or approaches shared, for example, in Catalonia, Scotland, Hungary, and Bohemia? Such an architecture would not be merely provincial or unsophisticated. Rather it would draw heavily on local ethnic traditions (or "invented traditions") and would mobilize religious and sacral motifs against the secularism of the administrative center. It would endeavor to assert for built space the celebration of ancestral province that Smetana and Dvořak or Sibelius sought in music. The architecture of subsidiarity might emphasize plasticity and asymmetry against the Neoclassical or Beaux-Arts program of the metropole, and those entrusted with its elaboration would seek inspiration from designers who operated on the same level of political space in other jurisdictions. Freed from the ruling ambitions of the center, the architecture of subsidiarity proposed by Antoní Gaudí or Lechner or Charles Rennie Mackintosh might reach more easily for elements of fantasy and folklore, experiment more readily with irregular space, offer variations on the less exuberant representations of empire and statehood.

IV

As the nineteenth century ended and the new one began, the tensions inherent in the Habsburg regime became more and more difficult to contain. From 1848 onward the Austrian Empire lurched from one unsuccessful expedient to another, in frequent crisis, but held in existence because it was obvious that without its cumbersome institutions even more endemic disputes would rage. Defeat in war—first in 1859 with the French and Italians, then in 1866 with the Prussians and Italians, and finally and catastrophically, after four years in 1918, at the hands of a vast coalition—was the major catalyst for attempted reforms and finally disintegration. The rapid and disastrous 1866 defeat allowed Bismarck to organize Germany under Prussian dominance, restored Venetia to the Italians, and, under the terms of the Compromise or Ausgleich of the next year, conceded the Hungarians the right to run their half of the Habsburg domains within an overarching Dual Monarchy. Just as the Austrian half included Czechs, Poles, and Ukrainians, southern Slavs, and Italians, the Hungarian half included peasant Slovaks and Ruthenians, restive Rumanians in Transylvania who resented Magyar landlords, and uncooperative Croatians (and some Serbs) in the formerly autonomous military border land who claimed their own parliamentary tradition. In each half the Jews served as a middle-class leaven, helping to organize business and finance, mastering the two ruling languages and dominating journalism, loyally supporting liberal politics and the dynasty as the major force against a rising ethnic antisemitism. The Jews were indispensable, above all in Hungary where intermarriage among the upper echelons of Magyar society and the Jewish bourgeoisie increased, and where far more than in Germany a real "symbiosis" occurred—but where their professional integration and success could only intensify preoccupation with their alleged domination of society.[12]

For half a century the new hyphenated Austria-Hungary retained a common dynasty, army, foreign office, and a tariff union renegotiated every decade, which in effect was a piece of imperial logrolling that protected the industrial producers of the German Austrian provinces and Bohemia in Cisleithania and the grain farmers of the Hungarian monarchy. Army issues were more troublesome, and when in 1903 the Magyars insisted on Hungarian as the language of command for their national militia as the price of authorizing contingents for the regular imperial army, they opened a profound two-year crisis. Elections returned a secessionist majority; the Emperor sent soldiers into the huge new parliamentary palace to dissolve the legislature, and his new minister brandished a universal male suffrage that would enfranchise the restive minorities. The suffrage reform threatened in Budapest was desired and introduced in Vienna—only to be withdrawn in Hungary when the Magyars gave in on the army issue. Hungarian liberals had to undergo their humiliation while watching the Russians successfully wrest a parliament from their autocrat just as Croats and Serbs were raising the specter of South Slav agitation. Young Budapest intellectuals, most celebrated among them the poet Endre Ady, sonorously evoked the melancholy of national cultural crisis.

Relations between the two halves of the monarchy were difficult enough to equilibrate: the role of Hungarian or German as the military language of command, the continuing dissatisfaction of Magyar radicals with the Compromise of 1867, and conflicting concepts for making South Slav or eventually Polish and perhaps Romanian regions into separate "crownlands" embroiled the partner regimes. But politics within each half of the Empire was even more wearying. Germans in Cisleithania—the "liberals" dominating in the 1860s and 1870s—believed that the whole complex structure was still essentially their Empire, and certainly Cisleithania was their half empire. But the German-speaking Emperor (titled "k und k," that is "imperial and royal" in the Dual Monarchy as a whole, "imperial" alone in Cisleithania, and "royal" alone as king of Hungary)—realized that he must in fact endeavor to represent every people, or the whole structure would collapse. For the Dual Monarchy to work it could not be a German puppet show. But paralysis resulted. Czechs wanted more schools and a larger budget, and made parliament unworkable if they were rebuffed, while Germans made it unworkable if concessions were made. Still, national rights were fairly tolerably preserved in the Austrian realms. In the Hungarian kingdom the Emperor's leverage was less, and Franz Josef was cautious by instinct; had the more autocratic Franz Ferdinand ever inherited the throne instead of dying in Sarajevo, he might have forced restructuring on the Magyars he detested—or he might have provoked outright secession.[13]

Language was the supreme issue of the monarchy, although language disputes were simultaneously contests over access to high office, the secure positions of state employment, and social prestige. The Habsburg Empire was a linguistic cartel, and as has been pointed out, language issues pervaded the culture.[14] Czech and Hungarian were reinvented during the course of the nineteenth century, while from Fritz Mauthner to Karl Kraus, the Vienna Circle, and Wittgenstein, German writers explored the capacities and limits of their precious language. Musil's epic was a rumination about life in the subjunctive mode; science was, in Mach's words, an "as if" enterprise—linguistic recognition remained the continuing prize of the Empire. By the new century, the Poles from Galicia had displaced the Czechs as the most troublesome minority, and some of the Germans envisaged separating Galicia into a third crown land—although the Hungarians vetoed such a development, fearing that it would set a precedent for their Romanian territories. Within a couple of years of the new century, a violent reorientation of Serbia's policies and the unleashing of Serbian ambitions to attract their ethnic brethren as well as Croatians and Slovenes made it appear that South Slav agitation might tear apart each half of the monarchy. Austria's annexation of Bosnia-Herzegovina (a territory it had been given as a sort of trusteeship since 1878) heightened the stakes in southeast Europe, and some of the key policy-makers, including the chief of the General Staff, surrendered to a disastrous fatalism about the preference of risking war rather than watching their country decompose piecemeal. As Conrad von Hötzendorf would later observe, we had the freedom to choose which way we would perish, and we chose the worst.

Looking backward from the denouement of 1918, when the armies of the Emperor decomposed on the battlefield and started the flight back from the front to their respective homelands (after, however, remaining remarkably cohesive and disciplined for four terrible years), historians often stress the inevitablity of the result. Much of the popular impression of the late Austro-Hungarian monarchy seems to be based, in fact, on the fictionalized image arising from Musil's *Man without Qualities* and Joseph Roth's *Radetzky March*—two brilliant but highly stylized evocations of the late monarchy. Cliches abound about the waltz to an inevitable destruction, when in fact the admittedly rickety and unwieldy institutions held together through four years of unparalleled military and economic testing. The point is that no territorial-based institutions could function easily given the ethnic intermixture of Central Europe, indeed southeastern and east Central Europe more generally. The old empires worked either by brokering or suppressing aspirations for linguistic self-consciousness. As Michael Walzer has recently written, empires have a special regime of tolerance; they encourage a pluralism and group consciousness that civic republicanism cannot easily accommodate.[15] But this toleration became increasingly difficult to preserve. For if at the educated levels of society, multilingualism had to be the rule of cultivated families, peasantries remained far more monolingual. By the turn of the century, moreover, country folk were migrating to the cities for new industrial employment. Underlying the periodic spectacular conflicts over schools or language ordinances was a less conspicuous but continual process by which the rural ethnicities of Bohemia or Slovenia or Slovakia encroached upon the multicultural identity of the medium-size Habsburg towns, undermining at the grass roots the pluralist existence that the regime required even to limp along from crisis to crisis.[16] Even then, as the philosophical reflection on language became ever more sophisticated, as the study of linguisitics deepened, and as German and Hungarian and Czech were reshaped as far more potent communicative tools for their aspiring communities, multilingual tolerance was forced to retreat in the Habsburg provinces. "Idioms," like "idiosyncratic," even originally "idiot": the root refers to particularity and incommunicability, the singularity of languages and language knowledge—the encroachment of monolingualism grew as liberalism declined.

It is against this increased brittleness and political complexity in which ethnicity and class both increased their salience, dividing society "horizontally" as well as "vertically," that the urbanists and architects wagered their own careers. But like the overall trends in the late Habsburg realm, they played two roles at once. On the one hand, interest alone suggested that they be supporters of the imperial project since the state was the source of so many contracts and commissions. But the supranational project was also the inspiration of representational architecture for the city. The Empire was an ideological commitment, and despite the conservatism of the Monarch and the Court, despite the imperfect liberalization of the regime, the Empire, with all its costumed flummery and pageants, legitimated modernism in its successive waves of anti-historicist reaction. Historicism was the style of the liberal-imperial phase of the sixties and seventies; Secession, rural rediscovery, and churches of vernacular inspiration provided the contending references for the early twentieth century. Architecture and urbanism insisted on cosmopolitanism because inspiration came from diverse sources, because the newest designs were shared with Baillie Scott, or Wright, or Berlage, or Gaudí—but at the same time architecture felt the pressure to be national, above all in the non-German regions which were asserting their claims for greater autonomy. The Hungarian national project was carried on fittingly enough by a Jewish Magyar architect, Béla Lajta.

To infer the intentions of architecture is a risky business, especially because the outcomes of design do not always carry out stated intentions. By 1914, the engagement with modernism could also—as in the case of Otto Wagner and his pupils—suggest a commitment to transnational values, which were values on which a multiethnic empire had to rest. At the same time architects also endeavored to incorporate local vitality. They cultivated *Heimat* localism, rural vernaculars, and even fanciful symbolic forms of "Asian" heritage for Hungarian art (whether expressed in the plastic, sculpted forms of small churches or portals or in the tiled exteriors and fanciful curves of Lechner). Design played a multilevel game: international, imperial, national, and ethnic, and any one practitioner over the course of a career could change the emphasis of his work. It was the multiethnic strains and diverse centers of vitality that ensured that this deeply conservative empire could and had to remain tolerant of innovation. Given the desire to preserve, one had to allow a framework for pluralism, both intellectual and stylistic. As Musil observed, after summoning up his image of the little toy city in the interstices of empire, insofar as national characteristics shaped character, they had done so in Kakania:

> … And in this Kakania was, without the world's knowing it, the most progressive State of all: it was the State that was by now only just, as it were, acquiescing in its own existence. In it one was negatively free, constantly aware of the inadequate grounds for one's own existence and lapped by the great fantasy of all that had not happened, or at least had not yet irrevocably happened, as by the foam of the oceans from which mankind arose.[17]

But there was a key difference between the planners of Central Europe and Musil's dreamy protagonists: the former were unwilling to drift along as passive protagonists and proposed instead the continuing remaking of their territories.

V

The often contradictory imperatives of architectural representation thus meant that there was no simple setback to the designers' imaginations when the Empire dissolved. But there was tremendous dislocation for politics and culture. Most immediately there ensued catastrophic poverty in the aftermath of blockade and defeat and the rupturing of the inner Habsburg trade flows. As early as the winter of 1917, the Allies' blockade, the economic exertions of the war, as well as the diversion of so many young active men to the armies meant scarcity of fuel and malnutrition. Without horses and farmhands, food production dropped. Infant mortality and tuberculosis, those unfailing indices of distress, rose sharply in the cold and hungry metropolises of the Empire.[18] The blockade continued through the winter and spring of 1919, and scarcity and poverty continued into 1920 and 1921. Even before it totally ravaged the German currency, hyperinflation in Poland, Austria, Hungary, and Soviet Russia meant that farmers hesitated to supply the cities with food for worthless paper. Precisely during this period the Viennese population intensified the cultivation of allotment gardens, vastly expanding household production of vegetables and eggs, and bequeathing the small plot as a topos for Loos's vision of post-war construction.[19] Until foreign capital began to enter the region after 1921—from League of Nations' credits for Austria, French and British investments, and American loans—poverty seemed chronic. Difficulties were augmented by the treaty settlements. Austria emerged as a small republic with six-million-odd inhabitants of whom two million were in a capital city that had lost its administrative vocation. The Hungarian grain belt became a land of small peasants whose prices and farm revenues (as elsewhere throughout the world) declined sharply. The massive migrations to North America that had relieved rural overpopulation in the decades before World War I could not resume, once the United States passed fundamental immigration restrictions in 1924.

Political difficulties were also rampant. The "winners" of the settlement included the new, restored Polish Republic with large German and White Russian minorities; the new Czechoslovak republic, which avoided financial disaster, but faced the timebomb of a three-million German minority; and a vastly enlarged Romania with a large Hungarian minority. Indeed, despite the Wilsonian effort at the Paris Peace Conference to enshrine the principle of national self-determination, of the 100 million inhabitants of east Central Europe as a whole, from the Baltic to the Balkans, 25 million lived as minority communities outside their own ethnic heartland and proved susceptible to irridentist appeals. The defeated centers of the old Empire faced political turmoil. In Hungary, the liberal magnates who had proclaimed an independent republic virtually surrendered power to a Bolshevik cadre under Béla Kun in March 1919 once it became clear how extensive would be the territorial cessions imposed by the Trianon Treaty. Following their three-month effort to install a communist order, a nucleus of far right military officers, supported by French and Romanian forces, seized power in the first counterrevolution of post-Versailles Europe.[20] For the next two decades Hungarian politics would oscillate between the Anglophile conservatives who emerged under the aegis of the so-called Regent, Miklós Horthy, and the more radical army officers and politicians who admired Hitler's anti-semitic populism and his restoration of German great-power status. No real Left-Right parliamentary alternation could take root in the semi-authoritarian political system whose élites remained self-imposed hostages to an obsessive sense of national victimization.

The Kingdom of the Serbs, Croats, and Slovenes remained riven by ethnic and historical rivalries from the outset; indeed from the moment that South Slav leaders understood that the world war might yield them a new nation-state, Croatian leaders resisted Serb ambitions to dominate the possible structure. Most Croatians, staunchly Roman Catholic, had lived within the Habsburg Empire, had remained loyal to the dynasty in Vienna, if distrustful of the Magyars in whose kingdom their semi-autonomous province formed the southern borderland. Most Serbs, Orthodox in faith, lived beyond the frontier in a state whose leaders even before 1914 had become ambitious to pry their Bosnian and Croatian kin from Habsburg control. Slovenia, wedged into the southeast corner of Cisleithania between Italian and German-speaking provinces, and rapidly industrializing, was relatively wealthy and remote from Belgrade. Its intellectuals felt themselves to be heirs of both Christian and humanist civilization, drawing on Latin and German as well as Slavic influences. The national tongues of Yugoslavia, so closely related, but including ten dialect variations of what outsiders would amalgamate as Serbo-Croatian from 1918 to 1990, were defended as three separate languages. Representatives of the "South Slavs" overcame their mutual rivalries sufficiently during World War I to plan a united kingdom after the projected defeat of the Austrian Empire. But after Serbian politicians imposed a centralized state structure in the constitution of 1921, tensions and confederal aspirations continued to simmer. Integral Yugoslavism was hard to differentiate from greater Serbian aspirations or, after a royal coup in 1929, from the authoritarian recourse of the monarch, himself assassinated in 1934. Briefly Croatian aspirations gained recognition in the late 1930s, and indeed the most xenophobic Croat claimants organized a murderous state under German and Italian auspices once Yugoslavia was occupied. After the Resistance struggle in World War II, the Communist takeover and then Marshall Tito's construction of a Communist federalism, Belgrade's intellectuals would appear most receptive to dialogue with the West. But between the wars, it was more likely that innovative artistic and planning impulses should emanate from the Slovenian and Croatian capitals and orient themselves toward Western modernism, above all when planners and architects were products of Viennese training.[21]

Elsewhere in Eastern Europe most of the parliamentary regimes established in the aftermath of the world war proved extremely fragile. The Polish Republic that debuted with such promise fell under the domination of its officer corps, as first in 1925 and then even more decisively a decade later, the military forces under President Piłsudski and then the junior officers progressively restricted parliamentary government. In Austria, the Social Democrats aspired to join their German party colleagues but were prevented by the Allies. Within a few years, legislative power passed from the left via a "great coalition" to rule by the Christian Social Party, representing the Catholic conservative forces of the countryside. The Social Democrats retained a strong majority in Vienna, determined to make its municipal and simultaneously federal-state regime into a showcase of socialist transformation. Confrontations moved to the street by the late 1920s as the Heimwehr, an aspiring authoritarian movement, deeply hostile to the Socialists and inspired in part by Italian fascist example, began to offer a more militant alternative to Christian Socialism. Under their impact, the Christian Socialists also gravitated toward antiparliamentary "clerical fascism," while a third current of outright Nazis emerged as an even more subversive force once Hitler's party came to power across the border. In a society where cross-class parliamentary coalitions seemed precluded, the Austrian Socialists retained a vision of Marxist transformation and a rhetoric of militance that was ill-designed to make their adversaries seek the sort of power-sharing arrangements that would become characteristic of post-World War II Austrian society. Instead the components of the Right outbid each other in proposing antiparliamentary tactics and formulas. The Heimwehr's appeal crested in the early 1930s as the Christian Socials themselves assumed an increasingly antidemocratic stance. In February 1934, the Social Democrats, convinced that fascism was coming in slow motion, attempted a disastrous rising in Vienna. In its aftermath the Dollfuss government imposed a virtual dictatorship, only to have the Nazis attempt their own ill-timed coup five months later. In part because of Mussolini's overt hostility, in part because of poor preparation, the coup leaders succeeded only in slaying the Chancellor. But within two years Hitler began to exert a far more skillful and relentless pressure on the Vienna government and finally secured the country's annexation in March 1938—the event and date (along with the autumn cession of the Sudetenland to Nazi Germany) that marks the *terminus a quem* of this study.

Only in Czechoslovakia, where prudent fiscal policies avoided the destructive post-war inflation and moderated the rigors of the world depression, had democracy survived the depression. But the German minority of about 23 percent, demoted from its status of ruling nationality in Bohemia and Moravia (where they constituted about a third of the population), also proved susceptible to the demagogic appeals of neighboring National Socialism and of their own opportunist politicians who exploited it in the old German ethnic settlements of the Czech borderland. Seconded by Poles and Hungarians, who coveted their own neighboring irridentist enclaves, and by clerical-populist Slovak nationalism, and abetted by British and French fear of European war, Hitler was able to dismember the state with a half year of resolute brinkmanship.[22]

It took twenty years to attempt to establish stable and independent states—whose interwar history begins with military collapse and financial turmoil—which then enjoyed a few brief years of restrained prosperity and foreign investment and democratic institutions before slipping into the renewed economic distress of the great world depression. It was natural enough that this barrage of difficulties made collectivist politics appear far more attractive than an apparently antiquated liberalism, which, except for President Tomáš G. Masaryk of Czechoslovakia, seemed to have few charismatic champions. Whether among Social Democrats, mobilizing their youth groups and activists, the Left intellectuals and Communists who accepted Moscow's discipline and inspiration, or the ranks of the small farmers and distressed middle classes who admired the German resurgence under Hitler, the epoch of liberalism seemed passé. Was it not time, they wondered, to fall in with modern regimented collectivism, to leave behind the feckless liberals who had no answer to the world depression, to abandon the parliamentary *Schwatzbuden* or talk-shops for the sake of real action, to cut back the growing Jewish influence that seemed to suck dry the countryside, reward bankers, and control the press?

VI

Still, it would be wrong to paint too uniformly bleak a picture before the late 1930s. The fact that independent republics were established with some effort to honor principles of self-deter-mination, the advent of even short-lived parliamentary government, and the belief that the League of Nations would help ensure a new international order, sanctioned an interval of hope. Intellectuals, including the urban planners and architects, wanted to contribute to the success of these auspicious experiments. If the great arena of Empire disappeared, local demo-cratic or populistic inspirations might replace it, as social democrats—having to renounce a brief moment of national political hegemony after the wave of post-war radical turmoil ebbed, but entrenching themselves in city and state governments and benefiting from a half decade of vigorous foreign loans—commissioned new housing projects and civic buildings. Hence urbanism and design bespoke some ambiguous objectives. Overtly it testified to the potential for progress, whether the elevation of the working class in Vienna or Prussia or the hope for democratic national independence in Prague. At the same time the focus on the urban labora-tories of democracy suggested the renunciation of more territorially extensive transformation, whether throughout Austria or Germany or in a spuriously multinational Yugoslavia. Most particularly in the Viennese Socialists' fall-back on the local, some critics have seen a sort of utopian melancholy, a radical distinction between the austere housing bloc and the buzz of the city outside its gates that enforced isolation, not community. More convincingly, the ambi-tious program of rebuilding settled districts has been defended as a rational strategy in light of the constitutional limits on land acquisition beyond the urban and simultaneously federal-state frontier; so, too, its aesthetics praised for their appropriation of the city's lively middle-class living patterns on behalf of a hitherto excluded proletariat.[23] At the same time, however, the regeneration of the metropolis as a proxy for a more extensive national transformation should also be understood as a new chapter of the multilevel negotiation of allegiances and territorial dialectics that Central Europe had nurtured since the late Middle Ages.

Nonetheless, the terms of territorial negotiation inherent in urban planning decisively shifted after 1918, as the territorial context was itself drastically altered. Architects still medi-ated between the assimilation of cosmopolitan values and the aesthetic representation of local ethnicity, but both influences had decisively evolved as a result of the war. Central Europe was fragmented. The great web-like influences left by three hundred years of Habsburg rule—a Catholic culture that could be cosmopolitan but was so often stultifyingly provincial; the fer-ment of the Jewish intelligentsia, challenging, conspicuous, and precarious all at once; the transnational pretensions to grace on the part of the aristocracy—now had to share the public sphere with soldiers and middle-class and peasant politicians. The rejection of the imperial center meant that styles no longer radiated so automatically from Vienna. The sources of mod-ernism, in any case, had become more diffuse. Czech architects had begun to look toward Paris and cubism even before the war.[24] Since the new Republic was created by exiles steeped in British, French, and German culture as well as dependent upon the French post-war security network (against a potential Austrian and Hungarian effort to reverse the Treaties), Western connections were preordained. In Croatia and Slovenia, too, the defense of national/ethnic autonomy within the structure of the new South Slav state encouraged the rapid assimilation of the international modernist style. In Zagreb a nucleus of almost sixty architects—among them Drago Ibler, Viktor Kovačić, Lovro Perković, Stjepan Planić, E. Steinmann, and Ernest

Weissman—many trained in capitals abroad, made their city a center for modern design and urban planning, even if economic realities condemned many projects to remain on paper.[25] For the Slovenian intelligentsia, who claimed both Latin and German cultural legacies, the idiosyncratic syncretism of Jože Plečnik, with its brilliant combinations of mythic vernacular rustic elements and Roman borrowings, its search for new combinations of primeval elements—a post-modernism *avant la lettre*—allowed the region to triangulate itself among Slav, Italian, and German inspirations.[26] Sensing this talent for encompassing multiple historical references even while creating new monuments, Czech President Masaryk asked Plečnik to help restore the new seat of government in the Prague castle, now to serve as the people's patrimony, not the dynasty's.

Thus the venerable Central European strategy of counter-balancing local and remote models on behalf of national self-representation still influenced inter-war design strategies. Of course, the specific program for national self-expression was perforce debated and often syncretic, just as the new political life of east Central Europe was turbulent and contested. Was national life to express the promise of Wilsonian self-determination, or be engulfed in nativist xenophobia and militarist yearnings? The ragged alignment of states and peoples endangered the democrats and advantaged the demagogues. "No country of Central or Eastern Europe had the wisdom to rise above territorial quarrels," wrote István Bibó, one of the region's shrewdest critics, in 1946. "They weren't 'fascist' or 'democratic' from principle but only because of the territorial advantages that fascism or democracy could secure for them."[27]

Still ideology counted. If the primary inter-war political influence on the context of urban design was the reshuffling of territory, the second was in fact ideological commitment. Although the great aesthetic innovations were already registered before the war—witness, among others, Wagner, Hoffmann, and Loos, or Gropius, Taut, and Behrens in Germany, just to cite architects from within Central Europe—the era that began with what we might call the Wilsonian moment ushered in widespread efforts to apply modernist innovations to social collectives. The aspiration to construct new societies, and the successive models on the Left—whether Moscow for the Communists, or Berlin and Vienna (and later Madrid and Paris) for the Socialists—meant that planners and architects could not finesse the political implications of their work. The social implications of construction had to be exhaustively articulated, even if the work itself might remain open to diverse interpretation. Before the war, Habsburg projects might encourage urban cosmopolitanism and modernist experiments; industrialists, too, patronized contemporary design in the Central European empires. But style became more polarized after 1918. An initial post-war period open to expressionist and fanciful design was succeeded by the earnest functionality of the "new objectivity" that fit the mission of the social democratic municipalities. Art Deco could serve the corporate client of the "golden twenties" in America, France, and the western-oriented Czechoslovakia (where it had naturally emerged in the pre-war years) but not the financially strapped social democratic city council. Wealthy clients still secured brilliant projects from avant-garde architects, whether Loos, Le Corbusier, or Mies van der Rohe. The garden city or suburban development emerged with a more pastoral or conservative valence. Great Britain—conservative, democratic enclave of the 1930s—turned to suburban housing, and occasional emulators of British civilization, as in Budapest, followed suit.

Nonetheless, the historian must caution again against ascribing any neat stylistic division along ideological grounds. It would be too simple to associate the exponents of Modernism simply with the forces of the democratic Left, and the conservatives with a historicizing or ruralist reaction. In an era when ideologies of Left and Right were deeply critical of liberal individualism, social aesthetics were also ambiguous. The powerful Americanist influence of Taylorism and Fordism allowed the modern design of industrial capitalism to win enthusiasts across the political spectrum.[28] Even in Weimar Germany, which now tended to displace Vienna as a major reference point, the advocates of modernism in the Bauhaus emerged from a craft-oriented ethos (as had inspired the Wiener Werkstätte and even earlier the Arts and

Crafts movement in Britain) that wove pre-industrial yearnings into its urban visions. Gropius declared that "We must destroy the parties. I want to establish here an apolitical *Gemein-schaft.*"[29] And the urban utopianism of a Le Corbusier, so powerfully expressed through writings and expositions in the mid 1920s, celebrated less the mass democracy of the city than an untrammeled authority for central planning. The new national collectivism of the Right would also enroll advocates of modernism: the architecture of Italian fascism (and to a degree of German National Socialism) also wanted to stress clean lines, massive volumes, housing and sport for the thousands. In the same decade the young American exponent of the "international" style, Philip Johnson, would himself experiment with fascistic commitments; and to cite another field of aesthetic endeavor, the great innovators in inter-war English-language poetry, T.S. Eliot and Ezra Pound, found rightist politics far more congenial. No matter where they were cited, urban design aspirations could be politically multivalent.

This does not mean that there were no political consequences for design and planning. From 1917 to the mid 1920s, admiration for the Russian revolution encouraged formalist experimentation, although thereafter Communist commitments would increasingly squeeze out innovation. By the mid 1920s, architectural conservatives sometimes harbored reactionary politics. Critics of the Bauhaus and champions of traditional German styles welcomed the destruction of the German Republic. In Hungary, where German and National Socialist influences could reinforce an ugly revisionist Right, some architects could intensify the search for a *völkisch* Magyar inspiration, now suggesting that even Lechner's efforts at national style had embodied too "oriental" (read Jewish) an influence.[30] Most consistently, reformist architects in Central Europe united social democratic aspirations for the working-class city with modernist design. In diverse ways, influenced by differing possibilities for land acquisition and the aesthetic traditions of their respective cities, the German *Siedlungen* and the apartment enclosures of Red Vienna became the characteristic endeavor of Central Europe's democratic decade.[31] The city thus remained the privileged arena of cosmopolitan inspiration. Social democracy and the working class remained heirs to the modernizing impulses that the Empire itself had allowed.

But in many ways it is the ambiguities of urbanism in Central Europe that remain the more intriguing and challenging legacy to decipher. As we distance ourselves from World War II (and as the collapse of Communism has liberated the historiography from a simple Left-Right confrontation), we can interpret the contradictory cultural currents of the inter-war period with more attention to shared or interwoven cultural traits. The architectural record of fascism emerges as more complex than granted earlier, above all the currents of modernism that emerged in the Italy of the 1930s.[32] Our own postmodern achievements may have begun by celebrating the vernacular "strip," but the historicizing impulse has become ever stronger and oriented toward classical retrievals. From the post-1989 reconsideration of inter-war ideological battles and in light, too, of the perspective afforded by Slovenia's early secession from a failing Yugoslavia in 1991—we can perhaps better understand the great accomplishment of Plečnik in Ljubljana.

By the end of the 1930s uniformity was arriving again—and in much of Central and Eastern Europe, the heavy hand of authoritarian decisions would not be lifted for half a century. With the Anschluss and, within a year, the destruction of the Czech state, quickly thereafter the conquest of Poland, and the ravages of an even more destructive war, the resources for new building projects were curtailed. After only a few years the styles of late Stalinism would become the order of the day. Nonetheless, it would be wrong to envisage the war and then the Cold War as imposing a total rupture. Planning for post-war reconstruction proved a main channel for the continuity of concepts and inspirations from the 1930s to the 1950s. Post-war German architecture owed more to the inter-war studios than the simplistic notion of "Stunde Null" allowed. Mussolini's Italy also incubated the seeds of a post-World War II modernism, including Pier Luigi Nervi's work at EUR (the exhibition outside Rome), and the apprenticeships of the neo-realist film-makers at the Cinecittà studios. British urbanism, exemplified in the 1943 London County Council plan, carried forward the inter-war aspirations with up-graded housing and new green belts. In Yugoslavia, enclaves resisting Nazism and then, to a degree, Stalinism, might continue innovation. This exhibit ends logically enough with the Nazi takeover of Central Europe, but many historical continuities in politics as well as culture link the 1930s with the two successive decades.[33]

In retrospect, it is clear why the territorial layering of Central Europe had proved so propitious for innovation and experiment. The Habsburg structure—that continually rickety and creaking compromise between localism and centralization—had nurtured the modern, because cultural innovation, as much as the assertion of traditionalism, provided the regime with a sort of tutelary legitimacy. This unacknowledged fact had been evident in the endorsement of the dynasty implicit in pre-war Austro-Marxism.[34] Without the grudging hospitality for Modernism, cosmopolitanism would have been extinguished far earlier, as the encroachment of populist nativism revealed. And without cosmopolitanism the two minorities that were ultimately removed from Central Europe—the Jews by murder, and, at last, the Germans of the Baltic, Silesia, the Sudetenland, by deportation—could not maintain their transnational presence. The Habsburg state defended imperial tradition by sponsoring or encouraging or tolerating the avant-garde, the international elements of social democracy, and the Jewish thrust toward Magyar and German Enlightenment. Kakania thus had to be innovative, but it could never be innovative enough. Suspended between a tolerance for cultural experimentalism, for language games or aesthetic innovation and a provincial conservatism that ultimately mobilized politically, it provided an asylum for innovative genius.

The republics that succeeded it initially seemed to offer the excitement of new birth, new commitment, and new openness. In fact their political systems, overburdened by ethnic conflict and by successive waves of economic dislocation, and their fragile territorial integrity, menaced by the giant and oppressive systems to the East and West and supported only fitfully by distant liberal regimes that did not want to risk conflict on their behalf, could not durably sustain a robust framework for invention. For half a century Central Europe faded into the category of memory or yearning—to be revived briefly as the Communist empire was disintegrating in turn, and then overshadowed anew by the attractions of NATO and the European Union. Its earlier modernistic impulses, seemingly buried like Pompeii by the political ash of Nazi and Soviet ambition, but now re-excavated, reveal to the city dweller today a promise of pluralist experiment that we encounter with a sense of kinship and recognition.

1 Robert Musil, *The Man Without Qualities*, trans. Eithne Wilkens and Ernst Kaiser, London, 1979, vol. 1, p. 34.
2 For a general survey see Gerhard Melinz and Susan Zimmermann, eds., *Wien–Prag–Budapest: Blütezeit der Habsburgmetropolen: Urbanisierung, Kommunalpolitik, gesellschaftliche Konflikte (1867–1914)* [Vienna-Prague-Budapest: Heyday of the Habsburg Metropolises—Urbanism, Local Policy, Social Conflicts (1867–1914)], Vienna, 1996.
3 Carl Schorske, *Fin-de-Siècle Vienna: Politics and Culture*, New York, Alfred A. Knopf, 1980. Taking up Schorske's metaphor of the enclosed garden of Viennese cultural life, then contrasting it with the young Hungarian intelligentsia's sense of activism and catching up, but ultimately viewing both in the grip of cultural crisis and morbidity, are Péter Hanák's final evocative essays: *The Garden and the Workshop: Essays in the Cultural History of Vienna and Budapest*, Princeton, N.J., 1998.
4 Ákos Moravánszky, *Competing Visions: Aesthetic Invention and Social Imagination in Central European Architecture, 1867–1918*, Cambridge, Mass., 1998, p. 22.
5 Robert A. Kann, *A History of the Habsburg Empire, 1526–1918*, Berkeley, Calif., University of California Press, 1974, pp. 345–56, or for more detail, Kann, *The Multinational Empire: Nationalism and National Reform in the Habsburg Monarchy, 1848–1918*, 2 vols., New York, 1950, II, pp. 125–207; also Arthur J. May, *The Hapsburg Monarchy, 1867–1914*, New York, 1968.
6 A sympathetic view of the Magyar elite and Hungarian political life is available from C. A. Macartney, *The Habsburg Empire, 1790–1918*, New York, 1969, and on a more impressionistic level from John Lukacs, *Budapest 1900: A Historical Portrait of a City and its Culture*, New York, 1988. For a harsh critique of Magyar backwardness and intolerance (echoing that of the novelist Joseph Roth in *Radetzky March*) see Oszkár Jászi, *The Dissolution of the Habsburg Monarchy*, Chicago, Ill., 1929. A balanced modern survey that stresses the relation of political history to social and economic development is provided by Andrew C. Janos, *The Politics of Backwardness in Hungary*, Princeton, N.J., Princeton University Press, 1982. In Hungary electoral gerrymandering allowed the Magyars to dominate parliamentary life despite their comprising only about half of the population (as of 1910: 48.6% of the Kingdom of Hungary and 20.2% of the Empire as a whole). Romanians constituted 14.1% of the Kingdom, Germans 9.8%, Croats 8.8%, Serbs 5.3%. Germans comprised

35.6% of Cisleithania in the same year (and 23.9% of the Empire as a whole), Czechs 23.0%, Poles 17.8%, Ruthenians 12.6%, Serbs-Croats-Slovenes, 2.7%. See Kann, *Habsburg Empire*, p. 607.

7 See Peter G.J. Pulzer, *The Rise of Political Antisemitism in Germany and Austria*, New York, Wiley, 1964; also John W. Boyer, *Political Radicalism in Late Imperial Vienna: Origins of the Christian Social Movement, 1848–1897*, Chicago, Ill., 1981.

8 A similar argument has been made for France by Schorske's student Debora Silverman, *Art Nouveau in Fin-de-siècle France: Politics, Psychology, and Style*, Berkeley, Calif., 1989, in which case the phenomenon testifies less to any Austrian particularities than general European trends.

9 See Eve Blau, *The Architecture of Red Vienna, 1919–1934*, Cambridge, Mass., and London, 1999, pp. 136–41.

10 On this theme in general, cf. Daniel T. Rodgers, *Atlantic Crossings: Social Politics in a Progressive Age*, Cambridge, Mass., 1998.

11 Cited in Moravánszky, *Competing Visions*, pp. 239–41.

12 See Robert S. Wistrich, *The Jews of Vienna in the Age of Franz Joseph*, New York, 1989; also the chapter on the Jews in Henry Wickham Steed, *The Habsburg Monarchy*, London, 1913. The Jews did not count as a nationality for the censuses of the Empire; if they spoke Hungarian, the Magyars counted them as Hungarian to increase their claims to jobs and resources; if they spoke Yiddish, they were tallied as part of the German minority.

13 For the Hungarian army crisis see A.J.P. Taylor, *The Habsburg Monarchy, 1809–1918*, London, 1948, pp. 206–11, (an opinionated but brilliant study that stresses the hopelessness of reform); for the inner life of a multinational military see the favorable verdict by István Deák, *Beyond Nationalism: A Social and Political History of the Habsburg Officers Corps, 1848–1918*, New York, 1990; on Ady and cultural melancholy, Hanák, *The Garden and the Workshop*; and on reform plans, Kann, *Multinational Empire*, vol. II, and May, *The Habsburg Monarchy*, pp. 479–92.

14 Allan Janik and Stephen Toulmin, *Wittgenstein's Vienna*, New York, 1973.

15 Michael Walzer, *On Toleration*, New Haven, Ct., 1997, pp. 14–19.

16 I am indebted to Jeremy King of Mount Holyoke College for sharing the findings of his research on these ethnic trends in the mid-size Habsburg cities.

17 Musil, *The Man Without Qualities*, p. 34.

18 See especially Clemens Pirquet, "Ernährungszustand der Kinder in Österreich während des Krieges und der Nach-kriegszeit" [The State of Children's Nutrition in Austria during the War and in the Post-war Period], Johann Bókay and Adolf Juba, "Ernährungszustand der Kinder in Ungarn," and Béla Schick and Richard Wagner, "Die Einwirkung der Hungerjahre auf die Tuberkulose des Kindesalters," [The Effect of the Years of Food Shortage on Tuberculosis in Children] all in Pirquet, ed., *Volksgesundheit im Krieg*, Vienna, Hölder-Pichler-Tempsky, and New Haven, Ct., 1926, part I, pp. 151–250. This is one of the volumes in the Carnegie Endowment's great series, Economic and Social History of the Great War, James T. Shotwell, general editor.

19 On allotments and Loos's concept see Blau, *The Architecture of Red Vienna*, pp. 83–8, 101; for the impact of wartime and post-war scarcity see Ilse Arlt, "Der Einzelhaushalt" [The Single Household] in *Geldentwertung und Stabilisierung in Österreich* [Currency Devaluation and Stabilization in Austria], Schriften des Vereins für Sozialpolitik, vol. 169, 1925, pp. 161–79.

20 For the revolutionary period in Hungary, see Oszkár Jászi, *Revolution and Counter-Revolution in Hungary*, New York, 1969; Pasquale Fornaro, *Crisi postbelliche e rivoluzione: L'Ungheria dei Consigli e l'Europa danubina nel primo dopoguerra*, Milan, 1987. For general political history see C.A. Macartney, *October Fifteenth: A History of Modern Hungary, 1929–1945*, 2 vols., Edinburgh, 1961. For a good study of Hungarian intellectuals who left after the counter-revolution, see Lee Congdon, *Exile and Social Thought: Hungarian Intellectuals in Germany and Austria, 1919–1933*, Princeton, N.J., 1991.

21 On the roots of inter-war Yugoslav politics see Ivo Banac's superb study, *The National Question in Yugoslavia: Origins, History, Politics*, Ithaca, N.Y., 1984, and the introduction to Audrey H. Budding, "Serb Intellectuals and the National Question, 1961–1991," dissertation, Harvard University, 1998.

22 For Austrian politics see Charles H. Gulick, *Austria from Habsburg to Hitler*, 2 vols., Berkeley and Los Angeles, Calif., 1948; Heinrich Benedikt and Walter Goldinger, *Geschichte der Republik Österreich* [History of the Republic of Austria], Vienna, 1954. For Czechoslovakia, Victor S. Mamatey and Radomir Luza (eds.), *A History of the Czechoslovak Republic, 1918–1948*, Princeton, N.J., 1973, esp. chapters 1–3; Jörg K. Hoensch, *Geschichte der Tschechoslowakischen Republik 1918 bis 1965* [History of the Czechoslovakian Republic 1918–1965], Stuttgart-Berlin-Köln-Mainz, 1966.

23 See especially Manfredo Tafuri (ed.), *Vienna Rossa: La politica residenziale nella Vienna socialista*, new ed., Milan, 1995, pp. 119–39; but cf. Blau's spirited defense in *The Architecture of Red Vienna*, pp. 400–01. For a contemporary critique of Berlin's insufficient social planning see Werner Hegemann, *Das steinerne Berlin* [The Berlin of Stone], Berlin, 1931. Critical discussions of Austrian socialist politics are offered by Helmut Gruber, *Red Vienna: Experiment in Working-Class Culture, 1919–1934*, New York, Oxford University Press, 1991; and Anson Rabinbach, *The Crisis of Austrian Socialism: From Red Vienna to Civil War, 1927–1934*, Chicago, Ill., 1983, among many others.

24 Again, Moravánszky, *Competing Visions*, pp. 333–63, who points out some of the bizarre results. For a useful guide to some of the artifacts see Stephan Templ, Michal Kohut, and Vladimir Stapeta, *Prag, Architektur des xx. Jahrhunderts* [Prague: Architecture of the Twentieth Century], Prague, Zlaty Fez, and Vienna, 1996. By the 1920s, Parisian and Western models more generally included not just the innovations of pre-war modernism but opulent Art Deco—open to colonial influences, swank and stylish, but hardly radical.

25 Tomislav Premerl, *Hrvatska Moderna Arhitektura izmedu dva Rata*, 2nd rev. ed., Zagreb, Nakladni Zavod Matice Hrvatske, 1990; also Stjepan Planić's 1931 guide to his contemporaries, *Problemi savremene Arhitekture*, with essays by Radovan Ivancevic and Tomislav Premerl, Zagreb: Biblioteka Psefizma, 1996.

26 Moravánszky, *Competing Visions*, pp. 389–405. On Plečnik see also Peter Krečič, *Plečnik, Une Lecture des formes*, Milan, Jaca, and Liège, Mardaga, 1992; and Jörg Stabenow, *Jože Plečnik: Städtebau im Schatten der Moderne* [Jože Plečnik: Town Planning in the Shadow of Modernism], Braunschweig and Wiesbaden, Vieweg, 1996.

27 István Bibó, *Misère des petits états d'Europe de l'Est*, trans. György Kassai, Paris, 1993, p. 175.

28 Cf. Charles S. Maier, "Between Taylorism and Technocracy: European Ideology and the Vision of Industrial Productivity in the 1920s," *Journal of Contemporary History*, vol. 5, no. 2, April 1970, pp. 27–61; also on German controversies Joan Campbell, *The German Werkbund: The Politics of Reform in the Applied Arts*, Princeton, N.J., 1978, pp. 211–42.

29 Cited by Marcel Franciscono, *Walter Gropius and the Creation of the Bauhaus in Weimar: The Ideals and Artistic Theories of Its Founding Years*, Urbana, Ill., 1971, p. 148 note.

30 Moravánszky, *Competing Visions*, pp. 274–75.

31 Blau, *The Architecture of Red Vienna*.

32 For orientation see Cesare De Seta, *La cultura architettonica in Italia tra le due guerre*, Bari, 1972; also Richard A. Etlin, *Modernism in Italian Architecture, 1890–1940*, Cambridge, Mass., 1991; Fabrizio Brunetti, *Architetti e fascismo*, Florence, Alinea, 1993; and the essays of Giorgio Ciucci, Marco Romano, et al. in Giulio Ernesti, (ed.), *La costruzione dell'utopia: architetti e urbanisti nell'Italia fascista*, Rome, Edizioni Lavoro, 1988; also Dennis Paul Doordan, "Architecture and Politics in Fascist Italy: Il Movimento Italiano per l'Architettura Razional, 1928–1932," dissertation from Columbia University, 1983, and Doordan, *Building Fascist Italy: Italian Architecture, 1914–1936*, New York, 1988.

33 For the German continuities, Werner Durth, *Deutsche Architekten: Biographische Verflechtungen 1900–1970* [German Architects: Biographical Interconnections], Munich, 1992; also Jeffry M. Diefendorf, *In the Wake of War: The Reconstruction of German Cities after World War II*, New York, 1993. Plečnik's post-war career—including after the establishment of the Tito regime a "retreat" to unrealized drafts and more church designs (which had long attracted him)—is treated in Krečič, *Plečnik*, pp. 171–91.

34 Hans Mommsen, *Die Nationalitätenfrage und die Sozialdemokratie im habsburgischen Vielvölkerstaat* [The Question of Nationalities and Social Democracy in the Habsburg Multinational State], Vienna, 1963. The two principal texts were Otto Bauer, *Die Nationalitätenfrage und die Sozialdemokratie* [The Question of Nationalities and Social Democracy], Vienna, 1907, and Karl Renner, *Der Kampf der österreichsichen Nationen um den Staat* [The Struggle of the Austrian Nations for a State], Leipzig and Vienna, 1902.

MULTICULTURAL COMMUNITIES: TENSIONS AND QUALITIES, THE EXAMPLE OF CENTRAL EUROPE

Moritz Csáky

Plurality in Postmodernism

To perceive the diversity and fragmentedness [*éclatement*] of the world we live in and to consciously accept this as a constitutive constant of the *conditio humana* is an essential demand of postmodern philosophy. If this demand is taken seriously, it follows that it is no longer possible to arrive at universally valid and binding statements and judgments by means of "grand narratives" [*grands récits*]. The great ideologies attempted to do just this. And the historiography which rested on nationalistic ideological premises also strove for just such universally valid interpretations. These "grand narratives," with the aid of which individual and collective legitimations and identities had previously been established (at least in intention), were now at an end, had lost all validity: As expressed most succinctly by Jean-François Lyotard, "Most people have lost the nostalgia for the lost narrative."[1] It has been replaced by a delegitimization of old standards of value and by the task—to be undertaken ever anew—of forming a constitution from variable, that is, changing points of reference and models of order. The global cultural discourse is based on this postmodernist insight, which it has further deepened. In one of his recent works Richard Sennett has taken up this thought, claiming that a situation of this kind demands instability and flexibility. Marcel Gauchet even states that today—in place of identification—it is increasingly dis-identification with traditional identification factors and a "dis-idealization" of familiar ideals that is being demanded of us.[2] This certainly does not lead to chaos or a new barbarism to which people would be forced passively to submit, but what results, rather, are multifarious forms of legitimization by means of "linguistic praxis and its communicative interaction."[3] One striking point made by Lyotard is that the experience of delegitimization is a phenomenon that did not first arise at the close of the twentieth century, but already played an essential role in the period around 1900, especially in Vienna. Admittedly, says Lyotard, people there were not yet able to come to terms with this experience, which encouraged a mood of pessimism and mournfulness [*travail de deuil*] that "was weaned on turn-of-the-century Vienna: not just artists such as Musil, Kraus, Hofmannsthal, Loos, Schoenberg, and Broch, but also the philosophers Mach and Wittgenstein."[4] Is this characterization of Vienna around 1900 correct, and if so, how is it to be placed within the larger sociocultural and historical context?

Modernization in Central Europe

Let me attempt to answer these questions by making two points. First, it would seem necessary to draw attention to the great economic and social changes (modernization) that have taken place over the past two hundred years. These changes had a considerable effect on culture and its self-definition. Second, we must ask whether the effects of modernization, which helped determine collective and individual identity formation, were not perhaps accompanied by further criteria that could be found precisely in Vienna and Central Europe. If we proceed from the fact that the rapid growth of urban centers was a Europe-wide consequence of industrialization, but that here the population streaming into the cities owed its ethnic and cultural diversity to the Central European region—that is, was more heterogeneous than elsewhere—then it is justified to inquire whether this fact might not have a special socio-cultural relevance, i.e., was ultimately constitutive of identity.

Modernization with its economic, technical, and scientific innovations altered and improved general living conditions for people in the nineteenth century. New means of transportation (railroad, bicycle, automobile) affected individual mobility and the exchange of goods; new forms of communication (telegraph, telephone) and the accelerated expansion of money circulation and finance (banks) contributed to a homogenization of society. In his study of the economic rise of the Habsburg Empire, the American historian David F. Good has convincingly demonstrated that in the Danube monarchy modernization initially had a unifying effect.[5] New and improved means of production increased the supply of commodities and improved the maintenance of the populace. All of these processes were accompanied and bolstered by ever-new scientific and technological innovations, for which people came to believe "progress" in general responsible. In many areas a faith in science and technology gradually supplanted earlier models of legitimization, such as the explanations provided by religion.

The increasing differentiation of means of production, aside from having a unifying tendency, also resulted in a new differentiation or segmentation of society. While traditional, feudal social structures were overcome, this went hand in hand with a general lack of orientation and increasing insecurity. Constant competition between heterogeneous social strata (workers, bourgeoisie) led to internal social conflicts which became visible above all in the burgeoning urban centers of concentration, and exacerbated the pervading sense of insecurity. In other words, the accelerated societal differentiation influenced individual and collective consciousness and effected a perception of internal societal difference. The various systems of reference by which people oriented themselves became ever more complex and the search for identities more manifold and arbitrary. The stylistic plurality of Historicism is a good example of how a completely heterogeneous social stratum, the new bourgeoisie, attempted to appropriate a new identity for itself: by turning to the most various, one might even say arbitrary, identifiers from the past.

A highly differentiated society or public also demanded a more differentiated and fragmented mode of argumentation from the producers of its art and culture. Not only the producers (the artists), but also the recipients of their products (the public) had a differentiated consciousness. In order to ensure that their works would be received by as broad an audience as possible, artists were compelled to include a multitude of decipherable codes in their works. This gave their art a fragmentary appearance. Linguistic expression became brittle and fractured; a literary product no longer gave the impression of being a consistent whole. "What is the sign of every literary decadence?" asked Nietzsche. "That life no longer dwells in the whole. The word becomes sovereign and leaps out of the sentence, the sentence reaches out and obscures the meaning of the page, the page gains life at the expense of the whole—the whole is no longer a whole."[6]

This observation is nothing other than the reflection of the changes caused by economic and societal transformations, which led to individual symptoms of crisis. "We have," noted Hugo von Hofmannsthal, "as it were no roots in life, and meander, clairvoyant yet day-blind phantoms, among the children of life."[7] In 1910 the philosopher Georg [György] Lukács wrote in *Nyugat* (*West*), the renowned journal of Hungarian modernism: "With the loss of the stability of things the stability of the ego was also lost; with the loss of facts, values were lost as well. Nothing remained but *Stimmungen* [moods, opinions]."[8] Such symptoms of crisis also made themselves felt in Baudelaire's Paris or Stanislas Przybyszewski's Berlin, and were a result of the modernization which had brought about a vertical differentiation of society and a fragmentation of individual and collective consciousness.

Cultural Heterogeneity of the Region

However, as the investigations of Jacques Le Rider have clearly shown, such symptoms of crisis, such "*crises d'identité*," were even more exacerbated in Vienna.[9] In this context Le Rider refers to the exemplary case of the identity crises of Viennese Jewry, who were involved in a process of emancipation and assimilation. Though the observation is certainly correct, in the overall social fabric of Vienna around the turn of the century Jews were a representative—but by no means the sole—constituent of that "foreign element" from which the populace was composed. Of the Viennese population in 1880, only 38 percent, and in 1900 only 46 percent, had actually been born in Vienna. The rest, the "foreigners," had come to the city for economic reasons. If they were to be successful they were compelled to adjust to the new urban milieu, to assimilate to the dominant stratum. Though an "internal colonization" of this kind resulted in an acceptance of immigrants, it did not remove their alien character, but rather stereotyped it and thus to a certain extent established it as fixed. Assimilation continually demanded the delegitimization of traditional ties or an oscillation between diverse value systems as standards of order, which further increased the insecurities fostered by modernization. And there was an additional aspect: the assimilating immigrants originated from a region which was determined by ethnic, cultural, and linguistic heterogeneity. That is, the general insecurity arising out of modernization's tendency to differentiation, the dilemma of having to come to terms with a life-world of multifarious relationships, was here magnified by specific regional conditions and thus took on an additional qualitative dimension.

Heterogeneous Urban Milieus

Hence the differentiation of society and the fragmentation of consciousness was bolstered by this additional factor in the urban centers of the Central European region. While the proportion of foreigners in Paris around 1900 was only 6.3 percent, that in Vienna was over 60 percent. The capital and royal residence had a population of 1.7 million at that time. It included over 500,000 immigrants from Bohemia and Moravia, 140,000 from the countries of the Hungarian Crown, approximately 100,000 from Galicia, Bukovina, and other parts of the monarchy, and 250,000 from the former patrimonial dominions (today's Austrian federal states). This influx led, as early as the 1850s, to the recommendation that Vienna be divided into national districts. As regards the capital of the Hungarian Monarchy, formed in 1872 by uniting Pest, Buda, and Ó-Buda into Budapest, Pest in 1851 had a population of 83,868, of which 33,884 were Germans, 31,965 Hungarians, 12,642 Jews, and 4,187 Slovaks. The situation in Buda was similar: 22,122 Germans, 6,182 Hungarians, 1,537 Jews, 1,145 Serbians, and 1,124 Slovaks. By 1890 Budapest already had 500,000 inhabitants, but only 39 percent had been born there; 52 percent originated from the ethnically and linguistically heterogeneous monarchy.[10] The percentage of the intrinsically heterogeneous Jewish population in Vienna increased by 1910 to 7.8 percent, in Budapest to approximately 24 percent, and in Černivci, a small town in the eastern monarchy, to over 30 percent of the total population.

This extreme diversity of ethnic and cultural traditions found in the cities provided the conditions for intense reciprocal influence, processes of cultural diffusion and acculturation, and a form of multiculturalism, albeit tied to certain social strata. The diversity of cultural traditions became an important impetus to cultural creativity, since one could choose from a range of cultural models or combine elements of various cultural origin in unprecedented ways. The richness in quotation in Viennese musical production around 1900 shows that this opportunity was not missed, and was indeed taken advantage of to a greater extent than ever before.

Yet in the narrow density of the urban milieu, regional heterogeneity was also seen as a threat. For here one experienced what was foreign, alien—i.e., difference—in one's immediate surroundings, felt a resulting sense of insecurity to which the dominant social group (which at times saw itself forced into the role of minority) reacted with increasing irritation. It attempted to get rid of these foreign influences, responding to the increasing ethnic and cultural fragmentation with forced linguistic and cultural assimilation, or violent marginalization and the suppression of alien elements. All of this was done on grounds supplied by the national ideology, namely that each individual possesses not several but only one national identity. For this purpose, of course, the concepts of nation or ethnic group first had to be defined. Language became the principal factor in this definition. But since linguistic assimilation led to continual changes in the number of people who belonged to a nation, it was constantly necessary to "reinvent" the ideas of "nation" and "ethnicity."[11]

To this end, nationalist and proto-fascist ideologies were increasingly enlisted. In this connection it is important to point out that these ideologies, which degenerated into radical forms of chauvinism and anti-Semitism, originated not in rural regions but in the densely populated urban areas, in which the heterogeneity of Central Europe not only became visible but was felt to be a threatening problem.

Pluralities in the Past

The Central European region had in fact been determined for centuries by a diversity of ethnic groups, languages, and cultures. It is from this characteristic trait, paradoxical as it may seem, that consensus in the region derived. This plurality of Central Europe can be demonstrated in a great variety of areas. It consisted in the ethnic variety and polyglot skills of its inhabitants, in a rich cultural differentiation, as well as in the presence of three monotheistic world religions—Christianity, Judaism, and Islam—in a rich range of forms. Plurality was manifested in the variety of political and governmental traditions, which could not be eliminated even in a state like the Habsburg Monarchy. On the other hand, this situation presented the opportunity for processes of exchange, ethnogenesis, and acculturation; on the other, it included the continual presence of differences and therefore of conflicts. This was true not only of the region as a whole but of its sub-regions—that is, individual countries, provinces, and cities. I would like to suggest that we view this ethno-cultural plurality as an inner (endogenous) plurality, that is, one present in the region, as well as viewing it as an external (exogenous) plurality, subject to overall European influences.

Endogenous Plurality

By endogenous plurality I understand the close coexistence of peoples, ethnic groups, cultures, and languages which has existed in the region for centuries and indeed persists to this day. Thanks to continual interaction there developed a range of cultural codes which were understood by everyone and which contributed to a super-ordinate regional identity. Even the so-called "national" folk cultures which were repeatedly viewed as the original custodians of cultural autonomy and authenticity were in truth pervaded by numerous "foreign elements"—codes adopted from neighboring cultures. Béla Bartók, with regard to the musical folklore of the region, pointed out a continual "crossing and re-crossing of melodies."[12] Thus, despite belonging to a certain cultural configuration ("national culture"), people participated in others as well, which facilitated the development of multiple identities.

This cultural multipolarity was reflected, for example, in the bilingualism or multilingualism of many inhabitants of the region. The idea of a "native language" was often not limited to fluency in any one language learned in childhood, but might encompass a knowledge of several languages. The consequences this could have were described by the linguistic philosopher Fritz Mauthner, who traced his early interest in the philosophy of language back to this fact:

> ... In other respects, too, many things could be said about the special conditions which heightened my interest in a psychology of language to the point of a passion. In my case this interest was very strong from my earliest childhood; indeed I do not understand how a Jew born in a Slavic area of

Austria could not find himself compelled into linguistic studies. Back then he learned … to understand three languages at once: German as the language of the officials, of education, literature, and its offshoots; Czech as the language of the peasants and servant girls, and as the historical language of the glorious Kingdom of Bohemia; a little Hebrew as the holy language of the Old Testament and as the basis of that vulgarized German which he heard spoken by Jewish junk dealers, but occasionally also by very well-dressed Jewish merchants in his environment, or even by his relatives. The Jew born in a Slavic region of Austria had, as it were, to simultaneously revere German, Czech, and Hebrew as the languages of his "ancestors." And the mixture of quite dissimilar languages in the common pidgin Bohemian and the much more vulgar Yiddish could not but draw the child's attention to certain linguistic laws, to borrowing and contamination, the full significance of which has yet to be understood by linguistics even today.[13]

Ethnic and linguistic heterogeneity characterized not only the region as a whole but also its sub-regions: kingdoms, countries, and many of their regions, and cities. Thus the multi-ethnic and multicultural situation in the Kingdom of Hungary was, in a sense, a mirror image of that which obtained in the Danube Monarchy as a whole. With the gradual realization of the educational ideals of the Enlightenment, which related to all strata of the population and thus aimed in effect at a "national" education, i.e., general education for all, there arose a situation of increasing competition among the languages and cultures of the monarchy, since development and maintenance of the various national languages were a precondition for the attainment of this educational goal. While the predominance of Latin as the generally binding administrative language (until 1842) initially delayed such conflict, the demand that Hungarian (Magyar) be introduced as an administrative and state language (a proposal first raised, in reaction to the Josephinian decree of 1784, by the Hungarian regional parliaments in the late eighteenth century and taken up in the first half of the nineteenth by part of the political intelligentsia) caused a polarization between the Magyar language and culture and the nationalities who spoke other languages. Only now did the ethno-cultural heterogeneity and inherent contradictions in the monarchy come to full awareness. These began to be problematized either by emphasizing a preference for Magyar (Hungarian linguistic nationalism) or by declaring the equal claims and rights of all languages in the region. Thus the Hungarian ethnographer Pál Magda could write in 1819:

> No matter how many in Hungary speak German and Slovakian, we still are not citizens of a German or Czech but of a Hungarian empire. Let it be at the discretion of a citizen of Hungary to speak and write Latin, Slovakian, and German as he wishes. But if a born Hungarian does not consider it beneath him to learn the Slovakian and German languages, a Slovak or a German should not be ashamed to learn Hungarian.[14]

Even prior to industrialization, cultural plurality or heterogeneity dominated in urban centers like Vienna, Budapest, and Prague. Already in the sixteenth century Wolfgang Schmeltzl, from the Palatinate, reported that the languages of Vienna were "Hebrew, Greek and Latin, German, French, Turkish, Spanish, Bohemian, Slovenian, Italian, Hungarian, good Dutch, naturally Syrian, Crabatian, Serbian, Polish, and Chaldaean."[15] Similar observations were made by foreigners such as Kaspar Riesbeck[16] or Johann Pezzl in the late eighteenth century, and by Frances Trollope[17] at the beginning of the nineteenth. Pezzl, a Josephinian man of letters who had emigrated from Bavaria, found the multi-ethnicity and polyglot character of the capital and royal seat of Vienna especially noteworthy.

> As far as the inner, imperceptible differences among the inhabitants of Vienna are concerned, it is true in this respect that no family can trace its native descent farther back than the third generation. Hungarians, Bohemians, Moravians, Transylvanians, Styrians, Tyroleans, Dutch, Italians, French, Bavarians, Swabians, Saxons, Silesians, Rheinlanders, Swiss, Westphalians, Lothringers etc. etc. incessantly flock in great numbers to Vienna, seek their fortune there, sometimes find it, and become naturalized. The original Viennese have disappeared. It is just this mixture of so many nations which creates that endless Babel of languages which distinguishes Vienna from all other European places.[18]

A similar situation existed in other centers of the monarchy. The multifarious nature of Budapest's population has been mentioned. Yet even smaller cities such as Ljubljana exhibited linguistic diversity, according to an entry in the Brockhaus encyclopedia of 1835: "The vernacular is Slovenian, a Slavic dialect interspersed with many German and Italian words; but much German, Italian, French and Modern Greek is spoken as well."[19] Cities less strongly involved in international trade had more homogeneous populations. But their hinterland tended to be as a rule ethnically and linguistically mixed, which was also true of many of the then patrimonial territories (now the federal states of Austria).[20]

Both the urban centers and the separate kingdoms and countries reflected the pluralistic character of the overall region. Germans, Hungarians (Magyars), Czechs, Poles, Italians, Ruthenians (Ukrainians), Romanians, Croats, Serbs, Slovaks, Slovenes, and Jews were the most important linguistic groups in the monarchy. These nationalities were not simply distributed according to the territoriality principle among the various kingdoms, countries, and provinces of the monarchy; they formed various mixtures above all in the great border zones, those places of "cultural encounter" which so interest cultural historians, such as Bohemia with its population of Czechs, Germans, and Jews.

Exogenous Plurality

By this term I understand the sum of those cultural elements which entered from outside and which contributed to the specific cultural and linguistic configuration of Central Europe. These pan-European processes of cultural diffusion were naturally often associated with certain social strata, but were nevertheless able to permeate the cultural consciousness of other broad sectors of the population.

The fact that the Habsburgs were not only possessors of their inherited patrimonial lands and kingdoms but simultaneously German kings and emperors of the Holy Roman Empire; that significant portions of the monarchy (such as the patrimonial territories or Bohemia) were part of this Roman Empire; and that the inhabitants of the patrimonial territories and leading social strata used German as the language of commerce and education in other regions of the monarchy—all these circumstances underscore the relevance of cultural codes which flowed into Austro-Hungary from the lands of the German Empire. In the context of the monarchy as a whole the "German element" was certainly only one among many, yet the fact that German had figured as a scholarly language since the eighteenth century made it a generally accepted and important instrument of cultural appropriation. Based on this widespread linguistic consensus there emerged a communication platform which especially furthered cultural exchange with the "foreign German countries."[21] In the monarchy, those who spoke German called themselves "Germans" without implying that clear orientation which was later, for those "Germans" of a German-nationalist stamp, to become an identity-defining criterion.

Habsburg Central Europe was exposed from the sixteenth century to a strong Spanish influence.[22] At that time many members of the Habsburg family had been educated in Spain, felt stronger ties to Spanish than to German culture, and were considered Spanish by their contemporaries. The propagators of re-Catholization were Jesuits who espoused a strict Spanish spirituality. Over the years this form of spirituality shaped the mentality of broad sectors of the population and was decisive in the development of a political culture based on submission to authority. Of similar importance was the reception of Spanish ceremonial, which influenced the quotidian culture of even the lower strata of the population. One can in fact speak of a continued presence of Spanish elements in the monarchy. The rediscovery of the Spanish Baroque in the late nineteenth century—the "Oracolo manual" of Balthasar Gracian, in Arthur Schopenhauer's translation, had become an important part of the education of the Viennese bourgeoisie—meant for many Austrian intellectuals (not least for representatives of Viennese modernism such as Hermann Bahr and Hugo von Hofmannsthal) a new conscious awareness of a tradition which could be considered part and parcel of one's own cultural memory.

During the Enlightenment period the French language took on relevance for all of Europe. The circle of scholars around Prince Eugen had already included many Frenchmen, such as the author Jean-Jacques Rousseau. The company of Franz Stephan of Lothringen included representatives of the Lorraine upper class, renowned scholars and artists who had a lasting influence on cultural life at the royal court and the cultural elites of Vienna. The great number of French borrowings in standard Austrian German and in colloquial Viennese—*vide* the writings of Ferdinand Raimund and Johann Nestroy[23]—is a reflection of an acculturation process enriched by these exogenous elements. French cultural influences also largely determined the emergence of one of the most popular entertainment genres at the end of the nineteenth century, the Viennese or Budapest operetta, a specific genre whose formation owed primarily to a reception of French vaudeville and Offenbach's Parisian operetta.[24]

Though the Italian influence, like the French, was effective throughout Europe, (one thinks, for example, of music, the visual arts, or literature), in Central Europe it became an inherent, formative cultural criterion. Especially intensive Italian cultural influences can be established in Dalmatia, Croatia, Hungary, Slovakia, and southern Poland since the heyday of the Pannonian Renaissance in the fifteenth century. Owing to the fact that entire Italian provinces were solidly integrated in the monarchy, the Italian element was indeed an inherent criterion of endogenous cultural plurality. The nobility, military, and officialdom traditionally contained a high proportion of Italians; Italian cultural codes became determinant even in everyday culture such as cuisine—in the nineteenth century the "Costolette Milanese" became the "Wiener Schnitzel."

When Naples was administrated by the Habsburgs for a few decades in the eighteenth century, Pietro Metastasio, a native of Rome, came from Naples to Vienna, where he held the influential post of court poet for over four decades. In the subsequent period Italian theater joined the French in setting the tone. Neapolitan opera, foremost in Europe, influenced the operas of the Viennese Classical School and the resulting "new sound" soon became a determining trait in music. Similar observations can be made regarding architecture throughout the territory of the monarchy. How formative the Italian style became not only for Vienna[25] and Prague but also for smaller towns of the monarchy may be seen from the example of Graz, whose Mediterranean look goes back predominantly to the activity of Italian architects, builders, and artisans both in the Baroque period and in the second half of the nineteenth century.

Finally I should like to point out a sphere of cultural influence which is almost forgotten today. The long presence of the Ottoman Turks in the Balkans helped shape the ethnic, cultural, and religious realities of the region and left traces that are still evident today. Parts of the eastern and southeastern countries of the monarchy were likewise long under Ottoman rule, which has influenced the cultural habits of the population right up to the present. The Hungarian shepherd's and magnate's costume, which are now presented as typical examples of Magyar national culture, went back in part to Ottoman models, and the so-called "Magyar National Style" in architecture that arose late in the nineteenth century employed Ottoman elements alongside elements derived from peasant building styles. Military music received its final configuration at the close of the eighteenth century through the reception of Turkish Janissary music, whose influence is evident not only in the music of the Viennese Classical School but in the operetta productions of the *fin de siècle*. The adoption of Mediterranean eating habits was largely due to the mediation of the Ottoman Turks; the term *Türkensterz* (roughly translated something like Turk's tail), still used in Styria to describe a cornmeal dish popular in rural areas, leaves no doubt as to its provenance.[26]

The Subjective Experience of Plurality

The endogenous and exogenous plurality of the region is not a retrospective product of the historian's imagination: it was perceived and described by many contemporary observers. "The situation and extent of the several main nations of the Monarchy has led to the idea of viewing these as a Europe on a small scale and positing, in addition to a European balance [of powers], a specially Austrian one." This remark, from a German encyclopedia of political science published in 1841,[27] was anticipated twenty years previously by Johann Csaplovics. Slovak in origin, Csaplovics wrote chiefly in German and Latin, and characterized Hungary as "Europe on a small scale" since "almost all European peoples and languages ... [were] at home there."[28]

Admittedly the cultural and linguistic heterogeneity of the region stood in the way of the homogenization tendencies of the nineteenth century. Emphasis was placed on the proneness to conflict and crisis of the situation, which was accordingly instrumentalized to serve national political interests. Yet to the thinking of broad sectors of the population, who had not yet experienced the imminent political demise of this ethnic and cultural plurality, such conflicts did not seem clearly to presage the end of the cohabitation of peoples and cultures in Central Europe. Men of the most diverse political affiliation, such as the political thinkers József Eötvös, František Palacký, Lajos Mocsáry, Karl Renner, Otto Bauer, or Oszkár Jászi, concerned themselves exhaustively in their works with various solutions, none of which envisaged a dissolution of the ethnically and culturally pluralistic state. Rather, in the face of extreme nationalist arguments, they all accepted as given the pluralistic constitution of the region, crisis-prone as it may be, and attempted to establish it firmly in the public awareness.

The immediate consequences of such a complex socio-cultural system were, on the one hand, the already mentioned continual processes of ethnogenesis, which on the micro-level of everyday life led to numerous mixed marriages between individuals of different origin and language group (a subject to which little research has yet been devoted). On the other hand, the meeting of different complex cultural traditions provided an opportunity for acculturation and the reception of "foreign" cultural codes and elements which helped shape the specific cultural configuration both of the entire region and of its sub-regions. The "cultural memory," that is, the specific framework of interaction which guides "behavior and experience" and "is available to generation after generation for repeated practice and initiation,"[29] grew increasingly permeable, both in the overall region and its sub-regions, to elements that owed their origin to regional (endogenous) and extra-regional (exogenous) sources.

A cultural life-world of such great if regionally differing heterogeneity formed an essential context for the formation of identity, be it of individuals or entire social strata.

> Our homeland is a polyglot country. Hungarians, Germans, Croats, Slovaks, Serbs, Slovenes, and Romanians live here, and who knows how many others besides? Though it is a small country, it possesses four to five independent literatures. Books, newspapers, schools in Italian, French, German, Latin, Hebrew, and five further languages are a necessity here.[30]

While Imre Gáspár was here describing the social situation of the Kingdom of Hungary in 1879, for intellectuals in the early years of the twentieth century this multi-polarity of their own identity became a key experience in their lives: "For a long, long time, ever since I have been conscious of my life and feelings, I have felt myself to be a Slav," wrote the Hungarian author Desző Kosztolányi to his Serbian colleague Veljko Petrović in 1909.

> My family is an old aristocratic family, but the Hungarian coat of arms gleams in vain over our ancestral home, because I know that in my father's family numerous intermarriages with Slavs took place, which has made me a poet and unhappy. When you read my writings, which I forward with today's post, you will notice that I have no Hungarian tone whatsoever. This beauty and this curse: they are Slavic. The Slavic seers of ghosts and dreamers. Indeed I have felt myself drawn to them since my childhood. I have sought my relatives not among the French and English but, very definitely, among the Russians, Polish, and later among the Czechs, and I have realized that the future belongs to them.[31]

An individual and collective reference system of this kind—shaped by a heterogeneous diversity—in which the separate elements may impinge on each other and interpenetrate yet still retain their autonomy, their foreignness, discloses the drama inherent in cultural processes. Even when they enter into a new configuration with others, the individual elements retain their authenticity and stand in competition with one another within the new cultural context. In this light, culture can be explained as a process in which the confrontation, merging, or rejection of various elements or codes take place in a dramatic mise en scène.[32] Recently the Bosnian author Dževad Karahasan illustrated this "fundamental relationship of tension" within apparent cultural symbioses by reference to the example of Sarajevo:

> Within the dramatically constituted cultural system an exciting game, its most marked characteristic, is being performed, a play of reciprocal commentary and contrasts of open and closed, of outside and inside, a game that of itself determines even the internal organization of the city, both the structure of every one of its parts and the business of daily life within it, including every individual element of this daily life, from dwelling to eating.[33]

Central Europe after the Fall of the Monarchy

In the decades around 1900 good use was made of this plurality, especially in the field of culture. It contributed fundamentally to the formation of individual and collective identities at that period. On the one hand, there developed a comprehensive, analogous cultural awareness that expressed itself, for instance, in a specific tradition of thought which likewise was indebted to analysis. What I have in mind is that tradition of thought which begins with Bernard Bolzano and extends to Ludwig Wittgenstein. On the other hand, the diversity of cultural offers was exploited, codes of the most varied nature were crossed and reworked to produce cultural goods of an identical or analogous nature. A glance at the architecture of the region, especially that of the decades around 1900, is enough to confirm this.

The enormous cultural creativity of the Central European modern movement can surely be traced back to this pluralistic background, yet it also evinces the conscious or unconscious reflection of a fragmented, "hybrid" life-world which owed its existence to the specific conditions of the region. The thoughts of the physicist and philosopher Ernst Mach, who attempted to interpret the ego in terms of its fleeting sensory impressions; the problematization of the relationship of individual percepts to the whole in the Gestalt philosophy of Christian von Erhrenfells or Alexius Meinong; the revolution in music initiated by Arnold Schoenberg's dodecaphonic system, in which every note is given equal relevance; the explanation of knowledge and its acquisition from a complex social context in Wilhelm Jerusalem or Karl Mannheim's sociology of knowledge, and finally, the psychoanalysis of Freud, who saw the causes of illness in a disregard (suppression, repression) of individual elements—all of these theories of Viennese or Central European modernity in the decades preceding and following the turn of the century cannot, I believe, be adequately explained without reference to the concrete regional conditions in which they emerged, the pluralistic, multicultural life-world of Central Europe.

The Austrian artist and art theoretician Peter Weibel recently based an entire exhibition on such considerations. Held in 1998 in Antwerp, Weibel's exhibition attempted to illustrate the comprehensive lines of development common to both art and science in the Central European region in the twentieth century.[34] The creative potential of the region was not bound up with national cultural premises; it was the result of cultural codes which pervaded the entire region. This insight leads to very general conclusions regarding cultural theory:

> Culture develops beyond the geopolitical and ethnic code; it is created by members of a community which transcends geographical, ethnic, linguistic, political, religious, state, and national borders. Culture is evidently a web, continually woven anew, overspanning geopolitical and national frontiers, a work of translation from generation to generation.[35]

The situation on the political level was admittedly different. Here, centrifugal tendencies fueled by nationalistic slogans and practices made continued cohabitation of the peoples and cultures of the region seem ever less likely. The alliance reached in 1879 between the Austro-Hungarian Monarchy and Wilhelmine Germany (Dual Alliance) was considered a threat in the rest of Europe, and thus arguments regarding the internal heterogeneity of the region, which the propaganda characterized as a "prison of nations," were given increasing emphasis in order to destabilize and thus politically dominate the region. The outbreak of World War I in 1914 confirmed, on the one hand, how precarious the situation in fact was, for the cause of the declaration of war on Serbia was the assassination of the Austrian heir to the throne who had suggested a political solution that did not take account of the idea of national autonomy: the amalgamation of the south Slavic peoples and a triple construction of the monarchy.

On the other hand, many people saw in the war a chance to restore a national unity that was growing increasingly shaky. War was viewed as a catharsis, a way to heal increasing internal political paralysis and to counteract the ever more threatening separatist tendencies. Many intellectuals thought this way and thus supported the war, from which they expected a strengthening of the unity of Austria, i.e., of the entire region of the monarchy. Thus the author Hermann Bahr wrote in his essay "Das österreichische Wunder" (The Austrian Miracle):

> Of all the surprises this war has brought us, the greatest is that Austria, so often declared dead, is still alive, and more so than ever. Of all the homilies current before the war the most inane was that concerning Austria's decay .... And now? What a different picture! All of Austria is of one and the same will, the same preparedness, the same readiness to make sacrifices; Germans, Slavs and Hungarians brothers, no more quarrels, unity everywhere: Austria is back again! ... It seems a miracle.[36]

That this was a deception would become apparent all too soon. Exploiting the situation of the vanquished, the victors dissolved the centuries-old political coexistence of the nations and cultures of Central Europe in the Paris peace accords of 1919.[37]

Thus the internal ethnic and cultural diversity of the region issued in a political differentiation which, under the banner of the self-determination of nations, gave rise to new nation-states. Apart from strategic political calculations relating to all of Europe, the point of the exercise was to quash those symptoms of conflict and crisis which could be traced back to regional heterogeneity. But did these new nation-states, such as Czechoslovakia, Hungary, Yugoslavia, truly reflect the aims of national autonomy? In reality almost every one of these new states saw itself confronted by the same problems as the previous larger conglomeration of states. The so-called successor nations simply mirrored, on a smaller scale, the ethnic and linguistic splintering that characterized the entire region. A few concrete examples may serve as illustration. In 1921 74.4 percent of the inhabitants of Yugoslavia were officially considered "Serbo-Croats"—an artificial lumping together of Serbs, Croats, and Bosnians; 8.5 percent were Slovenes, 4.3 percent Germans, 3.9 percent Hungarians, 3.7 percent Albanians, and 1.9 percent Romanians. The population of Czechoslovakia consisted of 65.5 percent "Czechoslovakians," i.e., Czechs and Slovaks; apart from this 23.4 percent were Germans, 5.6 percent Hungarians, 3.5 percent Ruthenians, and 1.4 percent (180,900) Jews. Hungary had lost two-thirds of its former territory in the Trianon Peace Treaty, and now contained 89.5 percent Magyars; the remaining 10.4 percent was distributed among minorities (above all Germans, Slovaks, and Romanians); the 473,000 Jews, the majority of whom had become assimilated to Magyardom, made up 5.9 percent of the population.

Such internal demographic imbalance made the inhabitants of these nations particularly susceptible to fascist and totalitarian ideologies, since they promised the removal of the "alien" element. And these became the triggering factor in revisionist and separatist movements, which both Nazi Germany and, after World War II, the Soviet Union were able to exploit for their own political interests. Today such ideologies once again provide a fertile soil for the emergence of autochthonous, irrational nationalistic tendencies which promise, with the aid of separation and ethnic cleansing, to remove the individual and collective tensions inherent to any complex, multicultural, i.e., hybrid system.

There is a further aspect that deserves consideration. As official demographic statistics of recent years indicate, minority groups have rapidly decreased in significance in many countries of Central Europe. In 1991 94.2 percent of the inhabitants of the former Czechoslovakia were Czechs and Slovaks, and in 1990 Hungary's population consisted of up to 97.9 percent Hungarians (Magyars). This picture of an ethnic and cultural homogeneity can be attributed, on the one hand, to the displacements that took place in the wake of World War II, but on the other, it reflects the phenomenon of "internal colonization," i.e., generally ascertainable tendencies as a result of which minority groups or individuals in such groups attempt to adapt to the dominant culture, not least for reasons of financial necessity or sheer survival.

Such assimilations, of course, need not necessarily be caused by direct social pressure; they can also have indirect motivations, such as the desire to participate in a supposedly higher, more advanced culture. A good example of this is the assimilation efforts of Jews in turn-of-the-century Vienna and other Central European urban centers, as well as people of other ethnic and cultural origins. The attempt to adopt a "different" culture often leads to an ambition to adopt this culture perfectly. Hence assimilated intellectuals frequently become pronounced propagators of the contents of the culture they have adapted to, and in the political field assimilated persons often become outspoken advocates of national cultural values. Perhaps this happens, partially unconsciously, because despite a range of assimilation tactics (down to changing one's family name) these would-be members of another culture are nevertheless still looked upon as "foreigners" by many of its representatives. This not infrequently leads to the attempt to suppress their former cultural context. Good examples are not only "Jewish self-hatred" (Theodor Lessing's phrase) but the fact that advocates of chauvinistic ideologies, especially in Central Europe, usually do not stem from the cultural context to which they have dedicated themselves.

But even the dominant cultures are enriched through assimilation processes by "alien" cultural components, which in turn continually alter the original cultural configuration while still remaining identifiable as "alien" elements. The cultural memory is charged with a variety of heterogeneous codes which constitute the richness of a culture, but which are also the cause of latent tensions. These codes naturally tend to become a problem when, for national political ends, they are instrumentalized, reinterpreted, or selectively marginalized. Their instrumentalization in the interest of re-establishing homogeneous individual or collective identities has been common political practice in Central Europe to this day; the marginalization of codes declared to be alien in the interest of some imaginary national concept is undoubtedly one of the causes of those crisis symptoms which have triggered many armed conflicts in recent times.

In view of such circumstances one might advance the hypothesis that Central Europe, owing to its ethnic and cultural differentiation, represents a "laboratory" in which processes are continually underway that today—in the age of globalization and cultural net-working have taken on a worldwide relevance. Rapidly increasing mobility and the expansion of new forms and systems of communication have made it possible to experience the "foreign" and "alien" on a daily basis. This might lead to socialization becoming more difficult and the formation of individual and collective identities more complex, i.e., more unstable and apparently more arbitrary. The complex cultural system of the Central European region was, and still is, a source of continuing insecurity, individual and collective conflicts and crises. This susceptibility to crisis was already perceived around the year 1900, and attempts to analyze and explain it were made in analogy to the procedures Freud applied to crisis symptoms in the individual personality. Though the crises and conflicts that arose from cultural heterogeneity could not be eliminated by such analyses, they could be mitigated by bringing them to consciousness. This insight would seem to hold valid for similar socio-cultural situations around the world today.

Against the sometimes one-sided notion of multiculturalism as a natural, "friendly," and harmonious interplay of diverse cultural codes, it is important to clearly point out—precisely in the example of Central Europe and its permanent "cultural" crises and conflicts—immanent differences. I believe that, based on this example, the demand "to rethink cultural diversity in terms of cultural difference" is not only possible but necessary: the cultural text of Central Europe should indeed be understood as a "concept of polyphonic and hybrid cultures." It should encourage us to go beyond a naive "utopia of cultural diversity."[38]

1 Jean-François Lyotard, *The Postmodern Condition: A Report on Knowledge*, translated by G. Bennington and B. Massumi, Minneapolis 1984, p. 41.

2 Richard Sennett, *The Corrosion of Character*, New York, 1998. Marcel Gauchet, "Essai de psychologie contemporaine I. Un nouvel âge de la personnalité," *Le débat*, vol. 99 (March–April 1998), pp. 164–81.

3 Lyotard, *The Postmodern Condition*, p. 41.

4 Ibid., p. 41.

5 David F. Good, *The Economic Rise of the Habsburg Empire 1740–1914*, Berkeley, 1984.

6 Friedrich Nietzsche, "The Case of Wagner "[1888] in *The Birth of Tragedy and The Case of Wagner*, translated by Walter Kaufmann, New York, 1967, p. 170, "Der Fall Wagner" [1888], in Giorgio Colli and Mazzino Montinari (eds.), Friedrich Nietzsche, *Kritische Studienausgabe*, vol. 6, Munich, 1980, p. 27. (Nietzsche indirectly quotes from Paul Bourget, "Essai de psychologie contemporaine," vol. 1 Paris, 1883, p. 25. See also Nietzsche, *Kritische Studienausgabe*, vol. 14, p. 405).

7 Hugo von Hofmannsthal, "Gabriele d'Annunzio" [1893], in Bernd Schoeller and Rudolf Hirsch (eds.), Hugo von Hofmannsthal, *Gesammelte Werke, Reden und Aufsätze I: 1891–1913*, Frankfurt am Main, 1979, p. 175.

8 Georg Lukács, *"Die Wege gingen auseinander,"* quoted in Aranka Ugrin and Kálmán Vargha (eds.), *"Nyugat" und sein Kreis 1908–1941*, Leipzig, 1989, p. 66.

9 Jacques Le Rider, *Modernité viennoise et crises d'identité,* Paris, 1994.

10 Michael John and Albert Lichtblau, *Schmelztigel Wien – einst und jetzt. Zur Geschichte und Gegenwart von Zuwanderung und Minderheiten,* Vienna and Cologne, 1990, p. 14ff.; László Gerevich (ed.), *Budapest története* [History of Budapest], vol. 3, Domokos Kosáry (ed.), Budapest, 1975, p. 399; vol. 4, Károly Vörös (ed.), Budapest, 1978, p. 378ff.

11 Werner Sollors, "Introduction: The Invention of Ethnicity," in Werner Sollors (ed.), *The Invention of Ethnicity*, New York and Oxford, 1989, pp. IX–XX.

12 Béla Bartók, "Race Purity in Music" [1942], in B. Suchoff (ed.), *Béla Bartók, Essays*, London, 1976, pp. 29–32.

13 Fritz Mauthner, *Erinnerungen*, Munich, 1918, pp. 32–33.

14 Quoted in Zoltán Ács, *Nemzetiségek a történelmi Magyarországon* [Nationalities in Historic Hungary], Budapest, 1984, pp. 230–31.

15 Wolfgang Schmeltzl, *Ein Lobspruch...* [1548], Vienna, 1913, facsimile, verses 332–38.

16 Kaspar Riesbeck, *Briefe über Deutschland*, Vienna, 1790, p. 6.

17 Frances Trollope, *Briefe aus der Kaiserstadt*, ed. and revised by Rudolf Garstenauer, Frankfurt am Main, 1980, pp. 174, 206f.

18 Johann Pezzl, *Skizze von Wien. Ein Kultur- und Sittenbild aus der josefinischen Zeit*, ed. Gustav Gugitz and Anton Schlossar, Graz, 1923, p. 22. According to Pezzl it was incorrect to assume, as did the poet Ramler, that only seven languages were spoken in the monarchy: "The indigenous languages of the Austrian patrimonial states are German, Latin, French, Italian, Hungarian, Bohemian, Polish, Flemish, Modern Greek, Turkish, Illyrian, Croatian, Slovenian, Walachian, and finally the Gypsy language" (ibid., p. 23).

19 *Allgemeine deutsche Real-Encyklopädie für die gebildeten Stände*, vol. 6, Leipzig, 1835, p. 449.

20 As late as the 1910 census, Tyrol and Styria, including the southern territories separated from them after World War I, were definitely mixed-language areas. Of the 916,216 inhabitants of Tyrol, 387,700 (42%) were Italian, and Styria contained a full 409,684 Slovenes (21.5%). See Moritz Csáky, "Die Gesellschaft," *Das Zeitalter Kaiser Franz Josephs*, exh. cat., Schloss Grafenegg, 1987, p. 41.

21 Particularly after the proclamation of an "österreichischer Kaiserthum," or Austrian Empire in the year 1804, those lands of the German Empire or German Bund which did not belong to Austria were referred to as "foreign." See *Oesterreichische National-Encyklopädie*, vol. 6, Vienna, 1837, p. III.

22 Ferdinand Opll and Karl Rudolf, *Spanien und Österreich*, Vienna, 1991.

23 Felix Kreissler, *Das Französische bei Raimund und Nestroy*, Vienna, 1967.

24 Richard Traubner, *Operetta: A Theatrical History*, New York, 1983; Franz Hadamowsky and Heinz Otte, *Die Wiener Operette. Ihre Theater- und Wirkungsgeschichte*, Vienna, 1947; Carlo Runti, *Sull' Onda des Danubio blu. Essenza e storia dell' Operetta Viennese*, Trieste, 1985; Moritz Csáky, *Ideologie der Operette und Wiener Moderne. Ein kulturhistorischer Essay*, 2nd edn. Vienna, Cologne and Weimar 1998; András Batta, *Träume sind Schäume. Die Operette in der Monarchie*, Budapest, 1992.

25 See Luisa Ricaldone, *Italienisches Wien*, Vienna and Munich, 1986.

26 As regards clothes and fashions, see Gabriella Schubert, "Die Rolle der Kleidung in den Nationalbewegungen der Donauvölker," in Moritz Csáky and Horst Haselsteiner (eds), *A magyar nyelv és kultúra a Duna völgyében. Die ungarische Sprache und Kultur im Donauraum*, Budapest and Vienna, 1989, pp. 314–32. On music, see Horst Reichenbach, *Zur Frage des Populären bei Mozart. Ein Beitrag zur Mozartforschung*, Halle and Wittenberg, 1975 (diss.); Bence Szabolcsi, *Die Exotismen bei Mozart*, Prague, 1956; E. Rameis, *Die österreichische Militärmusik, von ihren Anfängen bis zum Jahre 1918*, Tutzing, 1976.

27 "Oestreich," in Carl von Rotteck and Carl Welcker (eds.), *Staats-Lexikon oder Enzyklopädie der Staatswissenschaften*, vol. 12, Altona, 1841, p. 143.

28 Johann Csaplovics, "Das Königreiche Ungern [sic] ist Europa im Kleinen," in *Erneuerte Vaterländische Blätter für den Österreichischen Kaiserstaat*, vol. 13, Vienna, 1820, p. 410.

29 Jan Assmann, "Kollektives Gedächtnis und kulturelle Identität," in Jan Assmann and Tonio Hölscher (eds.), *Kultur und Gedächtnis*, Frankfurt am Main, 1988, p. 9.

30 Imre Gáspár, *Hazánk tót népe* [The Slovakian People of our Fatherland], Budapest, 1879, p. 6.

31 Dezső Kosztolányi, *Levelek-Naplók* [Dezső Kosztolányi: Letters, Diaries], eds. Pál Réz and Ágnes Kenyeres, Budapest, 1996, p. 186.

32 Wolfgang Lipp, *Drama Kultur*, Berlin, 1994.

33 Dževad Karahasan, *Tagebuch der Austreibung*, Klagenfurt, 1993, p. 14.

34 Peter Weibel, *Jenseits von Kunst* (exh. cat.), *Neue Galerie am Landesmuseum Joanneum Graz* (among other mueums),Vienna, 1997.

35 Peter Weibel, "Jenseits von Kunst," *Parnass* , (Vienna) vol. XVIII, no. 4, 1998, pp. 76–81; quotation p. 76.

36 Hermann Bahr, "Das österreichische Wunder," in Hermann Bahr *Schwarzgelb*, Berlin, 1917, p. 30.

37 The argument that the monarchy was "dismembered" by the Western Powers is advanced, among others, by the British historian Alan Sked, *The Decline and Fall of the Habsburg Empire 1815–1918*, Addison-Wesley, 1989.

38 Elisabeth Bronfen and Benjamin Marius, "Hybride Kulturen. Einleitung zur anglo-amerikanischen Multikulturalismusdebatte," in Elisabeth Bronfen, Benjamin Marius and Theres Steffen (eds.), *Hybride Kulturen. Beiträge zur anglo-amerikanischen Multikulturalismusdebatte,* Tübingen, 1997, pp. 12–13.

THE CITY
AS FORM AND IDEA

URBAN VISIONS, PLANS, AND PROJECTS, 1890–1937

Renate Banik-Schweitzer

Urban visions and utopias are rarely mere products of the imagination; they usually represent attempts to address issues specific to a certain time and place. The emergence of certain urban models can generally be conclusively related to specific social developments. If the most advanced ideas and models are absent from a particular geographical region, it can be assumed that the local society has not yet reached the corresponding level of development. Although the region of the former Austro-Hungarian Monarchy produced a few urban development models, they all shared a tendency to further develop the existing model rather than to break radically with it and advance a completely new conception. The fact that neither a disurbanization model like the Garden City nor a regional urban conception for a metropolitan agglomeration emerged there would seem to indicate that in the territory of the Habsburg Monarchy the urbanization process was not yet so far advanced as in other parts of Western and Central Europe.

Three of the town planning conceptions that originated in this region remained theoretical. Camillo Sitte's critical commentary on the city of 1889 and Otto Wagner's model of 1893–1911 are quite familiar. Less attention has been paid to Farkas Molnár's 1925 design for the KURI city (an acronym of Constructive, Utilitarian, Rational, International) which was intended as a political and ideological critique of Le Corbusier's Ville Contemporaine of 1922. Two further conceptions, on the other hand, were put into practice: first, the public housing projects of Red Vienna, built in 1923–34, which until recently were considered to be only a housing reform project and not a true urban development conception.[1] Second, there was the Baťa town, Zlín, in the Czech Republic, developed in 1923–39. Admittedly this project was not addressed to the theme of the metropolis, but embodied a "single company town" in the new form of a Fordist and functionalist industrial city. Though Zlín may have been modeled on Tony Garnier's Cité Industrielle (1901–04), it is more likely that the shoe manufacturer Tomáš Baťa was influenced by similar towns of the kind he had seen during his travels in North America, or even by earlier types of company towns in his homeland, such as the mining and smelting town of Ostrava. KURI city and Zlín certainly do not conform to the categories noted at the outset, since they were at the forefront of international developments. Molnár, however, developed his conception as a student of the Weimar Bauhaus and not in his native Hungary, and Baťa may well have been the absolute exception in all of Central Europe.

One of the contributions to town planning that continues to be most misunderstood is that of Camillo Sitte (1843–1903). This is partly because, without a knowledge of urban thinking and construction in Germany from about 1850 onwards, to which Sitte refers, his work can only seem incomprehensible, and partly because Sitte himself later became the object of widespread and generally accepted criticism which, however, treated his ideas in a highly unfair and selective manner. It is now generally recognized that Sitte's book,[2] despite its title, represents far more than an aesthetic critique of contemporary town planning. There is less agreement with regard to more far-reaching interpretations. In the context of this discussion, Sitte's book will be treated largely as a subjective commentary on the city as a material representation of the new bourgeois society, which, based on rules of liberalism and competitive capitalism, needed to overcome feudalistic and absolutist principles as well as to resolve its own internal contradictions.

New Planning Systems: Particularization and Functional Differentiation

After the bourgeois revolution of 1848, comprehensive urban planning in Central Europe faced the insoluble problem of private ownership of land. Whereas, previously, feudal lords had been in a position to develop an entire city district on their own land based on their personal ideas and in a unified building style (theoretically, still possible today in London, for instance), in Central Europe the abolition of the feudal system left city planners bogged down in negotiations with numerous small land owners whose diverse interests were nearly impossible to coordinate. At the same time, private property was one of the greatest achievements of the revolution and a fundamental pillar of bourgeois society. A respect for private property took precedence over considerations relating to the community at large.

Between about 1850 and 1870, two conceptions of urban planning were developed to resolve this dilemma. Either the persons and institutions involved in planning tried to buy up large areas, in order to be able to proceed along feudal lines (a variant that became increasingly important as time went on, becoming the dominant approach with the rise of organized capitalism), or—as was especially the case in the German-speaking countries—the state or one of its organs issued general guidelines (building code, regulation, and construction plan) within the framework of which various, mostly private property owners could reach individual decisions. This procedure naturally led to a loss of temporal and spatial continuity in planning. Such a system of development was unsuited to producing a unified, "beautiful townscape." For many architects and city planners—and Camillo Sitte, Le Corbusier, and Ludwig Hilberseimer had at least this in common—the city of competitive capitalism came to represent a chaos which it was the task of planning to order.

Now if there was no longer any temporal or thematic connection between public and private planning, city planning of the absolutist Grand Design variety no longer made sense. In the German-speaking countries the problem was addressed by introducing a two-phase planning process. The state (e.g., Prussian Alignment Act, 1875) or the community (e.g., General Building Line Plan for Vienna, 1866) established a street grid, usually perpendicular, and stipulated the admissible building height in a building code. The blocks defined by the street grid were then divided into smaller parcels, each one of a size suitable for building an apartment house of several stories.

The entire planning system rested on the fundamental acceptance of the traditional typology of urban buildings, not least because it favored small property owners as key supporters of competitive capitalism. Since in the capitalist city private ownership of property was one of the most important sources of taxation, it was regarded as a planning maxim to increase taxable private lands as much as possible, while minimizing the tax-consuming public domain. For urban planning typology this resulted in a demand for broad corridor streets, thoroughfares suitable for development, and a neglect of public areas and green spaces.

These changes with respect to absolutist planning practice were related to the triumph of what was probably the most important organizational principle of bourgeois capitalist society: the division of labor as a means of increasing productivity. From now on it was economically more efficient to spatially separate distinct activities and to concentrate related ones. The most rapid and lasting separation occurred between living and industrial manufacturing, though the service sector (trade, financial services, etc.) soon followed suit.

The new dislocation required the development of new mono-functional building types such as the factory, the purely residential building, the office building, the bank, the department store, etc. The negative side of this spatial separation of functions was a rapid increase in traffic, the costs of which were borne not by those responsible but by the urban populace as a whole, in the form of infrastructure development (building, maintenance, and operation of streets and mass transport, supply, and disposal networks) and increased demands on their private time.

In the rapidly growing metropolises of the second half of the nineteenth century, however, the differentiation of building types by use was soon no longer sufficient. More or less randomly developed conglomerates of mono-functional buildings, due to the enormous traffic load they produced, began to impair the functioning of the city as a whole. The bourgeoisie, no longer physically tied to their workplace, felt that they were being harmed by factory emissions. A spatial separation of industrial areas from business areas and middle-class residential areas of the city began. As early as 1876 the German planning theoretician Reinhard Baumeister pointed out how in the modern city large-scale functional differentiation—that is, the creation of city centers and of areas devoted to other specialized functions, such as industrial and residential areas—had come about in a "natural way."[3]

Critique of Town Planning: Between the Old and the New

In the former absolutist royal residence cities which, like Vienna, grew into *Großstädte* or large cities in the latter half of the nineteenth century, the contrast between "old" and "new" planning schemes was especially evident, and the desire to contain the modern "chaos" widespread. In addition, in such cities the emergent bourgeois society still had to assert itself on many levels, including that of symbolic representation *vis-à-vis* a still very real and ever-present absolutist feudalism.

It is only against this background that Camillo Sitte's critique of modern town planning can be properly understood. It was occasioned by a project that was a hybrid of the old and new: Vienna's Ringstrasse. Since the state owned the grounds of the former fortifications which had been razed to make way for its development, the Ringstrasse as grand design might have been planned as a sequence of Baroque plazas of the kind Sitte so favored. But in 1857, after the formation of bourgeois society, it was deemed sufficient to establish a sort of building line plan in which a few areas were to be set aside for public buildings and parks, while the largest proportion would be earmarked for development by private interests.

The modern planning system could not nearly do justice to Sitte's ideas of symbolic representation. Yet symbolic representation seemed to him indispensable, since modern society was only just emerging and "the people," the uneducated masses, had to be provided with architectural codes whose "reading" would help them find their place in this society and develop a *Heimatgefühl,* or sense of home. "One might think," wrote Sitte, "that art was completely and entirely appropriate precisely for municipal grounds, since it is this kind of work of art above all that, daily and hourly, has an uplifting effect on the great mass of the populace, while theater and concerts are accessible only to the more well-to-do classes...."[4]

Sitte did realize that this "work of art" tended to lose meaning with the progressive formation of civil society, as the middle classes withdrew from the physical public space as a result of increasing mediation.[5] Nevertheless, symbolic representation remained so important to him that he formulated his critique of the modern production process of the city, which no longer admitted of a Grand Design, in aesthetic terms. When he attacked the "dismal building block system" on account of its boring straight streets and broken-up street and site frontages, he tacitly refused to accept as the first priority the compulsion characteristic of capitalist planning—to maximize property rents on each individual lot, a manifestation of which was the block consisting of four corner parcels and surrounded by broad avenues, a type indeed seen in the Ringstrasse zone.[6]

On the other hand, Sitte knew that there was no reversing the modern planning process, and this, together with his adherence to the idea of the city as a (total) work of art, plunged him into an insoluble dilemma. This is clearly evident in the suggestions made in his 1899 book for the aesthetic improvement of the by-then existing Ringstrasse. The connection of the solitary building blocks by means of arcades, which at the same time concealed the intersecting streets, has an unconvincing, cosmetic look and would never have evoked the picture of a unified street or site frontage.

Sitte realized that, under the given conditions, the larger part of the city would have to be abandoned to the modern planning scheme. There is no complete overall plan for a

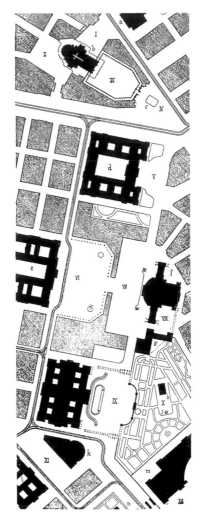

Camillo Sitte, project proposal for the alteration of the Vienna Ringstraße, 1889

Sitte proposes to replace the broad boulevard with a sequence of self-contained squares.

Repr. from: Camillo Sitte, Der Städte-Bau nach seinen künstlerischen Grundsätzen, Vienna, 1901 (3rd edn.)

metropolis from his hand. Instead, Sitte attempted to realize his conception of the city as a three-dimensional work of art in designs for small towns, city districts, or simply central public spaces (civic centers). Unlike most German city planners he provided three-dimensional designs for squares over which he could assume that the planning institution had aesthetic control.

The interest in a "beautiful cityscape" united Sitte with his near-contemporary Otto Wagner (1841–1918) and distinguished both of them from the majority of German town planners who, unlike Sitte and Wagner, were frequently not architects but engineers. Yet, despite their common interest in the city as a work of art, Wagner's urbanist conceptions differed considerably from Sitte's. Their ideas differed particularly in the way that the city of *laissez-faire* capitalism differed from that of organized capitalism, or the neo-absolutist royal residence city differed from the modern metropolis. For Sitte, the cultivated bourgeois, the "beautiful city" was to have an uplifting educational effect on the population and represent the *res publica* of the "citoyen." For the *haut bourgeois* Wagner, in contrast, the "beautiful city" was one which offered space for modern forms of life and whose architectural form conformed to the existential and functional requirements of the modern metropolis. It must offer high hygienic standards, facilitate rapid communication, ensure both anonymity and multifarious contacts, provide high information-density as well as a variety of possibilities for consumption, recreation, and entertainment—in a word, it must offer urbanity.[7]

For Wagner neither the trend towards a mass society nor its urban architectural manifestations had anything frightening about them. As early as 1893 he stated that the beauty of the cityscape arose not from a harmonious combination of heterogeneous elements but from the monumental effect of discrete elements merged into a grand, comprehensive form.[8] In 1896 he remarked that the modern eye had lost its feeling for the small, intimate scale and had become accustomed to images of less variety, to longer straight lines and larger masses.[9] In 1911, he concluded that "the art of our time has, by means of broad streets, raised this uniformity to the level of monumentality."[10]

The Metropole as a New Type of City

The epoch from 1890 to World War I was the epoch of the metropolis. This was the fastest-growing city type, center of organized capitalism and the modern society which had produced it. Yet to conservatives the Moloch of the metropolis was suspect, and the Left attacked it as the highest manifestation of capitalism. It was thus that both extreme poles of the political spectrum set their sights on deurbanization. On one side of the spectrum, Ebenezer Howard in 1898 advanced his Garden City model, intended to curtail the growth of big cities by establishing small, autonomous residential districts having a high proportion of green space; while on the other—for instance in the Soviet Union—this very same model was considered, until the end of the 1920s, to be the best form of settlement to counter the increasing opposition between city and countryside.[11]

In the other camp were advocates of the metropolis who, like Wagner, were of the opinion that "the most modern of modern things in architecture are certainly our contemporary metropoles."[12] The urbanists wanted to enhance the ability of the metropolis to function not by limiting its growth but by reorganizing its functional interrelations and thus improving communication by decreasing traffic density. They pursued, in many variants, the conception of "decentralized concentration." At any rate, the metropolis was the guiding theme of the epoch, and urban planning was no longer occupied with expanding the city (or parts of it), but focused on the city as a whole.

Around 1890, in the German-speaking countries, those who saw the problem in this light developed what were known as "building zoning plans." Such a plan was issued in 1893 in Vienna and at about the same time in Munich and other German cities. These zoning plans divided the entire city area into large zones devoted to different uses: pure residential area, mixed building zone, city center, and industrial zone. Actually none of these zones was strictly mono-functional. What was important, rather, was to eliminate the gravest conflicts of utilization, e.g., to free the downtown area from non-commercial uses, to separate the middle-class trade areas from industrial and working class districts, and thus to achieve a notable reduction in traffic density. Remarkably, this kind of functional zoning was quite compatible with the traditional typology of urban building, so that the multi-functionality of the sectors—i.e., the urban quality of the metropolis as a whole, far from being reduced, was actually enhanced.

Developmental Concept: Modular City versus Satellite Town

Otto Wagner, long before most of his contemporaries, viewed the metropolis as a highly complex system that obeyed its own, specific laws. Already in his competition design for the General Development Plan in 1893 he went a step beyond his competitors, whose submissions, based on the recently expanded planning instruments of building line and zoning plan, were addressed to the contingent situation of Vienna. Wagner, in contrast, attempted to outline a systematic solution to the problem of developing a modern metropolis. Proceeding from the observation that the growth of many metropolises followed a radial, concentric traffic pattern, he suggested basing any plans for expansion on just this scheme and, anticipating actual developments, laying a new ring around the existing body of the city with each stage of its growth. Wagner placed all public facilities at the points of intersection between the extended radial streets and the new ring roads—what he called "Stellen"—in order to ensure an equal provision of services to all the new districts and thus decrease the burden on the city center. "I...maintain," he wrote, "that in this way a rational method of modern city construction will develop."[13]

In his elaborated developmental model for a metropolis of 1911,[14] Wagner speaks with conviction of the necessity for a "systematic regulation of the metropolis" in its zone of expansion. His system, harking back to his proposal of 1893, consists of a comprehensive urban traffic scheme, a network of radial streets and concentric ring roads extending outwards from the city center, with multilevel constructions on intersections for rail and automobile traffic, and a modular, typological element for each area of "mesh" in the web—what he called a "district" for 100,000 to 150,000 inhabitants. Located in the center of the district were public and cultural facilities, which served the district alone and required no link to the larger traffic network, and a large green area for recreational purposes. The rest of the district was composed of smaller modules, each comprising eight blocks bordered by multi-story buildings arranged around a small park as an easily accessible recreation area. Wagner was able to dispense with large-scale functional differentiation of the German variety because his system was so open and flexible that, at the level of development of that time, every function could be adequately incorporated into the blocks. The retention of the traditional urban planning typology of block and corridor street, on the one hand, permitted further development to the perimeter block as needed, and on the other, made a separation of traffic into various levels possible but not necessary, so that a variety in forms of urban communication was retained.

This modular developmental model was for Wagner the result of the conditions of metropolitan growth:

> Since...the individual districts...will develop according to a well-considered plan at precisely predetermined intervals—that is, a group of smaller towns will form around the center—it would seem more appropriate to give each separate district sufficient open-air centers in the shape of parks, gardens, and playgrounds than to project a belt of woods and meadows, since laying out a belt around the city would only succeed in re-establishing a system of confinement, which surely should be avoided. To present-day perception, the expansion of a metropolis must be unlimited.[15]

In Germany too, almost concurrently with Wagner's "Großstadt," the same guiding principles informed a number of urban development models which no longer had anything in common

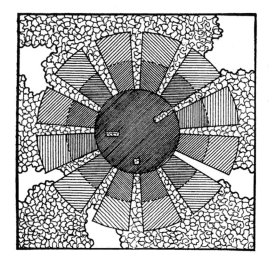 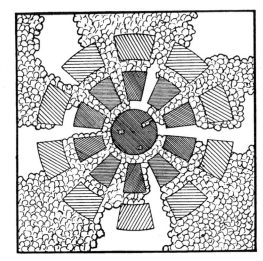 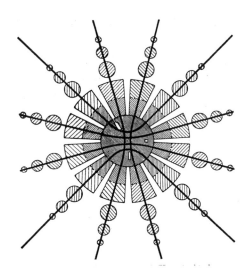

Distribution of green spaces in a larger city, after Eberstadt-Möhring (left), further development of this system (center), and satellite model by Richard Petersen, 1911 (right)

Repr. from: Joseph Brix, Felix Genzmer (eds.): Städtebauliche Vorträge aus dem Seminar für Städtebau an der Technischen Hochschule zu Berlin, vol. 5, no.3, Berlin, 1912

with the German two-phase planning concept. All of these so called "satellite models"—such as that submitted by Joseph Brix, Felix Genzmer, and the Hochbahngesellschaft (Interurban Rail Company) to the Groß-Berlin competition of 1909, or Gustav Langen's and Richard Petersen's differing further elaborations of the model developed by Rudolf Eberstadt and Bruno Möhring for the same occasion—aimed to relieve pressure on the city center by means of peripheral, relatively autonomous zones separated from the center by green areas. These zones were conceived as small towns with corresponding residential areas and, in part, employment opportunities, while the central metropolis was to contain only the higher-level workplaces and educational and recreational facilities.[16]

Wagner's urban model might be interpreted as an inversion of the satellite model to the extent that in the latter, the "small towns" were separated from the central city and from each other by belts or wedges of green, whereas Wagner separated his "districts" from the city center by streets and situated the green areas in the center of his districts. It certainly makes a difference whether streets or green areas are used to separate parts of the town. Green areas tend to isolate them from each other, as Wagner himself noted, while streets, even when they carry rapid traffic, represent connecting elements due to their circulation function. Another essential difference lies in the fact that Wagner's districts are metropolitan in character, differing from the city center neither structurally nor typologically, whereas the satellites are conceived as small towns that are structurally distinguishable from the central city. Thus Wagner's model is in fact a conception for the unlimited expansion of a metropolis, whereas the satellite models, depending on their degree of deconcentration, represent a gradual transition to deurbanization.

Functional Separation: Industrial and Residential City

In France at about the same time as these great-city models were developed, a proposal was made that, for the first time, applied a fundamental functional principle of modern industrial society—the division of labor—to urban development in the form of a complete spatial separation of functions: the *Cité Industrielle* of Tony Garnier (1869–1948).[17] Like Wagner, the architect Garnier sees his city as an abstract three-dimensional model. He designs an industrial city because in his eyes this represents the truly new type of city which will dominate urban planning in the future. As an example Garnier chooses a medium-sized town of 35,000 people which includes all building types that he regards as important, since—in his opinion—a metropolis is too complex to represent the relationships between its various building types in a model.

Actually Garnier operates with only very few functions, such as work (principally factory labor), living, health and recreation, i.e., production and reproduction in the most

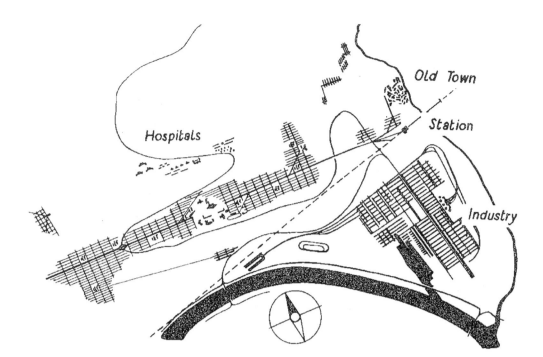

Tony Garnier, Project for the "Cité Industrielle", 1904–17

Schematic ground plan
Segregation on the basis of different types of usage; residential area, including a cultural center, to the south of the hospitals
Repr. from: Dora Wiebenson: Tony Garnier, The Cité Industrielle, New York, 1969

fundamental sense. In his view of the requirements of industrial production, areas such as education, administration, and other services, trade, and consumption play only a subordinate role and do not justify the creation of a traditional city. The city center is a civic center with public and cultural facilities located in the midst of the residential area. All individually perceived functions—manufacturing, living, services, and health/recreation—are assigned different sites, which are separated from one another by expansive green areas. Garnier separates not only functions but also types of traffic, permitting a purely pedestrian network in residential areas and an opening-up of the building blocks. Admittedly, however, the improvement in dwelling and living conditions sought by means of a separation of functions in his "industrial garden city" is achieved at the cost of a loss of urbanity.

It is surely no coincidence that a functionalist urban model first appears in the form of a developmental model for an industrial city. After all, it was industry that developed new forms of labor organization and thus gave the impetus to new forms of social behavior, which in turn demanded new forms of expression. Functionalism and zoning are the spatial forms of expression of industrial society. These demands were already fulfilled at an early date, and without planning, in the newly emerging manufacturing towns. From the *Cité Ouvrière* at Mulhouse, presented in London at the Great Exhibition of 1851, to the great mining and iron and steel regions of the Ruhrgebiet or of Ostrava in Austria-Hungary, there emerges a new typology of town planning which differs fundamentally from the old typology of block, row house, and corridor street.

In these "regional cities," which often did not even possess the legal status of autonomous communities, the (large) landowner was frequently identical with the mine or factory owner. Small scale land ownership, with the logic of ground utilization that is peculiar to it, played no role in these cases. Added to this was the fact that the service sector was under-represented in such regions. The only thing that counted was mass production and mass reproduction—the latter because there were hardly any social groups apart from workers. Property rents as an allocation mechanism were irrelevant. On the contrary, it was in the entrepreneur's interests to make more land available to his laborers, usually in the form of garden allotments, since (particularly in mining areas) employment for women was scarce, whereas—through gardening—these women could contribute to maintaining their families.

In spatial terms these needs could be better met by abandoning the block and corridor street, since the individual lot as unit of use had in any case become superfluous. Thus, for reasons of rationalization, these "cities" displayed a clear spatial separation of work from living. Their often enormous factory complexes were clearly demarcated from the housing settlements. The settlements, in turn, were designed solely as dwelling places. They consisted either of single-family houses (free-standing, duplex, quadruplex, or row house) with adjoining garden, or of freestanding, multi-story, multi-family houses in row or L-form with separate garden lots for each family. In the early designs the network of streets was usually strictly orthogonal, and there was no united street front because the houses required no access from the street. Designed solely to ensure the basic living functions of a socially homogeneous group, this model lacked all trace of urbanity, if this is understood to mean multifunctional and interwoven, highly concentrated communication.

It is Tony Garnier's achievement to have systematized examples of manufacturing-oriented functionalist worker settlements and developed them into a model for the modern industrial city. Yet his *Cité Industrielle*, made public for the first time in 1904, remained largely unknown outside the French-speaking world. Even in France very little notice was taken of it. One who did appreciate it, however, was the man who would help the functionalist urban model achieve its breakthrough and ultimately win worldwide acceptance. Le Corbusier had established contact with Garnier as early as 1907, and was also the first great architect to recognize the significance of the *Cité Industrielle*, which he presented to a broader public in *L'Esprit Nouveau* in 1921.[18]

Change in the Traditional Typology: The Birth of the Superblock

Functionalism found its way into the metropolis in another, indirect way—through housing reform. With the emergence of organized capitalism from about the 1890s onwards, the small property owner became an obstacle to the optimization of capital accumulation, which was achieved by restructuring the conditions of production and reproduction. In the housing system controlled by small property and home owners, the emergent "new middle class" of skilled workers, low and medium-ranking employees, and officials could not afford the living space necessary to meet the higher demands of reproduction.

Various approaches were taken to solve this dilemma. For one, the small property owner was eliminated by producing housing in larger units to be administered by non-profit organizations. Or attempts were made to create as much residential space as possible on the available lots, which, among other things, led to a suppression of other uses. Also, attempts were made to lower production costs by means of type-standardization, which again made financial sense only on large-scale lots. Finally, public subsidies for housing could be obtained in many cases. All of these factors combined to produce purely residential areas.

In the physical appearance of cities, this reorganization of the system of housing provisions manifested itself in the form of a change in the traditional urban building typology. The birth of the super-block was at hand. The first examples were to be seen at the Berlin City Planning Exhibition of 1910. In the multi-story housing projects in Steglitz and Niederschönhausen designed by Paul Mebes for the Berlin Beamten-Wohnungs-Verein, the connection between house and street is only seemingly direct, and even this connection exists only partially. At several points the courtyards open onto the street, but the resulting space thus created is not publicly accessible. In fact, the houses are accessed by pedestrian paths within the lot.

Inside the block, undivided by property boundaries, are one or more large green areas for common use. It is obvious that these improve the quality of the immediate living area and almost completely shut out the noise of motor vehicle traffic. Unlike the row house located on a corridor street, the quality of the flats oriented either toward the "inside" or the "outside" of the building is nearly the same.

Similar approaches were tried in the metropolises of the Habsburg Monarchy. In Vienna, at the request of the Komitee zur Begründung gemeinnütziger Baugesellschaften für Arbeiterwohnhäuser, the architect Leopold Simony in 1904 designed the so-called Engerth-Hof, which likewise had an internal access system, an only partially built-up perimeter, and green areas and playgrounds for the use of all tenants. An even more spectacular communal housing program based on similar organizational principles was launched in Budapest in 1910.

In 1917 in Holland, thanks to a highly developed planning code and experienced building contractors, Hendrik Petrus Berlage (1856–1934) was able to build an entire residential quarter of superblocks—Amsterdam Zuid. The orthogonal blocks display a four-story perimeter construction, and superficially resemble a traditional row housing block. Yet the block does not consist of individual plots and has a large internal green area accessible to all tenants. By using a perimeter block with which street spaces can be formed that are similar to the corridor street, and by choosing not to deconcentrate street traffic, Berlage succeeded in lending the entire neighborhood an urban quality.

Paul Mebes, Niederschönhausen Residential Estate for the Association for Civil Servant Housing in Berlin

The superblock is situated on one single site with private internal access roads and green spaces. Backyards have been dispensed with.

Repr. from: Werner Hegemann (ed.), Der Städtebau nach den Ergebnissen der Allgemeinen Städtebau-Ausstellung in Berlin, vol. 1, Berlin, 1911

Many metropolises could have been developed along the lines of Amsterdam Zuid, and some indeed were. A total separation of functions was still unnecessary. Though even the metropolis of the turn of the century was an industrial city, it was neither a single-company town nor the site of great heavy-industry operations, but rather of small or medium-sized innovative companies involved in finishing manufacturing. Both the metropolitan finishing industry and the at least equally important tertiary and quaternary sector were complexly interwoven and dependent on close spatial cooperation in their innovative activities. Thus after World War I, when European avant-garde planners and architects applied the model of the functionalist industrial town to the multi-functional metropolis, we may conclude from this that they expected a Fordist social configuration for the metropolis as well, though this would not come to pass until after World War II.

Le Corbusier's *Ville Contemporaine*: The End of the Traditional Metropolis

In the United States around the turn of the century, decisive steps were taken to improve the existing social system, which had been endangered by periodic crises of under-consumption. These reforms were associated principally with the names of Frederick W. Taylor and Henry Ford. The engineer and management expert Taylor had recognized that increases in productivity could be achieved not only through rationalization but through a strictly systematized organization of labor, and he believed that productivity increases would lead to increased wages and raise the standard of living throughout the country.[19] Henry Ford, for his part, fought poverty and social injustice by stimulating mass consumption, passing on a portion of profits from increased productivity to the workers involved in the mass production of consumer goods.

The message from across the Atlantic was as eagerly received by European industrial nations as it was by Lenin in the USSR, where Taylorism and Fordism were considered organizational models for the planned economy.[20] Its opponents in the West were the conservatives, but also the orthodox Left, who saw it only as an aggravated form of exploitation. During the inter-war years in the West, however, a modern consumer goods industry was not able to make much headway against the dominant investment goods industry, which had little interest in high salaries as an incentive to mass consumption. Even in France, which had gone into automobile manufacturing at an early date, the automobile had not yet become a mass product. All this may explain why the emergence of new urban models did not parallel social developments in the 1920s.[21] The European architectural avant-garde designed urban models for a Fordist society which did not yet exist in the metropolises of Europe. As a result, their visions remained on paper.

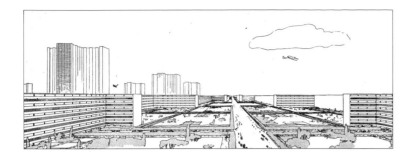

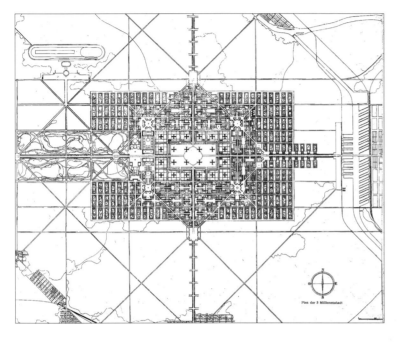

Le Corbusier, Project for the "Ville contemporaine pour 3 millions d'habitants", 1922

Functional separation of the city center, residential areas for employees and industrial and residential areas for workers (not shown). The high-rise superblocks contain maisonette-type flats with balconies and are situated in extensive green areas separated from street traffic. For this reason Le Corbusier referred to them as "vertical garden cities".
Repr. from: Oscar Stonorov, Willy Boesiger (eds.), Le Corbusier und Pierre Jeanneret. Ihr gesamtes Werk von 1910–29, Zurich, 1930

Le Corbusier, who in 1922 with his *Ville Contemporaine* designed the first functionalist big city for three million inhabitants, at the same time designed a city model for a Fordist society. A complete separation of functions was in fact the most rational form of spatial organization for a society in which a large number of people went to the same place at the same time, or undertook the same change of place. In his model Le Corbusier combined an efficient modular traffic network on several levels, no longer directly linked to the buildings, with complete functional and far-reaching social segregation and a new urban building typology.

Le Corbusier deals with the enormous increase in traffic caused by this total functional segregation, on the one hand, by spatially separating office employees in the core city from workers in industrial garden suburbs or towns; and on the other by adapting the high-rise building—previously used for business purposes only—for residential use. By this means part of the traffic flow is moved into the buildings, freeing up extensive spaces for use as green and open areas, so that Le Corbusier can speak of a "vertical garden city."

The *Ville Contemporaine* unmistakably marks the end of the traditional form of the city. With it died the traditional concept of urbanity, though of course the future Fordist society, with its standardized forms of life, will certainly not miss variety and complexity. Le Corbusier's conception caused a shock, but it simultaneously became a model against which avant-garde city planners measured themselves. There is hardly an urban model of the inter-war period which does not refer to it, more or less explicitly.

Counter-proposals: Hilberseimer, Molnár, Miljutin

Ludwig Hilberseimer, for instance, developed his own urban model out of a critique of a partial, if important, aspect of Le Corbusier's design. What Hilberseimer criticizes in Le Corbusier's plan is that it only displaces traffic without reducing it. Given the expansive area of the *Ville Contemporaine*, high-rise housing was not necessary, because the same amount of living space could be provided by traditional construction. Despite the high-rise concentration in the downtown area, Le Corbusier's city would remain a "horizontal city."

The various functional zones, in fact, lie next to one another on a plane. Hilberseimer's "Scheme of a High-Rise City,"[22] in contrast, is a plan that reduces traffic by avoiding it. He achieves this by arranging the two most important functions—working and living—not beside each other in juxtaposition, but one above another on different levels. "Since in this city the residential city lies over the business city, everyone will live over his workplace."[23] Hilberseimer is able to do without creating a city center or relegating industrial areas to the periphery since he does not typologically differentiate the work function. Factory and office work do not need to be situated in separate locations, but can in principle take place anywhere in the "lower city."

His new fundamental typological element is "the community building encompassing an entire block, which contains not only flats, work spaces, and business spaces but everything else necessary to life."[24] In its compactness and employment of the perimeter block for the "lower city," Hilberseimer's model approaches the traditional urban configuration, but differs

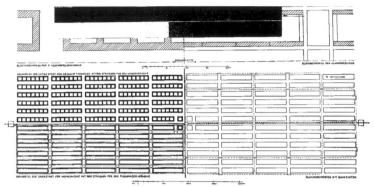

Ludwig Hilberseimer, Plan of a High-rise City, 1927

The "lower city" or commercial city follows the perimeter block and corridor road pattern, while the residential city located above it is accommodated on levels of high-rise buildings. The compact form suggests an urban character which is, however, contradicted by the inevitable reduction in mobility.

Repr. from: Ludwig Hilberseimer, Großstadt Architektur, Stuttgart, 1927

© 1999, The Art Institute of Chicago

from if fundamentally in its form of social organization. Since it ties living mobility to career mobility, it is primarily suited to a highly organized mass society.

Farkas Molnár similarly intended his model KURI city of 1925 to be understood as a critique of the *Ville Contemporaine*, which he had seen as a student at a Bauhaus exhibition in 1923.[25] A committed socialist, Molnár rejects a hierarchical model with a city center—of the kind Le Corbusier envisaged—as being an exemplary symbol of the capitalist metropolis. His KURI city is composed of a number of entirely identical modules, each a small city in itself, within which, to be sure, extensive functional segregation predominates. A module consists of a square street grid measuring 2000 meters on each side. Arranged along the streets are several parallel rows of slab-shaped residential high-rises. At the intersections are "plazas" with public buildings, point blocks where required. The areas enclosed by the street grid include parks, sports and cultural facilities, schools, health-care facilities, but also industrial plants.

Similarly to Hilberseimer, Molnár is able to retain the corridor street because his plan makes no provision for a city center as generator of increased traffic flow, and thus requires no separation into traffic types.[26] Owing to its consistent rejection of a city center—that is, of the service sector (financial capital) which the Left regarded as parasitic Molnár's model cannot be viewed as a developmental conception for a metropolis, despite the fact that it measures itself against the *Ville Contemporaine*. Formally and conceptually, it partially anticipates the linear town designs developed to enforce industrialization in the Soviet Union after the passing of the first Five Year Plan in 1929.

The original linear town conception, Arturo Soria y Mata's *Ciudad Lineal* of 1882, had exploited the potential of new means of rapid transport only by connecting two urban nodes by rail, thus making possible the development of band-shaped residential areas on both sides of the track. In 1930 Nikolay Milyutin modified this idea, under the influence of Ford's assembly lines, by discarding the centers and arranging all urban functions along the line of transport. Through a linear arrangement of industry along the central line of transport and energy supply, and a linear placement of housing and green bands with cultural, educational, and recreational facilities in parallel to the industrial plants, not only would the distances workers had to travel between home, workplace, and cultural and recreational facilities be reduced, but the rural population living on either side of the linear town would now gain access to cultural and health facilities. In Milyutin's design, the city was at least able to expand in two directions, but it still remained an industrial city, since, structurally, no place was foreseen for more complex urban functions.[27]

Zlín: Model of the Functionalist "Single Company Town"

While the many utopian projects were occupying center stage in the 1920s, it was often overlooked that a purely functionalist city already existed in Central Europe—not a metropolis, but a Fordist industrial town: Zlín in Czechoslovakia. Though it contained other manufacturing enterprises, Zlín can justifiably be called a single-company town, since it was completely dominated by the shoe company Baťa. Like Henry Ford, Tomáš Baťa produced mass-consumption commodities and passed on productivity increases in the form of higher salaries to his employees, who in turn stimulated local economic growth by increasing their consumption. Yet to organize not only a company but an entire city along Taylorist-Fordist lines, a few other specific conditions had to be met. Thus, Baťa acquired all of the land needed for urban development, and since he served as mayor of Zlín, he was able to keep taxes low so as to further the growth of trade and services.

The ground-plan which Baťa had drawn up in 1925 by his house architect, František Lydie Gahura—a pupil of Jan Kotěra, who had previously designed Baťa's family villa and the first workers' colony—clearly reflected his notion of a "factory in the garden."[28] Gahura's development plan for Greater Zlín of 1934 showed that he had attempted to combine elements of the European Garden City with American tendencies toward centralization and compression. The town was developed linearly along the hilly banks of the river. At one end of the city lay the factory, which consisted not of flat sheds but, of multi-story linear buildings arranged in strict parallel. Adjoining the factory grounds rose the city center, consisting of a central green area and, staggered up the slope, public and cultural buildings, likewise of open linear design. Then came extensive residential areas which, reflecting Baťa's motto, "work collectively—live individually," were built up with two-story single-family semi-detached houses with yards. Here a total separation of functions had been put into practice.

Baťa was interested in rationalization and systematization not only in his factory but in the "production" of the town. The standardization of building types, construction technology, and materials in all multi-story buildings produced an overall impression of great unity. The same held true of the residential areas, despite their quite different layout. Here, too, there were only a few house types, which were built in great numbers, albeit by the conventional brick masonry method, since serial production—not to mention prefabrication—was uneconomic in the field of single-family housing even when a large number of units was involved.

Zlín, whose population more than quadrupled from 1923 to 1930 and by 1940 had reached, at 37,000, about the size of Tony Garnier's ideal *Cité Industrielle*, was not the creation of a great planner or architect but of a Fordist entrepreneur. The great architects entered the picture only after the basic conception of Zlín had taken shape. In the mid 1930s the company mounted a competition for an urban expansion plan, in which Le Corbusier, among others, participated. Though he followed Gahura's basic linear town conception, his proposal to organize Zlín's housing into six high-rise complexes ran counter to the local "garden city" image and too greatly exceeded the local cost framework for it to be acceptable. Still, Le Corbusier placed great store in the urban planning and construction achievements of Zlín, which rested on the consistent application of Taylorist and Fordist principles to town planning.[29]

Satellite Towns and Social Housing

The German avant-garde, too, was strongly interested in Taylorism and Fordism. Most of its proponents, however, were not concerned with comprehensive urban models (Hilberseimer was the exception) but with that aspect of the city which was most in need at the time: housing. In the economically precarious situation of the Weimar Republic the building of new cities was unthinkable. Improving the housing conditions of the workers, on the other hand, was a realistic goal in the mostly Social Democratic-governed metropolises, and the State provided the means to do so. However, a key precondition for achieving the greatest possible improvement in housing conditions and the optimal use of technical advances was a total segregation of functions on the overall city level and mono-functional use at the actual construction site.

The most creative accomplishment of the German architectural avant-garde was the modern housing development and the satellite town serving housing needs alone. A leading role was played by Walter Gropius at the Bauhaus in Weimar and Dessau, along with Ernst May in Frankfurt and Martin Wagner in Berlin. Gropius was guided by Taylorism and Fordism particularly in connection with rationalization in building design and construction. In 1926, in the Dessau-Törten settlement with its small number of partially prefabricated housing types in the linear building style, Gropius was able to realize his idea of a "Ford dwelling."[30]

After Le Corbusier had provided the impetus for the Fordist conception of the metropolis and Gropius the impetus for the Fordist production of a city, the path seemed clearly marked out for the development of the modern metropolis. Yet one key thing was missing: a Fordist society. Thus when Social Democratic Vienna launched the most extensive public housing project of the period, it was guided not by the functionalist urban model, but by the building typology of the multi-functional city. Red Vienna opted for urbanity over functionalist determinism. Though the target group was indeed the new middle class (skilled workers and employees, single wage-earners, small families), the "*neuer Mensch*" was not to be reduced to the status of producer and consumer of commodities, but, through improved living conditions, was to be enabled to participate fully in the cultural achievements of the age.

After the disastrous outcome for Vienna of World War I, the possibility of a Fordist development was even more remote here than in the rest of Europe. Industry had to adjust to completely altered manufacturing and market conditions; unemployment was on the increase; the preconditions for the mass production of consumer goods and the transfer of productivity increases to the workforce were simply not given. Since rationalization in the construction industry would have been counterproductive, the City of Vienna logically took the opposite tack and chose traditional (brick) construction, with an eye to creating as many jobs as possible.

The avoidance of new building materials, construction methods, and typologies led many critics to reject the public housing projects of Red Vienna as behind the times, unmodern. By comparison with international modernism this was certainly true, yet the modernity of Red Vienna lay not in its aesthetics but in its social quality. For the purpose of facilitating the equitable participation of the inhabitants of public housing in the life of the metropolis, the building model chosen represented the most progressive avenue possible under the local contingent conditions.

One factor contributing to the decision to adhere to the perimeter block and corridor street was undoubtedly the fact that by this means reserves of already opened-up building land could be put to use, thus cutting costs. Structurally, the "new" city had to be capable of development within "building gaps" ranging in size from a single traditional lot to a superblock comprising several traditional blocks. It was to provide better and equitable living conditions for all, yet instead of consisting of mono-functional housing blocks the Viennese buildings were infrastructurally at least as rich and functionally as differentiated as the surrounding urban area. The "new Vienna" was no "dormitory town" but a locally contingent contemporary metropolis, that was not spatially concentrated but spread out over the entire existing urban area.

Prospects

Was there, then, as maintained at the outset, a congruence between social development and urban configuration? Or was the form of the city a matter of arbitrary choice? Two cases would seem to suggest conflicting conclusions: the comprehensive functionalist urban models of a Le Corbusier, Hilberseimer, or Molnár appear to be premature while the architectural form of Red Vienna, appears to be belated. On closer scrutiny, however, the contradictions might be resolved.

If the functionalist city is to be regarded as the architectural manifestation of a Fordist society, then it essentially remains an industrial city which can fulfill only a limited range of social functions, if on a relatively high average level for a large number of people. Zlín is an excellent example of this. The partial functionalism of the housing developments in large German cities also fits this pattern. The functionalist model, on the other hand, does not provide an adequate overall conception for a multifunctional metropolis. The comprehensive models of Le Corbusier and other avant-garde planners did not come too early, in so far as a few examples of Fordist social organization indeed already existed—*vide* Zlín. Yet these must surely be regarded as dead ends, since, when the social configuration of the Fordist welfare state finally triumphed in the European industrial nations after World War II, this development did not occur synchronically, but diachronically, in smaller, mono-functional units. By this time the metropolises no longer conformed to the multifunctional type of the turn of the century, but had simply become large (industrial) cities.

Red Vienna, in contrast, can not be considered belated when it is seen not just as a series of housing projects, but as an entire city. Since the joys of consumerism were out of people's reach in Vienna in the period between the wars, the Viennese also did not have to bear its limitations. Instead, the city attempted to encourage as far as possible the participation of its previously underprivileged citizens in urban life, and this was easier to do if one did not stray too far from the traditional form of the city. After 1945, when Austria, too, went the path of the welfare state, the architectural form of Vienna's urban development no longer differed at all from that of other European metropolises. If today, after the end of the Fordist society and the functionalist city, the desire for urbanity should once again be felt, the supposedly defunct multifunctional metropolis might be able to provide us with some inspiration—not least of all in the field of town planning.

1 Eve Blau, *The Architecture of Red Vienna, 1919–1934*, Cambridge, Mass., and London, 1999.

2 Camillo Sitte, *Der Städtebau nach seinen künstlerischen Grundsätzen*, Vienna, 1889 and 1963, 6th ed.

3 Reinhard Baumeister, *Stadt-Erweiterungen in technischer, baupolizeilicher und wirtschaftlicher Beziehung*, Berlin, 1876.

4 Sitte, *Der Städtebau*, p. 120.

5 Ibid., pp. 112f.

6 Ibid., pp. 91f.

7 Otto Antonia Graf, *Otto Wagner. Das Werk des Architekten*, 2 vols., Vienna, Cologne, and Graz, 1994, vol. 2, II, pp. 641f.

8 Ibid., vol. 1, p. 93.

9 Ibid., vol. 2, p. 281.

10 Ibid., vol. 2, p. 641.

11 Selim O. Chan-Magomedow, *Pioniere der sowjetischen Architektur. Der Weg zur neuen sowjetischen Architektur in den zwanziger und zu Beginn der dreissiger Jahre*, Dresden, 1983, p. 273.

12 Quoted in Graf, *Otto Wagner*, vol. 2, p. 279.

13 Ibid., vol. 1, p. 101.

14 Otto Wagner, *Die Großstadt. Eine Studie über diese*, Vienna, 1911. Reprinted in Graf, *Otto Wagner*, vol. 2, p. 640.

15 Quoted in Graf, *Otto Wagner*, vol. 2, pp. 643f.

16 Gustav Langen, "Stadt, Dorf und Landschaft," in Joseph Brix and Felix Genzmer (eds.), *Städtebauliche Vorträge aus dem Seminar für Städtbau an der Technischen Hochschule zu Berlin*, vol. 5, no. 3 (Berlin, 1912).

17 Dora Wiebenson, *Tony Garnier: The Cité Industrielle*, New York, 1969.

18 Ibid., pp. 98, 105.

19 Thomas P. Hughes, *American Genesis: A Century of Invention and Technological Enthusiasm, 1870–1970*, New York, 1989 (quoted from the German edition, *Der technologische Aufstieg der USA seit 1870*, Munich, 1991, p. 205).

20 Ibid., pp. 255f.

21 Charles Maier, "Zwischen Taylorismus und Technokratie. Gesellschaftspolitik im Zeichen industrieller Rationalität in den zwanziger Jahren in Europa," in Michael Stürmer (ed.), *Die Weimarer Republik: Belagerte Civitas*, Königstein, 1980, p. 191. (A shorter version appears in *Journal of Contemporary History* [London], vol. 5 [1970], pp. 27–61.)

22 Ludwig Hilberseimer, *Groszstadt Architektur*, Stuttgart, 1927, pp. 17f.

23 Ibid., p. 17.
24 Ibid., p. 18.
25 Oliver Arpad Istvan Botar, *Modernism in Hungarian Urban Planning: 1906–1938*, (University of Toronto) Ph.D. thesis), 1985, pp. 73f.
26 Ibid., pp. 76ff.
27 Chan-Magomedow, *Pioniere der sowjetischen Architektur*, pp. 338f.
28 Dusan Riedl, "Zelený rys Zlínského urbanismu – Der grüne urbanistische Zug von Zlín," in *Zlínský funkcionalismus. Funktionalismus von Zlín*, Zlín, 1993, p. 47.
29 Iloš Crhonek, "Zlín, die Stadt des Konstruktivismus," in *Zlínský funkcionalismus*, p. 42.
30 Hughes, *American Genesis*, pp. 321f.

Planning in Two and Three Dimensions, 1890–1910

The new science of town planning in the 1890s was driven by the need to find a model for growth that would deal comprehensively and "scientifically" with the urban terrain. The emphasis was on circulation, sanitation, and social hygiene and on the new German concept of zoning, in which the city was organized along functional lines. Examples of this two-dimensional "engineer's" planning appeared in cities throughout Central Europe in the form of *Regulierungspläne*, which considered the city in its entirety and put in place infrastructures such as municipal railways and tramways, gas and electricity services, sewage systems and drinking water; they also analyzed the city in terms of its constituent parts and uses—residential and commercial sectors, streets, building blocks, public places, recreational space—and reassembled them into a rational, extendable, urban grid.

At the turn of the century, two notable Viennese critics of the concept of planning through engineering, Camillo Sitte and Otto Wagner, were offering radically different concepts of urban planning in which the city was seen as an architectonic unity and a cultural artefact that evolved out of custom, use, and habit. Although their approaches were markedly different—Sitte focused on the discrete square, view, and prospect, while Wagner was concerned with the dynamic expansion of the modern metropolis—both attempted to reconcile the conditions of modern urban life with traditional concepts of place-making.

Otto Wagner, Presentation Drawing,
View of the Aspernplatz, Vienna,
1897

Perspective
Indian ink and watercolor on paper,
mounted on card, 98.7 x 71.7 cm
HM Vienna

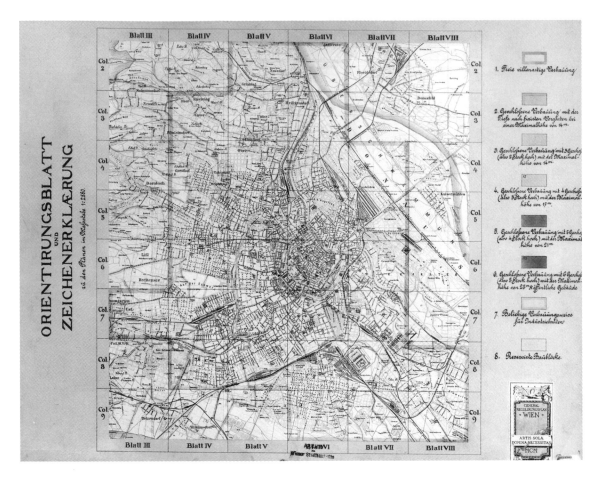

Otto Wagner, Project for a General Plan for the Regulation of Vienna, 1892–93

Orientation sheet and key to symbols, scale 1 : 2880
Colored print, mounted on card, 58 x 71 cm
WSTLA Vienna

View of Elisabethplatz showing integration of proposed municipal railway station into old city center
Indian ink, opaque white on paper, 29.4 x 49.7 cm
HM Vienna

Otto Wagner, Nußdorf Weir and
Lock, Vienna XX, 1894

Preliminary project
Pencil, indian ink, and watercolor, on
paper, 45 x 61 cm
HM Vienna

Otto Wagner, Quayside, Danube Canal,
Augartenbrücke to Franzensbrücke,
Vienna, 1896–99

Sheet 53, Plans and sections of the
metropolitan railway station at the Ferdi-
nandsbrücke, the arrangement of platform, quays, new bridge construction,
at the level of the upper quays
Heliogravure
Repr. from: Otto Wagner: Einige Skizzen. Projekte und
ausgeführte Bauwerke, vol. 2, Vienna, 1897

Otto Wagner, Metropolitan Railway,
Vienna, 1894–1908

Study for the title page of publication on
elevated section of municipal railway over
the Gumpendorferzeile
Indian ink and watercolor on paper,
61.8 x 44.8 cm
HM Vienna

Camillo Sitte, Development Plan for
Ostrava-Marianské Hory, 1904

Plan to scale 1 : 5000
Multicolor print, 35.5 x 56 cm
TU Vienna

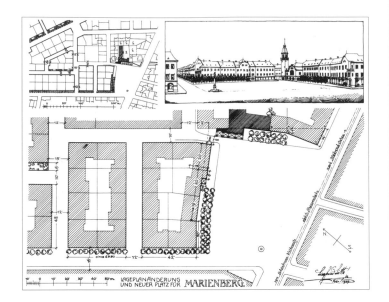

Siegfried Sitte, Ground Plan Alteration
and new square for Ostrava-
Marianské Hory
Version 3, 1909

Site plan, perspective
Indian ink on transparent paper,
47.5 x 41 cm
TU Vienna

Camillo and Siegfried Sitte, Church
Square, Ostrava-Marianské Hory
Perspectival view, 1909

Indian ink on paper, mounted on card,
37 x 28.5 cm
TU Vienna

Maks Fabiani, Design for a monumental square in front of the new Palace of Justice (now Miklošičev Park), Ljubljana 1899

Perspective
Repr. from: Der Architekt, VI, 1900

Maks Fabiani, Project for a General Development Plan, Ljubljana, 1895
Repr. from: Regulacija deželnega stolnega mesta Ljubliane, Vienna, 1899

The Großstadt, 1910–14

Adolf Loos's *Plan von Wien* (1909–12) was a theoretical proposal for transforming the old inner city of the imperial capital into the business and cultural core of a modern Großstadt. Loos's plan took as its starting point the street plan of Vienna in 1859—just after the old city walls had been razed, and before the *Ringstrasse* was built. It combined the planning principles of Sitte—carefully framed squares, views, and prospects with the modernizing program of Wagner—broad avenues and new cultural and financial institutions that facilitate communication and foster a cosmopolitan life. Loos visualized his plan in freehand sketches of the streetscapes, banks, railways stations, courthouses, theaters, apartment houses, and other buildings he proposed. Loos's most famous built work, the *Haus am Michaelerplatz* (1910), represented the type of sophisticated, metropolitan architecture that he envisioned as the vernacular for his modern capital city.

Otto Wagner, Die Großstadt, 1911

Vienna as a model regulatory plan of a city with districts divided by ring and radial roads, scale 1 : 100,000

Repr from: Otto Wagner, Die Großstadt. Eine Studie über diese, Vienna, 1911

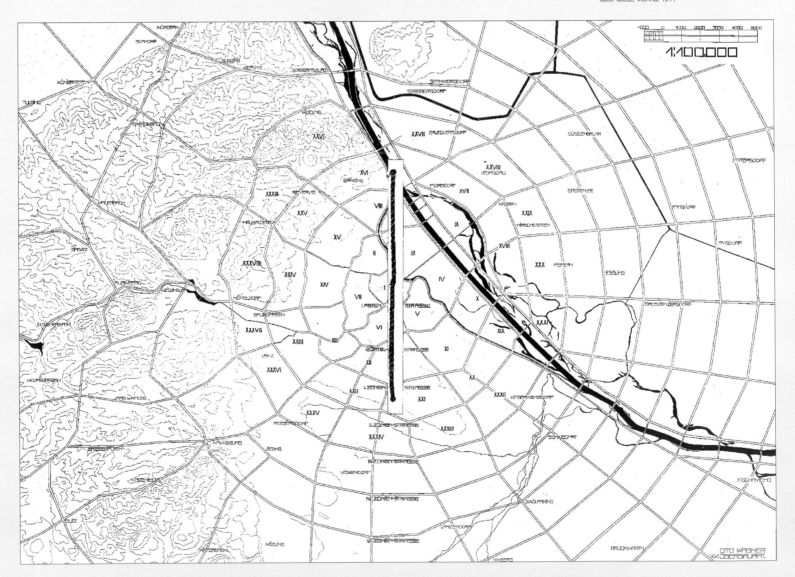

Otto Wagner, Die Großstadt, 1911

Aerial perspective of the Center of the
Future
XIIth district of Vienna
Pencil and indian ink on paper,
61 x 82 cm
HM Vienna

Otto Wagner, Die Großstadt, 1911

Plan of the projected XXIIth district of
Vienna, scale 1 : 27,500
Repr from: Otto Wagner, Die Großstadt. Eine Studie
über diese, Vienna, 1911

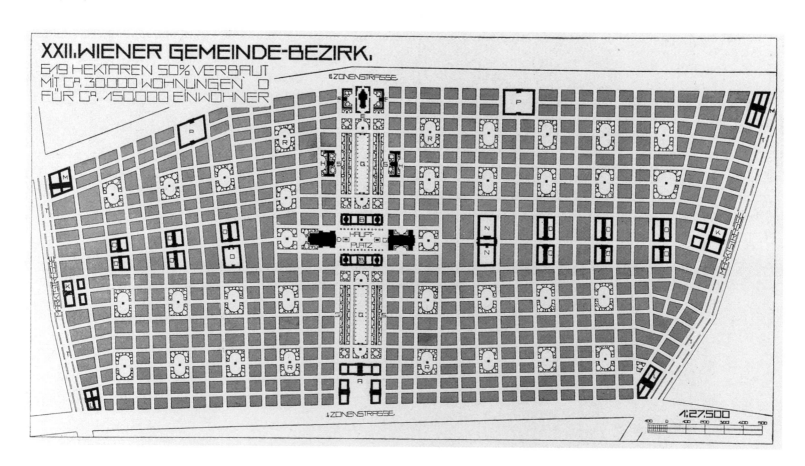

Otto Wagner, Apartment Building, Vienna VII, Neustiftgasse 40, 1909

Sheet 4, view
Heliogravure
Repr. from: Otto Wagner, Maks Fabiani, Einige Skizzen, Projekte und ausgeführte Bauwerke, vol. 4, Vienna, 1922

Otto Wagner, Project for an Industrial Exhibition Hall, Vienna I, Zedlitzgasse, 1913

View
Pencil and indian ink on paper, 53.5 x 54.5 cm
HM Vienna

Otto Wagner, Project for the "Hotel Wien," Vienna I, Kolowratring, 1910

Perspective
Pencil and indian ink on paper,
57.5 x 65 cm
HM Vienna

Otto Wagner, Relocation of the "Naschmarkt" at the "Zeile," Vienna, 1905

Sheet 49, perspectival view
Heliogravure
Repr. from: Otto Wagner, Einige Skizzen, Projekte und
ausgeführte Bauwerke, vol. 3, Vienna, 1906

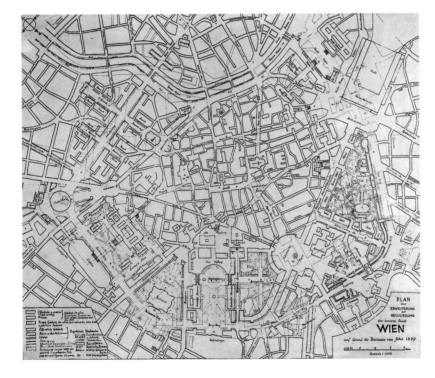

Adolf Loos, Goldman & Salatsch
Building, Vienna I, Michaelerplatz,
1909–11

Perspective, 1912
Colored print, 50 x 43.5 cm

Planning on a New Scale, 1920–37

By the 1920s the new political and economic realities of the post-war period had made the traditional architectural conception of Wagner's *Großstadt* obsolete, and opened the region to experimentation, new architectural ideas, and theoretical models of the city (including Le Corbusier's City for Three Million, 1922, and Ludwig Hilberseimer's Highrise City, 1924–27) which addressed what were perceived to be new problems of scale, density, and urban economic organization.

In social housing, industry, and public building, a larger scale of urban construction and architectonic form (the super-block and megastructure) emerged in the 1920s as municipal and federal governments in new nation states strove to reshape the spaces of production and public life in the cities they had inherited.

Jaromír Krejcar, Competition Project for a New Government
District on the Letná Plain, Prague, 1928

Bird's-eye view
Indian ink and watercolor on card, mounted on canvas, 100 x 220 cm
NTM Prague

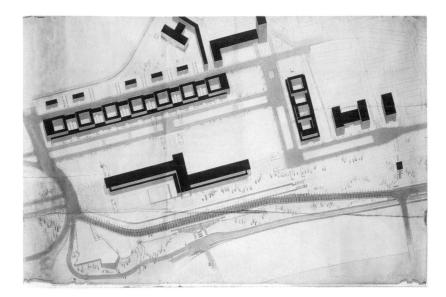

Josef Štěpánek, Competition Project for a new Government District on the Letná Plain, motto "Green", Prague, 1928

Bird's-eye view
Colored print, 99 x 148 cm
NTM Prague

Aerial perspective
Indian ink on transparent paper, 50 x 38 cm
NTM Prague

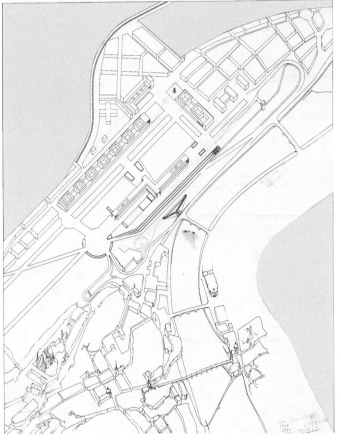

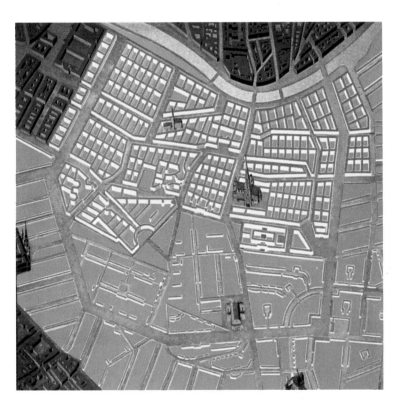

Otto Neurath, Gerd Arntz, The New Vienna, c. 1927

Plan of old inner city Vienna overlaid with the footprint of the new socialist housing blocks
Chromolithograph, 19 x 20 cm
IC Reading

Hubert Gessner, Karl-Seitz-Hof, Vienna XXI, Jedlesser Straße 66–94, 1926–29

Bird's-eye view of one of Red Vienna's largest buildings
Pencil and indian ink on paper, 31 x 69 cm
Albertina Vienna

Jozef Gočár, Projet for a General Development Plan, Hradec Králové, 1925–28

Inner City
Indian ink and watercolor on paper, mounted on canvas, 91 x 107 cm
MVČ Hradec Králové
© Miroslav Beneš

Regulation of the city between the Elbe (Labe) and the Jungmannova, 1925
Indian ink and crayon on card, 63 x 102 cm
MVČ Hradec Králové
© Miroslav Beneš

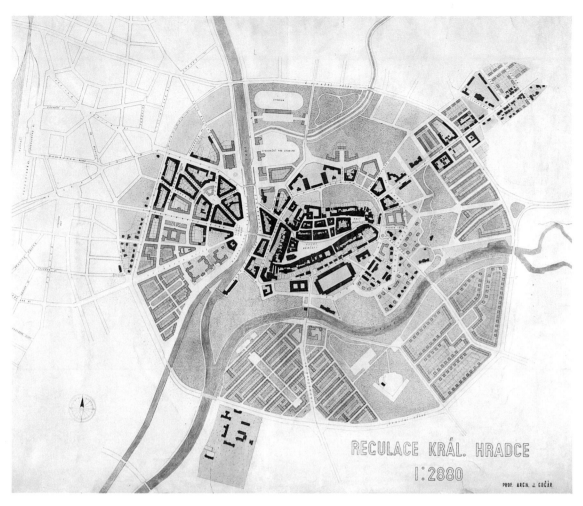

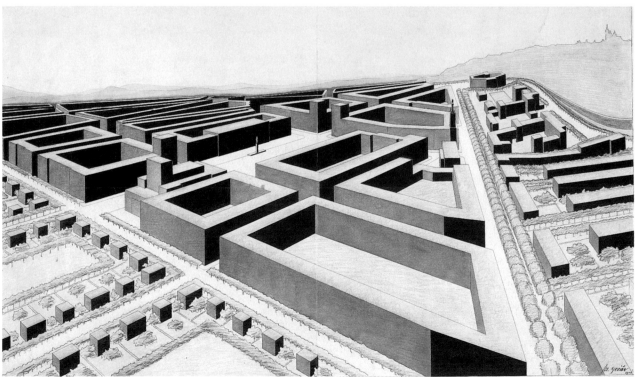

Farkes Molnár, KURI-Straße, 1923

Perspectival view of two apartment blocks
Postcard
MEM Budapest
© Gábor Barka

Farkas Molnár, KURI-Stadt, 1923

Site plan
Repr. from: Molnár Farkas munkái /The Works of the
Architect F. Molnár 1923–33, Budapest, 1933

Urban Topography: Texture and Fabric of the City, 1890–1930

As the commercial life of the city expanded, its traditional markets, meeting places, and recreational spaces were supplanted by modern services, and the texture of the city street changed. The storefront, hotel, park gate, and café became vehicles for innovation in design, for the rationalization of the streetscape, and for the expression of a metropolitan life. With the use of plate glass and new graphic techniques, the urban wall became increasingly a focus for display. Typical of the Central European

city was the implantation of standardized street furniture and other urban amenities. Planning for the city railway systems of the region's two largest cities, Vienna and Budapest, began in the 1880s. By the turn of the century, Wagner's *Stadtbahn*, constructed above, below, and at grade around Vienna's inner districts, studded the urban environment with bridges, viaducts, tunnels, and 36 monumental municipal railway stations. Integrated with the new ring road [*Gürtelstrasse*] and

regulated waterways running through the city, it was a major feat of engineering and urban design. In Budapest an electric subway—the first in continental Europe—with highly ornamented entrance pavilions was built along the Andrássy út in 1896 as part of the Millennial celebrations in the Hungarian capital. As cities responded to growth, the increasingly mechanized distribution of water, power, sewage, and traffic provided opportunities for architects to experiment with completely new building types

(such as water towers, gas stations, and electrical plants) or to rethink the form of older types (such as roads, bridges, and dams) at a new scale and with new materials. Here, the representation of advanced technology might be allied—as in Ödön Lechner's water tower for the city of Kecskemét, built in concrete but faced with colored ceramic tile—with assertively rooted indigenous folk art forms.

Ödön Lechner, Water Tower, Kecskemét, 1909–12

View
Pen and watercolor on paper,
76 x 132.5 cm
BKMÖL Kecskemét

**István Medgyaszay, Project for a
Department Store, 1902**

Perspective
Indian ink and watercolor on paper,
55.5 x 33 cm
Medgyaszay collection, Budapest
© Gábor Barka

**Ludvík Kysela, Lindt Office Premises,
Prague I, Václavské náněti 4, 1926–27**

Perspective
Pencil on paper, 99 x 51.5 cm
NTM Prague

Otto Wagner, "Anker" Apartment House, Vienna I, Graben 10, 1894

Perspectival view
Indian ink and watercolor on paper,
32.8 x 23.5 cm
HM Vienna

Joseph Maria Olbrich, Project for Café Niedermayer, Oprava, 1898

Perspectival view
Pencil, pen, and watercolor on paper,
28 x 17.5 cm
Kunstbibliothek Berlin

J. Sykora, Design for shop front of an Imperial Tobacconist, c. 1905

View of façade
Indian ink and watercolor on paper,
44 x 53.8 cm
HM Vienna

Competition Design for Advertising Pillars, Vienna, 1917

Motto 'U-Boat', various views
Indian ink and watercolor on paper,
52.5 x 73.5 cm
HM Vienna

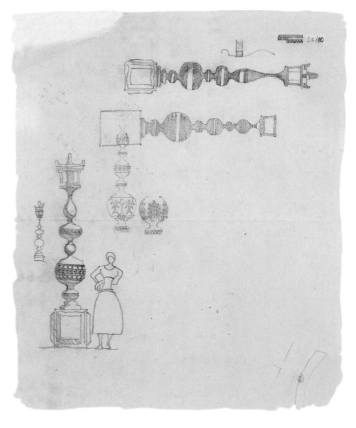

Jože Plečnik, Study for the Street Lighting in front of St Bartholomew's Church (Cerkev Sv. Jerneja), Ljubljana c. 1933

Various design sketches
Pencil on paper, 31.5 x 18.4 cm
AM Ljubljana

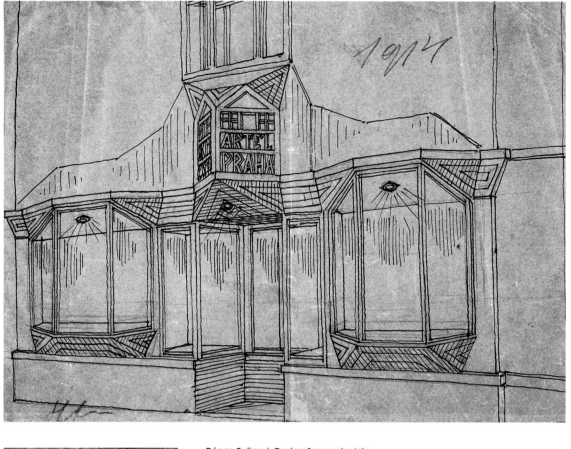

Vlastislav Hofman, Design for a shop front of "Artěl," Prague, 1914

Perspective
Pencil and indian ink on paper,
26.3 x 37 cm
CCA Montréal

Dénes Györgyi, Design for an electric street lamp, from the 1930s

Perspective
Pencil on transparent paper, 110 x 38 cm
Budapesti Történeti Múzeum
© Judit Szalatnyay

Wilhem Beetz, Design for Iron Public Conveniences for Men (Urinals, Pissoirs)
With patented "Beetz" oil system

Matrix for a folder
Print, 45 x 58.7 cm
Beetz Company, Vienna

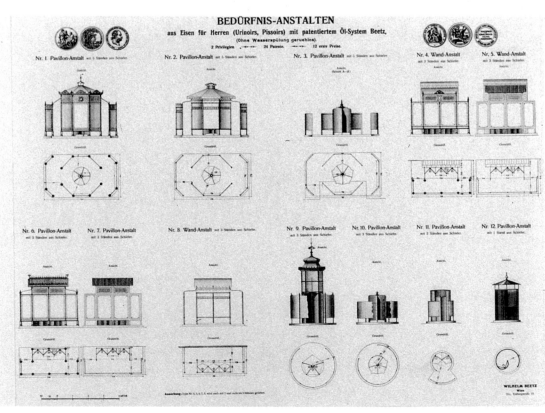

Otto Wagner, Stadtbahn, Metropolitan Railway, Vienna, 1884–1900

Station at Akademiestraße, Vienna I, Karlsplatz, 1895
Indian ink and watercolor on paper on card, 65 x 45 cm
HM Vienna

Millennium Underground Electric Train, Budapest, 1889

Cutaway view of the electric underground train
Watercolor on paper, 83 x 108 cm
Közlekedési Múzeum, Budapest
© Gábor Barka

István Medgyaszay, Design for a Lock Installation, 1901

Study
Indian ink and watercolor on paper, 58 x 45 cm
Medgyaszay collection, Budapest
© Gábor Barka

MODERNITY AND PLACE

THE PLURALISM OF MODERNITY:
THE ARCHITECTONIC "LANGUAGE PROBLEM"
IN CENTRAL EUROPE

Friedrich Achleitner

Opening Remarks

The present essay can do no more than advance a number of hypotheses, suggestions, and conjectures regarding a topic to which little attention has been devoted: the multilingual character of the Habsburg Empire and, in particular, the role played by the linguistic aspects of what are known as the non-verbal arts, especially architecture, in the complex and conflict-ridden network of relations between the nations within this state.

In the wake of the Counter-Reformation, the Josephinian Enlightenment, the 1848 Uprising, and Metternich's police state—waves of revolution and restoration—it was a political concern of the ruling dynasty to further non-verbal arts such as music and architecture while controlling and suppressing philosophy and literature, thus defusing the more rational and politically effective instruments of a culture. This inadvertently resulted in drawing special attention to language and to the linguistic per se, which became an object of research in philosophy, psychology, and psychoanalysis, and it perhaps even sparked a more widespread general interest in the semantic aspects of architecture and music. It was possibly as a result of this policy that the linguistic aspects of the non-verbal arts came to occupy the center of attention in such a way that these arts—at the height of their expression—could just as easily be "read" and employed as a political medium, that is, as a political or social statement. The following discussion is based on this hypothesis. Still, we should always keep in mind that in architecture we are not dealing with language, but rather with an analogous mode of expression, or with the "linguistic use" of a non-verbal medium.

I wish to spare the reader (and myself) the unfruitful debate as to whether architecture is a language. I proceed on the assumption that it possesses levels of communication which are related to linguistic levels; but it certainly has no binding grammar, no more or less securely defined vocabulary, no abstract concepts. All that can be said to exist are cultural constellations in which combinations of architectural "vocabulary" (forms, techniques, materials, etc.) can be read in a way comparable to verbal communications. We also know (at least since Alberto Manguel) that reading itself far surpasses the boundaries of verbal communication, that information can be derived from any organized or repetitive phenomenon. To this extent, architecture too can be "read" in various ways and from the most diverse viewpoints.

The Language Problem in the Austro-Hungarian Monarchy

In the territory of the Austro-Hungarian Monarchy a full ten recognized national languages were spoken: German, Italian, Magyar (Hungarian), Bohemian (Czech), Polish, Ruthenian (Transcarpathian, Ukrainian), Slovenian, Serbo-Croatian (with Latin and Cyrillic alphabet), and Romanian.[1] This multilingualism was a cultural reality—in some countries, such as Galicia, classroom instruction was conducted in as many as four languages. So there must have arisen, alongside the conflicts this involved, something in the nature of a collective linguistic consciousness.

Though it would surely be mistaken to view architecture as a sort of mirror image of this situation, there are doubtlessly analogous phenomena relating to the "use" of architecture. The very existence of multilingualism in a nation-state engenders a different "reading behavior," a cultural relativity whose background, though constant, was certainly changing and

previous page:
Zagreb, Jelačićev trg
Title page (extract)
Repr. from: Svijet, V, 1930

multi-layered. Moreover, this multilingual situation surely must have augmented the significance of individual languages as identification factors, while at the same time emphasizing the role of universal or official national languages.

As early as 1784 Joseph II issued a decree for Hungary and Transylvania concerning the "Introduction of the Use of the German Language in all Government Departments of the Kingdom of Hungary," which also extended to Transylvania. Yet the decree had to be rescinded in 1790. Under Franz II/I the languages of commerce were German, Latin, and Italian. The Hungarian aristocracy and provincial legislatures spoke Latin, which was also the official government language until 1848. It was possibly Joseph II's edict that helped trigger the wave of Magyarization in Hungary. Though the equality of all languages was declared (especially in 1848–49) in numerous announcements, manifestos, statements, even constitutional charters, from 1851 with the *Silvesterpatent* (rescinding the March Constitution) the "primacy of the German language" was assured under neo-absolutism.

In her study *Die Vertreibung der Mehrsprachigkeit* [The Expulsion of Multilingualism], Hanna Burger points out a remarkable development that took place in the wake of the Compromise Agreement [*Ausgleich*] with Hungary. On the one hand, in the field of school planning and construction, the authorities reacted sensitively to diverse linguistic contexts, yet on the other, more and more prejudices were cultivated against multilingualism and bilingualism (even for scholarly and pedagogical reasons). As a result, by the end of the monarchy monolingual schools by far predominated in the Habsburg Empire. As Hanna Burger notes:

> This language battle fought by all nationalities—if with differing intensity and in quite changing constellations—was, in Otto Bauer's eyes, nothing other than a "covert class struggle"…which both the socialist and the nationalist camps around the turn of the century believed could be resolved only by the greatest possible segregation of the nationalities. In the field of education this meant the constitution of autonomous school systems administered by the nationalities. This model, first realized in Bohemia and Moravia, contributed considerably to culturally prepare and facilitate the political separation which took place after the First World War. In a paradoxical development, the transnational state produced specific, national educational systems and thus foreshadowed a key element of future nation-states.[2]

In this development, spreading from linguistic into cultural policy, there were naturally wide areas of contact with architecture. While west of the Leitha River, on the Austrian side, German became the universal or official national language, to the east it was Hungarian. This division would prove to be a grave political mistake, for it entailed, despite all the promised rights of national languages, both the actual and symbolic suppression of Czech and Slovakian. These cultural circumstances found their expression in other arts as well, especially in architecture.

The Language Problem in Architecture

Owing to the nature of the art, conditions in architecture were somewhat different. For one thing, as a consequence of humanistic ideals, there existed in this field a clear hierarchy and an unchallenged dominance of the Greek and Roman revival styles. The declaration made by Gottfried Semper (1803–79) in his capacity as a juror in the competition for the Vienna City Hall, that he would have to repudiate his entire life's work if he voted for Friedrich von Schmidt's neo-Gothic project (which was eventually built), indicates the still precarious position of Gothic in 1868 in Central Europe. When Adolf Loos, around 1900, defined the architect as "a mason who has learned Latin," this pointed to a similar acceptance of the cultural predominance of Athens and Rome, or rather of the reception of these ancient cultures. This predominance was challenged only towards the end of the nineteenth century, especially by the German National "Los von Rom" movement, but also by a partial shift of interest in art history from Rome to Byzantium (e.g., through Josef Strzygovksy) and by the increasing influence of Anglo-Saxon architecture on the Continent.

Thus the theme of a universal architectural language was more or less related to the Italian Renaissance or the styles derived from it, including Neoclassicism—in any case, sources that lay outside the "German cultural community" (a term still current on the political Right). In Austria, for instance, the so-called "Old German Style" around 1900 projected the diffuse image of a "German Renaissance". In Vienna, as is still evident from the present-day cityscape, this style enjoyed no great popularity, being employed primarily by a German national clientele.

So if the role and use of languages had enormous social and political meaning, even amounting to a labeling, it is perhaps not too daring to assume that similar processes took place in other cultural fields, including architecture. But it would probably be wrong to conclude that the political and administrative dominance of the German language west of the Leitha stood in conflict with the cultural dominance of Mediterranean antiquity, since the propagation of this cultural heritage was likewise in German hands (at least in Vienna and the lands of the monarchy). After all, the German stylistic discussion (as in Heinrich Hübsch's *In welchem Style sollen wir bauen*, 1828) or the search for a "modern style" initiated in Bavaria by King Maximilian II (around 1850), and finally Semper's unfinished magnum opus *Der Stil in den technischen und tektonischen Künsten, oder praktische Aesthetik* [Style in the Technical and Tectonic Arts, or Practical Aesthetics] (1860) exerted incomparably more influence than, say, Viollet-le-Duc's theories pertaining to the "constructivist" aspects of Gothic, since the nationalistically tinged and misguided reception of Gothic as a "German art" weakened the discussion, if it did not actually preempt it.

If the language of government officials and military officers was German, similarly the styles of the bureaucracy (court buildings, prisons, regional administration offices, museums, schools, etc.) and the military (barracks, casinos, etc.), in their dry, formulaic, and very painstakingly produced variants of the Renaissance, amounted to a sort of universal architectural language for all of the crown lands. Particularly interesting in this context is the construction of the *Staatsbahnen*, or National Railways, on the basis of whose stations one can still gauge the extent of former Austrian territory. The *Staatsbahnen* represented a "closed system." Not only in terms of the typology of stations (whose size was an indicator of the significance of a village or town), but in the clear typology of their auxiliary structures, too (locomotive sheds, storage buildings, switch towers, switchmen's cottages, etc.), the railways displayed a very rigidly organized system of technological territorial occupation which could be read as the official presence of a German (i.e., solid and reliable) administration. The stylistic models (regional trappings appearing only after the turn of the century) were "universal styles," preferably the equally hierarchical and easily combinable system of the "Renaissance" (or interpretations thereof). Orientation was provided by the grand, "eternal" styles, preferably taken from antiquity, which were legitimated by the aura of history and which in the "Nation of Many Peoples" were initially untainted by nationalism.

In other words Austria, not surprisingly for a multinational state, did not produce any national style, but rather a universal style suited to state-funded public and official buildings. Even today one can recognize former territory of the Austro-Hungarian monarchy by its regional government headquarters, court buildings, museums, hospitals, and schools.

In this connection one should perhaps also recall that the populace of the period, still largely illiterate, was much more practiced in reading such hierarchically organized images and their meanings than is today's literate society. Above all clothing, whether uniform or folk costume, had an irreplaceable information and communication value. Every child was capable of immediately recognizing not only the numerous regiments (and the elite troops as a matter of course), but even the ranks of officers and enlisted men. That is, the "non-verbal communication" of a pictorial language (from which Otto Neurath would later develop the progressive system of visual statistics) was accessible to the majority of people; in fact it was the only orientation and information system that existed in this not so simply structured society.

Heinrich von Ferstel, Votive Church,
Vienna IX, Rooseveltplatz, 1856–79

The Architectural Languages of the Imperial, Capital, and Royal Residence City of Vienna

Although the period covered by the discussion is set from 1890 to 1937, the situation in Vienna and indeed Central Europe as a whole makes it imperative to review briefly the development of the so-called Historicism of the latter half of the nineteenth century. The categories introduced by Renate Wagner-Rieger, "Romantic Historicism" (about 1830–60), "Strict Historicism" (about 1850–80), and "Late Historicism" (about 1880–1914), are of limited use here, because Viennese developments conformed only loosely to sequential periods. The "polyglot" approach of architects (who generally employed two or more "languages" or styles) and architectural schools bears a greater analogy to a network than to a chronological process. So it is a fundamental question of interpretation whether one focuses more on a linearity of developments or on a description of reciprocally influential forces.

Already in the period of liberalism, the Gründerzeit, and the first wave of industrialization (that is, in the second half of the nineteenth century), the Viennese situation diverged from a linear development towards modernism. The attitude of its architects to architectural history, despite an intimate knowledge of the material, was a detached, linguistic one. Calculation of effects was not only permissible, it was considered a virtue. This explains why one and the same Heinrich von Ferstel could have conceived the Votive Church (as a religiously tinged memorial) on the basis of a High Gothic model, clothed the university building in resplendent Renaissance (glorifying the humanistic tradition in the sciences), and designed a museum of art and industry with an affiliated school of decorative art (now the Museum and University of Applied Art) in what appears superficially to be Renaissance forms, but which on closer examination turns out to be an example of the Schinkelesque reception of English industrial architecture.

The real message of these structures (and also of the Chemical Institute on Währinger Strasse) lies in their anticipation of a "functional style," in their rigorous, hierarchical consistency of materials (clinker, terracotta, ceramics), and in the pronounced handcrafted nature of the execution—in this respect, emulating Schinkel's Building Academy in Berlin. The arguments advanced with respect to content (including iconography) for Vienna's City Hall and Parliament have often been discussed. Of particular interest here is Theophil von Hansen's advocacy of the ancient Greek style as being the one which was especially capable of expressing the connection between "order and freedom."

An analysis of Viennese styles from 1848 to 1900 that would place them solidly in their sociopolitical and "linguistic" overall context has yet to be undertaken. An interesting subject of inquiry would be the fact that most of these styles did not reflect any political conception but were pragmatic, personal styles, or "private languages" of great adaptability. This circumstance also goes far to explain the architects' great inventiveness (formal, not merely typological), which frequently led them far from their historical models. Thus one can find, for example, in the ornamentation of the Kunsthistorisches Museum (1871–82) by Gottfried Semper and Karl Hasenauer, modern elements that might have come from the hand of a Josef Hoffmann (1870–1956), around 1900. One is tempted to see in the architecture of the latter half of the nineteenth century the anticipation of an "architectural corporate state"—which aesthetically never came about—with an astonishing networking of visual functions that remain legible even today.

Heinrich von Ferstel, University, Vienna I, Dr.-Karl-Lueger-Ring 1, 1873–84
View of main façade

Heinrich von Ferstel, Chemical Institute of the University of Vienna, Vienna IX, Währingerstraße 10, 1868–72
Detail of façade

The Situation around 1900

What the generation of the late nineteenth-century Gründerzeit, (corresponding roughly with the first students of Otto Wagner), scoffingly referred to in the 1890s as a "carnival of styles," is for us today an interesting example of the coexistence of diverse cultures, strata, groups, languages, and political positions. The fact that it was accompanied by the phenomenon of "mixing" was perhaps characteristic of the leading bourgeois strata, which, as a new class that had only recently attained power and respectability, had its own problems of cultural orientation.

An interesting issue for investigation in this connection would be the phenomenon of assimilation, especially with regard to Viennese Jews. Whereas Jewish students were apparently not welcome in the Otto Wagner school (or were not attracted by the master), a group of those young intellectuals and doctors of architecture (such as Josef Frank and Oskar Strnad) gathered around Carl König who would subsequently play a key role in the critique of modernity (i.e., the German avant-garde).

Carl König (1841–1915), perhaps more successful as a teacher than an architect, was a representative of neo-Baroque, that "Maria Theresian Style," which around 1900 was on the verge of establishing itself as a national style—a fact which, in view of König's position as a Jewish architecture professor, might also be interpreted as an "assimilation style" (emphasizing loyalty to the House of Habsburg). By contrast, later in the 1920s, the Czechs (about 200,000 of whom lived in Vienna in 1900) avoided the pressure of linguistic assimilation (Vienna's mayor, Karl Lueger, was a notorious "Germanifier") and, by building schools and gymnasiums through the Sokol associations, managed to retain their Czech character for a generation longer, at least in terms of building and architecture.

Viennese stylistic pluralism around 1900 is truly difficult to describe. Apart from Otto Wagner's great project of developing a modern (imperial) universal style (with all its secessionist and constructivist inclusions), just after the turn of the century there was, in addition to the "pure" Secession, a lively Biedermeier reception which was partly supported by Secessionists such as Josef Hoffmann. However, this involvement with Biedermeier, being associated with a movement known as Heimatschutz [preservation league] (one of whose Viennese

Carl König, Agricultural Exchange (formerly Corn Exchange), Vienna II, Taborstraße 10, 1887–90

View of main façade

Friedrich von Schmidt, Parish Church Maria vom Siege, Vienna XV, Maria-vom-Siege 3, 1868–75

View into dome

advocates was Joseph August Lux) was more a phenomenon of the Zeitgeist than a true stylistic movement. It was intermingled with forms of Late Classicism, reflecting Hansen's tradition of a striving for clarity, order, and freedom, as well as clerical or German national relics of neo-Romanticism, neo-Gothic, and neo-Renaissance ("Old German Style").

The architecture subsumed under the category of Late Historicism generally consists of pathos-filled and overloaded combinations of ornamental scraps of Renaissance, Baroque, Rococo, and Gothic, in which, for economic reasons, the industrial manufacture of ornamentation played a role. Naturally Jugendstil, Secession, and even Biedermeier approaches also entered into this mélange. It should not be forgotten that around 1910 even the Secessionists (again, foremost among them Josef Hoffmann) unfolded a new, imaginative magnificence in the field of ornament, making it possible today to read and analyze the public housing projects built shortly before the First World War in particular as a collective psychograph of the bourgeoisie.

Only modern tendencies such as the Otto Wagner school are generally credited with exhibiting a high degree of imagination. But if we look more closely, we find that even supposedly arch-conservative buildings like the neo-Romanesque and neo-Gothic churches in the districts outside the Vienna Belt, denigrated as "building-block architecture," often evince considerable spatial and constructive inventiveness, which simply does not register on the stereotyped perception of the enemies of Historicism.

The Role of Otto Wagner and His School

Otto Wagner began teaching at the Academy of Visual Arts in the midst of a *Sprachenstreit* [language battle] raging in the Vienna Parliament (the German-speaking officials refused to learn Czech as a second administrative language). So one may assume that this cradle of talent, which congratulated itself on being the most modern architectural school on the Continent and which attracted the most gifted young people in the Monarchy, cannot have remained uninfluenced by these events. Wagner's architecture, which combined history with progress, doubtless represented a culturally stabilizing and unifying force, no matter how loudly it claimed, with the rise of the Viennese Secession in 1894, to be a driving, transforming force. Wagner's architecture attempted once again to achieve an imperial universal style, if one that focused on technical and aesthetic innovations, directed to a so-called "modern society" that was on the verge of staging the collapse of the monarchy as a technological inferno.

So if Wagner—despite the enmity of members of the royal house such as heir to the throne Franz Ferdinand—represented a centripetal force for the Habsburg family, his students, especially the Czechs, became in the course of the vehement debate concerning a national style, the dominant centrifugal movement. One might also discuss the hypothesis of whether the non-recognition of Czech as the third official language might not have encouraged this "compensatory act" of creating an architectural national style.

Of course the Czechs were too intelligent to conduct this debate solely or obviously on a nationalistic level. The famous essay by Pavel Janák (with Jan Kotěra and Josef Chochol, one of the most prominent of Otto Wagner's students), *From Modern Architecture to Architecture* (Prague, 1910), criticized Wagner's utilitarian stance and urged that form—as opposed to functionalism and constructivism—was an intellectual, spiritual product whose content was made up of elements far more complex than a rationalistic view of architecture was willing to admit.[3]

Jože Plečnik, whose origins were in the Catholic Slovenian *petit bourgeoisie*, was similarly shocked by the utilitarianism of metropolitan society in Vienna. Perhaps it was the experience of the metropolis that first made the many students from the crown lands aware that the regions they had left were not only narrow and provincial, but possessed specific and irreplaceable qualities.

Wekerle Estate, Budapest XIX, Kós Károly tér, 1909–29
Entrance gate, 1909–12

The Construction of National Styles: Arbitrariness and Tragedy

While the development from "folk languages" to national or "high languages" represented collective processes of discovery, revival, research, even polishing and refining, the development of so-called national styles was usually an idea pursued by individual artists or small groups. Such attempts have an air of the arbitrary and random, are extremely bound up with a certain period, and often represent mere episodes in the oeuvres of the architects involved. However, things look different when it is a matter of the perception of these individual styles, their recognition as national styles—that is, when their proponents were able to create a new national frame of reference or some basis for collective identification.

Before I tread the thin ice of conceptions of national architecture in conflict with, or without, Vienna, I should first like to attempt to describe the features shared in common by these various architectures. Their romantic potential surely lay in a recollection of the forms of life and expression of the "common people": rural life in general; craftsmanship and its techniques, partially oriented towards the English Arts and Crafts movement; the search for authentic symbols (such as national colors) and folk ornaments, preferably emerging from "the depths of history" or relating to primal myths. The models included peasant buildings and their archaic construction methods. These resources were naturally not very extensive, and in any

Ödön Lechner, Museum and College of
Arts and Crafts, Budapest IX, Üllői út
33–37, 1891–96

Entrance hall

case not particularly suitable as patterns for the new, stately building tasks; the most they could supply were decorative details. Moreover, the national historical sources, where they could be found at all, were very limited, forcing architects to rely on more global ideas.

National Romantic Movement in Hungary: Ödön Lechner and Károly Kós

Thanks to the Austro-Hungarian Agreement of 1867, Hungary successfully established itself as a state with Hungarian as the official language and with dominion over considerable minorities (Slovaks, Croats, Romanians, Germans). It would seem no coincidence that this independence from Austria should have fostered the emergence of a broader spectrum of artistic and architectural approaches. Of course the development of Budapest into a metropolis in competition with Vienna played no small role here. In a word, a national romantic focus quite naturally emerged in Hungarian architecture (embodied above all in Ödön Lechner, Károly Kós, Lajos Kozma, Aladár Árkay, and many other Jugendstil architects), but there were also tendencies that made freer play with modernism and technical advancements (with, say, Béla Lajta, József Vágó, or István Medgyaszay) and thus suppressed the national romantic aspect to some extent.

Lechner's construction of a national architecture took place in absolute independence from Vienna. Beginning in Paris, where he studied and produced his first works, Lechner then embarked on a "search for sources" in the "ornamental cultures" of the Near and Far East. In this regard, the myths concerning the origin of the Hungarian people both aided Lechner and put him off the track. His construction is both a synthetic and highly individual invention in one. One might also say that it represents an attempt to develop an architecture that occupied the same outsider position as the Hungarian language (and its primal myths) held in the concert of European languages. But its yardstick and background remains, in its spatial design and typology, the "Latin" culture of the French. All in all, Lechner's project was an enormous artistic effort, quite without parallel. It was surely no accident that he received important commissions in Budapest and other cities, and produced results that symbolized a new high-level Hungarian culture.

Károly Kós, to name another national romantic, worked closer to the people, seeking out, much as Béla Bartók would later do in music, its soul in Transylvania and the Carpathian arc. His architecture remained closely tied to society, being oriented to the life of the "simple folk," whose needs it attempted to serve (as in the Wekerle-Siedlung, 1909–12, Budapest). In a word, it was less an attempt to build a new national architecture than a campaign of renewal mounted from national conditions. As mentioned, by 1900 Hungary was already too large and culturally stable, and had a potent metropolitan culture in Budapest, so that by the 1920s it was able to develop its avant-garde more effectively than Vienna.

Czech Cubism: A Struggle with Vienna?

The spread of the ideas of Pan-Slavism and the language conflict raging in the Vienna Parliament doubtless spurred the discussion about a Czech national architecture. Although Jan Kotěra (1871–1923), a student of Otto Wagner and an admirer of the Dutchman Hendrik Petrus Berlage (1856–1934), was still engaged in the attempt to adapt the doctrine of the Wagner school for Prague, his younger fellow students, such as Pavel Janák (1882–1956) and Josef Chochol (1880–1956), mounted an opposition to Wagner's imperial rationalism. However, Alena Kubova points out a Viennese influence here,[4] namely Alois Riegl, who with the concept of *Kunstwollen* took up a decidedly intellectual position with respect to the theory—probably

Josef Chochol, Apartment Block, Prague II, Neklanova 30, 1913–14
Entrance

Pavel Janák, Crematorium, Pardubice, Pod břízkami 990, 1921–23
Detail of side gallery

going back to Gottfried Semper (1803–79)—of a collective creation of form or process-related formation

In the development of Cubism the young Czechs emphasized the intellectual aspects of the creation of form, referring back to Bohemian Baroque (especially to the "expressionism" of a Giovanni Santini-Aichel, [1667–1723]), and thus became the sharpest critics of "Viennese utilitarianism," their view of the Wagner doctrine distilled into a phrase.

The brief heyday of Cubism—and the immediately following "Rondo-Cubism"—indicates that it could not provide a very firm basis on which to build a national style. Rather, Cubism represented a radical break with the conventions of modernism, in order to place them, in the early emergent avant-garde, on new social or socialist, functional or functionalist, constructive or constructivist foundations. The 1920s and 1930s in the force-field between Prague and Brno were characterized by a tremendously dynamic development and a great receptiveness to happenings on the international stage (Paris, Berlin, Moscow). Bohemia and Moravia had "inherited" extensive modern industrial areas from the monarchy and, thanks to their president and philosopher, Tomáš Garrigue Masaryk (1850–1937), had become a modern, prospering republic.

Jože Plečnik: Universalist or Slovenian Special Case?

Plečnik's œuvre does not reflect an attempt to create a clearly declared "national architecture." His architectural conception—as far as he can be said to have had one—tends rather to a universal language, though Plečnik had no ambition to develop a new language, instead employing the vocabulary of the old language to think new thoughts. Hence to the conservatives he appeared an innovator, and to the modernists a conservative. Plečnik's forms were the result of transformations, which he undertook with the greatest care and responsibility. As a Catholic and devout artist he remained loyal to Roman culture, to which he returned again an again and which provided him with the basic typological patterns for his thought constructs. The modernist *tabula rasa* disgusted him; Viennese utilitarianist culture (synonymous with modern metropolitan culture) frightened him.

Jože Plečnik, Reconstruction of
Prague Castle, Prague, 1920–34

Balustrade of stairs to Powder Bridge
(Prašný most)

Plečnik as it were came of age on the frontier between the Roman and Byzantine worlds: linguistically speaking, between Romanic, Germanic, and Slavic cultures. His unbounded architectural inventiveness seems to have drawn its power from these fields of tension, to which others were added, such as the social tensions between his background (in a Slovenian artisans' milieu) and his artistic socialization in the *haute bourgeoisie* of Vienna. His path by way of Prague, where before returning to Ljubljana he designed seminal buildings (not least among them the conversion of the Hradschin on commission from Tomáš Masaryk), likewise brought him into contact with a tri-polar (Czech, German, Jewish) and thus conflict-rich metropolitan culture.

To remain with the analogy to the language situation in the multinational empire, one might call Plečnik the creator of a "universal language from below"—which was closer to the people, rejected imperial affectation and gestures, sought common links among all cultures, and rather than compressing time into developmental lines perceived it in terms of diverse constellations. It is perhaps exactly because he was not a national—not to mention nationalist—artist that Plečnik became a kind of symbolic figure. His architecture evinces virtues that explode the national frame of reference, and transcend regional conditions, that indeed even represent a conception of culture which leaves far behind it the nationalistic conflicts of the nineteenth and twentieth centuries.

Dušan Jurkovič: "Poetry of the People"

If one were to interpret the work of Dušan Jurkovič solely with reference to the political situation in Slovakia, which on the one hand was a strongly dominated component of the Hungarian half of the empire and, on the other, stood in close dialogue with Czech and German culture, this would be enough to explain the strange dualism of his orientation: in part a reception of English country house architecture and a reworking of Central European Secessionism, yet also a turn to the folk sources of Slovakian—and Polish—wood architecture. Although his war cemeteries (in mid World War I) arose by order of the Austrian military, they are homages to the Slovakian countryside and its "folk architecture." Perhaps Jurkovič was only able to succeed in making such impressive transformations due to the continued existence in these areas of an unbroken peasant culture which had still escaped decorative appropriation by the educated middle class (an appropriation evidenced by the health resorts built around 1900). Naturally the building task of the funerary monument can be treated by more direct reference to historical models, and its emotional symbolism (commemoration, remembrance) lies closer to the cultural roots of a people.

An analysis of these various "language situations" can, in my view, only be begun at the present moment with regard to the work of a few outstanding architects. This would require an intimate knowledge of the political and cultural situation of the cities and regions involved. Especially in the case of the work of someone like Dušan Jurkovič, we can see that it is already a matter of subjective "commentaries," of evaluations and reactions to specific political and cultural circumstances. And these could be one-sided, spontaneous, and above all, rapidly changing. Perhaps this is the very reason why the projects of national romanticism were so short-lived. The outbreak of World War I, the collapse of the Austro-Hungarian monarchy, and the founding of independent nation-states only accelerated their demise.

The Margins: Openness or Ossification

There is a linguistic theory according to which languages tend to ossify at the margins of their territory. While the centers remain mobile, receptive, and involved in a process of continual change, the margins prove highly resistant to change. This may have something to do with the situation of the "province," which possesses a different, temporal rhythm or it may have to do with the existence of a heightened "language awareness," whatever that may be.

Applied to architecture, this hypothesis can be equally well defended and refuted. If we take the regions of South Tyrol and Trentino, or even the Adriatic coast (Dalmatia) as examples,[5] the borderlines between center and margins prove very indefinite and permeable, and the Historicist architecture there is rife with Italian (Roman) influences. Now one might argue in terms of climate and other regional factors, but the only secure fact is that the Adriatic-Venetian culture had already been present in these regions for centuries and "modernism" must have felt itself an intruder. So in this case there was no formation of margins or frontiers. In this context, Trieste provides an example that is both intriguing and certainly difficult to decipher.

Quite a different situation obtained in L'viv, the capital of Galicia, which was alternately Polish, Ukrainian, and, from 1772 to 1918, Austrian. The face of this city, as all observers agree, betrays the strong influence of architecture. One might explain this phenomenon by the theory of "ossified margins," were it not for more logical explanations such as the strategic occupation and, as it were, "colonization" of a marginal land.

Avant-Garde: Constructivism, Functionalism, and International Style as Variants of a New Universal Style?

It is remarkable that after national independence and autonomy had been achieved by the former "crown lands" (disregarding the continuing conflicts with larger minorities) and after the brief heyday of concepts of national styles, the thrust of modernism should have led for the first time to a "universal style" independent of regional factors. Doubtless the distance traveled in formal development away from regionalist styles was so great that the new architecture could only appear to be a homogeneous, broad movement. But if one analyzes the developments and their results in the various countries more closely, one can detect (helped by hindsight) great differences; one might even reverse the proposition and speak of the first truly regional building culture. The Hungarian avant-garde (connected with the Bauhaus, De Stijl, and other avant-gardes through Marcel Breuer, László Moholy-Nagy, Farkas Molnár, Alfréd Forbát, etc.) is no less fresh than that of Brno or Prague, despite the fact that local traditions, even the specific building culture of the country, are in evidence there.

But this brings us to a new chapter of architectural history, in which the "linguistic reference" level—at least that between the nations—plays little if any role. One might even, with a touch of cynicism, maintain that hardly had these nations been given freedom with regard to their languages, or these languages been articulated as nations, when their best minds set out to develop a new universal language. The national aspect had ceased to be an existential theme. Architecture as a whole had been dismissed from the service of national identity; or, put differently, the representation of national progress shifted to the levels of technological, social, hygienic, and generally communitarian development. Constructivism celebrated the technological standards, functionalism the social and hygienic ones, the "International Style" the new standards of civilization.

The conceptual birth of the "International Style" at the eponymous 1932 exhibition curated by Henry-Russell Hitchcock and Philip Johnson was also its funeral. The actual existence of a movement, was, as it were, changed into an historical concept. At the "gateway of history" stood other, more ominously vital figures who practiced "universal styles" of a special brand: the architecture of fascism, National Socialism, and Socialist Realism. Stalin and Hitler (and perhaps Mussolini in a different way) had been both damaged and inspired by the culture and architecture of the Habsburg multinational empire. The liaison of Nazi architecture with regionalism and the skewed relation of Stalin's architecture to national cultures might even be interpreted as reprises of the old Danube monarchy theme within new political constellations. But that would be, and is, another story.

Epilogue

If the first Republic of Austria, the remnant "German Austria," "the state nobody wanted," produced no avant-garde as fresh and active as those of the countries liberated from the "prison of nations," this may have been due not solely to the country's hopeless economic situation, the doubtful viability of the new state on whose narrow shoulders tottered "hydrocephalic" Vienna, whose now surplus buildings would take decades to fill with life. Nor was the stagnation merely due to the desperate search for identity on which the "Alpine Republic" was forced to embark. Perhaps the explanation is much simpler: Austria saw no need for an aesthetic future. After all, it inherited not only a metropolis of the Dual Monarchy but the rubble-heap of an aesthetic revolution that had taken place around 1900.

Viennese public housing [*Gemeindebau*], with its radical economic and social program, could permit itself the luxury of adhering to the traditional rules of a metropolitan bourgeois architecture, because the new political forces saw no reason to compound their social experiments with the risk of aesthetic ones. In the "Volkswohnpalast" or palatial tenement which Josef Frank opposed with such brilliant rhetoric, one could demonstrate a cultural continuity that served to safeguard and legitimate comprehensive reforms on another level. Still, there gravitated to these public housing schemes (though admittedly under altered conditions) that diversity of architectural languages which was still possible in Vienna, and only in Vienna, and from which the new community could draw from old sources the identity it so gravely needed.

The conservative-dominated "Alpine Republic," the "black provinces" as opposed to "Red Vienna," sought in new sources of meaning—the Alps, the scenery, history, culture, tourism—not simply a new–old identity but a basis for economic survival. The architecture of the provinces, from the Salzburg Festival buildings to the Grossglockner Alpine Highway and the new funicular structures, replied to the situation with a regionally tinged modernity. Here, too, the theme of architectural language was addressed anew, if on old foundations.

One might maintain, in conclusion, that the semantic, that is, linguistic component of architecture becomes particularly active or effective at the point when communities urgently require its means of expression, and when such manifestations can also be read and understood. Without a doubt, the Austro-Hungarian Monarchy, the Central European multinational state, was a construction that also ascribed special roles to architectural languages, and it is by no means certain that in a unified Europe, where dissolution of nation-states goes hand in hand with increasing regionalist tendencies, architecture might not again be expected to assume similar tasks.

1 In this brief discussion I rely entirely on the work of Hanna Burger, in particular her essay "Die Vertreibung der Mehrsprachigkeit am Beispiel Österreichs 1867–1918," in Gerd Heschel (ed.), *Über Muttersprachen und Vaterländer, Zur Entwicklung von Standardsprachen und Nationen in Europa*, Frankfurt am Main, 1997, and on personal communications.

2 Ibid., p. 44.

3 Pavel Janák, "Od moderní architektury k architektuře" [From Modern Architecture to Architecture] in *Styl* (Prague) II, 1910, pp. 105–09.

4 In a lecture on Czech Modernism held at the Universität für angewandte Kunst, Vienna. See also Alena Kubova, *L'avant-garde architecturale en Tchécoslovaquie, 1918–1939*, Liège, 1992.

5 See for example the documentation in *Arhitektura secesije u Rijeci. Arhitektura i urbanizam početka 20. Stoljeća 1900–1925* [Secessional Architecture in Rijeka. Architecture and Town Planning at the Beginning of the 20th Century 1900–25], 2 vols., exh. cat., Moderna Galerija Rijeka, Rijeka, 1997.

All the photos in this article are by Friedrich Achleiter.

Budapest, 1890–1914

THE URBAN DEVELOPMENT OF BUDAPEST

Budapest, View of Town Center with Elizabeth Bridge [Erzsébet-híd]
Postcard
Gerle collection, Budapest

Budapest, Andrássy út
Opera house, second building from the right (Miklós Ybl, 1874–84)
Postcard
Gerle collection, Budapest

The development of the urban structure of Budapest was largely complete by the turn of the twentieth century. Changes that were made around 1900 in the appearance of the city can be seen as an organic continuation of earlier trends, and their significance becomes clear if one looks back over the preceding decades. Their beginning can be traced back to the initiatives of Count István Széchenyi in the 1830s. Széchenyi was a leading figure of that circle of liberal aristocrats who championed the political, social, and cultural development of Hungary and who tried to extend these endeavors through architectural and urban development. He consequently proposed to have those public institutions that were initiated by him built on sites which would be critical for the future development of the urban topography. It was also his idea to join the two cities lying to the right and left of the Danube. He took a pragmatic step in this direction by constructing the

Chain Bridge (Lánchíd) (1839–49) as the first permanent bridge across the river.

The first Prime Minister of Hungary after the Austro-Hungarian Compromise of 1867, Count Gyula Andrássy, was a great follower of the socio-political ideas of Széchenyi. Concurrent with the rise of the middle classes Andrássy's activities focused on institutional establishment rather than on private initiatives by the aristocracy. Following the example of England in 1870, paralleling the London Municipal Board of Works, he founded the Municipal Council of Public Works, which organized and supervised urban development in Budapest right up to the years after World War II.[1] The Council prepared the union of the cities Buda, Pest, and Ó-Buda into Budapest (1873), and in 1871 laid the foundation for urban development over the next decades by launching a major international competition. On the basis of the designs

Flóris Korb, Kálmán Giergl, Klotild Palace, Budapest V, Szabadsajtó út 5, 6, 1900–02
Postcard
Gerle collection, Budapest

Budapest, Szabadság tér

On the left, residential and business premises of Géza Kármán and Gyula Ullmann (1900–01), on the right (cut out), the Austro-Hungarian Bank (now Hungarian National Bank, Ignác Alpár, 1902–05)
Postcard
Gerle collection, Budapest

chosen, a system of radial and ring roads was developed, partially integrating and enlarging existing roads and partially incorporating new ones into the old city structure. In this way Andrássy út, running from the city center to the city woods, came about in 1876, though its development was only completed by the mid 1880s.

The rise of mass transport also raised the question of whether to install tramlines on this representative boulevard (Andrássy út). In order to preserve the elegance of the Budapest boulevards, London was once again taken as the model and the first underground railway on mainland Europe was laid in 1896. Today's underground lines are still largely in their original form, while the station buildings by Albert Schickedanz were later demolished.[2]

The project of constructing a Major Ring Road [Nagykörút] parallel to a Minor Ring Road [Kiskörút], which followed the line of the old Pest city wall, was begun in 1871, but its route was gradually changed up to 1896. Around the turn of the century, as a consequence of the rapid development of the city, the construction of further bridges across the Danube (with the urban adjustments resulting from this) became necessary. As early as 1876 a second permanent bridge, the Margaret Bridge [Margit-híd], was opened as a northern continuation of the Major Ring Road onto the Buda side. This was followed in 1894–96 by the Franz-Joseph Bridge, the present Liberty Bridge [Szabadság-híd], at the southern end of the Minor Ring Road. The eastern continuation of the Elizabeth Bridge [Erzsébet-híd] into Pest's city center, which took place between 1897 and 1903, involved major urban reconstruction. As the numerous existing narrow, twisted lanes could not possibly cope with the traffic, almost the entire complex of buildings in the old Pest city center had to be demolished and the old country road

[the present Rákóczi út] widened and extended towards the eastern railway station.

Owing to their simultaneous construction, the buildings in the vicinity of the bridgehead of the Elizabeth Bridge on the Pest side are typical of the stylistic diversity around the turn of the century, which extends from the two buildings of the Clothilde Palace (Budapest V, Szabadsajtó út 5, 6, Flóris Korb and Kálmán Giergl, 1900–02), with their combined forms of Baroque and Jugendstil, to the block of apartments and stores at Ferenciek tere 5 (Budapest V, Henrik Schmahl, 1909–13), where the architect brought together elements of Venetian Gothic with forms from Ödön Lechner's architecture. After serving several temporary functions (as an amusement quarter, among other things) the rapid development of the Southern part of Buda began with the construction of the Franz Joseph Bridge. A regional planning scheme for this area was drawn up as early as 1871, based on the geometric grid of American cities. The final building zone of 1876 followed the basic layout of the earlier plan, organizing the developed region by means of a geometrical network of streets, circular open spaces, and wide radial roads.[3]

The former industrial area in the north of the city center of Pest also underwent radical changes. A competition held in 1883 for the design of the new Parliament, in which Otto Wagner also participated, gave the decisive impetus to the further development of the area bordering directly on the Danube.[4] The first prize was awarded to Imre Steindl for his design in a neo-Gothic style—no doubt influenced by Gyula Andrássy's anglophile preferences. The construction work on this 265-meter-long building lasted until 1904. The smooth collaboration between the planning authorities and the workers set the standard for the sophisticated and qualitatively outstanding arts and crafts activities of the turn of the century.

Ödön Lechner, Museum and College of Arts and Crafts, Budapest IX, Üllői út 33–37, 1891–96

Postcard
Gerle collection, Budapest

Adjacent to the Parliament building were the former barracks of the Austrian army, the so-called New Building [Újépület]. This unpopular edifice posed an obstruction to further development and was therefore demolished in 1899. As a result of a competition, a generous open square was created in this vast area, surrounded by prestigious public buildings. Similar to the buildings around the bridgehead of the Elizabeth Bridge, this complex of buildings around the present Liberty Square [*Szabadság tér*] offers a good cross-section of the diverse architectural styles in use around the turn of the century. The northern side of the square is bordered by various private palaces in a historicist style forming a crescent. From Vécsey utca, one of the lanes emanating radially from the square, the view opens on to the dome of the Parliament.

The square is flanked on its western and eastern sides by the former Stock Exchange (1902–05), an imposing building comparable in size only to the Berlin Stock Exchange, and by the former Austro-Hungarian Bank (the present Hungarian National Bank, 1902–05). The story of the development of both buildings is once again evidence of the historicist trend which was dominant in the design of prestigious public buildings around the turn of the century. In the competition for the Stock Exchange the first prize and building contract were awarded to Ignác Alpár for his historicist design, whereas Ödön Lechner, the originator of modern Hungarian architecture, was runner-up. With his proposals, which combined a well-organized structure and his own idiosyncratic stylistic devices with elements of Indian architecture, Lechner would have surpassed the construction of his Post Office Savings Bank by far (Budapest V, Hold utca 4, 1899–1901).

The scenario of the competition for the Stock Exchange was repeated when the Austro-Hungarian Bank was built:

again Alpár was given preference over Lechner and was awarded the building contract. Once again his voluminous Beaux-Arts style was able to assert itself successfully against innovative trends, resulting in two buildings in the historicist style which still dominate the Szabadság tér today.[5]

Ödön Lechner, on the other hand, represented a totally different concept of architecture, as is shown to great effect by his first major building in Budapest, the Museum and School of Arts and Crafts [Iparművészeti Múzeum és Iskola] (Budapest IX, Üllői út 33–37, 1891–96).[6] This complex, built on the occasion of the Millennial anniversary of the Magyars' land acquisition, was intended to present the culture that existed prior to the land acquisition as a model worthy of imitation for those seeking new directions in architecture. For Lechner, Indian architecture was the authoritative model for monumental buildings, and he believed that he had discovered in the similarity of their motifs a kinship to the extinct original architecture of the Magyars. Based upon their specific characteristics Lechner chose motifs from rural craft, and through his artistic imagination he created gigantic three-dimensional decorative elements and architectural spatial forms out of these diminutive two-dimensional ornaments.

The search for a national identity, however, was not to be confined to a new form of ornament, but with it also went a structural renewal of architecture based on functional criteria. After building the Church in Kőbánya (1893–96), the Institute of Geology (Budapest XIV, Stefánia út 14, 1896–99), and the already mentioned Post Office Savings Bank, the Hungarian Secession was officially rejected by the government and as a consequence Lechner was not given any more public assignments (a few years later a similar official treatment was meted out to Otto Wagner). Lechner's architectural language as well as his ideas had many followers who continued his aspirations to formulate a specific Hungarian architectural language or, later on, turned toward Neoclassicism.[7]

István Medgyaszay became Ödön Lechner's most influential supporter.[8] His anthropological interest in the origins of the Hungarian people led him as far as India. He, too, developed an architectural language based on archetypal forms of folk architecture combined with reinforced concrete construction, the modern methods of which he had studied in detail during his collaboration with François Hennebique in Paris. This combination of folk-based ornamentation and innovative engineering resulted in the first "modern" buildings in Hungary, such as the studio houses in Gödöllő (1904–06), the Theater in Veszprém (1907–09), and the Church and Mausoleum in Mul'a (formerly Rárósmúlyad; 1908–10).

The end of this short *tour d'horizon* around the Budapest Liberty Square consists of a group of buildings between Lechner's Post Office Savings Bank and the square grounds. Formerly residential buildings and shops (Géza Kármán, Gyula Ullmann, 1900–01), these buildings demonstrate in their architectural form a clear indebtedness to the Viennese Secession, but this was to remain the exception. In their efforts to break free from Vienna and in their search for independent forms of artistic expression, Hungarian architects orientated themselves more toward the Belgian *art nouveau* or the English Arts and Crafts movement.[9] One of the best examples of these trends is the residential building at Honvéd utca 3 (Emil Vidor, 1903) running northward from Szabadság tér.

In the context of the search for a national identity two other types of building are of central importance for Hungarian architecture of the turn of the century: the Exhibition Pavilion and the Monument or Mausoleum. While attempts were made outside Hungary to acquaint the general public with national mythology and tradition in the Hungarian Pavilions at the International Arts and Crafts Exhibition in Venice (Géza Maróti, 1909) and at the International Exhibition in Turin (Emil Tőry, Móric Pogány, 1911), in Hungary itself such buildings were intended to function as prestigious memorial buildings. The construction of a National Pantheon on the Gellért Mountain in Budapest [*Gellérthegy*] (1902) by István Medgyaszay is much influenced by Indian temple buildings. Covered by a large dome imitating the Hungarian crown, it was intended as a tomb for Hungarian kings and national heroes.

Apart from the neo-Romanesque architecture of the United States and the architecture of Finland, it was the peasant architecture of the Middle Ages which, after 1905, became a primary source of inspiration for the latest generation of young architects—the so-called "Young Ones" [*Fiatalok*].[10] These architects were concerned with creating a new urban environment on the foundation of traditional conceptions of values and morals. As part of a building program to provide small apartments, and with the support of Mayor István Bárczy, there arose in Budapest—in contrast to other Central European cities—very extensive housing estates.[11] Parallel with this project, more than fifty schools were built between 1909 and 1912 to make up for the massive shortfall in primary schools. Some of the most impressive examples of these are the schools in Városmajor utca 59 (Budapest XII, Károly Kós, Dénes Györgyi, 1910–11) and in Áldás utca 1 (Budapest XII, Dezső Zrumeczky, 1912). As an integral part of the architectural program, these buildings through their conscious imitation of traditional village architecture were meant to instil in children living in an urban environment a feeling of national unity—a strategy which was not only confined to the buildings themselves, but was, in a wider context, aimed at creating a new national identity.

This contribution is based on an article by János Gerle.

1 For more details about urban planning and the activities of the Municipal Council of Public Works see László Siklóssy, *Hogyan épült Budapest? (1870–1930). A Fővárosi Közmunkák Tanácsa története* [How was Budapest built? (1870–1930): The History of the Municipal Council of Public Works], Budapest, 1931, reprint 1985; András Sipos, "'Stammeshäuptlinge' und Reformer. Kräfteverhältnisse und Strukturen in der Budapester Kommunalpolitik 1873 bis 1914" ["Tribal Chiefs" and Reformers: Power Relationships and Structures in the Municipal Politics of Budapest 1873–1914], in Gerhard Melinz and Susan Zimmermann (eds.), *Wien-Prag-Budapest. Blütezeit der Habsburgermetropolen. Urbanisierung, Kommunalpolitik, gesellschaftliche Konflikte (1867–1918)* [Vienna-Prague-Budapest: The Heyday of the Hapsburg Metropolises—Urbanization, Municipal Politics, Social Conflicts (1867–1918)], Vienna, 1996, pp. 108–22.
2 Schickedanz together with Fülöp Herzog completed such significant buildings of the Budapest *fin de siècle* as the Art and Exhibition Center [Műcsarnok] (1895–96), the Millennium Monument (1898–1902) and the Museum of Fine Arts [Szépművészeti Múzeum] (1900–06).
3 See *A XI. kerület építészeti emlékei* [Monuments of the XI. district], Issue no. 1, Budapest, 1993, issue no. 2, Budapest, 1999.
4 Otto Wagner designed his entry for the competition in collaboration with Mór Kallina, who was already overseeing the building of Wagner's synagogue at Rumbach Sebestyén utca 13 (Budapest VII, 1871–73).
5 See János Gerle, *Paläste des Geldes* [Palaces of Money], Budapest, 1994.
6 For Lechner see Jenő Kismarty-Lechner, *Lechner Ödön*, Budapest, 1961; Tibor Bakonyi and Mihály Kubinszky, *Lechner Ödön*, Budapest, 1981; *Ödön Lechner 1845–1914*, exh. cat. Hochschule für Angewandte Kunst Wien [College of Applied Art Vienna], Heiligenkreuzerhof, Budapest, 1991. For the Arts and Crafts Museum see Piroska Ács, *Az Iparművészeti múzeum palotájának építéstörténete* [The History of the Art and Crafts Museum], Budapest, 1996.
7 Among the many pupils and followers of Lechner were Sándor Baumgarten, Marcell Komor, Dezső Jakob, Zoltán Bálint, Lajos Jámbor, Albert Körössy, Artúr Sebestyén, Henrik Böhm, and Ármin Hegedűs. They popularized Lechner's style particularly in the rural areas; see also János Gerle, "Hungarian Architecture from 1900 to 1918" in Dora Wiebenson and József Sisa (eds.), *The Architecture of Historic Hungary*, Cambridge, Mass., and London, 1998, pp. 223–43, 304–05); Béla Málnai, József and László Vágó, Dávid and Zsigmond Jónás as well as Béla Lajta as the most influential architect (cf. Ferenc Vámos, *Lajta Béla*, Budapest, 1970) later distanced themselves from Lechner's ideas.
8 See Imre Kathy, *Medgyaszay István* [István Medgyaszay], Budapest, 1979.
9 Through travel, specialized journals and periods of study abroad, the Hungarian architects were well informed about international trends. Those who spent part of their years of study abroad were Lipót Baumhorn, Ernő Förk, István Medgyaszay (Wagner School, Vienna), Flóris Korb, Kálmán Giergle, Ödön Lechner, Gyula Pártos, Emil Tőry, Emil Vidor (Berlin), Géza Kármán, Gyula Kosztolányi, Albert Körössy, Zsigmond Quittner, Emil Vidor (Munich), and Aladár Árkay, Albert Körössy (Paris).
10 The "Young Ones" (Fiatalok) group was formed from students at the Budapest School of Arts and Crafts. The artists' colony at Gödöllő played an important part in spreading their ideas. The most important member of this group was Károly Kós; other members were Dezső Zrumeczky, Béla Jánszky, Dénes Györgyi, and Lajos Kozma. Later some architects of the older generation also joined this movement, including Aladár Árkay and Emil Vidor.
11 Cf. Gyula Kabdebó, *Budapest székesfőváros kislakás és iskola építkezései* [Blocks of Small Flats and School Buildings in Budapest], Budapest, 1913; András Sipos, "Stammeshäuptlinge," pp. 118–22; Gerhard Melinz and Susan Zimmermann, "Die aktive Stadt. Kommunale Politik zur Gestaltung städtischer Lebensbedingungen in Budapest, Prag und Wien (1867–1914)" [The Active Town Municipal Policy Affecting Urban Living Conditions in Budapest, Prague and Vienna (1867–1914)], in Melinz and Zimmermann, *Wien—Prag—Budapest*, p. 169.

Inventing a Hungarian Architecture: Budapest

In the years before World War I, architects in Budapest and the cities of the Hungarian plain searched for ways to draw out expressions of modernity from indigenous traditions. Focusing on building types such as savings banks and commercial schools, artists' colonies and craft centers, museums and theaters that served an ascendant urban middle class and expressed the force of national arts, crafts, and literature, they incorporated folk themes and explored the fusion of color, materials, painted decoration, and tactility with modern building techniques. This national consciousness was boldly presented in two representational projects: István Medgyaszay's ambitious proposal to rework the Gellért Hill as a national pantheon, and the Hungarian pavilion designed by Móric Pogány and Emil Tőry for the great Arts and Crafts Exhibition at Turin in 1910–11. Other architects, such as Aladár Árkay, Károly Kós, and Lajos Kozma, joined investigations underway in literary, art, and musical circles of the region's folk cultures and ethnic roots, rich sources from which to develop modern forms of expression divorced from the international historicism of the academic tradition. Borrowing from woodcut and folk-carving to illustrate their propositions and concentrating their work on synagogues, reformed churches, and cemeteries in the small towns and cities of Hungary, these architects looked as far afield as India and Finland for formal schemes and ornamental motifs.

J. Benedict, *Plan of Budapest*, 1896

Bird's-eye view
Multicolored print, 57 x 80 cm
Budapesti Történeti Múzeum
© Judit Szalatnyay

Ödön Lechner, Post Office Savings
Bank, Budapest V, Hold utca 4,
1899–1901

View, 1900
Print, 55 x 74 cm
MEM Budapest
© Gábor Barka

Section, 1900
Print, 56.5 x 61.5 cm
MEM Budapest
© Gábor Barka

Móric Pogány, Emil Tőry, Hungarian
Pavilion at the International Arts and
Crafts Exhibition in Turin, 1910–11

Section through entrance hall, 1911
Print, 66 x 50.4 cm
MEM Budapest
© Gábor Barka

Béla Lajta, School of Trade, Budapest
VI, Vas utca 11, 1909

Gymnasium
Photo
MEM Budapest
© Gábor Barka

View from street
Photo
MEM Budapest
© Gábor Barka

Móric Pogány, Emil Tőry, Hungarian
Pavilion at the International Arts and
Crafts Exhibition in Turin, 1910–11

View from street, 1911
Heliogravure, 50.2 x 66.1 cm
MEM Budapest
© Gábor Barka

István Medgyaszay, Project for a National Pantheon on the Gellért Mountain [Gellérthegy] in Budapest, 1902–03

Perspective
Watercolor on paper, 58 x 193 cm
Medgyaszay collection, Budapest
© Gábor Barka

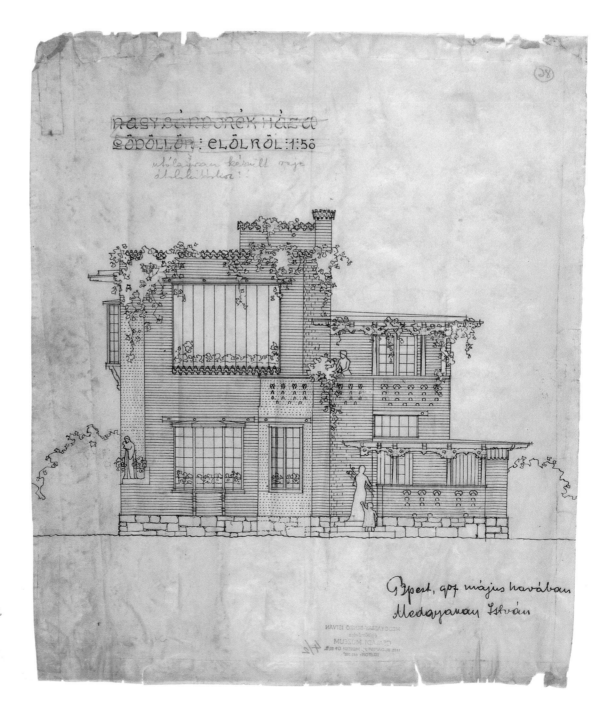

István Medgyaszay, Studio Apartment, Gödöllő, Kőrösfő utca, 1904–06

Elevation
Indian ink on transparent paper,
36 x 30 cm
Medgyaszay collection, Budapest
© Gábor Barka

SZÖVŐ ISKOLA≋≋
GÖDÖLLŐN≋≋≋≋≋
ELÖL NÉZET 1:100

István Medgyaszay, Studio Apartment, Gödöllő, Kőrösfő utca, 1904–06

Elevation with section of weaving school
Indian ink on transparent paper,
23 x 41.5 cm
Medgyaszay collection, Budapest
© Gábor Barka

View from Garden
Photo
Sammlung Medgyaszay, Budapest

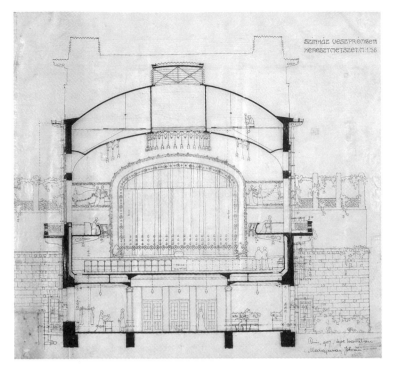

István Medgyaszay, Theater, Veszprém, 1907–09

Section
Indian ink on transparent paper,
53.5 x 59 cm
Medgyaszay collection, Budapest
© Gábor Barka

Aerial photograph
Photo
Gerle collection, Budapest

Section elevation
Indian ink on transparent paper,
32.5 x 53 cm
Medgyaszay collection, Budapest
© Gábor Barka

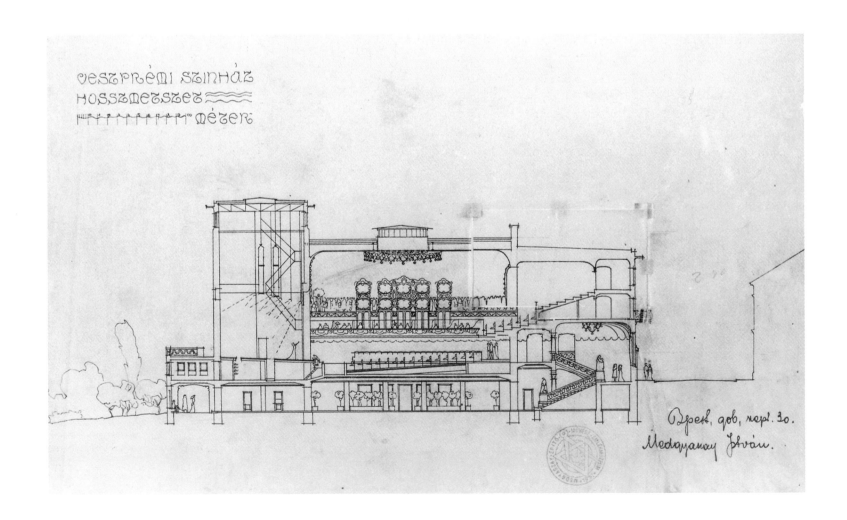

Prague, 1908–18

THE ARCHITECTURAL AVANT-GARDE IN PRAGUE

Petr Krajči and Rostislav Švácha

Thanks to the initiative of a student of Otto Wagner, Jan Kotěra,[1] the architectural conception of the Wagner school became a driving force in the countries of Bohemia around the turn of the century. Kotěra was concerned to develop further the theories of his teacher. Following the examples of other advocates of the modern movement such as Victor Horta, Hendrik P. Berlage, or Frank Lloyd Wright, by 1908 Kotěra had arrived at a kind of pre-constructivism marked by a reduction in façade decoration in favor of an emphasis on tectonics and building materials. (Similar paths were taken by Béla Lajta in Budapest, Robert Örly in Vienna, and, within the Wagner school, by Josef Hoffmann, Hubert Gessner, and Otto Wagner himself.) This phase in Kotěra's work is illustrated by the architect's own villa and the Laichter House in Prague-Vinohrady (1908–09), and by the City Museum in Hradec Králové (1909–13) as well as the Urbánek House (the so-called "Mozarteum") in the Prague Jungmannova street (1911–13). Kotěra's moralistically tinged architectural program, which demanded the active participation of the architect in bringing about social reforms (in this connection we mention only the projects for the workers' estates in Louny [1910] and Zlín [1915]), as well as his severe tectonic style, which strove for architectural truthfulness, were traits which also characterized the work of his pupils and collaborators alike. Apart from Josef Gočár and Otakar Novotný, the Wagner pupil Pavel Janák in particular was much influenced by Kotěra.

It was precisely Janák, however, who around 1910, together with a few younger Prague architects, began to voice opposition to the views of Otto Wagner and Jan Kotěra. The accusation of an exaggerated architectural rationalism and materialism that was directed against Kotěra should not be regarded merely as an isolated incident on the Prague

Jan Kotěra, Laichter House, Prague II, Chopinova 4, 1908–09
Photo: Jan Štenc, 1909
NTM Prague

architectural scene, but was a phenomenon concurrent with parallel trends in the international context: the circle of young Dutch architects that had formed around the newspaper

Josef Gočár, Spa Hotel, Bohdaneč, 1912–13
Photo: Jan Štenc, 1913
ÚDU AVČR Prague

Pavel Janák, Fára House, Pelhřimov, Masarykovo náměstí 13, Conversion, 1913–14
Photo: Jan Štenc, 1914
ÚDU AVČR Prague

Wendingen, as well as the German expressionists and, in his own particular manner, Jože Plečnik also set themselves in opposition to the generation of Berlage, Behrens, and Wagner.

What Pavel Janák, as spokesman and main theoretician of the Prague opposition, criticized in the modern movement was that it had until then been too one-sidedly governed by considerations of function, construction, and social questions. A possible way out of this impasse toward a real architecture whose forms would be based on artistic design Janák believed to have found in the work of Jože Plečnik. Janák himself sought to further refine his ideas and to develop his own conception of architecture. The path he took on the way to such a conception can be traced in the changes he made to the project for the Hlávka Bridge in Prague (1909–12), in his many drawings and sketches, in the theoretical essays he published in the newspaper *Umělecký měsíčník* [Artists' Monthly] and, in particular, in his extensive diaries.[2] The attempt to overcome the conventional orthogonal system consisting of load-bearing and supporting elements by supplementing these with a third—diagonal—force was to become the focal point of Janák's theory. This third, oblique movement, which Janák saw as an active intervention by the creative mind, became from 1912 onwards the structural basis of the architect's further work. The outer shell and the inner life of a building were to become a dynamic interplay, a mixture of matter and space.

Janák's first work in the new Cubist style, the Jakubec Villa in Jičín (1911–12), became the model which, from 1912 onward, other architects tried to aspire to: Josef Gočár with his U Černé Matky Boží [*To the Black Madonna*] department store in Prague (1912), the spa building in Bohdaneč (1912–13), the villas in Prague-Hradčany (1912–13) and

Libodřice (1912–14); Vlastislav Hofman with the cemetery in Prague-Dýáblice (1912–14); and Josef Chochol with his villas (1912–13) and apartment blocks (1913–14) in Prague-Vyšehrad. Janák himself built Villa Drechsel (1912–13) and undertook the renovation of the Fára House in Pelhřimov (1913–14) as well as the dam in Předměřice nad Labem (1913–15) which was destroyed by floods in 1929. While in some of these buildings the conception of architecture is revealed solely in the modification of traditional types of building and the shaping of the façade (something that can almost be likened to a new phase in the "façade architecture" of the nineteenth century[3]), other projects demonstrate quite clearly the architects' attempts to see the building as a purely abstract, geometric form—a feature that links these projects to aims that were later to be pursued by the post-war avant-garde.[4] The ground plans of these buildings show a preference for the polygon. Although in principle Janák held the view that the sculptural façade design sufficiently characterized the interior space of the building, there exists from his hand a few important drawings of interiors which reveal that he conceived these spaces to be like the inside of crystals. In contrast to the German Expressionists, however, neither Janák nor the other Prague Cubists were given the opportunity to convert this vision into architectural reality.

Towards the end of 1911 Janák, Gočár, Hofman, and Chochol joined the Skupina výtrárných umělců [Group of "Plastic" Artists]. The painters of the group—Emil Filla, Josef Čapek, Antonín Procházka, Vincenc Beneš, and the sculptor Otto Gutfreund—tried to develop further the Paris Cubist program of Picasso and Braque. This circumstance still leads people to interpret the architecture of the circle around Janák as a more or less naive and factually unachievable attempt to translate the "analytical" method of arranging objects and space on a two-dimensional plane into three dimensions.[5] The Prague Cubists were undoubtedly aware of the revolutionary significance of Picasso's work and drew conclusions from it for their own. From contemporary photographs of Skupina's exhibitions we can discern a tendency towards a new kind of *Gesamtkunstwerk*: the crystalline architectural frame was to accommodate suitably shaped furniture with sloping surfaces, small craft objects, sculptures by Otto Gutfreund, and Cubist paintings by Emil Filla as well as by Picasso. The inspiration drawn from cubist paintings, however, characterizes only one aspect of the work of Janák, Gočár, Hofman, and Chochol. Of much greater importance to these architects was a concern to solve problems endemic to the European architectural scene of that period—that is, to find a way out of the crisis of rationalism at the end of the first decade of the twentieth century.

Essential to the development of Prague Cubism were its theoretical foundations, which were based on a thorough knowledge of current Austrian and German art theories. The Cubists were convinced that their work fulfilled the "objective" laws and principles that had been laid down by Alois Riegl and Wilhelm Worringer for the science of art. They felt strongly tied to those historic epochs when, in their view, the creativity of the artists had conquered the limitations of materials and tectonic possibilities: the Gothic or the Borrominian Baroque. Hofman was, moreover, interested in Indian architecture; Gočár, in the classicism of the early nineteenth century. Even Riegl's theory of the preservation of monuments, with its program of integrating new forms into a historic environment, left visible traces in the work of the Prague Cubists. Experiments in context-related architecture can be seen in the U Černé Matky Boží House of Josef Gočár or in Pavel Janák's renovation of the Fára House in Pelhřimov.

Around 1912 a split occurred within the Skupina výtvarných umělců. Janák and Gočár remained members, but Hofman and Chochol transferred to an older association, Mánes. From this point an architectural cubism lost the character of a collective movement, and its followers confined themselves to differentiating their individual points of view from those of the others. The four Cubist architects with their own personal stylistic development were later joined by other architects such as Bedřich Feuerstein, Vladimír Fultner, Otakar Novotný, Rudolf Stockar, and, surprisingly, even Jan Kotěra. By 1914 Josef Chochol had arrived at a Czech variant of Purism, Vlastislav Hofman's drawings and linoprints approached the style of organic architecture, and after 1914 Josef Gočár designed projects in an almost purely Neoclassicist style. Pavel Janák's diary sketches from between 1914 and 1919 show some interesting metamorphoses. Crystalline, cylindrical, prism-shaped, and segment-like elements, here and there arranged in neo-plasticist compositions,

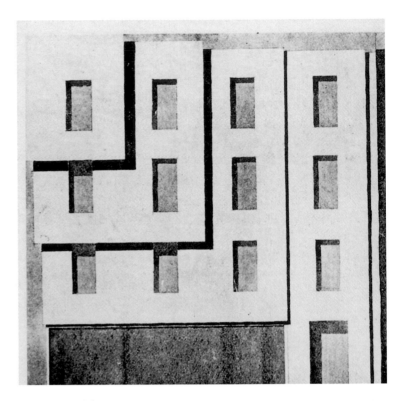

Josef Chochol, Façade Study, 1914
Repr. from: Stavba, II, 1923

gradually show an increasing tendency to take the shape of load-bearing and supporting elements—the very model which Janák had once so vehemently opposed.

From the very beginning the program of architectural Cubism had been completely apolitical. We hardly detect any trace of a nationalist tendency in Janák's polemics against the views of Otto Wagner. If we read Janák's writings and notes from the years 1910–20 more closely,[6] we are surprised to find that in those places where the architect does concern himself with a political delineation of Cubism, this is directed more against Germany than Vienna. And yet it was precisely in Germany that architectural Cubism found the widest resonance on an international level, with the exception of certain peripheral phenomena like the Paris sculptor Raymond Duchamp-Villon's project for a Cubist House (1912). Herwarth Walden, the most influential theoretician of Expressionism, exhibited a selection of projects by Pavel Janák and Josef Gočár at the Berlin Autumn Salon of 1913, and published designs by Vlastislav Hofman in his journal *Der Sturm* [The Storm]. The Austrian Pavilion at the exhibition of the Deutscher Werkbund in Cologne (1914) contained two Cubist rooms which Novotný, Janák, and Gočár helped to design and arrange.

It is probable that the German Expressionists saw in the Czech Cubists welcome allies against the emerging objectivity of architecture. Against this trend, which he saw as leading to coldness and dehumanization, Janák emphasized the specific Czech sense of the lyrical and sculptural elements of objects.

Josef Gočár, Bank of the Czechoslovak
Legions, Prague I, Na poříčí 24, 1921–23

Photo: Jan Štenc, 1923
NTM Prague

After World War I these "Czech" values would be expressed by the "National Style" (also known as Rondo-Cubism) as we know it from Josef Gočár's Bank of the Czechoslovakian Legions in Prague (1921–23) or Pavel Janák's Crematorium in Pardubice (1921–23).

1 For Kotěra see also Otakar Novotný, *Jan Kotěra a jeho doba* [Jan Kotěra and His Epoch], Prague, 1958 and the recently published essay by Rostislav Švacha and Dita Robová, "Jan Kotěra et ses élèves," in *Prague Art Nouveau*, exh. cat., Palais des Beaux-Arts, Brussels, 1998, pp. 173–83. A catalogue of Kotěra's work is in preparation at the Architectural Archives of the National Technical Museum in Prague under the direction of Petr Krajči.
2 For a more detailed account of the theories of Janák and the other architects of Prague Cubism see Rostislav Švacha, "Die Kunstauffassungen der Architekten" [The Architects' Conceptions of Art], in Jiři Švestka and Tomáš Vlček (eds.), *1909–1925 Kubismus in Prag. Malerei, Skulptur, Kunstgewerbe, Architektur* [1909–1925: Cubism in Prague—Painting, Sculpture, Arts and Crafts, Architecture], exh. cat., Kunstverein für die Rheinlande und Westfalen, Düsseldorf, Stuttgart, 1991, pp. 202–11; Irena Žýantovská Murray, "The Burden of Cubism: The French Imprint on Czech Architecture 1910–1914," in Eve Blau and Nancy J. Troy (ed.), *Architecture and Cubism*, Cambridge, Mass., 1997, pp. 41–57.
3 For the aspect of "Fassadenarchitektur" [façade architecture] see especially Friedrich Czagan, "Kubistische Architektur in Böhmen" [Cubist Architecture in Bohemia], in *Werk* [Work], Zürich, vol. LVI, 1969, pp. 75–79.
4 For more on this connection see Miroslav Šik, "Modern anti-Modernism: Bohemian Cubism 1910–1920," in *Domus* (Milan), no. 782, 1996, pp. 64–69.
5 For a critical analysis of this phenomenon see Wolf Tegethoff, "Kubismus mezi Paříží a Prahou" [Cubism between Paris and Prague], in Bayrische Vereinsbank (ed.), *Stavební umění. Kubistická architektura v Praze a jejím okolí* [Architecture: Cubist Architecture in Prague and Its Surroundings], Mnichov, 1994, pp. 8–13. See also the review of this publication in *Umění* [Art] (Prague), vol. XLIV, 1996, pp. 213–15.
6 See the bibliography of Janák's writings in Kateřina Dostálová, "Pavel Janák," in Jiří Šetlík (ed.), *Acta UPM*, vol. XIX, C 4, Commentationes, Prague, 1985, pp. 72–83. The manuscript and typescript essays of the architect are kept in the Architectural Archives of the National Technical Museum in Prague (the estate of Pavel Janák).

Czech Cubism

Czech architects began to experiment with Cubism in the years before World War I, and the originality of their work was widely observed in the modern circles. Ignoring Wagner's doctrine of construction, rationality, and dynamism, the Prague Cubists adopted as governing principles the ideas of form and dynamism. The core concept in the Cubist perception of architecture, particularly as expressed in the essays of Pavel Janák, is "animation," the bringing to life within a building of both its material and substance, and its "third element"—the lines, space and spirit implicit in the form. Key notions are that matter is influenced from the outside, that materials can be shaped by artistic feeling within the artist himself, and that the surface and inner life of a building can fuse in a dynamic play between matter and space. How such theories could be realized can be seen in Janák's many façade sketches and in the design of the Prague Vyšehrad (1914–15) by Vlastislav Hofman. Prague's historical fortifications, known since 1900 as the "Acropolis," were under pressure from speculative developers envisioning it as a site for new residential properties. Hofman's proposal (a garden city of row housing with monumental exterior stairs) aimed to take into account the aesthetic and typological character of the historical environment. Similar concerns with context are evident in Josef Gočár's department store At the Black Madonna (1912) and Josef Chochol's apartment house in Neklanova Street (1913–14). These buildings all endeavor to establish a dialogue with a cityscape shaped by the Baroque and Gothic.

Vlastislav Hofman, Project for the Development of the Vyšehrad, Prague II, 1914–15

Western elevation, perspective
Pencil, crayon, and watercolor on card,
39 x 56 cm
AUR Prague

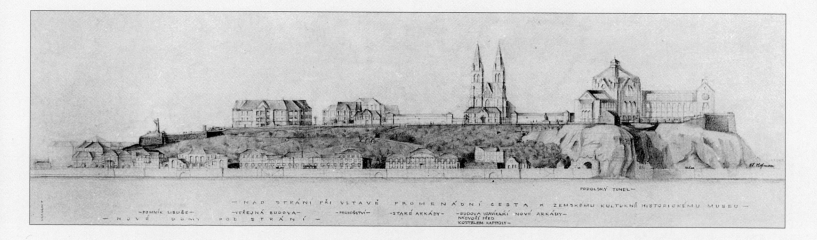

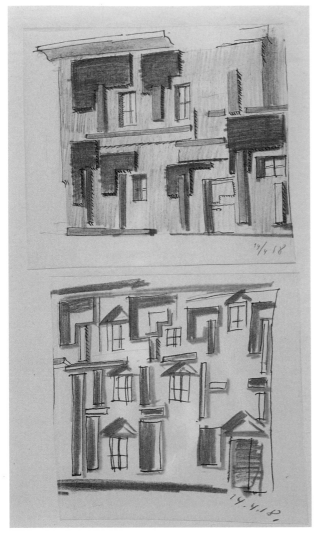

Vlastislav Hofman, Project for the Development of the Vyšehrad, Prague II, 1914–15

View of staircase in front of the ramparts
Pencil and crayon on card, 42.5 x 52.5 cm
AUR Prague

Vlastislav Hofman, Project for Redesigning the Palackého náměstí, Prague I, 1913

View from the park across the House Bridge to the Palackého náměstí
Indian ink on paper, wash, 58 x 96 cm
Getty Los Angeles

Pavel Janák, Façade Sketches, 1912–18

Indian ink and crayon on paper,
13.4 x 15 cm, 13.8 x 14 cm
NTM Prague

Pavel Janák, Façade Sketch, 1912

Pencil and indian ink on paper,
16.5 x 25.2 cm
NTM Prague

Jiří Kroha, Study for a Villa, Kroměříž, 1917

Pencil, crayon, chalk, indian ink, and water-color on paper, 22 x 40 cm
MMB Brno
© Karel Šabata

Bedřich Feuerstein, Design Sketch for a Memorial, Prague, 1914

Pencil and indian ink on paper,
21.6 x 30 cm
NTM Prague

Jiři Kroha, Architectural Study, 1915

Pencil and watercolor on paper,
36 x 34.5 cm
MMB Brno
© Karel Šabata

Josef Chochol, Apartment Block,
Prague II, Neklanova 30, 1913–14

Photo, 1914, 23 x 16 cm
© Štenc Archives, Prague

Pavel Janák, Sketchbook, 1911–18

Design sketch, 1912
Pencil on paper, 16 x 10 cm
NTM Prague

Vienna around 1910

VIENNA BETWEEN MEMORY AND MODERNITY

Iain Boyd Whyte

With the dubious benefit of hindsight, Viennese society in the years around 1910 has been characterized as enfeebled and decadent, waltzing towards the inevitable apocalypse that was unleashed with the outbreak of war in August 1914. To a degree, this general picture holds true. As the 1911 edition of the *Encyclopaedia Britannica* noted in its article on Vienna: "A decline of its importance similar to that within the larger sphere which it influenced prior to 1859 has continued uninterruptedly within the Habsburg dominions until the present day."[1] This decline, however, was only relative, and Vienna was still a booming city around 1910. With the incorporation of Floridsdorf in 1905, it became Europe's second largest city by area, covering 27,120 hectares.

The population of greater Vienna also expanded, increasing from 842,951 in 1869 to 1,927,606 in 1910, greatly stimulated by immigration from the eastern territories of the dual monarchy. This growth had economic effects, and a conspicuous increase in national wealth marked the decade before the outbreak of war. With a burgeoning population and a growing economy, the prospects for architectural production were excellent.

Central to the cultural life of the city in the first decade of the century was a creative dialogue between modernity and memory, in which architectural design held a pivotal role. Within this discussion the only common conviction was an absolute rejection of dogmatic historicism, in which Otto Wagner had played a seminal role. As his former student, Otto Schönthal, wrote in 1908:

> If we think back to twenty years ago we can measure how far behind us we have left the age of stereotyped design. Our thanks for this are due, above all, to Otto Wagner. For it was he who cleared away the rubbish, or the degrading business of copying, and shook the multitude out of their indolent slumber.[2]

The radical modernism proposed by Wagner in the Post Office Savings Bank (1903–06) took specifically urban form in two schemes at the end of the decade. With the apartment house at Neustiftgasse of 1909, and the 1911 lecture text on the *Großstadt* [the metropolis], Wagner argued for a rational design process in which the artist was challenged to give symbolic form to the economic and material demands of the great city. Yet historical precedent was always admissible as the enriching factor that creates the *Stadtphysiognomie*, the face of the city. History for Wagner did not mean the stylistic rules and imperatives of nineteenth-century eclecticism, but rather a discourse with the masters of the past, and with their solutions to comparable questions.[3] This conviction informed the cover illustration that Wagner's former student and assistant Emil Hoppe designed for *Der Architekt* in 1906, in which Wagner's Kirche am Steinhof of 1902–04 is joined by a view across Rome toward St. Peter's and by a Doric temple. The major, if unbuilt, projects designed by Wagner around 1910 must be understood in this light.[4]

The all-embracing dialogue between modernity and memory not only offered a multiplicity of resting points between the two poles, but also proposed many possibilities of synthetic resolution, all of which could claim to be modern, while still grounded in Viennese tradition. Wagner's position within this spectrum was only one of many, and even his ex-students looked for alternative strategies. Denying its Hennebique concrete frame, the heavy marble-clad presence of Jože Plečnik's Zacherl-Haus (1903–05) challenged Wagner's rationalism in its compelling mixture of menace and magic. Leopold Bauer also abandoned the austere, Wagnerian stance of his early works and adopted a pluralist position shared by the great majority of his architect contemporaries in Vienna. In an interview published in 1910 he explained:

Josef Hoffmann, Villa Skywa-Primavesi, Vienna XIII, Gloriettegasse 18, 1913–15,
View from the west
Repr. from: Eduard F. Sekler, Josef Hoffmann. Das architektonische Werk, Salzburg, Vienna, 1982,
(second edition 1986)

As I originally come from a rigidly modernist and materialist school, these ideas have only slowly gained a hold with me.... It is undoubtedly quite impossible to create something that is tradition-less.... In our buildings we can happily make use of all known styles, of all those countless artistic treasures left by our predecessors...the strength of the artistic personality reconquers them for our own age.[5]

Three key issues emerge from Bauer's interview: history is accessible through artistic intervention rather than academic knowledge; the goal of history, thus understood, is twofold. On the one hand, it should uncover primeval and thus universal patterns of form, scale, and rhythm. On the other, it should identify how these universal patterns are informed by a specifically local spirit. Finally, formal devices exist in a free relationship both to their historical context and to each other, and can be employed at the will of the architect to create new combinations that have never before existed and which, by this definition, are new and thus modern.

Within the work of a particular architect, these propositions allow enormous freedom to adopt varying styles for different commissions, functions, and sites. Ernst von Gotthilf, for example, favored a palatial, rather French, Baroque for the Haus der Kaufmannschaft on the Schwarzenbergplatz (1905), but a much more austere Neoclassicism for the Credit-Bankverein on the Schottengasse (1909–12). Such freedom was also exploited within the same building: in Leopold Bauer's unbuilt scheme for the Österreichische-Ungarische Bank (1911–18) classical columns and pilasters support a Romanesque drum, which in turn is capped by a neo-Baroque dome.

According to Ferdinand von Feldegg in 1908, contemporary Viennese architecture had "an inventive, heuristic character, with a predilection for primitive forms."[6] A return to the classical canon was an obvious path, and one highly symptomatic of an age for which Jugendstil and Arts and Crafts had lost their charms. In 1910, for example, Peter Behrens was appealing to classical order in his designs for the AEG factories in Berlin, with the young Le Corbusier working as one of his assistants. A year later, Le Corbusier visited the Parthenon in Athens every day for three weeks in order to comprehend its supreme mathematics and ascetic self-control. A similar move toward the authority of Classicism can also be found in Vienna. Josef Hoffmann intimated a stripped-down classical revival in 1905–1906 with his project for an extension to the Kunstgewerbeschule in Vienna, and developed it triumphantly with his designs for the Ast House and the Villa Skywa-Primavesi. In contrast to the sturdy Prussian Classicism of Behrens, or Le Corbusier's monk-like asceticism, however, this Viennese version was more playful and inventive. Although Hoffmann refers to pediment, architrave, and pilaster, they never quite fulfill their traditional function: literal quotation is avoided in favor of "simplifications, elisions, transformations, and metamorphoses of every kind."[7]

To the inventive spirits of the period the local Baroque was another obvious point of reference in the search for an architecture appropriate to Vienna in 1910. Indeed, a successful Baroque revival was already well underway by the turn of the century, stimulated by the very positive popular response to the neo-Baroque gateway leading from the Michaelerplatz to the Hofburg, which had opened to traffic in September 1893. Directly across the Michaelerplatz, Carl König, Professor of Architecture at the Technische Hochschule, designed the Palais Herberstein (1893–95) in a sculptural neo-Baroque considered appropriate to its site opposite the Hofburg. This regal manner also found favor in König's Haus der Industrie, built on the Schwarzenbergplatz in 1906–09, and articulated with imperial Roman pilasters. A similar motif was adopted by König's former pupil Maks Fabiani in his design for the Urania building (1909–10), which sports Corinthian pilasters with no bases. As private advisor to Crown Prince Franz Ferdinand, Fabiani found himself at this point in a uniquely privileged position, located somewhere between the iconoclasm of his Portois and Fix building (1899–1900) and the innate conservatism of the court. His design for the Urania building represents a brilliant response to this challenge. In setting the two main auditoria one above the other, Fabiani anticipated Adolf Loos's theory of flexible vertical space—"Raumplan"—within a whimsical neo-Baroque envelope.

Other König students played a significant role in giving the historical core of Vienna a more metropolitan face. A strong example is the Residenzpalast, a seven-story block with a reinforced concrete frame, built in 1909–10 to the design of Arthur Baron. Three stories of commercial space were layered within exposed iron frames, which were in turn

Maks Fabiani, Wiener Urania, Vienna I, Uraniastraße 1, 1909–10
Repr. from: Der Architekt [The Architect], XVI, 1910

Carl König, Herberstein Palace (left), 1893–95, Adolf Loos, Goldman & Salatsch House (right), Vienna I, Michaelerplatz, 1909–11

enframed by signboards—a truly metropolitan gesture in which the display window focuses the act of commodity exchange. Two auditoria were installed in the basement, one for the Residenztheater—with an interior by the fashionable architects Krauss & Tölk—the other for a cinema. Just as Otto Wagner's city railway (1894–1901) had heralded the age of mass transit in Vienna in the 1890s, so complex urban buildings like the Residenzpalast ushered in the age of mass entertainment and consumption.

Away from the commercial heart of the city, domestic building favored a neo-Biedermeier manner whose lack of decorative ostentation commended it as an obvious precedent for the simple austerity of the modernists.[8] The threeman practice of Emil Hoppe, Marcel Kammerer, and Otto Schönthal—all former students and assistants of Otto Wagner—produced a series of distinguished apartment houses around 1910 in which the ground bass of Biedermeier austerity was enriched with detailing derived from a variety of sources. For the Palais Fischer in the Frankenberggasse, of 1910, they created a perfectly mute façade that gave no inkling of the functions or disposition of the interior spaces. Another house from the same year in the Martinstrasse hinted at

English influences, and employed a geometrical system of façade composition based on the golden section, a typically Biedermeier technique that had dominated the Vienna streetscape in the 1830s.[9] The rural equivalent of Biedermeier—the vernacular architecture of the outlying suburbs of Vienna and the surrounding countryside—was also favored around 1910 as an antidote to the pattern-book *Heimatstil* that threatened to turn every suburban railway station and post office from Hamburg to Vienna into an imitation Bavarian farmhouse. Both the Biedermeier façades in the city and the vernacular architecture of the Vienna hinterland became a favored subject of the new, portable cameras that were used by architects to study and record historical motifs. Further afield, the camera also captured the traditional architectures of the Mediterranean and Aegean, an important source for the domestic work of Hoffmann, Loos, and Josef Frank. Joseph August Lux famously condemned pan-Germanic *Heimatkunst* as "a detour leading to the boondocks."[10] The way forward, he insisted, lay with the new technologies of the engineer, in which he detected "a new artistic beauty…naked utility, the fleshless skeleton of functionality and objectivity."[11] As in every other major city, this "new beauty" could be found in Vienna in the quotidian structures of commerce and industry. The best Viennese examples, however, resist "fleshless functionality." In the grain silo designed for the Hammerbrot factory in Schwechat in 1909 by the brothers Gessner, for example, the blandness of the simple container is relieved by tile cladding and expressive fenestration. On a larger scale the concrete-framed grain store built on the Handelskai in 1911–13 to the design of Friedrich Mahler and Albrecht Michler created a powerful architectural statement that went far beyond the dictates of its ferro-concrete frame. Unsurprisingly, Mahler, Michler, and the brothers Gessner were all former Wagner students.

Griechengasse, Vienna I, c. 1910
Photo: Otto Schönthal

Emil Hoppe, Project for an Apartment Block, Vienna XVIII, Martinstraße 17, 1910
Perspective
Pencil, indian ink, and watercolor on paper, 30 x 19.5 cm

Wagner with a hint of Americanism, Classicism, Biedermeier, or Baroque: all were proposed around 1910 as the solution to the search for a specifically Viennese "modernism." Adolf Loos's pre-war work can best be understood as a critique of these claims. In his domestic designs of this period—the Steiner, Scheu, or Horner houses, for example—Loos placed the comfort of the inhabitants and the traditional wisdom of the carpenter above the transient fads and fashions of the artist-architect. The Looshaus on the Michaelerplatz took the protest against architectural self-indulgence and *Künstlerphantasie* into the city center, with its merciless critique of the diverse blandishments of current Viennese architecture. The classical canon was present in the basic scheme of base, column, capital, and architrave. The Viennese Baroque echoed in the plastic treatment of the entry space, in the bay windows, and in the choice of highly finished marble on the exterior and the mirrors within. Biedermeier is there in the simple stucco and undecorated openings of the upper stories. English Arts and Crafts pragmatism, Mediterranean vernacular, and American know-how are also part of the equation. Yet none of these claims the ascendancy, as all are played off against each other under Loos's ironic gaze. The Looshaus offers an acerbic enquiry into the nature of architecture and into its claims to be an art. It does not propose any resolution to these questions, and might be read as the ultimate confirmation of Friedrich Achleitner's trenchant proposition:

> Vienna was never a site of architectural inventions. Rather, it was an emporium of ideas, a spacious factory for processing ideas. It is a place for the reception, adaptation, contemplation, and co-existence of alien or even mutually exclusive systems. The strength of the Viennese lies in reacting, weighing up, connecting, and qualifying systems that are or behave as if they are absolute. Nothing is more suspect to the Viennese than something that takes itself seriously.[12]

1 "Vienna," *Encyclopaedia Brittanica*, Cambridge, 1911.
2 Otto Schönthal, "Die Kirche Otto Wagners," *Der Architekt*, vol. 14, 1908, p. 1.
3 See Peter Haiko, "Otto Wagner: Von der Renaissance der Renaissance zur Naissance der Kunst" in Tilmann Buddensieg (ed.), *Wien und die Architektur des 20. Jahrhunderts, Akten des XXV Internationalen Kongresses für Kunstgeschichte*, Vienna, 1983, p. 118: "Wagner's discussion with history is less an object-bound appeal to the artistic production of the past than a subjective discourse with those architects from history who were, in his eyes, artistically the most productive and best qualified."

Franz Gessner, Hubert Gessner, Grain Silo for the Hammerbrot Factory, Schwechat nr. Vienna, 1909
Repr. from: Der Architekt, XVI, 1910

4 The central block for the proposed Academy of Fine Arts, for example, designed for a site outside the city on the Schmelz, pays clear homage with its flanking pylons to Fischer von Erlach's Karlskirche. Not only does it pull the new academy back from the suburbs toward the city's cultural and spiritual heart, but critiques the long and difficult history of the City Museum, also consigned to the Schmelz, following the dismissal of Wagner's earlier schemes for the Museum on the Karlsplatz, directly beside the Karlskirche. For the long saga of the City Museum see Peter Haiko and Renata Kassal-Mikula (eds.), *Otto Wagner und das Kaiser Franz Josef-Stadtmuseum: Das Scheitern der Moderne in Wien*, Vienna, Museum, 1988. On the related discussions on the remodeling of the Karlsplatz see Hans Schmidkunz, "Wiener Baufragen," *Der Städtebau*, vol. 6, 1909, pp. 49–51; and Alfred Castelliz, "Die Vollendung des Karlsplatzes in Wien," *Der Architekt*, vol. 16, 1910, pp. 51–56.
5 Leopold Bauer, interview given in Berlin, 1910; quoted in Edmund Wilhelm Braun, "Einige Gedanken über Leopold Bauer," *Moderne Bauformen*, vol. 9, 1910, pp. 68–69.
6 Ferdinand von Feldegg, "Über die inneren Grundlagen moderner Architekturauffassung," *Der Architekt*, vol. 14, 1908, p. 102.
7 Eduard F. Sekler, *Josef Hoffmann: The Architectural Work*, Princeton, N.J., 1985, p. 140.
8 See Joseph August Lux, "Biedermeier alz Erzieher," in *Das Interieur*, vol. 10, 1909, p. 45: "The domestic architecture shows no clamorous façades. They are entirely undecorated. If anyone were to summon up today the moral seriousness to build an entirely flat façade without any superfluous decoration, people would be scandalized by it. We no longer have any idea of how charming the cityscape must have looked when the houses parade plain faces with flat, light, pure and undecorated walls, and how powerful the impact of the truly monumental buildings must then have been."

9 See Iain Boyd Whyte, *Emil Hoppe, Marcel Kammerer, Otto Schönthal: Three Architects from the Master Class of Otto Wagner*, Cambridge, Mass., 1989, pp. 70–73.
10 Joseph August Lux, "Über die Aufgaben und Ziele einer Architekturzeitschrift," *Der Architekt*, vol. 15, 1909, p. 2.
11 Ibid., p. 1.
12 Friedrich Achleitner, "Pluralismus und Mehrsprachigkeit in der Wiener Architektur," in Achleitner, *Wiener Architektur*, Vienna, 1996, p. 16.

Reworking Traditions

Two powerful figures—Otto Wagner and Adolf Loos—dominate historical accounts of Viennese architecture at the turn of the century. They have been favored for specific reasons. With his radical simplicity and insistence on flat planes and engineering technology, Wagner was seen as a forerunner of the international modernism that blossomed in the 1920s. Loos, in contrast, linked architecture to contemporary debates on language, representation, and truth—the central concerns of a specifically Viennese *Moderne* that emerged around 1900. While both Wagner and Loos were enormously significant figures, the story of Viennese architecture in the first decade of the century is too diverse and complex to be encompassed by these two positions alone. The search for an architecture appropriate to the new century was marked by a vigorous dialogue between modernity and memory, in which the demands of the modern metropolis were constantly measured against the imperatives of site and history. On one side, the examples of Berlin, London, or New York were cited in support of the requirements of the engineer and the traffic planner. On the other side came calls for Neoclassical and neo-Baroque revivals, for a return to the simplicity of the Viennese Biedermeier of the 1830s and 1840s, or for the re-evaluation of vernacular architecture as a possible model for contemporary housing. All of these positions were seen as "modern." Far from favoring one of these impulses to the exclusion of all others, however, the leading architects such as Otto Wagner, Adolf Loos, Leopold Bauer, Karl König, Josef Hoffman, and Maks Fabiani drew from many of these options in their own designs. It is precisely this rich and often contradictory mix that lends the Viennese architecture built around 1910 its extraordinary fascination.

Otto Schönthal, Project for a Jubilee Memorial, 1908

View
Indian ink and chalk on paper, 25 x 25 cm
Albertina Vienna

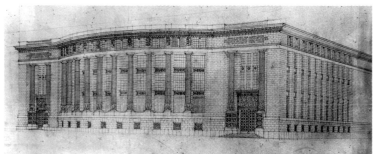

Leopold Bauer, Project for the Austro-Hungarian Bank, Vienna IX, 1911–18

Perspective, view from point M
Pencil on paper, 65.5 x 76.2 cm
Albertina Vienna

Perspective, lower part of main façade
Pencil on paper, 42.5 x 97.7 cm
Albertina Vienna

Cross-section through the main hall
Pencil on transparent paper,
136.5 x 115.5 cm
Albertina Vienna

**Carl König, House of Industry,
Vienna III, Schwarzenbergplatz 4,
1906–09**

Sketch of façade
Pencil on paper, 21.5 x 34 cm
TU Vienna, Archives

**Carl König, House of Industry,
Vienna III, Schwarzenbergplatz 4,
1906–09**

View from Schwarzenbergplatz
Plate 67
Repr. from: Bauten und Entwürfe von Carl König, edited
by his pupils, Vienna, 1910

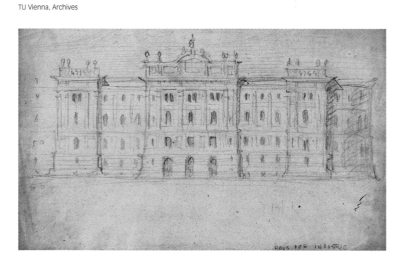

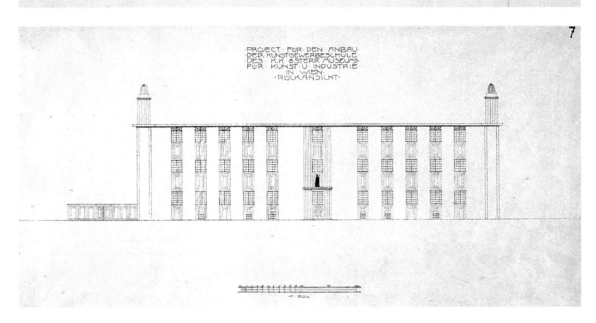

Josef Hoffman, **Project for the Extension of the College of Arts and Crafts, Vienna 1, 1905–09**

Façade towards Marxergasse
Colored print, 31.5 x 52 cm
UAK Vienna, Archives

Rear view towards Wienfluß
Colored print, 28 x 52 cm
UAK Vienna, Archives

Adolf Loos, **Project for a Housing Complex with Equestrian Monument, c. 1909**

View
Processed print, 36.5 x 87 cm
Albertina Vienna

Josef Hoffman, Project for a Villa

Perspective
Watercolor on paper, 24.8 x 31.5 cm
CCA Montréal

Jan Kotěra, Villa Lemberger, Vienna XIX, Grinzinger Allee 50-52, 1913–14

Photograph of model
NTM Prague

Design sketch, perspectival view, and ground plan
Pencil and indian ink on paper,
22 x 31.5 cm
NTM Prague

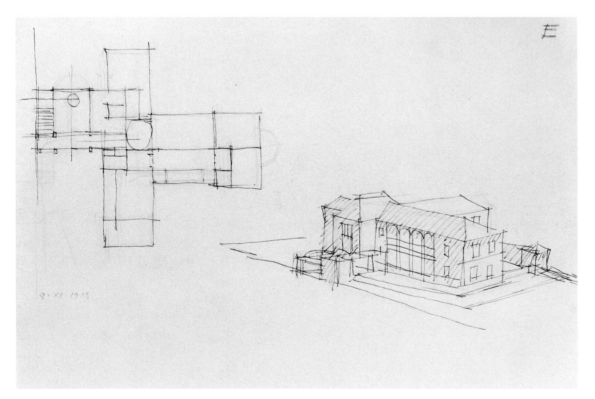

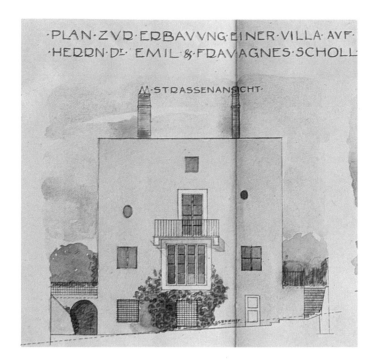

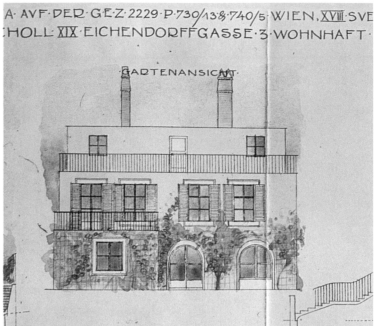

Josef Frank, Scholl House, Vienna XIX, Wilbrandtgasse 3, 1913–14

View from street and garden, ground plan of living floor area
Colored print, 61 x 105 cm
MA 37 Vienna
© Hermann Czech

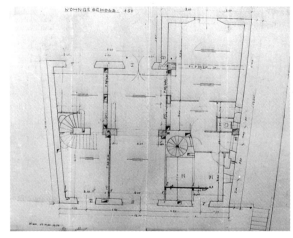

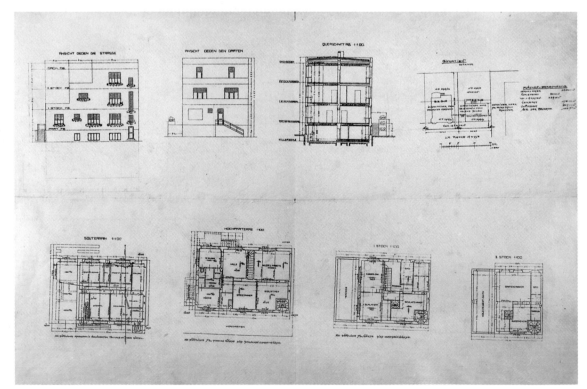

Adolf Loos, Scheu House, Vienna XIII Larochegasse 3, 1912–13

Views, section, and ground plans
Print, 65 x 101 cm
Albertina Vienna
© VBK Vienna 1999

Arthur Baron, Residence Palace,
Vienna I, Fleischmarkt 1, 1909–12

Plate 100, 45 x 32 cm
Repr. from: Die Architektur des XX. Jahrhunderts, XII,
1912

Jože Plečnik, Zacherl House, Vienna I,
Wildpretmarkt 2–4, 1903–05

Plate 81, 45 x 32 cm
Repr. from: Die Architektur des XX. Jahrhunderts, VI,
1906

Pierto Palumbo, Residential and
Business Premises, Vienna I, Graben 16,
1909–11

Plate 84, 45 x 32 cm
Repr. from: Die Architektur des XX. Jahrhunderts, XII,
1913

Zagreb, 1880–1918

MODERN ARCHITECTURAL TOWN PLANNING IN ZAGREB

Aleksander Laslo

Plan of the city of Zagreb, scale 1:4000, 1911
Colored print, 63 x 95 cm
DA Zagreb

The history of modern Zagreb begins in the mid nineteenth century.[1] In 1850, following an Imperial Decree, the two municipalities of Gradec and Kaptol which had been in existence since the Middle Ages were joined to the surrounding settlements to form the Royal City of Zagreb. Below these two historic cities the Lower City (Donji Grad) developed and soon became the center of the new Zagreb.

The first building regulations were passed in 1857 and initiated the first phase of a general process of modernization and urbanization. The urban and socioeconomic changes ran parallel with a rapid population growth[2] and took place in three major historico-cultural stages.[3] Two *Regulierungspläne* [regulatory plans] formed the basis for the territorial expansion of the city. The first plan of 1865 concentrated primarily on the layout of the new Lower City as the future center of the new Zagreb. The architectural concept of the Vienna Ringstrasse served as a model in this process. The so-called Green Horseshoe [*Zelena potkova*] was laid out—a site on which prestigious monumental buildings such as the Academy of Sciences and Fine Arts, the University, the Central Station, Technical School, National Theater, urban villas and houses of prosperous citizens as well as extensive parks were arranged in such a way as to form a singular *Gesamtkunstwerk* of architectonic historicism.

In 1880 Zagreb was hit by a severe earthquake. As a direct consequence the building activities were intensified during the 1880s and in 1887 a second regulatory plan was prepared. Between 1880 and 1890 around 400 new buildings were constructed and the new urban areas gradually merged with the heart of the city. The period of the most intense urbanization and construction, however, came in the last decade of the nineteenth century. Apart from the development of the most important traffic axes and the construction of more than 2,300 new buildings, the plumbing system for the water supply, begun in 1878, was extended and several streams within the urban areas were filled in. The construction of extensive housing estates for workers and civil servants at the town periphery which had been part of the second regulatory plan was postponed until after World War I.

The intensive construction work carried out in Zagreb at the end of the nineteenth century also led to changes on the local architectural scene. An important factor in this was the establishment in 1878 of the Association of Croatian Engineers and Architects. Already by 1880 the first issue of their specialist journal was published. In 1882 a foundation course was introduced at their Technical College and in 1892 a course at the intermediate level was set up at the associated Architectural College. The guest architects and foreign architects who had become temporarily resident (Friedrich Schmidt, Ferdinand Fellner, Hermann Helmer, Kuno Waidmann) were soon joined by a self-confident group of young Croatian architects who had been educated at the Vienna Academy of Fine Arts or at the Technical Universities in Vienna: Josip Vancaš, Martin Pilar, Ciril Metod Ivaković, or Janko Holjac.

A special place among these architects was occupied by the naturalized former German Hermann Bollé and the most significant Zagreb architect duo of the time, Leo Hönigsberg and Julio Deutsch. Although initially unpopular due to his neo-Gothic infringements on local churches, Bollé made important contributions in expanding the educational system for the building profession and in his museum-related and educational work at the newly founded Industrial Museum. Hönigsberg and Deutsch later devoted themselves to establishing basic regulations for the architectural profession, which resulted above all in improved competition procedures, increased publication of important public projects, and in a closer collaboration between architects and their respective building contractors.

These circumstances helped to make the last decade of the nineteenth century—in spite of its continued commitment to architectural historicism—the most significant period of architectural and urban development in the history of Zagreb architecture. Among the buildings that are important for their use of new buildings techniques (including steel-frame construction) are to be counted the "Octagon" in the First Croatian Savings Bank (Josip Vancaš, Ilica 5/Preobraženska 1–3/Bogovićeva 6, 1897–99) and the Arts Pavilion at Tomislavov trg 22. The Pavilion, a steel-frame structure, designed by the Budapest architects Korb & Giergl for the Millennium Exhibition in Budapest (1896), was dismantled after the ceremonies and transported to Zagreb as a gift from the Hungarian government. There the studios of Fellner & Helmer as well as Hönigsberg & Deutsch undertook its reconstruction (1897–98).

Thanks to its sufficient geographic distance from the metropolises of Vienna and Budapest, Zagreb was able to develop more or less autonomously at the periphery of the Monarchy. Here too, however, the fundamental conflict between historicist trends and the modern style was interrupted by a schism: Jugendstil. The programmatic prelude to the Zagreb Secession was represented by the first exhibition of the young generation at the Arts Pavilion (December 1898, organized by the Association of Croatian Artists. In addition, the journal *Hrvatski Salon* [Croatian Salon] briefly appeared modeled on Vienna's *Ver Sacrum*. The first signs of Jugendstil architecture can be found in the house of Eugen Rado and Mira Reiching (Trenkova 2/Strossmayerov trg 7, Ignjat Fischer, 1897). With its freely applied ornamentation, it follows in

Fellner & Helmer, Hönigsberg & Deutsch, Arts Pavilion, Zagreb, Tomislavov trg 22, 1897–98

The pavilion was originally built by the Budapest architects Korb & Giergl with a steel-frame structure for the Millennium Exhibition in Budapest (1896). It was then dismantled and transported to Zagreb, and there rebuilt according to the instructions of Fellner & Helmer, and Hönigsberg & Deutsch.
Postcard
Laslo collection, Zagreb

Otto Wagner's footsteps and symbolizes by its break with tradition—quite literally—the Secession, in the sense of a separation of modern architecture from historicism. Other new buildings in Zagreb such as the Pečić House (Ilica 43, Vjekoslav Bastl, 1899) and the Tišov Villa and Studio (Pantovčak 54, Aladar Baranyai, 1900–01)—already begin to show characteristics of early modernism.

Wagner's pupil Viktor Kovačić was the leading figure on the path to a new architecture. In 1900 he joined the circle of Croatian Secessionists and published his programmatic article "Modern Architecture," a personal paraphrasing of Otto Wagner's manifesto of the same title.[4] Kovačić's essay formulated for the very first time in the Croatian context the basic principles of a conception of architecture that was primarily based on building materials, tectonics, and functionality: "Modern architecture must be logical and practical. Logical means that the building is composed in conformity with the laws of its building materials, and method of construction; practical means that it in fact satisfies the needs and suits the environment in which it was constructed."[5] The style of this short excerpt points, incidentally, to a further figure who played an influential role in the development of Croatian architecture: Adolf Loos. Kovačić had met Loos while working on his essay; Loos for his part was well-informed about the work of his Zagreb colleague.[6] As a consequence, characteristic elements of Loos's conception of architecture were incorporated into the essay, which, up to then, had been written completely under the influence of Otto Wagner.

Although Victor Kovačić did not establish an architectural school in the formal sense, his influence made a strong and lasting impact on various levels of the architectural scene and

Aladar Baranyai, Tišov Villa and Studio,
Zagreb, Pantovčak 54, 1900–01

Indian ink and watercolor on paper,
23.7 x 35 cm
Lambert collection, Zagreb

social life. In 1905, together with Vjekoslav Bastl, Edo Šen, and Stjepan Podhorsky, he founded the Club of Croatian Architects [*Klub hrvatskih arhitekta*], an independent professional association whose main objectives were the promotion of architecture through public activities and the preservation of the legacy of historic buildings. Kovačić was also a leading figure in the "internationalization" of Zagreb architecture. He demanded that foreign architects and specialists should also be represented on the jury of national competitions—a practice that proved beneficial and was maintained during the inter-war years. The framework thus established for an active international exchange soon resulted in the successful participation of Croatian architects in competitions not merely in the whole of Yugoslavia, but also internationally (Aladar Baranyai in Banská Bystrica, Sibiu, and Oradea; Vjekoslav Bastl in Prague and Belgrade). It is ultimately to Kovačić's credit, as well, that the young Croatian architectural scene—in spite of a marked tendency towards individualism —ventured to undertake a series of formal and functional experiments, and—under the influence of Kovačić's views— took a firm stand against the development of an autochthonous "National Style," such as was typical of Hungarian architecture around the turn of the century.

The first phase of the Zagreb modern style is characterized, on the one hand, by the attempt to break loose from the customary method of embedding the town house within rows of houses, in order to achieve a freer and more dynamic solution. An example of this is the Kallina residential and office block (Gundulićeva 20/Masarykova 19, Vjekoslav Bastl, 1903–04). In its formal language clearly indebted to

Jugendstil, it is a kind of Zagreb version of Otto Wagner's Majolika House in Vienna (1898–99). On the other hand, several houses were built under the influence of the "Domestic Revival." When Victor Kovačić built the Robert Auer Villa and Studio (Rokova 9, 1904–06) he adopted a free building arrangement and tried to create a cultural topography which stands consciously within tradition.

At the same time, however, Kovačić himself was attempting to arrive at a new, more abstract language of form, following Loos's dictum of the ornament-free façade. His residential and office block for Oršić & Divković (Masarykova 21–23, 1906–07) and the Lustig House (Kumičićeva 10, 1910–11) are evidence of this. The residential and business premises for Deutsch (Masarykova 20, 1910–11) designed by Otto Goldscheider take up Kovačić's geometric and tectonic mode of architectural expression, while the National and University Library (Marulićev trg 21, Rudolf Lubynski, 1910–13) presents a technological innovation in the form of a flat roof. The Kastner & Öhler Department Store, formerly the Hotel "Kaiser von Österreich," (Ilica 4, Ignjat Fischer, 1911–13) represents the new type of modern, urban department store. It is part of that need for a new main core of buildings and, especially, for a technological infrastructure, which emerged in the wake of changed ways of urban life: the need for buildings for health care, cultural/educational and administrative institutions, plants for gas supply, social facilities, residences, and new buildings for recreation and social life.

An important factor running parallel with these "progressive trends" was the reception of Biedermeier (three blocks of flats for the Croatian Real Estate Bank, Dečelićev prilaz

4 The role of Kovačić as an "ambassador" of the Wagner School may be compared to that of Jan Kotěra in Bohemia and Moravia. Kotěra also commented on the views of Otto Wagner in a programmatic essay, "O novém umění" [About New Art], in *Volné směry* [Free Directions], Prague, vol. IV, 1900, pp. 189–95.
5 Viktor Kovačić, "Moderna arhitektura" [Modern Architecture], in *Život* [Life], Zagreb, vol. I, 1900, no. 1, p. 26, here quoted from Ehgartner-Jovinac, "Zagreb um die Jahrhundertwende," pp. 105–6.
6 See Adolf Loos, "Aus der Wagner-Schule" [From the Wagner School] (*Neue Freie Presse*, Vienna, 31 July 1898), in Adolf Opel (ed.), *Adolf Loos. Das Potemkin'sche Dorf. Verschollene Schriften 1897–1933* [Adolf Loos: The Potemkin Village, Lost Manuscripts,1897–1933], Vienna, 1983, pp. 50–52. On the friendship between Kovačić and Loos see Tihomil Stahuljak, "Ein Klatsch über den Architekten Adolf Loos" [Some Gossip about the Architect Adolf Loos], in *Peristil*, Zagreb, vol. XXXIV, 1991, pp. 115–26.

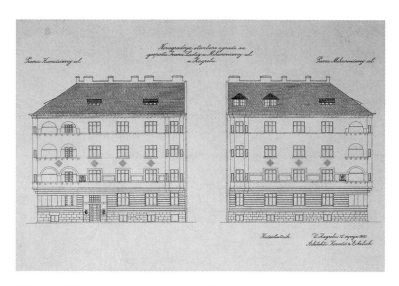

Viktor Kovačić, Lustig House, Zagreb, Kumičićeva 10, 1910–11
Elevation
Indian ink on transparent paper, 48 x 68 cm
MKRH Zagreb

42–46, Rudolf Lubynski, 1910) and of cottage estates of the Wiener Werkstätte variety (Villa Frangeš, Rokovperivoj 2, Victor Kovačić, 1910–11). Other buildings in which this trend is clearly visible are the Harnisch House and the housing estate "Mali Pantovčak" by Benedik and Baranyai (Nazorova 17, 1907, and Hercegovačka/Istarska/Bosanksa, 1911–12, respectively) or the upper-class Villa Feller (Jurjevska 31a, Mathias Feller, 1909–11).

With its clearly targeted urbanization process directed toward a "provincial metropolis" with positive connotations, and with lines of development in the areas of architectural form and type, Zagreb Modernism defined the framework as well as the essential questions of planning and layout for the next generation of architects. After World War I these considerations were to be supplemented by a focus on the social component, which was integrated into Zagreb's future architectural development, above all *Neues Bauen*.

1 For Zagreb's urban development, see the contributions to Gerhard M. Dienes (ed.), *"transLOKAL," 9 Städte im Netz (1848–1918): Bratislava/Preßburg, Brno/Brünn, Graz/Kraków/Krakau, Ljubljana/Laibach, München, Pécs/Fünfkirchen, Trieste/Triest, Zagreb/Agram* ["transLOKAL," 9 Towns in the Network (1848–1918)], Graz City Museum, Graz, 1996; Snješka Knežević, *Zagrebačka zelena potkova* [The Green Horseshoe of Zagreb], Zagreb, 1996, or more recently Eugenia Ehgartner-Jovinac, "Zagreb um die Jahrhundertwende: ein Ort der Moderne?" [Zagreb around the Turn of the Century: A Center of Modernism?], in Heidemarie Uhl (ed.), *Kultur—Urbanität—Moderne. Differenzierungen der Moderne in Zentraleuropa um 1900* [Culture – Urbanity – Modernism: Differences in Modernism in Central Europe around 1900], Vienna, 1999, pp. 83–137.
2 The population of Zagreb rose from approximately 14,300 (1851), 39,000 (1890), and 58,000 (1900) to 75,000 (1910).
3 The stages referred to here are the so-called "Neo-Lyricism" of the 1860s, the "Mažuranić" Era at the beginning of the 1870s and 1880s (period of industrial expansion) and the breakthrough of modernism around 1890–1910 (cf. Ehgartner-Jovinac, "Zagreb um die Jahrhundertwende," pp. 86–91).

The Cosmopolitan Ideal

It was not only great cities such as Vienna, Budapest, and Prague that were caught up in urbanization and the great city aspirations that appeared with it. Smaller centers of the monarchy were also drawn in. Modern Zagreb arose after 1900, through the efforts of a new generation of architects returning from studies in Vienna, Graz, and Budapest with ideas that would reshape the structure of the city. The example of dynamic expansion set by the western European capitals stimulated new planning ideas in the city, while architects such as Vjekoslav Bastl, Aladar Baranyai, Otto Goldscheider, and Rudolf Lubynski brought the international art nouveau style currently *en vogue* to new residential and commercial buildings. On an aesthetic and typological level, these activities not only prepared the way for the planning and design concepts of the next generation, but asserted Zagreb's progress in urban development toward the status of a "sub-capital."

Vjekoslav Bastl, Hönigsberg & Deutsch, Kallina Residential and Business Premises, Zagreb, Gundulićeva 20, 1903–04

View
Indian ink on paper, 41 x 68.5 cm
DA Zagreb

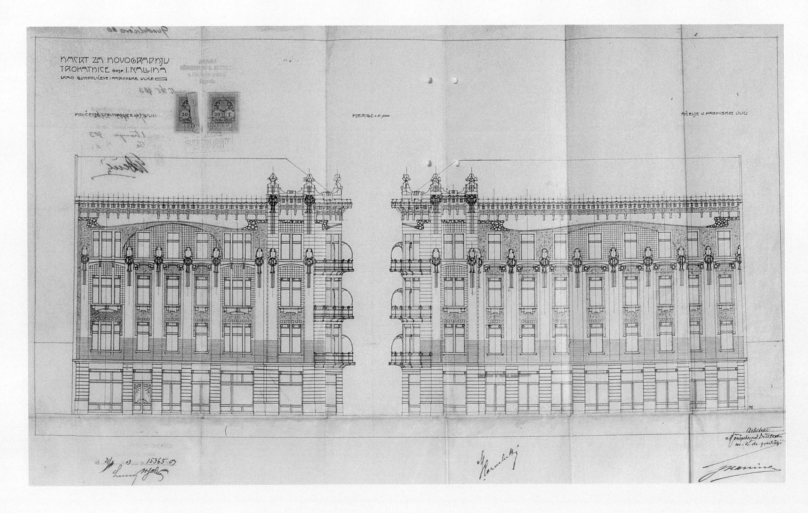

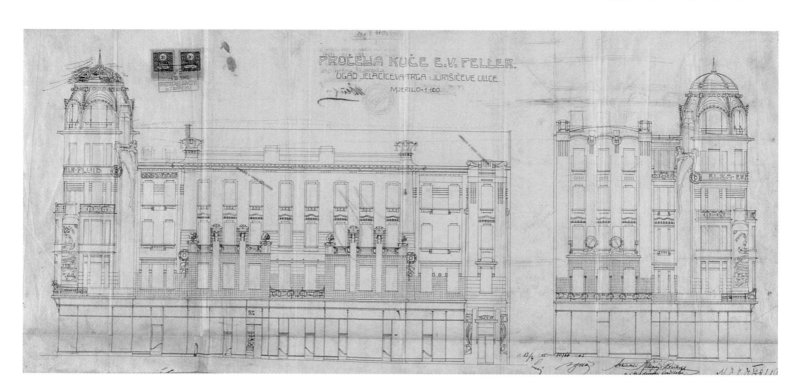

**Vjekoslav Bastl, Hönigsberg & Deutsch,
'Elsa Fluid' buildings, Zagreb,
Jurišićeva 1, 1905–06**

Elevation
Indian ink on paper, 37.5 x 84 cm
HDA Zagreb

View with Jelačićev trg after building was
completed
Postcard, c. 1906
MGZ Zagreb

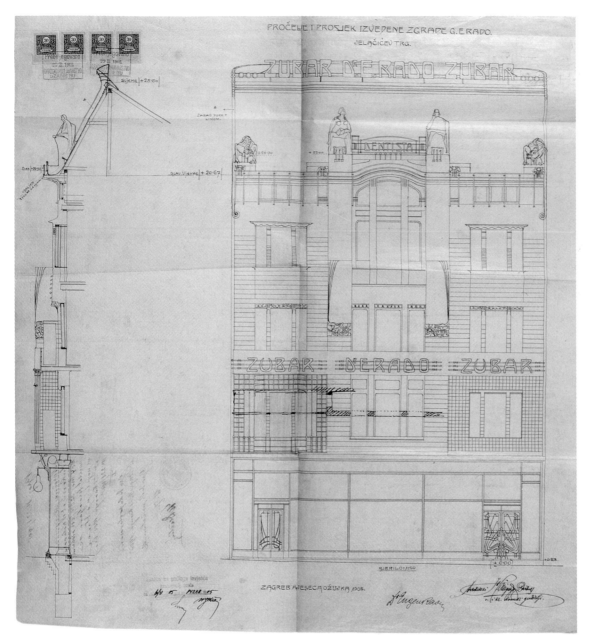

Vjekoslav Bastl, Hönigsberg & Deutsch,
**Rado Residential and Business
Premises, Jelačićev trg 5, Zagreb
1904–05**

Façade, Section
Indian ink on transparent paper,
65 x 60.5 cm
DA Zagreb

Detail of façade
Indian ink on transparent paper,
46.5 x 32 cm
DA Zagreb

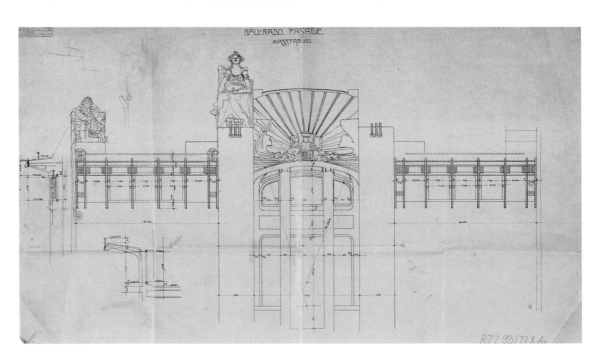

**Otto Goldscheider, Hönigsberg &
Deutsch, Deutsch Residential and
Business Premises, Zagreb,
Masarykova 20, 1910–11**

Elevation, section plan of front façade
Indian ink on paper, 71 x 55 cm
MKRH Zagreb

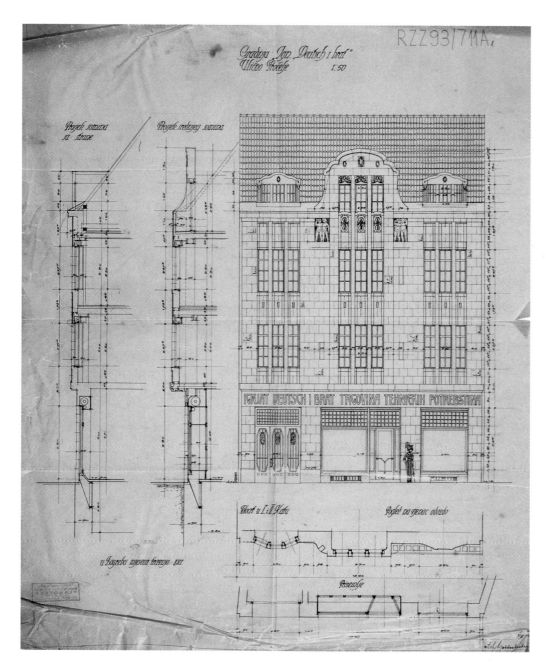

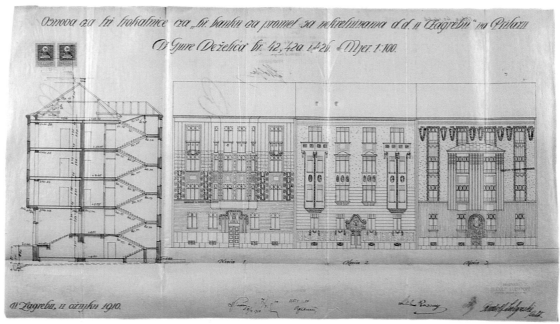

**Rudolf Lubynski, Three Apartment
Blocks of the Real Estate Bank of
Croatia , Zagreb, Dečelićeva 42-46,
1910**

Façade, Cross-section
Indian ink and watercolor on transparent
paper, 42 x 74 cm
DA Zagreb

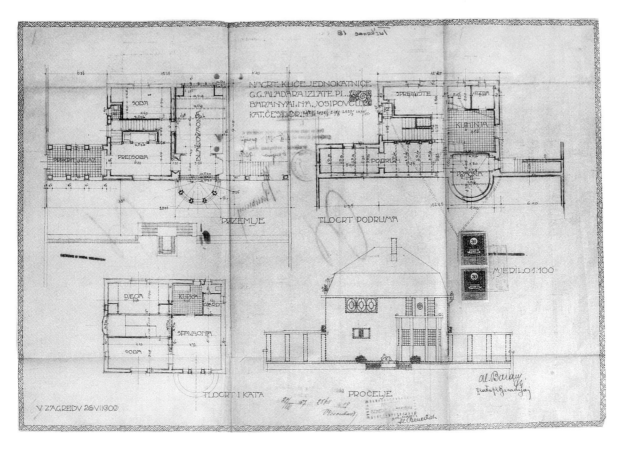

**Benedik & Baranyai,
Villa Baranyai, Zagreb,
Tuškanac 18, 1909–10**

Sketch
Blue ink and watercolor on
transparent paper, 36.5 x 26 cm
Lambert collection, Zagreb

View of street façade and
front garden
Contemporary photograph
Photo: Rudolf Mosinger, Zagreb
Lambert collection, Zagreb

Floor plans and façade
elevation, scale 1 : 100
Indian ink and crayon on paper,
41 x 59.5 cm
HDA Zagreb

Ľviv, Kraków, and Timişoara, 1897–1914

THE ARCHITECTURE OF L'VIV

Ihor Žuk

The intensive building activity and architectural developments which took place in Ľviv [Lwów, Lemberg] in the years 1890–1910 were unprecedented in the city's history and would elicit great admiration from contemporaries in the following years. Administrative and political reforms made in the Danube monarchy in the late 1860s resulted in changes of the status of Ľviv, capital of Galicia, which was the easternmost crownland of the Austro-Hungarian empire.[1] In 1870 the city was given a new statute guaranteeing wide-ranging autonomy and self-rule which allowed it increasingly to respond to the enormous population influx and to regulate the subsequent territorial expansion of the town as well as the growing demand for new buildings of various designated functions.[2]

The architecture of Ľviv around 1900 made use of the achievements of past decades. The 1870s were marked by the construction of numerous monumental buildings having programmatic character for Galician architecture. Buildings such as the new Polytechnic (Bandery 12, Julian Zachariewicz, 1874–77) or the building of the Galician Landtag [Regional Diet] (Universytets'ka 1, Juliusz Hochberger, 1877–81, now a university) were orientated towards the historicist style of the Vienna Ringstrasse. The School of Architecture which developed out of the architecture department of the Polytechnic achieved some very impressive successes.[3]

In 1885 building zone regulations were passed in Ľviv. Concurrent with the territorial expansion of the city, the foundation for a modern, urban infrastructure was laid. The year 1880 saw the first horse-drawn tram cars and in 1894, on the occasion of the Galician National Exhibition, the first electric tram system began operation. Ľviv was the fourth city in Europe possessing such means of transport. By vaulting the Poltva river, which divided the city but was slowly threatening to become the town's sewer, the foundation for a modern sewer network was laid. A viaduct was constructed and came into operation in 1901. The construction of the first power plant in 1894 brought electrification to Ľviv, to be followed by a further plant in the Persenkivka region in 1908. A special chapter in the history of Ľviv's urban development is represented by the laying of a diadem of parks and green spaces in the second half of the nineteenth century. The largest of these municipal green parks, the Stryjs'kyj Park, created in 1887 following plans of the Inspector of Municipal Green Spaces, Arnold Röhring, became in 1894 the venue for the Galician National Exhibition, which was also attended by the Emperor Franz Josef. Following the model of Vienna's Ringstrasse, a boulevard was laid around the city's historic center.[4]

While the 1880s in Ľviv's architectural history was a period totally dominated by a neo-Renaissance style based on Italian models (among other "veterans" of Ľviv's School of Architecture, prominent architects in this period include Alfred Kamienobrodzki, Wincenty Rawski, and Jan Schulz) the end of the century was characterized by a diversity of historic styles aspiring to independent and more picturesque and Romantic interpretations of the historical models (as can be seen in the buildings of Teodor Talowski and Kazimierz Mokłowski).

In the context of the city development of this period, special attention must be drawn to several designs from the later career of Julian Zachariewicz, the leading figure in Ľviv architecture in the late nineteenth century.[5] In his later works Zachariewicz devoted himself to the design of private houses, whose architecture displays features clearly borrowed from the Arts and Crafts movement (the architect's own villa, Metrolohična 14, 1891–93).

Ivan Levyns'kyj, Alfred Zachariewicz, Mikolasz Arcade, L'viv, 1899–1901
(destroyed 1939)
Žuk collection, L'viv

Tadeusz Obmiński, Segal House, L'viv, Čajkovs'koho 6, 1904–05
View
Žuk collection, L'viv

In the 1880s the architect and building contractor Ivan Levyns'kyj was a close collaborator of Zachariewicz. The design studio of Levyns'kyj's company played an important role in the architectural development of Galicia as, in the years between 1890 and 1910, he succeeded in recruiting the best architects of L'viv either as assistants or as partners. At the turn of the century, the company, founded by Levyns'kyj in 1881, was by far the largest of its kind in L'viv, while the building supply company which was part of the same firm was considered to be the leading industrial enterprise in Galicia.[6]

A process of architectural modernization occurred in L'viv as totally new types of buildings, such as shopping arcades, were introduced to enhance the town. Plans for the largest of this kind of commercial building, the Mikolasz Arcade (Kopernika 1, 1899–1901, destroyed 1939) were drawn up by Ivan Levyns'kyj and Alfred Zachariewicz, the son of Julian Zachariewicz. New technology such as reinforced concrete construction ensured that important large buildings in the urban infrastructure were completed swiftly.[7] Reinforced concrete was used, for example, in the construction of the Municipal Theater (Prospekt Svobody, Zygmunt Gorgolewski, 1897–1900) and in the impressive new Central Station (Władysław Sadłowski, 1901–04).[8]

The development of new building types was intended to lead to the discovery of new forms of stylistic expression. The Mikolasz Arcade and the new Central Station represented the first buildings in L'viv showing the influence of Jugendstil. Again it was the Levyns'kyj studio that played the main role in spreading Jugendstil, when it built the group of buildings in Bohomoľcja 3–11 around 1905 (the main building was constructed in 1905–06) and in Pavlova 1–4 (1905–06) as well as completing numerous other projects.[9] Tadeusz Obmiński,

working as an architect in Levyns'kyj's office, played a crucial role in these projects.[10]

Obmiński's signature is unmistakably present in numerous designs originating from the Levyns'kyj studio as well as in a few major projects completed by the architectural and building firm of Michal Ulam, which was founded in 1904. Among the latter is Segal House (Čajkovs'koho 6, 1904–05).

Apart from those buildings that adhere to the architecture of "cosmopolitan" Jugendstil (the Segal House falls into this category), the buildings in which Obmiński—often in collaboration with Ivan Levyns'kyj—achieved a national style of architecture carried out in the spirit of Jugendstil constitute an important part of his creative work. The most outstanding example of this is the building of the Dnister insurance company (Rus'ka 20, 1905–06, now a polyclinic). Besides Tadeusz Obmiński, the two young architects Olkesandr Lušpyns'kyj

Alfred Zachariewicz, Tadeusz Obmiński,
Chamber of Commerce and Industry,
Ľviv, Prospekt Ševčenka 17–19, 1907–11
Žuk collection, Ľviv

and Lev Levyns'kyj, who were also working in Ivan Levyns'kyj's office, were also adherents of the "national style."[11]

During the years 1907 and 1908, recurring periods of economic decline occurred, leading to the consequent stagnation of the building industry. By 1910, however, the building industry had recovered and in 1912 construction reached an all-time record. At the same time a new phase in the architectural development of Ľviv began.[12]

After 1908 the formal vocabulary of Jugendstil was to disappear rapidly from the repertoire of Ľviv's urban architecture, to be replaced everywhere by Neoclassicist motifs of the dawning twentieth century. Concurrent with this, a number of designs pointed unmistakably towards the evolution of the early modernist style.[13] The intensive search for new building materials and methods persisted. Their use in the construction of the Polytechnic found strong advocates in Professors Maksymilan Thullie (theory of steel reinforced concrete) and Jan Bogucki (metal construction).

The most productive phase of Alfred Zachariewicz's work coincided with this period of revolutionary change in architecture.[14] His work is inextricably linked with the development of reinforced concrete construction in Galicia. The Sosnowski-Zachariewicz company, founded in 1903 together with Józef Sosnowski, followed the Hennebique system of construction.

Among the most important buildings of Alfred Zachariewicz are to be counted the building of the Chamber of Commerce and Industry (Prospekt Ševčenka 17–19, 1907–11), a prime example of an architectural *Gesamtkunstwerk* at the

beginning of the twentieth century,[15] or Ballaban House (Halyc'ka 21, 1908–10), part of what is probably architecturally the most interesting housing complex in Ľviv (Valova 9–13, 1908–13). Zachariewicz's bank and office buildings constitute an important part of his work. The most significant of these are the building for the Assucurazioni Generali Insurance Company (Kopernika 3, 1908–10) and that for the Real Estate Bank (Kopernika 4, 1912–13), whose main transaction hall is clearly reminiscent of Otto Wagner's design for the Vienna Post Office Savings Bank.

Next to Zachariewicz, Roman Feliński, head of the Ulam architectural office, is considered to be one of the most important architects in Ľviv in the period around 1910. The modern department store at Špytaľna 2 (1911–13), revealing in its form a clear leaning towards *Neues Bauen*, has gone down in the architectural history of Ľviv as Feliński's masterpiece.[16]

Due to a number of circumstances, there was no general regulatory plan for the city of Ľviv until the beginning of World War I. The first attempt up until then to develop such a plan and to bring it before the public was made by Ignacy Drexler in a series of lectures and publications.[17] He modelled his plans of 1910 on the Garden City concept and continued to be active throughout the 1920s.[18]

With the outbreak of World War I and during the subsequent Ukrainian-Polish war (1918–19) Ľviv was for a long time a frontier town. This had serious consequences for the local building industry and thus was also reflected in the city's architectural development. Many architects who had been active prior to the war stopped working in Ľviv altogether after 1914. Some architects, however, remained active even

Roman Feliński, Department Store, Ľviv, Špytaľna 2, 1911–13
Žuk collection, Ľviv

during the war, among them Witold Minkiewicz, who had begun his career in the Levyns'kyj company around 1900 and later made a name for himself as a member of the Zespół group and as an outspoken architecture critic.[19] Eugeniusz Czerwiński, another member of the staff of the Levyns'kyj office, was one of the main designers of the Lysenko Music Institute (Plošča Šaškevyča 5, 1914–16) and subsequently designed several buildings showing a Neoclassicist influence.[20] Among other architects of the inter-war years who had made a name for themselves prior to the war are Józef Awin, Jan Bagieński, Maksymiljan Burstin, and Ferdynand Kasler.

After the collapse of the Danube monarchy Ľviv was annexed to Poland and in 1939, together with East Galicia, became part of the Soviet Union. During the many centuries of its history Ľviv played an important role as a center of economic and cultural exchange between East and Central Europe. As long as Ľviv was fulfilling this function effectively, and the exchange took place on a basis of freedom, equality, and tolerance, the town prospered, cultural life and artistic creativity blossomed, and many impressive architectural achievements were to be recorded. In the disastrous times of war and political despotism Ľviv lost its importance, turning into a no-man's-land, whose architecture had degenerated to the status of provincial architecture. World War II (1939–45) ushered in a second difficult "grey" period. Having attained such great heights and highly promising architectural achievements Ľviv's urban development now experienced a rupture. Only time will tell whether during the next millennium Ľviv can regain its role as an architectural center of European rank in an independent Ukraine.

1 Cf. *Lemberg / Ľviv 1772–1918. Wiederbegegnung mit einer Landeshauptstadt der Donaumonarchie* [Lemberg / Ľviv 1772–1918: Revisiting a Provincial Capital of the Danube Monarchy], exh. cat., Museum of History Vienna, Vienna, 1993, cf. also pp. 64–104.

2 Cf. Stanisław Hoszowski, *Ekonomiczny rozwój. Lwowa w latach 1772–1914*, Ľviv, 1935, pp. 61, 107.

3 Cf. Zbysław Popławski, *Dzieje Politechniki Lwowskiej 1844–1945*, [The History of the Polytechnic of Ľviv 1844–1945], Wrocław, Warsaw, Kraców, 1992, p. 59.

4 Cf. Tetjana Trehubova and Roman Mych, *Ľviv. Architekurno-istoryčnyj narys* [Ľviv: An Outline of Its Architectural History], Kiev, 1989, pp. 114–19.

5 Cf. Ihor Žuk, *Julian Zachariewicz 1837–1898. Alfred Zachariewicz 1871–1937. Wystawa Twórczosci. Katalog* [Julian Zachariewicz 1837–98, Alfred Zachariewicz 1871–1937: Exhibition of Works, Catalogue], exh. cat., Warsaw, 1996, pp. 6–12.

6 Cf. Ihor Žuk, "Ivan Levyns'kyj. architektor-budivnyčyj Ľvova" [Ivan Levynsk'yj: Architect and Builder in Ľviv], in *Architektura Ukraēny* [The Architecture of the Ukraine], Kiev, 1992, no. 2, pp. 20–28.

7 Cf. *Czasopismo techniczne* [Technical Journal], Ľviv, XVI, 1898, no. 6, table IV.

8 Cf. "Nowy dworzec kolei państwowej we Lwowie" [The New National Railway Station in Ľviv], in *Architekt* (Kraców), V, 1904, pp. 101–04.

9 Cf. Franciszek Mączyński, "Najnowszy Lwów" [The Latest Ľviv], in *Architekt* (Kraców), IX, 1908, pp. 91–97.

10 Cf. "Necrologja," in *Czasopismo techniczne* [Technical Journal] (Ľviv), L, 1932, no. 21, pp. 318–19.

11 Ihor Žuk, "Historismus, Secession und Neoklassizismus in Lemberg— Grundzüge der Architektur der Jahre 1870-1910" [Historicism, Secession, and Neoclassicism in Ľviv—Principal Features of the Architecture of the Years 1870–1910], in *Lemberg / Ľviv 1772–1918*, note 1, p. 37.

12 Cf. Hoszowski, *Ekonomiczny rozwój*, p. 62.

13 Cf. Trehubova, Mych, *Ľviv. Architekurno-istoryčnyj narys*, pp. 128–33.

14 Cf. Jerzy Nechay, "Pierwsze kroki żelbetu w Polsce" [The Beginnings of Steel Reinforced Concrete in Poland], in *Cement* (Warsaw), 1937, no. 8, pp. 113–15.

15 Cf. Ihor Žuk, "Das Gebäude der Handels- und Gewerbekammer in Lemberg" [The Building of the Chamber of Commerce and Industry in Ľviv], in Hanns Haas, Hannes Stekl (eds.), *Bürgerliche Selbstdarstellung. Städtebau, Architektur, Denkmäler* [Bourgeois Self-Representation: Town Planning, Architecture, Monuments], Vienna, Cologne, Weimar, 1995, pp. 145–51.

16 Andrzej K. Olszewski, *Nowa forma w architekturze polskiej 1900–1925* [The New Form in Polish Architecture 1900–25], Wrocław, Warsaw, Kraców, 1967, p. 87.

17 E.g., Ignacy Drexler, *Wielki Lwów* [Great Ľviv], Ľviv, 1920.

18 Cf. Trehubova, Mych, *Ľviv. Architekurno-istoryčnyj narys*, p. 119.

19 Cf. Romana Cielątkowska, "Architekt Witold Minkiewicz (1880–1961)," in *Kwartalnik architektury i urbanistyki* [Architecture and Urbanism Quarterly], Warsaw, XXXII, 1987, no. 2, p. 107–30.

20 For Czerwiński cf. *Album inżynierów i techników polskich* [Album of Polish Engineers and Technicians], Ľviv, 1932, pp. 50–51.

THE URBAN DEVELOPMENT OF KRAKÓW

Jacek Purchla

Kraków did not conform to the typical pattern of city development in the nineteenth century. This was observed by many contemporaries, but was most aptly expressed on the threshold of the present century by Tadeusz Boy-Żeleński, one of the creators of the myth of "Young Poland" [Młoda Polska], in a well-known and oft-quoted section of his book *Znasz-li ten kraj?* [Do you Know this Country?] Turn-of-the-century Kraków was a "unique creation," indeed, though perhaps "not the most original city under the sun" and "the world's greatest rarity of all times," as Boy-Żeleński would have it.[1]

The peculiar and unique character of Kraków around 1900 resulted from a combination of various factors. Understanding the limitations, complexity, and chronology of Kraków's development in the nineteenth century is the key to analyzing the phenomenon of "Young Poland" and Kraków's artistic development at that time.[2]

The development of Kraków at the turn of the century was beset with many contradictions. The general weakness of the city's economy was offset by Kraków's exceptional cultural and intellectual importance for the Poles. Its role as the nation's spiritual capital was at variance with its function as a frontier fortress town and provincial garrison for a foreign occupying army. Seen from the perspective of Vienna, which had been transformed into a great cosmopolitan metropolis at the turn of the century, Kraków was merely a medium-sized city on the periphery of the multicultural empire of Austria-Hungary. Seen from the political perspective of the Polish people, Kraków, poverty-stricken as it was, performed the function of the national capital of their non-existent Polish state. These and other contradictions helped create "the phenomenon of Kraków" and its specific situation under Austrian rule.

The early 1890s were for Kraków doubtless a turning point in the autonomous period. Two events which happened almost concurrently represented a symbolic break with the past: the opening of the new Municipal Theater on plac św. Ducha in October, 1893, and Jan Matejko's death one month later in November. While Matejko was a symbol of Kraków in the second half of the nineteenth century, the new theater marked the beginning of a new phase in the city's development, although from an aesthetic and architectural point of view it was more a recapitulation of nineteenth-century historicism than a herald of the nascent Jugendstil movement. It was no coincidence that Matejko, as a representative of a passing era of reverent reflection on the past, and as figure symbolizing the declining importance of the Stańczyks, immediately took a stand against the idea of building—on the site of a medieval monastery—a monumental theater anticipating the power and modernity of approaching capitalism (the theater was the first building in Kraków to have electric lighting!). Attention should also be paid to the antinomy between Matejko and his work on the one hand, and the cosmopolitanism and academic pomp of the theater's architecture on the other, in which Siemiradzki's and not master Jan's curtain was raised.

The new theater thus became not only a symbol of conflict between matter and spirit, but above all a sign that Kraków had entered its metropolitan phase of development. In 1890 there were 70,000 inhabitants living in Kraków (not including members of the army garrison) who were squeezed into an area of only 5.77 square kilometers.[3] However, from the 1880s, despite the restrictions imposed by the military authorities, sixteen boroughs surrounding Kraków, of which only Podgórze enjoyed municipal status, began to develop rapidly. Already at this time a number of these areas could be regarded as city districts, partly because of their building density, but perhaps mainly because of the benefits they brought to Kraków and the professional profile of their inhabitants. By 1900 the quickly growing population of these fifteen boroughs (excluding Podgórze) amounted to one-third of Kraków's inhabitants.[4]

Kraków's urban development after 1900 was closely tied to the emergence of capitalist economic structures in Galicia

Jan Zawiejski, New Municipal Theater, Kraków, plac św. Ducha, 1888–93
Photo
MH Kraków

as a whole. The decision, made by Kraków's then mayor, Juliusz Leo, entailed not only incorporating a dozen or so external boroughs and a considerable extension of the city's administrative area (from 5.77 km² to 46.90 km²), but above all forcing Kraków onto a path of capitalist development based on industry, trade, transportation, and financial capital.[5] Implementation of these plans between 1909 and 1915 signaled the final abandonment of the idea of Kraków as a non-industrial city. The fact that the city at the turn of the century was marked externally by great dynamism and modernity also led to rapid changes in the social consciousness of its inhabitants.

Early twentieth-century Kraków thus found itself in the process of fundamental transformation. The hitherto dominant national perspective and force of tradition were now confronted by the rising stars of liberalism, universalism, and cosmopolitanism, which emerged victoriously toward the end of the multinational Habsburg state. Stagnation and a backward social framework were challenged defiantly by the openness and dynamism of large-scale capitalist urbanization. The pervasive historicist attitude now had to contend with modernism of a European dimension.

The Kraków section of the "Young Poland" movement represented not only the local variant of a universal response to historicism emerging around 1900, but also the city's belated entry into its capitalist and metropolitan phase of development, the achievement of liberalism. This entailed that the quasi-feudal, clerical, and paternalistic model of Kraków of the Stańczyks, which still adhered to the city's enclosure within the Austrian fortifications, would have to be discarded.

In this situation, complex and full of discrepancies, Kraków between 1890 and 1914 also became the center of Polish architectural thinking, despite the fact that Warsaw, Łódź, L'viv, and Poznań were all better off economically, and were experiencing far more intensive urban development and construction activity. The primacy of Kraków and the creation of an influential architectural scene there were based more on the efflorescence of intellectual and artistic life on Wawel Hill than on any building boom.[6] For architects active in Kraków, Poland's former capital was still a laboratory for artistic experiment rather than a fast-growing metropolis. Therefore, as a rule, major building commissions were awarded by competition, which provoked creative discussions that went beyond the confines of local concerns. After a period during which urban concentration and building activity in the city had been influenced by various architectural schools (Munich, Berlin, Vienna, Paris), Kraków's architects in the nineteenth century entered a stage of creativity, developing their own architectural form of expression. This was a result both of inspiration from abroad and of a creative treatment of local traditions. Through the buildings of these architects, Kraków developed its unmistakable character and stood out to advantage from other Polish cities.[7]

Historicism in Kraków lasted longer than in other cities, thanks to the fact that it was enhanced here through the addition of symbolic themes just before World War I. Lack of independence gave rise to an almost cult-like enthusiasm for a "national style" in art and architecture, thus both strengthening and prolonging the city's historicist orientation.[8]

Around 1895 Kraków became the center of the Polish avant-garde, which consisted of a group of literary figures and artists gathered around Stanisław Przybyszewski. In its attempt to break with traditional middle-class culture, this group also broke with historicism as a symbol of that culture. These young artists and architects already regarded themselves as a generation of modernists.

New forms of ornament provided initial means for overcoming historicism and eclecticism in art and architecture, and were the main form of expression of Kraków's most prominent Jugendstil architect Franciszek Mączyński (1874–1947). His pavilion for the Society of Fine Arts in Szczepański Square (1898–1901) was the first programmatic work of Kraków's Jugendstil. Its massive form betrays a certain classicist tendency, yet in its detail it is clearly inspired by the Viennese Secession. Mączyński's design is in a direct line of descent from the work of Otto Wagner and the architecture of Josef Maria Olbrich's Secession Building in Vienna (1897–98).[9] The spectacular reconstruction of the nearby Old Theater [Stary Theatr], carried out between 1903 and 1906, was the work of Tadeusz Stryjeński (1849–1942) and Franciszek Mączyński, who at the time operated an architectural office together. The latter spent almost the whole of 1902 on a study tour of Germany, France, and Italy.[10]

By preserving the large windows of the second floor—a trait characteristic of 1840s Munich architecture—Stryjeński and Mączyński were able, with great sensitivity, to transform the façade of the Old Theater in Szczepański Square into a distinctive example of Jugendstil architecture. An extended frieze, decorated with the leaf motifs characteristic of the "Munich" style and running beneath a powerful cornice, forms the building's main highlight. The frieze, the work of Józef Gardecki, was clearly inspired by August Endell's designs. However, the importance of the Old Theater's reconstruction is not due solely to its façade. The architects also completely reconstructed the building's interior, introducing, for the first time in Poland, a ferroconcrete structure to form the roof of the concert hall. A new conception of architecture is also evident in the building's free ground plan and in its interior design. Although classical elements are still maintained and even added (Attic elements), the reconstruction of the Old Theater can rightly be regarded as Kraków's best example of Jugendstil architecture, with Szczepański Square as the city's unquestionable center for this style.

In addition to the exhibition pavilion for the Society of Fine Arts and the Old Theater, there is a third outstanding example of Jugendstil architecture: the former headquarters of the Technical Society (Ulica Straszewskiego 28, 1905–06), designed by Sławomir Odrzywolski (1846–1933), who had studied in Berlin. Its distinguishing features are the consistently maintained asymmetry between its interior and façade and a reduction in its use of ornament. The whole composition is based on the contrast between the noble simplicity of the building's white glazed-brick façade, with its varied and asymmetrical placement of windows, and its mosaics and ornaments, which are limited to a few select areas.[11]

The "myth of Kraków" as the capital of the Polish Jugendstil may be disappointing in view of the city's small number of clear examples of this new style. For many Kraków architects—especially from the generation raised in the historicist tradition—Jugendstil was just another stylistic costume, and often merely a pretext for extending their eclectic palette of decorative motifs. Hence the buildings of Kraków architects after 1900 are marked by a mixture of historicist, Jugendstil, and folkloristic forms, as well as by a clear tendency towards modernism. This approach was exemplified by Jan Zawiejski (1854–1922), the architect of the new Municipal Theater, Sławomir Odrzywolski, and Władysław Ekielski (1855–1927), who had worked in Kraków since the 1880s.

An important example of this direction is the Academy of Commerce, which Zawiejski planned and designed in Kraków in 1904–06. Its style was described as "Romantic and indebted to Jugendstil." To establish the latter as the building's defining style, Zawiejski made use of the classical repertoire of late-historicist structural elements, thus giving it a sumptuous and dynamic presence. This apparent turn of Kraków architects towards new formal principles, while at the same time maintaining the historical forms and canons, can be seen very clearly when we compare the façade of the Academy of Commerce with that of its neighboring building (built around the same time)—the House of the Technical Society designed by Sławomir Odrzywolski.[12]

Kraków's Jugendstil architecture should not be viewed in isolation, without taking into consideration its historical sources, as well as the fact that it came about within the context of a utilitarian (applied) art. The revival of Arts and Crafts and the integration of art into all aspects of building were among the principal demands of the "Young Poland" movement, and were most consistently put into practice in Kraków. These ideas were given additional support by Kraków's monthly journal *Architekt*, which had been in publication since 1900. Kraków's architects were also active in the Polish Society for Applied Art, founded in 1901, and later in the Kraków Workshops. Both groups followed in the footsteps of the English Arts and Crafts movement.[13] The most outstanding artists of the "Young Poland" movement, Stanisław Wyspiański (1869–1907) and Józef Mehoffer

(1869–1946), created many splendid interior designs. It may be said that Kraków's Jugendstil found its fullest and most individual expression in these interiors.

Wyspiański made an important contribution towards the goal of a synthesis of art and architecture. As a co-founder of the Polish Society for Applied Art, he was involved in creating new stylistic forms, in the spirit of ornamental Jugendstil but based in folk art. Wyspiański designed interiors, furniture, polychrome decor, and stained-glass windows. He helped to revive polychromy and glass painting as an art. The interior of the Medical Society building of 1904 is Wyspiański's most successful realization of the *Gesamtkunstwerk* idea. The railings of the staircases and balustrades, with their use of chestnut leaf motifs, became a symbol of Kraków Jugendstil. Wyspiański also introduced new art into historical church interiors. He helped restore the medieval Church of the Franciscans in Kraków, which contains his best stained-glass work, the monumental composition, *God the Creator*.[14]

The most beautiful achievement in interior decoration in early twentieth century Kraków is the meeting room of the Chamber of Commerce and Industry, located at Utica Długa 1. It was designed by the painter Józef Mehoffer, Wyspiański's colleague since their training together at the Academy of Fine Arts in Kraków. Mehoffer later became famous for his design of a series of monumental stained-glass windows for Fribourg Cathedral in Switzerland, a project he began in 1906.[15] Mehoffer's Chamber meeting room echoed the local tradition of wooden church interiors. Borrowing motifs from folk art, the artist created an architectural work of pure Jugendstil.[16] Also strongly inspired by Jugendstil were the interiors of the Old Theater, designed in 1896 by a group of artists from the Polish Society for Applied Arts. A different form was given to the interior of the "Jama Michalika" café on Ulica Floriańska, a meeting place of the "Young Poland" group and the home of the "Green Balloon" cabaret. The designer, Karol Frycz, had studied at the Kunstgewerbeschule [School of Applied Arts] in Vienna, and was obviously influenced by the work of Charles Rennie Mackintosh.

The strikingly original building of the Chamber of Commerce and Industry (Tadeusz Stryjeński and Franciszek Mączyński, 1904–06), with its corner-tower crowned by a globe, is perhaps the best example of the search for new forms, which also took place in Kraków, and of the artistic dilemmas associated with it, clearly heralding the advent of modernism. The cubist-like and asymmetrical form of the building, made of unbaked brick, can be counted—in spite of betraying the influence of picturesque historicism—as a true example of early modernist design. These characteristics, along with a free interpretation of Romanesque and Gothic forms, are reminiscent of Hendrik P. Berlage's Amsterdam Stock Exchange building, which was opened in 1903. The Chamber

Ludwik Wojtyczko, Józef Czajkowski, Central Pavilion of the "Exhibition of Architecture and Interiors in Garden Settings," Kraków, 1912
Repr. from: Architekt, XIV, 1912

of Commerce and Industry design concentrates on two divergent themes: the cubist modernism of the structure and the Jugendstil style of the decoration, enriched by elements of the local folk art tradition. In addition to the above-mentioned meeting room, designed by Józef Mehoffer, all other rooms of the building were also designed in Jugendstil. The Chamber of Commerce and Industry is Kraków's best realization of the modernist demand that a work of art be unified, and brings together superior achievements of architecture, painting, sculpture, and applied art.[17]

The supreme achievement of Polish modernism was the construction by Tadeusz Stryjeński of the Museum of Technology and Industry (Ulica Smolensk 9, 1908–14), particularly in its façade of 1908. Adam Miłobędzki wrote of it:

> The division of this façade corresponds to the bays of the ferro-concrete skeleton and is the work of Tadeusz Stryjeński. It is supplemented with folkloric and even historical elements, which have been subjected to a Purist, sharp-edged and almost constructivist manner of stylization. The "anti-decoration" presented here in large scale is the work—not of an architect—but of two painters: Józef Czajkowski and Wojciech Jastrzębowski. They are among the most active representatives of "applied art" and of modern architecture in Kraków—both movements having a strong connection to this "art in building."[18]

The achievements of the Kraków school with its search for a style at once national and modern, culminated in the Kraków "Exhibition of Architecture and Interiors in Garden Settings" organized in 1912 by the Polish Society for Applied Arts. One of the goals of the exhibition was to bring about an application of the idea of the English Garden City in Poland. All the leading Kraków architects took part. The exhibition was a success not only because it summarized the achievements of the Kraków school and confirmed its position in the forefront of Polish architecture, but, perhaps above all, because it laid down the direction to be taken: a shift towards the Polish country estate as constructive proposal for a compromise

between modernism and regional architecture. The idea of the Polish country estate not only satisfied the Romantic longing for the self-affirmation of a national architecture and the demands of modernism, but it also went to the heart of social evils, developing into a universal solution to the housing problem that married new building forms to national traditions.[19]

The exhibition of 1912 also reflected the growing interest of Kraków's citizens in town-planning issues. This interest sprang, on the one hand, from Kraków's gradual development into a metropolis, but it was also the result of the withdrawal of the Austrian garrison from Wawel Hill, in 1905, and the partial razing (on the western side) of the internal walls of Kraków's fortifications, which opened the way for new construction projects.

In 1904 Stanisław Wyspiański, with the support of Władysław Ekielski, began work on an exceptionally bold project which went by the name "Acropolis." Its aim was to transform Wawel Hill into the hub of Polish political and cultural life—an altogether visionary idea that set the standard for all later large-scale urban development schemes. This plan was preceded in 1908 by a competition for the design of a small colony of singel-family houses in Salwator. It was the first competition of its kind in Poland, and provoked a stormy debate among architects. The result was a design which recalled the English Garden City concept. The following year saw the announcement of a competition for a regulatory plan for Greater Kraków. The resulting projects, published in 1910, represent the beginning of modern town planning in Poland. Many important principles were established by this competition, including that of urban zoning. The competition was also the occasion of a comparison between different European urban planning models existing on Polish territory, whose effect on the creative imagination of Polish architects was highly stimulating.

The competition for the regulatory plan of Greater Kraków confirmed the superiority of Kraków's modern urban planning and of Polish architectural theory. It also provided a unique laboratory for developing the principles of a national Polish architecture within the context of foreign influences. The "Kraków School," formed just before World War I, continued its work in the first years of Poland's independence, achieving its greatest successes outside Kraków.[20]

1 Tadeusz Boy-Żeleński, "Znasz-li ten kraj?" [Do You Know this Country?], in *Boy o Krakowie* [Tadeusz Boy-Żeleński on Kraków], Kraków, 1973, pp. 3–4.
2 In the following article I have made use of information contained in my earlier publications, including *Jak powstał nowoczesny Kraków* [The Emergence of Modern Kraków], Kraków, 1990, and *Matecznik Polski. Pozaekonomiczne czynniki rozwoju Krakowa w okresie autonomii galicyjskiej* [The Polish Shrine: Non-economic Factors in Kraków's Development During the Period of Galician Autonomy], Kraków, 1992.
3 Jacek Purchla, *Jak powstał nowoczesny Kraków*, p. 122.

Stanisław Wyspiański, Władysław Ekielski, Project for the Wawel "Acropolis,"
Kraków, 1904

Photo of model
© Stanisław Michta

Józef Czajkowski, Władysław Ekielski, Tadeusz Stryjeński, Ludwik Wojtyczko,
Kazimierz Wyczyński, Competition project for the regulatory plan of Greater
Kraków, 1910

Repr. from: Architekt, XII, 1910

4 Jacek Purchla, "W sprawie granic aglomeracji miejskich" [The Limits of Urban Agglomerations], in *Rocznik Dziejów Społecznych i Gospodarczych* [Yearbook for Social and Economic History], vol. 41, 1980, pp. 284–86.

5 Cf. C. Bak-Koczarska, *Juliusz Leo—twórca Wielkiego Krakowa* [Juliusz Leo—The Creator of Greater Kraków], Wrocław, Warsaw, Kraków, Gdańsk, Łódź, 1986.

6 Jacek Purchla, *Jak powstał nowoczesny Kraków*, passim.

7 Jacek Purchla, "Formowanie się środowiska architektów krakowskich w drugiej połowie XIX wieku" [The Emergence of the Kraków Architectural Scene in the Second Half of the 19th Century], in *Rocznik Krakowski* [Kraków Annual], vol. 54, Kraków, 1988, pp. 117–36. (Cf. also J. Purchla, "Kraków's Architectural Circle at the Turn of the 19th Century," in *I Biennale Architektury*, Kraków 1985, Kraków [1989], pp. 11–18.).

8 Cf. the work of Kraków's leading architects during this period: Władysław Ekielski, Jan Zawiejski, and Teodor Hoffmann.

9 Andrzej K. Olszewski, *Nowa forma w architekturze polskiej 1900–1925* [New Form in Polish Architecture 1900–1925], Wrocław, Warsaw, Kraków, 1967, p. 58.

10 K. Nowacki, *Architektura krakowskich teatrów* [Theater Architecture in Kraków], Kraków, 1982, pp. 237–65.

11 A. K. Olszewski, *Nowa forma*, pp. 58f.

12 J. Purchla, *Jan Zawiejski. Architekt przełomu XIX i XX wieku* [Jan Zawiejski: An Architect in the Transition from the 19th to the 20th Century], Warsaw, 1986, p. 294.

13 I. Huml, *Warsztaty Krakowskie* [The Kraków Workshop], Wrocław, Warsaw, Kraków, Gdańsk 1973; I. Huml, *Polska sztuka stosowana XX wieku* [Polish Applied Art in the 20th Century], Warsaw, 1978, pp. 9–64.

14 H. Blum, *Stanisław Wyspiański*, Warsaw, 1969.

15 T. Adamowicz, *Witraże fryburskie Józefa Mehoffera* [Józef Mehoffer's Stained-Glass Windows in Fribourg], Wrocław, Warsaw, Kraków, Gdańsk, Łódź, 1982.

16 Zbigniew Beiersdorf and Jacek Purchla, *The Globe House—the Former Headquarters of the Chamber of Commerce and Industry*, Kraków, 1997.

17 Zbigniew Beiersdorf and Jacek Purchla, *The Globe House*, passim.

18 A. Miłobędzki, *Zarys dziejów architektury w Polsce* [An Outline of Architecture in Poland], Warsaw, 1978, p. 304. For a discussion of the building, see also Zbigniew Beiersdorf, "Muzeum Techniczno-Przemysłowe w Krakowie" [The Museum of Technology and Industry in Kraków], in *Rocznik Krakowski* [Kraków Annal], vol. 57, 1991, pp. 129–64.

19 A.K. Olszewski, *Nowa forma*, pp. 68–70.

20 The most important works of the Kraków School in the inter-war period include the imposing church of St. Roch in Białystok, designed by Oskar Sosnowski, and the Exhibition Pavilion of the Glass Works Union at the General Polish Exhibition in Poznań. The development of the geometric form

of ornament characteristic of the Kraków School culminated in the Polish Pavilion at the Exposition Internationale des Arts Décoratifs et Industriels Modernes in Paris in 1925, designed by Józef Czajkowski and other members of the school. The Pavilion's enormous success led to the Kraków School's being acknowledged as the obligatory national style.

IN THE CENTER OF THE PERIPHERY: TIMIŞOARA'S URBAN ARCHITECTURAL EVOLUTION

Ileana Pintilie

The study of the development of art and architecture most often suggests a complexity that is based on the interaction between a center, "radiating" outward, and a surrounding periphery that responds to it. The intensity with which impulses received from the center are appropriated and interpreted depends—as a basis for further interaction—on the existing cultural-historic context. This may, in the domain of architecture, lead to the development of a style which then serves as a model for smaller towns. If "provincial art" exists in "the shadow" of the large centers, then "peripheral art" is far removed from them and receives a multitude of impulses from all directions. By reworking these influences into new forms and using them for different applications, "peripheral art" assimilates and transforms them according to its own traditions.[1]

The phenomenon of peripheral development was displayed particularly clearly in the Austro-Hungarian monarchy, a multinational and multicultural state, whose capital provided the urban model which the provinces adopted and adapted to their own traditions. This complex situation became even more multifaceted in the second half of the nineteenth century when the multifarious political, economic, and cultural conditions of "imperial cosmopolitanism" (which was opposed to nationalism or internationalism) were balanced out and ultimately established themselves as new "national features." In 1718 Banat, together with other territories, became a "crown land" of the Habsburg monarchy similar to Bukovina, another Romanian province annexed by Austria in 1774. Both provinces cultivated the idea of a "territorial" rather than a "national autonomy" and espoused a "provincial patriotism" which stood in sharp contrast to the centralism of Vienna. If one further compares Banat and Bukovina one can see a resemblance between their two capitals—Timişoara and Černivci—which developed into "metropolises of the province" in the second half of the nineteenth and especially at the beginning of the twentieth century as a result of ongoing urban development and a general process of "modernization."

The Compromise Agreement [*Ausgleich*] of 1867 between Austria and Hungary and the creation of the dual monarchy brought about important changes in the history of Banat—foremost among these being the replacement of the Imperial Austrian administration by the Royal Hungarian one. However, as capital of Banat, Timişoara retained its status of "free Imperial town" which it had been granted in December 1781 and which entitled it to autonomy in internal affairs and the right to put to its own use the revenues it gained from taxes and other sources. Against this background of political and administrative transformation a massive wave of Hungarian settlers moved into Banat. As a result, Timişoara saw a significant increase in its Magyar population, though this was never sufficient to form a majority. As the census of 1851 and that of 1880 showed, it was the Germans and Austrians who remained the major group.[2] The census of 1851 showed the Romanians to be the second largest ethnic group, and only after the town came under Hungarian administration did the Magyars became the second largest group after the Germans, with the Romanians in third place. The fact of its German-Austrian majority ensured that, with respect to urban planning and architecture, Timişoara would follow the example of Vienna and—due to the owner's preferences—Jugendstil of a Viennese provenance became the predominant feature of its cityscape.

The citadel-like "Cetate" [city center] of Timişoara constructed in the eighteenth century had, by the end of the nineteenth century, become an anachronistic structure.[3] The fortifications had not been in use since the siege of 1848. The high walls and the entire moat system, the glacis or open slopes outside the walls separating the Cetate from the rest of the city, and the various drill grounds and military installations remained untouched, being kept in reserve for use by the army. All this stood in the way of the city's normal development. The three city gates contributed to traffic congestion because they were very narrow and kept closed at night. The city gates were finally demolished only in 1891. At the same time the city council began to negotiate with the army, leading in 1892 to the decision to abandon the city's fortress image. Demolition work began in 1898 and lasted until World War I. In compensation, the army received annually a significant sum in instant payments from the city. The sites made available by demolition of the fortifications, as well as the glacis and an adjacent vacant site, were divided into plots and sold to the highest bidder. The proceeds were used partially to offset the compensation paid to the army and partially to finance new city planning and development. As in Vienna, a trust was set up in Timişoara for financing the expansion of the city. The city council now had development area at its disposal right in the city center and the opportunity to establish wide boulevards linking the center with the outer districts, which were approximately 2.5 to 3 kilometers away from the

Timişoara, Demolition of the
Fortifications
Photo, 1908
MB Timişoara

Cetate. As early as 1867 it had been decided to set up a regulatory committee with special responsibility for urban planning. In 1892 the first planning meetings took place and various models for the layout of the city were discussed. One proposal was to extend the regular street grid of the Cetate by means of straight roads; another considered it necessary to comply with the excessive demands of the army for an extensive drill ground which would block the development of the entire northern part of the city leaving only two important districts—Josefin and Fabric—connected with the Cetate.[4]

The regulatory committee finally decided that all areas should be made available for planning in order to ensure a unified cityscape, while preserving the Cetate in the center of a new urban fabric.[5] The Budapest architect Lajos Ybl was consulted in the general planning. Ybl had studied architecture in Vienna and Stuttgart and was familiar with the various planning models of the time, preferring Otto Wagner's proposal to that of Camillo Sitte.

Wagner's urban planning conception was based on the constant growth of the modern metropolis, interlaced by wide radial boulevards and concentric thoroughfares. Another reason why Ybl favored Wagner's model was that the city "fathers" of Timişoara gave preference to practical and expedient solutions and had an open attitude towards modernism. Thus to a certain extent it was empathy which dictated that the objective solution would be part and parcel of the image and spirit of the "provincial metropolis." Between 1893 and 1895 several alternative plans were prepared based on a radial-concentric street grid with two ring roads around the Cetate—a wider inner ring road in place of the

walls of the old fortress, and a narrower boulevard along the boundary of the former glacis. The outer districts were connected to the center by large access roads and public buildings were placed in such a way as to form the end points of the street perspectives. The advantage of this design lay above all in its geometric and functional clarity.

The second planning stage (1901–03), headed by László Szcsztay from Budapest, took on a more definite shape and took into account previous proposals to confine urban development to the Cetate region, including the glacis. Of the two ring roads, only half of one, south of the old town, remained. Szesztay, like Ybl, did not want to touch the existing structure of the old town. The merit of his proposal lay in the fact that he offered a variation to the then "modern" notion of a continuous belt by adding generous green spaces.

Based upon these two plans, in 1911 the regulatory committee headed by Emil Szilárd devised a general land subdivision plan for Timişoara. This plan divided the town into two zones, set limits to the number of floors and roof height of its buildings and designated areas to be developed in the block system and the streets where houses were to have front yards. The width of streets and boulevards was also determined, the maximum width being 45 meters. In front of the theater (where the fortifications had once stood), a square-like avenue (340 x 53 m) was created. Workers' housing estates were to be built next to the North Station.

Plans for a water supply and sewage systems were drawn up for the entire town area within the framework of this project. They were carried out between 1904–07 by the engineer Stan Vidrighin and supplemented in 1910–14 by various

Timișoara, Hunyady út (now Piața Victoriei)
View towards the theater
Postcard, around 1915
MB Timișoara

László Székely, Hungaria Baths, Timișoara, Strada Galați 2, 1913–14
Contemporary photograph from László Székely's album
Fogarassy collection, Timișoara

additions to the infrastructure (water purification plant, encasements for the springs and water towers) by the Budapest architects János Lenarduzzi and Richard Sabathiel. The technical quality of these works was excellent (some of the installations are still in use today); in architectural terms they show the influence of Viennese Jugendstil.

Following the straightening of the Danube in Vienna, Emil Szilárd, chief engineer of the regulatory committee in 1900–15, undertook to regulate the course of the Bega (1902–07). In this context there emerged upriver one of the first small hydro-electric plants of the region [László Székely, 1907–10] (initially it supplied only the town with power, but later also the electric tram system) as well as a number of parks such as the Pădurea Verde [Green Woods—formerly, Hunting Woods] located 4 kilometers away from the town center and measuring approximately 800 hectares, which developed into an important recreation area in the town's immediate vicinity.

Multi-story residential buildings of the "tenement palace" type [*Mietspalast*] were built on the sites which had been freed up by the razing of the old fortress walls—these sites no longer being subject to building restrictions. The *Mietspaläste* were large blocks with side wings fronting several streets. At street level they held shops, restaurants, and cafés while the two upper floors consisted of apartments (the number of floors depended, according to the regulatory plan, on the building's location). The style in which they were built at the beginning of the century followed the Jugendstil, which was then popular throughout the Monarchy. Timișoara developed no really original stylistic variants and the Viennese model prevailed, preferred by the chiefly German and Austrian owners.[6] However, since Budapest architects were involved in the design of a few representative buildings, some Hungarian influence is also evident.

Two phases can be distinguished in the development of Jugendstil architecture in Timișoara: the first, falling between 1900 and 1908, shows the very pronounced influence of *art nouveau*, with its floral décor and sinuous lines; the later stage, occuring between 1909 and 1914, is characterized by an emphasis on architectonic volumes and simplified and geometric forms as well as a reduction in decorative elements. The first buildings constructed on the vacant sites, however, were public buildings essential for the town infrastructure, such as the Gymnasium for Boys (Ignác Alpár, 1902–03) and the Gymnasium for Girls (Lipót Baumhorn, Jakob Klein, 1902–03), which, in their plain brick construction, pay obvious homage to the neo-Gothic style. Another important building of this time was the Gymnasium of the Piarists [a religious teaching order] (László Székely, 1907–09), which was erected on a trapezoidal site on the former glacis. The façade of its main building runs at an angle to two adjacent streets. On the opposite side or the site the façade of the chapel—as if a mirror image—also runs at an angle to these streets. The most spectacular group of buildings, including the prestigious city palace, was constructed around 1910 along the wide avenue in front of the theatre: the Lloyd Palace together with the Agricultural Exchange and the Café Lloyd (Piața Victoriei 2, Lipót Baumhorn, 1910–12), and, at the opposite end of the same street, the Széchenyi Palace (Piața Victoriei 8, László Székely, 1910–12). One striking feature is common to both buildings here: their main façades are arranged diagonally to one another and are further emphasized by a tower which catches the eye from a distance.

A new boulevard [now Bulvardul Revoluției] established the connection between the Cetate and the Factory district. Work on this boulevard—running from the Piața Traian towards the Bega—was begun around 1900. Due to the fact that it was coordinated with work on the Bega, here it was

Timişoara · Bulev. Regele Ferdinand cu palatul Lloyd · Ferdinánd király-út Lloyd palótával

Timişoara, Hunyadi út (now Piaţa Victoriei)

On the right, Lloyd residence with the agricultural exchange and Café Lloyd
Postcard
Bogner collection, Vienna

possible to achieve a unified architectural whole. A striking accent along the boulevard's further course in the Factory District is provided by the imposing building of the Hungaria baths (Strada Galaţi 2, László Székely, 1913–14). This building, easily noticeable from a distance, takes on a dynamic appearance through the diagonal placement of its façade, which incorporates the street line, thereby emphasizing the importance of its location in the city's urban development.

At the beginning of the twentieth century many "provincial metropolises" were miniature replicas of Vienna. This is true, for example, of Timişoara, Černivci, and Ľviv.[7] The capital of the Habsburg monarchy, without any doubt, served as a model for these towns quite in contrast to cities like Budapest and Prague, which competed "jealously" with Vienna. This is evident from the fact that communal politics took over city planning and—last but not least—from the stylistic features of municipal architecture and their use for representational purposes.

1 On this aspect cf. e.g. Marco Pozzetto "Modernistička Arhitektura u Rijeci / Modernistic Architecture in Rijeka," in *Arhitektura secesije u Rijeci. Arhitektura i urbanizam početka 20. Stoljeća 1900–1925 / Secessional Architecture in Rijeka. Architecture and Town Planning at the Beginning of the 20th Century 1900–1925,* exh. cat., Moderna galerija Rijeka, Rijeka, 1997, pp. 16–25.
2 Between 1851 and 1880 the total population of Timişoara increased from 20,500 to 33,700. The proportion of Romanians fell by about half from 18.5% to 10%, while that of Germans and Austrians rose quite steeply (43% to 57%) as did that of Hungarians (from 11% to 22%). Regarding the fact that Timişoara is not a center of Hungarian culture and art, cf. also Ilona Sármány-Parsons, "Die Rahmenbedingungen für 'die Moderne' in den ungarischen Provinzstädten um die Jahrhundertwende" [The Conditions for 'Modernism' in Hungarian Provincial Cities around the Turn of the Century], in Andrei Corbea-Hoisie and Jacques Le Rider (eds.), *Metropole und Provinzen in Altösterreich (1880–1918)* [Metropolises and Provinces in Old Austria], Vienna, Cologne, Weimar, Iaşi, Romania, 1996, p. 209.
3 For a detailed description of the fortified inner city of Timişoara cf. Mihai Opriş, *Timişoara. Mică monografie urbanistică* [Timişoara: A Brief City Monograph], Bucharest, 1987, especially chapter 2, pp. 25ff.
4 The names of the districts of Timişoara still in use today follow the examples of Vienna and Budapest: Cetate [inner City], Josefin [Joseph Town], Elisabetin [Elizabeth Town], Fabric [Factory Town].
5 Cf. Josef Geml, *Alt-Temesvár im letzten Halbjahrhundert. 1870–1920* [Old-Temesvár in the Last Half-Century], Timişoara, 1927, pp. 10–11.
6 The Viennese influence is visible especially in the architecture of villas, which adopts, in many cases, elements deriving from J. Hoffmann's style which spread among his pupils: balanced volumes, with their interplay between verticals and horizontals; high mansard roofs; few decorative elements. Accidentally, one can notice the influence of Olbrich's flowery style, too, but the few examples represent an exception.
7 Cf. Jacques Le Rider, "Die Erfindung regionaler Identität: Die Fälle Galiziens und der Bukowina" [The Invention of Regional Identity: The Cases of Galicia and Bukovina], in Andrei Corbea-Hoisie and Jacques Le Rider, *Metropole und Provinzen,* p. 12.

Urban Aspirations on the Edge of Empire

Three smaller cities, each on the edge of the empire, illustrate the varied responses and conditions of great city urbanism. Close to the political boundaries of a nation long contested by the great powers of Europe, Ľviv, at the heart of the empire's oil producing regions, was a major manufacturing and financial center as well as the capital of Galicia. The city's optimistic cosmopolitan drive was expressed in the large-scale development of new residential and commercial districts and of mixed-use/middle-class apartment houses—a sophisticated art nouveau architecture drawing on the examples of Vienna and with little interest in regional or folk-derived connections—and similarly urbane initiatives to modernize the city through public open space and cultural monuments.

Kraków served as a critical part of the imperial defensive system. Still fortified until 1918, its status as a garrison town inhibited its aspirations toward modernization, expansion, and an industrial infrastructure. At the same time, this ancient city served as a prime locus of Polish national memory. The architectural self-expression of this mythic status was exemplified by the construction of a "national" theater in 1893 as a repository of the Polish language. For the most part, the nationalist architects associated with the "Young Poland" movement in the arts looked for sources of modernity in an often fanciful medievalism (visible in the new chamber of commerce 1904–06) or motifs from the rural vernacular (as in the pavilions of the *Gesellschaft für bildende Kunst* exhibition of 1898–1901). Reflecting a determined cosmopolitanism, the city's other progressive forces adopted a self-consciously international "art nouveau," evidenced in the form and ornament of its new trade school. Once liberated from the planning restrictions of a military outpost, an extraordinarily expansive, but largely abortive, city plan was adopted, drawing on international planning models in an attempt to catch up with modernization.

Timişoara, at the eastern edge of the Hungarian-ruled Banat, consciously envisaged itself as a giant metropolis of the future with monumental city-block-sized new buildings, modeled on Vienna but overlaid with Magyar-derived motifs, built in the city center. Its development plan, adopted in 1893, forecast the infrastructure for a massive urban population and production. The huge scale of its projected water systems, for example, becomes apparent from the design and construction of concrete tanks and reservoirs at once futuristic and drawing on local Transylvanian forms, while its focus on mass educational facilities indicates aspirations to a technological future. Timişoara, the metropolis that never was, is powerfully illustrative of Austria-Hungary's belated attempt to catch up with the industrial revolution and to fabricate and "regulate" a great city almost from scratch.

Previous page:
Levyns'kyj Company, Zygmunt
Gorgolewski, Municipal Theater, Ľviv,
Svobody Prospect, 1897–1900

Photographed during construction,
17 x 23 cm
LIM Ľviv

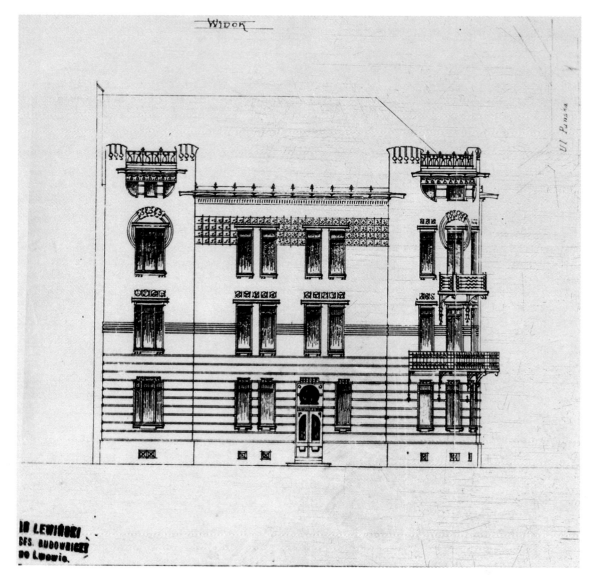

Ivan Levyns'kyj, Pappee House, Ľviv,
Bohomoľcja 3, 1905–06

Elevation, 1905
Print, 34 x 62 cm
DALO Ľviv

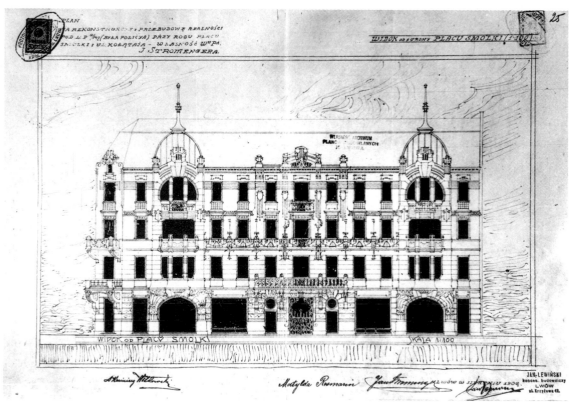

Ivan Levyns'kyj, Tadeusz Obmiński,
Stromenger Building, Ľviv,
Plošča Hryhorenka 4, 1906–07

Elevation, 1906
Print, 41 x 61 cm
DALO, Ľviv

Alfred Zachariewicz, Józef Sosnowski,
Bałaban Building, Ľviv, Halyc'ka 21,
1908–10

View of street front
Photo
Žuk collection, Ľviv

Elevation
Print, 37 x 36 cm
DALO Ľviv

**Alfred Zachariewicz, Land Credit
Institute, Ľviv, Kopernika 4, 1912–13**

View of interior
Żuk collection, Ľviv

Cross-section
Print, 63 x 62 cm
DALO Ľviv

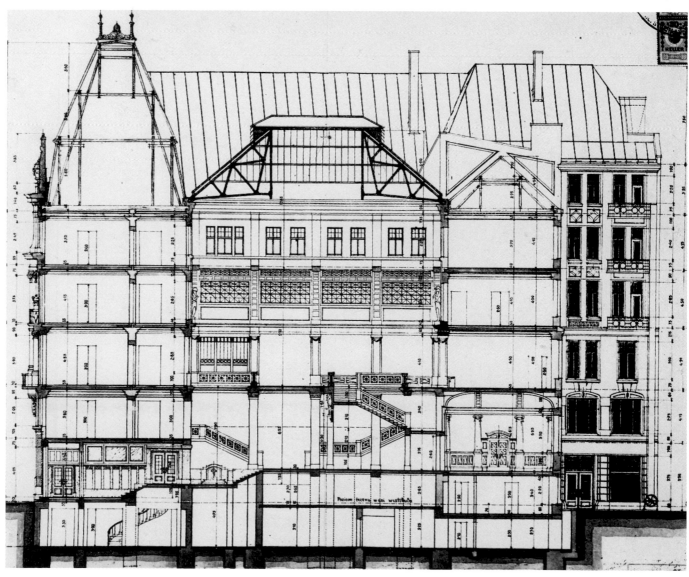

Towarzystwo Przyjaciół sztuk pięknych w Krakowie   Künstlerhaus in Krakau

Franciszek Mącyński, Exhibition Pavilion of the Society of Fine Arts, Kraków, Plac Szczepański, 1898–1901

Postcard, c. 1901
MH Kraków

Perspective
AP Kraków

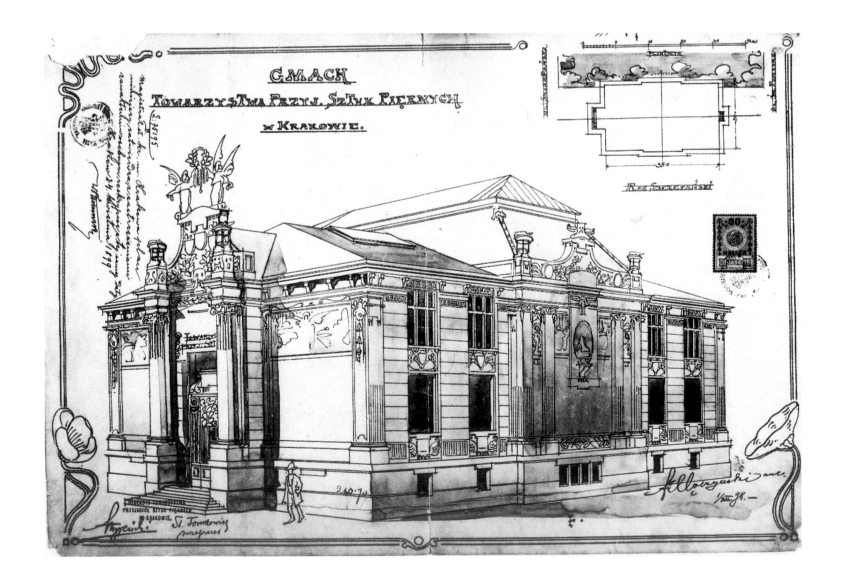

Jan Zawiejski, Academy of Commerce,
Kraków, Ulica Kapucyńska 2–4, 1904–06

Photo
MH Kraków

Elevation
AP Kraków

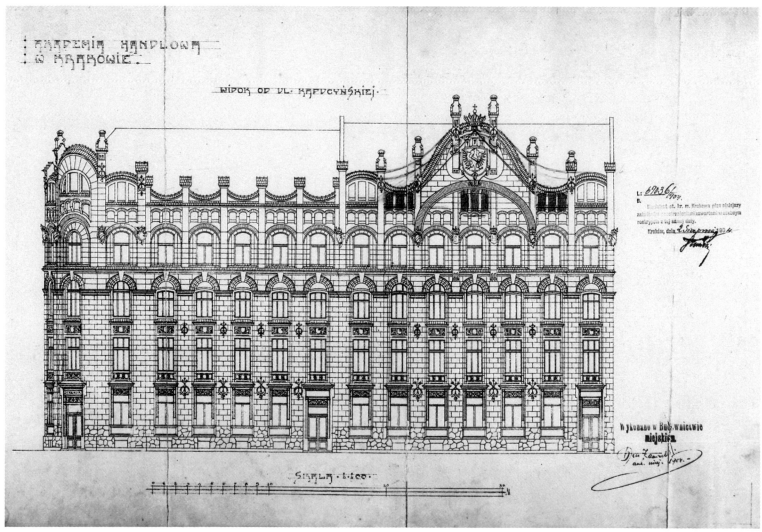

Tadeusz Stryjeński, Franciszek
Mączyński, Reconstruction of Old
Theater [Stary Teatr], Kraków,
Plac Szczepański, 1903–06

Photo
MUJ Kraków

Tadeusz Stryjeński, Franciszek
Mączyński, Chamber of Commerce and
Industry, Kraków, Ulica Długa 1,
1904–06

Photo
MUJ Kraków

Ludwik Wojtyczko, Czynciel Building,
Kraków, Rynek Główny 4, 1906–08

Photo
MUJ Kraków

Lipót Baumhorn, Lloyd Palace,
Timişoara, Piaţa Victoriei 2, 1910–12

Postcard
Bogner collection, Vienna

Lajos Ybl, Project for a General
Development Plan of Timişoara,
1893–95

Plan of city with proposals for
development, 1893
Colored print, 82 x 112 cm
AM Timişoara

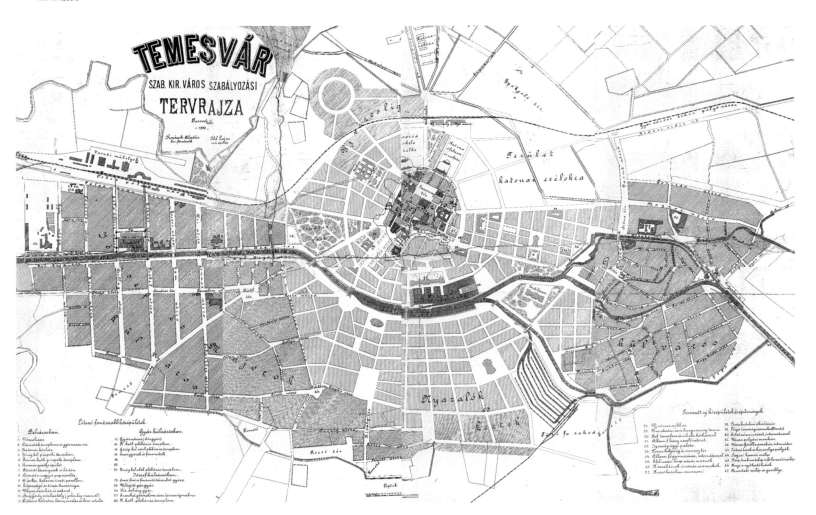

János Lenarduzzi, Richard Sabathiel,
Water Supply System, Timișoara,
1910–14

Building for encasement of natural
springs, Calea Urseni, 1910–12
View
Photo: Petru Teleagă

László Székely, **Hydroelectric Plant on
the Bega,** Timișoara, Str. Chopin 11,
1907–10

Photo, after 1910
MB Timișoara

Interlude: Ideas for a New World, 1919–27

REVOLUTIONARIES OF THOUGHT: THREE SITES OF INNOVATION

Monika Platzer

After World War I architecture and art, serving a new society, represented a source of spiritual renewal. Following the traumatic experience of the war, it was a question of making an entirely new beginning. The two revolutions in Russia (1918) and in Germany (1919), with their call for a new classless society, had repercussions throughout the entire art world and, ultimately, led to a series of avant-garde initiatives which also took root in the states emerging from the Austro-Hungarian monarchy. A number of short-lived, mostly radical groups of artists were formed, consisting of painters, architects, writers, poets, and critics. In the pages of their journals and anthologies (mostly published by the groups themselves), they responded swiftly to the events of the day through manifestos and pamphlets. The goal of this flurry of literary activity was to stimulate the public into adopting a more "proactive" lifestyle. In architecture, as in all other artistic fields at this time, the implementation of projects was a secondary matter—the primary concern was the proclamation of a new beginning.

Lajos Kassák and the Journal *MA*

In November 1915 the first volume of the journal *A Tett* [The Deed] appeared in Budapest, with Lajos Kassák as its editor. This journal soon became a forum for young, left-wing authors who proclaimed themselves pacifists and were opposed to the prevailing policies.[1] By October 1916 the journal had been banned for political reasons and only one month later *A Tett's* successor appeared, again initiated by Lajos Kassák. This was the first volume of the journal *MA* [Today]. It pursued the same objectives, but the means of bringing about social change were now broadened. New perspectives that would effect social change were now not only

propagated in literature, but also in the fine arts, music, theater, and architecture. In addition, texts by foreign authors (among them Henri Guibeaux, Karl Otten, Ivan Goll, and Ludwig Rubiner) were translated into Hungarian.[2] Many of these contributions had already appeared, from 1911 on, in the journal *Die Aktion* [Action], edited in Berlin by Franz Pfemfert. Kassák's interest in the latest trends in art, such as Expressionism, Cubism, and Futurism, also linked *MA* to Herwarth Walden's *Der Sturm* [The Storm].[3]

From his youth Lajos Kassák had been a member of the Social Democratic Party of Hungary, which in 1919 amalgamated with the Communist Party. For a short period he was involved, as a publisher and a member of the People's Commissariat for Education, in establishing a Hungarian Commissarial Republic. However, he became embroiled in a dispute with Béla Kun, co-founder and chairman of the Hungarian Communist Party, about the social function of art. During a party congress Kun attacked the authors of the journal *MA,* accusing them of bourgeois decadence. This generated a direct response from Kassák, which appeared in *MA* in June 1919 in the form of "A Letter to Béla Kun in the Name of Art."[4] The next issue of *MA* appeared without government permission. In August 1919 Kassák was arrested, and some six months later he managed to escape to Vienna hidden aboard a ship.

In the following May, *MA* was published once again—but now in Vienna. The first issue of this new edition, which was to appear until 1925, contains an essay by Kassák in Hungarian and German in which he articulates his attitude and objectives regarding the autonomy of art:

The motto is: The Human Being. We are human beings in our art and, not having served the bourgeoisie in the past, we do not intend to serve any class in the future—not even if that class is

László Moholy-Nagy, Glass Architecture
Cover of MA, VII, 1922, nos. 5-6
© VBK Vienna, 1999

the proletariat.... In opposition to all forms of class rule, we proclaim the triumphant community of man. In opposition to all state morality, we proclaim a communal ethics. This revolution can succeed only through a moral and cultural education suited to the proletariat, which alone provides a healthy raw material for the future! Therefore, culture. And more culture![5]

The artist, in his view of himself, had advanced to take on the role of educator of the people, and his contributions are to be seen as the work of social enlightenment, serving more the new political order than actual reconstruction. Kassák's contribution of *Bildarchitektur* [image architecture] should also be understood in this sense. The term *Bildarchitektur* first appears in an introduction to a portfolio of six linoprints by Sándor Bortnyik,[6] and in October 1922 a manifesto bearing this title appeared in *MA*, containing three illustrations of "image architecture" by Kassák himself.[7] "Not the image of the world but the essence of the world: architecture. The synthesis of pure order."[8] Kassák was not concerned with mastering space or the world, but with representing creative energies: "The artist with a world view is able to create, whatever it may be. Creating is the constructive, noble act.

Construction is architecture."[9] The "construction on a surface," composed of geometric forms existing in a network of spatial interrelations, becomes the synonym for a new way of seeing and living. The polarity between space-constructing and space-destroying functions which characterizes architecture becomes the leitmotif in a design of life that permeates all spheres. In the center stands the artistic act, which—together with the urge to shape—is seen to be closely allied to human "sensation."

Hungary at the Bauhaus

If Kassák's decision to settle in Vienna was initially due to it's geographical location, it was later the Bauhaus in Weimar which became an important focal point for the Central European avant-garde. The Hungarians represented one of the largest national groups among the students of the Bauhaus. In 1921 Marcel Breuer, Farkas Molnár, and Andor Weininger, to name only a few, came to Weimar on the initiative of Alfréd Forbát, who was working as architect for Walter Gropius. Under the leadership of Molnár, seventeen Bauhaus students jointly set up the KURI group. Influenced by Theo van Doesburg's "De Stijl" course held in Weimar (March–July 1922) they spoke out against the "expressionist degeneration" of the Bauhaus caused by Itten's students, formulating their demands in a manifesto written by Farkas Molnár: "the fortuitous is to be replaced by that which is governed by laws, the decorative and the desire for expression by the constructive, utilitarian, rational, international.... Long live the new cube: the first cubic house in the world—Kuri—world—Kuri!"[10] Molnár's famous design of the red cubic house is an architectural translation of these ideals. The projected one-family house, with it's rational ground plan and it's garden and pergola (attached for health reasons) embodies the principles of a new conception of architecture. The shape of the house, the orientation of the ground plan, as well as its projected method of construction (prefabrication) are based on the primacy of rationality.

Concurrent with the Bauhaus, the De Stijl group, Russian Constructivism, and French Purism were pursuing similar aims. They all served as catalysts for a new conception of architecture. This was not to be confined merely to the aesthetic and form a sphere, but was to be translated directly into social practice, for instance, in the taking of an active stand with regard to one of the most urgent problems of the time—that of housing. A just, social solution was central to this issue. In his design for a frieze (around 1923) Molnár espoused a "cooperative solution": it was not the manufacturer who should determine the distribution of goods to consumers, but an organization serving the needs of the general public.

In this context the design for the town KURI, created in 1925, should be mentioned. This model of a "new town,"

Farkas Molnár, Remembering the Bauhaus Week in Weimar, 1923
Etching, 24.3 x 19.8 cm
CCA Montréal

which is able to do without any definite town center, must be seen as a counter-model to Le Corbusier's *Ville Contemporaine* of 1922.[11] Quite apart from the claim of being the concrete translation of an idea, this represents a utopian town model created for a society that is able to exist without any formal or social segregation.

Architecture and town planning thus became an ever more important issue at the Bauhaus. After the great Bauhaus exhibition of 1923 Molnár, together with Breuer and Muche, began an initiative to create an architecture department at the Bauhaus. In the end, this plan would have to wait until 1927, when the first architecture department was set up in Dessau by Hannes Meyer.

Devětsil

Apart from the Bauhaus exhibition of 1923, Walter Gropius also organized an international architecture exhibition, whose aim was to provide an overview of the current trends in European architecture. With the participation of Jaroslav Fragner, Bedřich Feuerstein, Karel Honzík, Jaromír Krejcar, Jan E. Koula, Evžen Linhart, and Vít Obrtel, Czechoslovakia was among the countries most strongly represented. With the exception of Koula, all these architects were members of the artists' group Devětsil [Butterbur, Coltsfoot],[12] founded in Prague in October 1920 by Karel Teige. While in its first phase Devětsil was characterized by a political orientation and position in the direction of the "New Proletarian Art" championed by Teige, a re-orientation took place in 1922. Karel Teige, the group's organizer and ideological leader, went to Paris in the summer of 1922, where he came into contact with the current trends in art, painting, and literature, and among other things became acquainted with Le Corbusier's and Amédée Ozenfant's ideas and concepts of Purism. As a direct result of his impressions, Teige, together with Jaromír Krejcar, compiled the almanach *Život II* with the programmatic subtitle *Sborník nové krásy* [Almanach of New Beauty] dedicated to the forward-looking "beauty of gigantic ocean liners, American steel structures, of sky scrapers, machines, turbines, automobiles, aeroplanes, of city crossroads with illuminated advertising signs, and of cinemas."[13] The members of the artists' group Devětsil expressed their enthusiasm for the new era in their own journals *Disk* and *Pásmo* [The Zone] and in the architecture magazine *Stavba* [The Building], edited by the Association of Architects, which, at the same time, became a forum for a broad, international dialogue.

In three architectural drawings of 1921–22 (designs for a department store, a hotel, and a provincial railway station[14]) which testify to the new faith in the metropolis, civilization, and technology, Jaromír Krejca articulates for the first time a language of form which can be described as specific to the aesthetics of Devětsil. The polarity of building and poetry, i.e., construction and the lyrical character of forms, makes here its very own contribution to the European avant-garde.[15] Krejcar's architectural vocabulary of form for the department store design takes it's bearings, on the one hand, from Purist formal principles, while its massive use of advertising signs (which in their arrangements, however, still adhere to a geometric order) points to a direct kinship with the typical "image poetry" of the Devětsil group. The montages of written texts herald a better future to be brought about by the mechanization of the world. The view of architecture as a pure science in the service of functionality, divested of all aesthetic ambitions, formulated by Teige in *Stavba* from 1924, was rejected by Jaromír Krejcar and the other Devětsil architects. In place of this, geometric forms were imbued with a lyrical character. The use of suggestive forms and bare symbols to indicate elements of color were meant to invoke free associations in the viewer and to expand the spectrum of human perception. It was precisely this aspect that Teige wished to remove from architecture and reserve as a form of free artistic expression for the Poeticism initiated in 1924.[16]

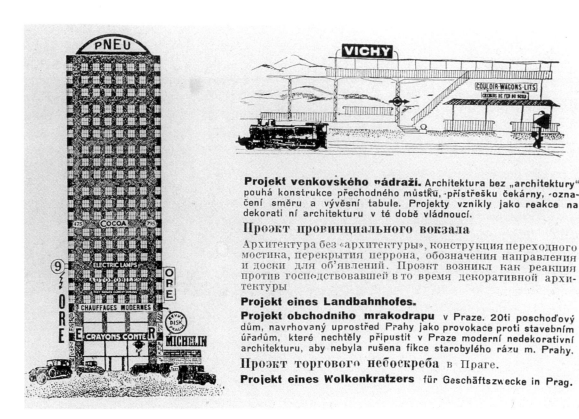

Jaromír Krejcar, Designs for Business
Premises and a Provincial Station,
1921–22

Repr. from: Karel Teige: Práce Jaromíra Krejcara [The
Works of Jaromír Krejcar], ESMA, vol. 2, Prague, 1933

Jaromír Krejcar's project for the Olympic Department Store in Prague may be considered the main work of "architectural Poeticism" (1925–26). Here a standardized formal language is imbued with poetic content, in keeping with the tradition of Lyrical Constructivism. The combination of advertisements, whose messages are not always unambiguous, is meant to stimulate the imagination of the viewer. The awnings and the railings, reminiscent of ships, hint at travels past or future. Similarly, the advertisements reflect an enthusiasm for the wireless. With the inscription TSF [Télégraphie sans fil], Krejcar makes allusion to the 1925 book of Jaroslav Seifert, *On the Waves of TSF*.[17] To sum it up in the words of Zdeněk Primus: the department store Olympic was a "cathedral of quivering life."[18]

At the "Wiener staatliche Schule für Expressionismus" [State School of Expressionism, Vienna]

The almanach *Buch neuer Künstler* [The Book of New Artists] edited by Kassák and Moholy-Nagy and published in Vienna in 1922 is a further collection of articles expressing enthusiasm for the technological achievements of the new era. Kassák's preface states: "art, science and technology meet at one point. There is a need for change! There is a need to create, for movement is creation."[19]

From 1919 the Kunstgewerbeschule [School for Arts and Crafts] in Vienna became the model of an institution where the boundaries between conventionally defined disciplines were dissolved. "The idea without action is dead," Franz

Čižek proclaimed.[20] His course on the theory of ornamental form, comparable to the *Vorkurs* [preliminary course] at the Bauhaus, became the seed for a renewal process of universalist inspiration. Central to the course was the direct and untainted rendering of sense impressions on the picture plane. In 1922 a book by Leopold Rochowanski was published in Vienna entitled *Der Formwille der Zeit in der angewandten Kunst* [The Current Desire for Form in the Applied Arts]. The tone throughout this publication was that of an aggressive, activist pamphlet in which central importance is attached to the younger generation as the driving force toward a new and better world. Franz Čižek was appointed leader of this revolutionary group and was expected to prepare the way for the new art. Contacts with Béla Uitz, Enrico Prampolini, Filippo Tomasso Marinetti, and Theo van Doesburg, as well as with the Bauhaus, provided the link to the international scene.

In 1923—almost exactly paralleling similar developments at the Bauhaus—the course on Ornament underwent an artistic change away from the expressive, individualistic period to a formally reduced constructivist phase. "The Artist as Technician" is the title Lucia Moholy gives to her photograph of her husband, in which he appears in the red "mechanics" outfit that he wore at the Bauhaus. A Čižek student can be seen wearing similar dress during work on one of the three-dimensional material studies that, from 1923, became the core of the student's training. Drawing courses were streamlined, rationalized, and amended to include sculptural art and material collages, allowing the student to explore spatial balance and the relations of tension existing between various materials.

The inclusion of materials and tectonics in the elementary course culminated in the 1926 exhibition on the theme "Construction of Space." The tectonic element was further promoted through the establishment in 1923 of a carpenter's workshop (led by Karl Witzmann), where a large number of models and strictly tectonic wood constructions were made.

This development should be seen in connection with the architectural courses given by Josef Hoffmann and Oskar Strnad at the Kunstgewerbeschule in Vienna.[21] In addition to the course on the general theory of form, Oskar Strnad was responsible for the architecture course, while Josef Frank was professor of building construction. The main theme of the architecture course was the formal break-up of the "cube" into an expansive network of autonomous surfaces and plates. In the Bauhaus book *Internationale Architektur* of 1925, Walter Gropius published models of a country-villa executed by the students of Otto Niedermoser and Julius Jirasek (each student being represented by one model). It was Josef Hoffmann who, as Commissioner of the Austrian section of the *Exposition Internationale des Arts Décoratifs et Industriels Modernes* in Paris in 1925, entrusted Friedrich Kiesler

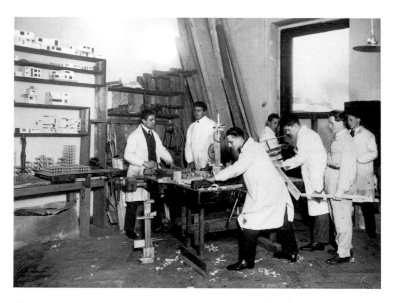

Čižek School, School for Arts and Crafts, Vienna, c. 1923
Pupils in the workshop making a model
Photo, 23 x 17 cm
HM Vienna

with the design of the exhibition for the theatrical contribution at the Grand Palais. Kiesler developed the concept of a "city in space," consisting solely of a wooden structure suspended from the ceiling. In a contemporary manifesto, Kiesler describes the overcoming of gravity as "the creation of new possibilities of living, and, by means of these, of the demands which will remold society."[22]

In Vienna, the process of artistic renewal was, from the very start, closely linked with concurrent educational reform movements. If, around the turn of the century, the main concern was an all-encompassing quest to integrate aesthetics into everyday life (i.e., craft and art became synonymous), by the beginning of the 1920s there was a detectable shift in emphasis towards educational objectives, whose driving force was a determination to reform life. Strnad understood his teaching to be "an education" towards a certain way of thinking.[23] Above all else, it was the role of architecture to exert a positive influence on man's spiritual feelings—in other words, architecture as a way of establishing a harmonious environment for the mental and physical welfare of people, as spatially visualized emotion and a possibility of experience. Strnad, moreover, speaks of a "moral duty of architectural training."[24]

This view of architecture as a physical translation of spiritual content invested with a cultural and political mission is reminiscent of Bruno Taut. Taut's project of 1919–20 for the Folkwang School is considered to be the model of an "activist" architecture, whose goal is the creative education of the community.

László Moholy-Nagy, Lajos Kassák, *Book of New Artists*, Vienna, 1922
Print
Private collection, Vienna

1 See Lajos Kassák, "Program," in *A Tett* [The Deed],Budapest, 1916, no. 2, p. 10; German translation in József Vadas (ed.), *Lajos Kassák. Laßt uns leben in unserer Zeit: Gedichte, Bilder und Schriften zu Kunst* [Let Us Live in Our Time: Poems, Pictures and Writings on Art], Budapest, 1989, pp. 17–19.

2 See Esther Levinger, "Lajos Kassák: *MA* and the New Artist, 1919–1925," in *The Structurist*, Saskatoon, 1985–86, nos. 25–26, p. 82.

3 *Der Sturm* [The Storm], Berlin, vol. I, 1910–11 to vol. XXI, 1932. In *MA* [Today], works by Franz Marc, Vincent van Gogh, Max Pechstein, Pablo Picasso, Henri Derain, and Umberto Boccioni can be seen along with works by Hungarian artists such as Béla Uitz, János Máttis-Teutsch, János Kmetty, Lajos Tihanyi, and György Ruttkay.

4 Lajos Kassák, "Levél Kun Bélához a művészet nevében," in *MA*, Budapest, vol. IV, 1919, no. 7, pp. 146–48; German translation, "Brief an Béla Kun im Namen der Kunst" [Letter to Béla Kun in the Name of Art], in Vadas, *Lajos Kassák*, pp. 55–58.

5 Lajos Kassák, "An die Künstler aller Länder!" [To Artists of All Countries!], in *MA*, Vienna, vol. V, 1920, nos. 1–2, pp. 2–4, quoted here from Vadas, *Lajos Kassák*, pp. 59–61.

6 Lajos Kassák, "Einführungstext zur Bildarchitektur-Mappe von Sándor Bortnyik. Wien 1921" [Introductory text to the Image Architecture Portfolio of Sándor Bortnyik. Vienna 1921], in Hubertus Gassner (ed.), *Wechselwirkungen. Ungarische Avantgarde in der Weimarer Republic* [Mutual Influences: The Hungarian Avant-Garde in the Weimar Republic], exh. cat., Neue Galerie, Kassel and Museum Bochum, Marburg, 1986, p. 221.

7 Lajos Kassák, "Bildarchitektur" [Image Architecture], in *MA*, Vienna, vol. VIII, 1922–23, no. 1, pp. 5–6 (heavily abridged German version of the Hungarian original "Képarchitektúra," in *MA*, Vienna, vol. VII, 1922, no. 4, pp. 52–54; available in German in Vadas, *Lajos Kassák*, pp. 105–10).

8 Lajos Kassák, "Bildarchitektur" [Image Architecture], quoted from Vadas, *Lajos Kassák*, p. 106.

9 Ibid., p. 108.

10 Farkas Molnár, "KURI-Manifest," in Gassner, *Wechselwirkungen*, p. 268.

11 See also the contribution by Renate Banik-Schweizer in this volume.

12 See also František Šmejkal and Rostislav Švácha (eds.), *Devětsil, Czech Avant-Garde Art Architecture and Design of the 1920s and 30s*, exh. cat., Museum of Modern Art, Oxford, and Design Museum, London, 1990.

13 Jaromír Krejcar, "Co se chystá" [What One Prepares], in *Československé noviny* [Czechoslovakian Newspaper], vol. I, 1922, no. 212, p. 6.

14 Published for example in Karel Teige, *Práce Jaromíra Krejcara* [The Works of Jaromír Krejcar], ESMA, vol. 2, Prague, 1933, p. 18.

15 See for example Rostislav Švácha, "V čem spočívá originalita české avant-gardy?" [What Constitutes the Originality of the Czech Avant-Garde?], in *Zlatý řez*, *Golden section* Prague, 1996, no. 13, pp. 4–11.

16 See Karel Teige, "Poetismus" [Poeticism], in Karel Teige, *Liquidierung der "Kunst"* [Liquidation of Art], Frankfurt am Main, 1968, pp. 44–52.

17 Jaroslav Seifert, *Na vlnách TSF* [On the Waves of TSF], Prague, 1925.

18 Zdenek Primus (ed.), *Tschechische Avantgarde 1922–1940. Reflexe europäischer Kunst und Fotografie in der Buchgestaltung* [Reflections of European Art and Photography in Book Design], exh. cat., Kunstverein Hamburg, 1990, p. 77.

19 Lajos Kassák, "Preface," in Ludwig Kassák and László Moholy-Nagy, *Buch neuer Künstler* [Book of New Artists], Vienna, 1922, p. 4 (facsimile printed Budapest, 1977).

20 Manuscript note of Franz Čižek, Historisches Museum der Stadt Wien, Literary Estate of Franz Čižek. See also Monika Platzer, "Die Idee ohne Tat ist tot" [The Idea without Action is Dead], in *Abstracta Austria Germania Italia 1919–1939. Die andere "entartete Kunst" / L'altra "arte degenerate"* [The other "Degenerate Art"], exh. cat., Museum of Modern Art, Bozen (etc.), Milan, 1997, pp. 38–46.

21 See also the exhibition architecture of the following exhibitions: *School Exhibitions*, May, 1924; artistic design for the exhibition of the classes of Strnad and Hoffmann at the Museum of Applied Art; exhibition architecture by Oswald Haerdtl for the *Exposition Internationale des Arts Décoratifs et Industriels Modernes* in Paris, 1925; *Anniversary Exhibition*, 1929.

22 Friedrich Kiesler, "Manifest: Vitalbau – Raumstadt – Funktionelle Architektur" [The City of Space], in Dieter Bogner, *Friedrich Kiesler 1890–1965: Inside the Endless House*, exh. cat., Historisches Museum der Stadt Wien, Vienna, Cologne, Weimar, 1997, p. 33.

23 For this see Otto Kapfinger and Matthias Boeckl, "Vom Interieur zum Städtebau. Architektur am Stubenring 1918–90" [From the Interior to Town Planning: Architecture on the Stubenring], in Hochschule für angewandte Kunst in Wien (ed.), *Kunst: Anspruch und Gegenstand. Von der Kunstgewerbeschule zur Hochschule für angewandte Kunst in Wien 1918–1991* [Art: Requirement and Object—From the School of Arts and Crafts to the Academy of Applied Art in Vienna], Vienna and Salzburg, 1991, pp. 109–18.

24 Ibid., p. 111.

Manifesto Architecture

In the wake of revolution and political reconstruction, progressive architects in the new capitals of the immediate post-war years of political upheaval and economic crisis joined the ferment of cultural activism, experiment, and propaganda. Architects saw themselves as a leading force in generating a new social and aesthetic order and in proposing new patterns of urban living. The image, form, and features of the modern city became as important to the plastic arts and the new literature and photography as it was to architecture. For Lajos Kassák and the *MA* Circle (Hungarian radicals operating in Budapest, and later Vienna), the city as an abstract leitmotif lay at the base of their *Bild-architektur*, while the Devětsil group in Prague embraced the icons of modern city life in skyscrapers, signage, and industrial plants as new aesthetic values for an Industrial Age. Looking to take their place with the modernizing states to east and west, members of the cultural avant-garde in the former empire joined a much wider discourse on architectural ideas and social ideology. Their central texts (such as Farkas Molnár's KURI Manifesto or Karel Teige's Poetism) and organs (like *MA* or *Život*) became founding documents in the evolution of an international debate on Modernism.

Jiří Kroha, **Primary Plan**, 1919

Pencil, charcoal, and chalk on paper,
42 x 50.5 cm
MMB Brno
© Karel Šabata

Alfréd Forbát, Composition,
c. 1920

Chalk on paper, 20.5 x 20.5 cm
JPM Pécs
© István Füzi

Lajos Kassák, Image Architecture,
1922

2 compositions
Print, 31 x 31 cm
Repr. from: MA, VIII, 1922

Farkas Molnár, Design for a frieze: the manufacturer—the consumer, c. 1923

Pencil, wash, and watercolor on paper, 32,6 x 50,2 cm
DAM Frankfurt / Main

Farkas Molnár, The Red Cube, 1923

Indian ink and watercolor on paper, 59 x 91.5 cm
DAM Frankfurt / Main

Farkas Molnár, ›KURI‹-Collage, 1929

Mixed media, oil on paper, 33 x 50 cm
Kassák Múzeum, Budapest

Oswald Haerdti, The Austrian Museum of Art and Industry (now Austrian Museum of Applied Art), 1924

Spatial arrangement for an architecture exhibition at the School of Arts and Crafts Vienna, the classes of Josef Hoffman and Oskar Strnad

Repr. from: Deutsche Kunst und Dekoration, XXVII, 1924

Elisabeth Karlinsky, Concert Hall, 1924

Chalk and watercolor on paper,
38 x 42.7 cm
HM Vienna

Friedrich Kiesler, City in Space, 1925

Installation at Exposition Internationale des Arts Décoratifs et Industriels Modernes, Grand Palais, Paris

Bogner collection, Vienna
Photo: Photo-Art J. Rosemann, Paris

Karel Teige, 'Mrkvička Hotel', 1922

Pencil, indian ink, and watercolor on paper,
19.3 x 16.9 cm
NG Prague

Jaromír Krejcar, Olympic Department
Store, Prague I, Spálená 16, 1925–28

1925
Repr. from: Stavba, IV, 1925–26

Budapest, 1927–37

NEUES BAUEN IN BUDAPEST

András Ferkai

The urban development of Budapest during the years between the two wars is characteristic for development as a whole in Central Europe. As the political, economic, and cultural center of Hungary, the city was destined for rapid expansion. During this expansion, however, the inner-city that had developed between 1870 and 1914 remained largely unchanged. The growth of the city concentrated, on the one hand, on extending the suburbs and building single-family houses on what had previously been green belts (particularly in the Buda mountains) and, on the other hand, on constructing new apartment blocks in densely built-up inner-city areas (mainly on the Pest side).[1] While the former development was mainly spontaneous, subject only to the existing building zone regulations, the latter was to a very large degree carried out on orders of city councilors and planning authorities.

It is surprising that most competitions in Budapest town planning only had a very small influence on the city's actual development. Thus competition plans for major building projects were either not carried out (the competition of the Budapest-Fórum for redesigning the city center of Pest, 1936; József Vágó's utopian plans for the architectural redesign of Budapest, 1936) or remained fragmentary (Madách út, 1930–38, the Buda bridgehead of the Petőfi bridge, 1935; a new design for Ó-Buda [Old Buda], 1936.)[2] Intervention by the municipal authorities was generally confined to certain squares, sections of streets, or a few blocks of houses, and was concerned with larger, interconnected areas only in the Újlipótváros district on the Pest side, the Lágymányos quarter in Buda, and in the suburbs.[3]

The strong influx from the Hungarian minority territories in Czechoslovakia, Yugoslavia, and Romania was only one factor that led to an acute housing shortage in the mid 1920s. The municipal authorities failed to respond adequately to this situation, and the provision of social housing remained inadequate, limited to a few estates and apartment blocks of a type and style which showed no significant innovations. The construction of blocks of small flats, undertaken in 1933–34 by the OTI (Országos Társadalombiztosító Intézet [the National Institute of Social Security]) at the Köztársaság tér, with its consistent slab development and uncompromising formal language, was one of the rare exceptions.[4] By offering tax relief, the municipal authorities attempted rather to induce private builders to move away from the traditional tenement blocks with small courtyards ringed by circular galleries and to use the healthier system of perimeter blocks.

This led to the growth of the hitherto provincial main traffic arteries of the inner-city areas into large urban radial and ring roads, lined by modern, often luxuriously equipped apartment blocks with cinemas, cafés, and elegant shops at street level. In this way, from the mid 1930s onward, the Margit körút, the Krisztina körút, and the Attila út in Buda as well as the uniform, modern building complex of the Szent István Park in Pest (1933–42) were developed.[5] The block of residences and the Átrium Cinema at the Margit körút (Budapest II, Lajos Kozma, 1935–36) or the block of apartments and shops with the Café Dunapark at Pozsonyi út (Budapest XIII, Béla Hofstätter, Ferenc Domány, 1935–36) amply demonstrate what the Budapest upper classes of the 1930s understood by a sophisticated, modern metropolitan infrastructure.[6]

Initially the modern architecture movement in Hungary met with considerable resistance. A deeply rooted conservatism coupled with political and economic insecurity fostered an attitude of scepticism towards new trends at the beginning of the 1920s. The Hungarian avant-garde was forced to emigrate (Berlin, Weimar, Paris, the Kassák-circle in

Lajos Kozma, Átrium Cinema and Residence, Budapest II, Margit körút 55, 1935–36
Photo: Zoltán Seidner
OMVH Budapest

Béla Hofstätter, Ferenc Domány, Residential and Business Premises with the Duna-park Café, Budapest XIII, Pozsonyi út 38–42, 1935–36
Repr. from: Dénes Györdyi et al. (eds.): Új magyar építőművészet [New Hungarian Architecture], vol. 2, Budapest 1938

Vienna), and the first modern buildings were built only around 1927–28.[7] It is not surprising, then, that right from its beginnings Hungarian modernism regarded itself as a pluralistically orientated movement designed to integrate diverse views and variations, from the radically technological functionalism of the avant-garde to aestheticizing modernism and regional aspirations.

Followers of *Neues Bauen* gathered in the Hungarian CIAM group around the Bauhaus pupil Farkas Molnár and the Social Democrat József Fischer.[8] Members of the group also included the former colleague of Walter Gropius, Alfréd Forbát, and, as a result of his short stay in Hungary in 1934–35, Marcel Breuer.[9] Due to a lack of contracts in the social housing sector (other than the OTI apartment blocks already mentioned), the majority of the group's work was in the area of villas and apartment blocks which were built according to the requirements of *Neues Bauen* (e.g., Villa Dálnoki-Kovács, Budapest XII, Lejtő utca, 1932; Villa Bajai, Budapest II, Pasaréti út/Trombitás utca, 1936–37, both by Farkas Molnár). The group's failure to receive commissions for major public building projects was largely due to the left-wing political commitment of its architects.

Contact with other countries helped to refine the architectural vocabulary. Several Hungarian architects, for instance, worked in the Paris office of Le Corbusier.[10] His influence can be seen clearly in János Wanner's family house in the Szilágyi Erzsébet fasor (Budapest II, 1936), Károly Dávid Jr.'s own house in Somlói út (Budapest XI, 1932, destroyed in 1945), and the Stühmer chocolate factory by Aladár and Viktor Olgyay in Vágóhíd utca (Budapest IX, 1941). Several architects maintained their links with Vienna: Bertalan Árkay, for instance, was a student in the masterclass of Peter Behrens. His charcoal drawings and some of his buildings cannot disguise the influence of the German master (e.g., the villa in Virágárok utca, Budapest II, 1927).[11] Manó Lessner was a close friend of Josef Frank and Oscar Strnad, and shared their critical views of the dogmas of modernism. Similar to the work of the Viennese architects, modern, traditional, and playfully accidental elements combine harmoniously in his designs and in the few projects that he realized (e.g., the villa on the Somlói út, Budapest XI, 1928).[12] The churches and villas of Bertalan Árkay and Gyula Rimanóczy, the public buildings by István Janáky, László Lauber, and Lajos Hidasi, as well as the blocks of flats by Gedeon Gerlóczy are evidence of the favorable reception that was given to the Italian *razionalismo* (Terragni, Libera), the *novecento* in Rome, and the more moderate French architects (Roux-Spitz, Mallet-Stevens, Ginsberger).

Of great importance for development from the mid 1930s were the growing efforts to create a modern architectural language that, by taking into account existing structures and local building traditions, would assume its own regional character.[13] Points of reference in this departure from the radical dogmatism of *Neues Bauen* were provided above all by the Stuttgart School (where Pál Virágh had spent a year studying

in 1930), the Scandinavian architectural scene (Alvar Aalto, Gunnar Asplund), and representatives of a moderate modernism such as Paul Bonatz, Willem M. Dudok, and Otto Rudolf Salvisberg. These regionalistic trends in Hungary manifested themselves most originally in the efforts of a group of architects gathering around Jenő Padányi Gulyás who, through ethnographic studies, wanted to determine the locally inherent building style of each respective region and use this as the basis for current architectural design. During the 1940s several estates were completed based on such models, which, like the German "Heimatschutz" movement reflect the drive to preserve the homeland as well as a strong, nationalistically tinged body of thought.

1 For a more detailed account of developments in suburbanization see András Ferkai, "Hungarian Architecture between the Wars," in Dora Wiebenson and József Sisa (eds.), *The Architecture of Historic Hungary*, Cambridge, Mass., and London, 1998, pp. 245–74, 305–06.
2 See Ferenc Bodor, "A Megépíthetetlen város" [The City That is Impossible to Build], in *Budapesti Negyed* [Budapest Quarterly], Budapest, vol. 1, 1993, no. 2, pp. 174–79; András Román, "Madách Imre, avagy egy sugárút tragédiája" [Imre Madách or the Tragedy of a Radial Road], in *Budapesti Negyed* [Budapest Quarterly], Budapest, vol. V, 1997–98, nos. 18–19, pp. 69–82; András Hadik et al., "Képek a meg nem épült Budapestről" [Pictures of a Budapest that was Never Built], in ibid., pp. 208–26; *Budapest művészi újjáépítése Vágó József elgondolása szerint* [The Artistic Recreation of Budapest Based on the Concepts of József Vágó], Budapest, 1936.
3 See Ferenc Harrer, *A Fővárosi Közmunkák Tanácsa 1930–1940* [The Municipal Council of Public Works 1930–1940], Budapest, 1941.

4 Architects of the OTI houses: Bertalan Árkay, Sándor Faragó, József Fischer, Károly Heysa, Pál Ligeti, Farkas Molnár, Móric Pogány, Gábor Preisich, Mihály Vadász. Innovative ground plan proposals offered by the architects— all members of the Hungarian CIAM group except Árkay, Faragó, and Heysa—were rejected by the OTI management.
5 See András Ferkai, *Buda építészete a két világháború között* [The Architecture of Buda in the Inter-war Years], Budapest, 1995, pp. 13–14.
6 Published in *Tér és forma*, Budapest, vol. IX, 1936, pp. 127–59, and vol. X, 1937, pp. 111–42.
7 For more details on the political and cultural circumstances see note 1.
8 See Eszter Gábor, *A CIAM magyar csoportja (1928–1938)* [The Hungarian CIAM Group (1928–1938)], Budapest, 1972.
9 Other members of the CIAM group were Pál Ligeti, György Masirevich, Máté Major, Gábor Preisich, György Rácz, Zoltan Révész, Zoltán Kósa.
10 See András Ferkai, "Le Corbusier és Magyarország" [Le Corbusier and Hungary], in *Magyar Építőművészet* [Hungarian Architecture], Budapest, vol. LXXVIII, 1987, no. 6, pp. 50–51. Károly Dávid, János Wanner, János Weltzl, László Málnai, and Aladár and Viktor Olgyay all worked with Le Corbusier.
11 See László Pusztai, "Árkay Bertalan (1901–1970)" [Bertalan Árkay (1901–1970)], in *Magyar Építőművészet* [Hungarian Architecture], Budapest, 1972, no. 5, pp. 60–61.
12 See Márta Branczik, "Lessner Manó építész. A Kiscelli Múzeum építészeti gyűjteményéből" [The Architect Manó Lessner: From the Architecture Collection of the Kiscelli Museum], in *Magyar Építőművészet* [Hungarian Architecture], Budapest, vol. LXXXV, 1994, no. 6, pp. 37–39.
13 See András Ferkai, "Vzdáleno rýstřednostem (Poznámky k modernismu v Mad'arsku)/Away from the Extremes (Remarks on Hungarian Modernism)," in *Zlatý řez/Golden Section*, Prague, 1998, no. 18, pp. 9–15.

Postwar Avant-Garde

As Hungary's political winds shifted between revolutionary socialism, democratic liberalism, and a quasi-fascist strain of Magyar nationalism, so modern architectures with varying degrees of social reformism, national inflection, and Italian borrowings flourished and faded. This episode focusses on the left-leaning, Bauhaus-trained architects Farkas Molnár and Virgil Bierbauer, editors of the journal *Tér és forma*. It was principally the promotion of the simple, efficient dwelling to which these architects devoted their intensive campaigns of demonstration projects, publications, exhibitions, and lectures. Built as modest suburban villas and apartments and borrowing their materials and palette from the industrial world, the "new architecture" of the *Tér és forma* group contributed as much to the developing ideas of their progenitors (Walter Gropius, Marcel Breuer, Josef Frank, and Le Corbusier) as they had drawn from them. Molnar's functionalist villas, in particular, became archetypal models of modernist dwelling space.

Virgil Bierbauer, László Králik, Airport, Budapest XI, Kőérbereki út 36, 1936–37

Detail
Photo, 25 x 35 cm
MEM Budapest
© Gábor Barka

Virgil Bierbauer, László Králik, Airport, Budapest XI, Kőérbereki út 36, 1936–37

View of the Passenger Handling Building
Photo, 25 x 35 cm
MEM Budapest
© Gábor Barka

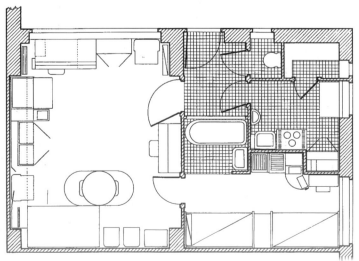

Farkas Molnár, apartment, Budapest I, Mihály utca 11, 1929

View into living room and study
Photo mounted on card, 24.5 x 34 cm
MEM Budapest
© Gábor Barka

Floor plan
Repr. from: Ottó Mezei, Molnár Farkas, Budapest, 1987

Farkas Molnár, Villa Dálnoki-Kovács, Budapest XII, Lejtő utca 2a, 1932

Plan of ground floor and first floor .
Repr. from: Ottó Mezei, Molnár Farkas, Budapest, 1987

South side
Photo, 23 x 17 cm
MEM Budapest
© Gábor Barka

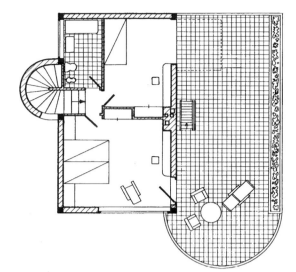
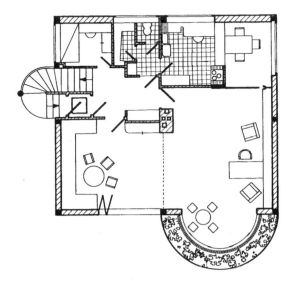

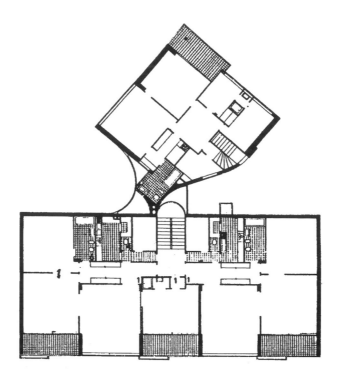

Farkas Molnár, Pekanovich Apartment Block and Villa Bajai, Budapest II, Pasaréti út 7, Trombitás utca 32, 1936

Floor plan
Repr. from: Tér és forma, X, 1937

View from street of apartment block
Photo mounted on card, 24 x 33 cm
MEM Budapest
© Gábor Barka

Bertalan Árkay, Sándor Faragó, József Fischer, Károly Heysa, Pál Ligeti, Farkas Molnár, Móric Pogány, Gábor Preisich, Mihály Vadász, Housing complex of the Department of National Social Security (OTI), Budapest, Köztársaság tér 14-16, 1933–34

Section, floor plan
Repr. from: Tér és forma, VIII, 1935

View of completed blocks
Photo mounted on card, 24 x 33 cm
MEM Budapest
© Gábor Barka

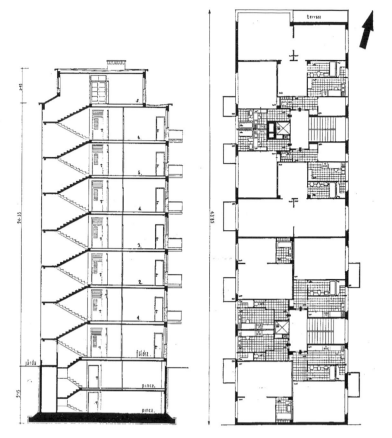

Zagreb, 1923-37

ARCHITECTURE OF INTER-WAR ZAGREB

Aleksander Laslo

The end of the Austro-Hungarian Monarchy and the founding of the Kingdom of the Serbs, Croats, and Slovenes in 1918 established a new framework for the development of Zagreb. As the social, political, and cultural center of the Croats, the town was faced with a rapid growth in population and with ensuing social and political problems. To find a solution to these problems it was essential that contact and subsequent cooperation between community interests and the ambitions of the private industrial sector be established, and this was also echoed in the architectural field.[1] Now it was no longer merely the private entrepreneurs who stood behind architecturally ambitious projects, but also the municipal authorities, who were now attempting to deal with the housing shortage by carrying out an extensive social building program.

During the 1920s several municipal housing estates were built which were based on a combination of two fundamentally different models: the urban super block, which followed the example of Viennese communal building complexes ["courtyards"], and the *Siedlungen* [housing estates], which were built particularly in Germany and had their roots in the ideas of the Garden City movement. The urban housing estates "Ciglana" (Klaićeva 9–11b, 1920–21) and "Kanal" (Radnička cesta 16–18a/Botićev trg 1–2, 1925) by Pavao Jušić and "Gogoljin brijeg" (Petrova 69–79/Medovićeva 2–26/ Kovačevićeva 1–17, 1927–28) by Edo Mikloš-Schreiner are evidence not only of the socially motivated efforts of the Zagreb architectural scene, but also of its striving to find a more concise and pared-down formal language. These examples of municipal support for residential housing were also exhibited at the International Congress on Housing Construction and Town Planning in Paris in 1928.

The private entrepreneurs, too, were anxious to foster and expand their international contacts. Thus the jury of the 1921

competition for the Zagreb Stock Exchange and Esplanade Hotel also included Hermann Muthesius. Viktor Kovačić managed to win the contract for the Stock Exchange. His masterpiece, built at Trg Burze 3 between 1923 and 1927, is notable for its simplicity and strength, and, in its use of Doric elements, recalls the Loos House on Vienna's Michaelerplatz. Shortly after completion, it achieved the status of protected site. Meanwhile, the Esplanade Hotel by Dionis

Bogan Petrović, Gomboš & Kauzlarić, Slavko Löwy, Villa Colony, Zagreb, Novakova, 1931–1938
Photo: Tošo Dabac, c. 1937

Josip Pičmann & Josip Seissel, Project for the building of the so-called 'Zakladni blok' [block funded by an endowment], Jelačićev trg, Zagreb, 1932

Perspective view

Repr. from: Josip Pičman, Josip Seissel: Izložba projekta za izgradnju Zakladnog zemljišta na Jelačićevom trgu [Exhibition of the project for the construction of ' Zakladni zemlište' on the Jelačićev trg], exh. cat., Salon Ulrich, Zagreb, 1932

Sunko (Mihanovićeva 1, 1922–24) became a center of liberal, middle-class life and was the venue for press balls and beauty contests, provocative stage appearances by Josephine Baker, and a visit by Frank Lloyd Wright, long since forgotten.

The 1920s in Zagreb's architectural history was a period of rapid and important change. In 1919 the Technical University was founded (up to this point qualification as a *Baumeister* [master builder] had been the highest degree attainable in architectural studies) and in 1926 the competing *Meisterschule* [training school for master craftsmen] was established at the Academy of Fine Arts. At this time the last generation of architects who had been educated in other countries returned to Zagreb: Ivan Zemljak and Marko Vidaković from the Czech Technical University in Prague, Zlatko Neumann from Adolf Loos in Vienna and Paris, Drago Ibler from Hans Poelzig in Berlin, Juraj Neidhardt from Peter Behrens in Vienna and Berlin and, somewhat later, Stjepan Gomboš from the Technical University in Budapest, Antun Ulrich from Josef Hoffmann in Vienna, Slavko Löwy from Martin Dülfer in Dresden, and Zdenko Strižić from Hans Poelzig in Berlin. Their influence in the spread of the ideas and concepts of *Neues Bauen* in Zagreb was crucial. Ibler was head of the school at the Academy of Fine Arts which was striving to achieve reforms, and Zemljak, as the city's chief builder and architect, supervised the work of the municipal building department and executed almost all of the city council's building commissions (including a series of modern elementary schools: Jardanavac 108 and Selka 95, both from 1930–31).

Neidhardt and Vidaković were first and foremost striving to achieve an objective form of expression in their work (Theological Seminary, Voćarska 106, 1926–29, and the Pfeffermann Villa, Jurjevska 27a, 1928–29). In his manifesto-like program of *Neues Bauen*, *Architektur und Zeitgeist* of 1930[2] Zlatko Neumann broke decisively with the traditonal view of architecture, presenting a new volumetric conception of space (the Deutsch apartment block, Vukotinovićeva 5, 1928–29), as well as the basis for a new conception of interior design (König-Fuchs apartment, Palmotićeva 18, 1928).

The fundamental changes in views of architecture brought about in the wake of *Neues Bauen* held a potential that was exhausted by the next generation of Zagreb architects, leading to an "alignment" with modern architectural production. The initiative here did not come from a representative of Zagreb architecture but from a pioneer of the modern movement — Peter Behrens. With his redesign for the façade of the Stern House (formerly "Elsa Fluid," Jurišićeva 103, 1927–28), he once and for all paved the way for a general public recognition of the new architecture. The Behrens project is, in other respects, too, not a unique case. At this time Zagreb's pluralistic architectural scene, with its pronounced international orientation, offered foreign architects scope for intense and multi-faceted architectural work. A few examples of this can be seen in the new Municipal Abattoir by the German architect Walter Frese (Heinzelova 64–68, 1926–30), the French and the Czechoslovakian Pavilion for the Zagreb Exhibition grounds by Bernard Lafaille, Robert Camelot, and Ferdinand

Zagreb, Jelačićev trg

Elevation of the old hospital of the Brothers of Mercy with the comtemporaneous building of the first residential and business premises in the 'Zakladni blok'
Photo, c. 1933, 15×11cm
MKRH Zagreb

Stjepan Planić, Tower block of the Cooperative Bank 'Napretkova zadruga', Zagreb, Bognovićeva 1, 1936

Photo: Tošo Dabac, c. 1937
© Tošo Dabac archives, Zagreb

Fencl (Savska cesta 25, 1937–38), and the building of the insurance company "Assicurazioni Generali" by Marcello Piacentini (Jelačićev trg 3, 1937–40).

In 1930–31 special interest was generated abroad by three competitions in which an invited jury including Josef Gočár, Paul Wolf, Wilhelm Kreis, and Henry-Roger Expert examined entries by Paul Bonatz, Ludwig Hilberseimer, and Alvar Aalto.[3] Concurrent with this, Zagreb architects published their works in international specialist journals[4] and exhibited them in Paris, Berlin, London, and at the Milan Trienialle. They received prizes in competitions in Charkiv (Zdenka Strižić) and in Baťa's shoe town Zlín (Vladimir Potočnjak). Several architects who had qualified at the Zagreb College of Technology went abroad to work under distinguished representatives of modernism (Ernest Weissmann with Le Corbusier in Paris, Vladimir Potočnjak with Ernst May in Frankfurt, Josip Pičmann with Hans Poelzig in Berlin). A few architects in Zagreb joined the association of artists called "Zemlja" [The Earth] (Drago Ibler, Stjepan Planić, Mladen Kauzlarić, and

Lav Horvat) or were active within the "Zagreb Association" (Weissmann, Pičman, Antolić, Seissel, among others), which functioned as the Yugoslav regional group of the CIAM.

The principal characteristics of Zagreb architecture of the 1930s can be seen most clearly, perhaps, in a few major projects in the International Style, such as the complex of villas in the Novakova (Bodan Petrović, Stjepan Gomboš & Mladen Kauzlarić, and Slavko Löwy among others, 1931–38),[5] a new residential district along Zvonimirova or the unrealized project for a uniform arrangement of the so-called "Zlakladni blok" [a block funded by an endowment] (Josip Pičman & Josip Seissel, 1932) in the immediate town center.[6] Here, in contrast to the idealized model estates, a real spatial context for real consumers was realized that, besides exhibiting the characteristic traits of a consistently abstract morphology, also developed a great variety of individual and local means of expression.

Zagreb architecture of the 1930s did not merely cultivate the compositional rules of the classical discipline (seen in such buildings as the Academy of Commerce and Industry by Zvonimir Vrkljan, Krešimirov trg 1, 1931–35, or the Administrative Building of the Municipal Services by Juraj Denzler, Gundulićeva 32, 1932–35) or offered a broad field of activity to its *genius loci* (the apartment and business block of the Foundation for the Construction of the new polyclinic by Anton Ulrich and Franjo Bahovec, Petrićeva 1/Ilica 1a, 1932–33); it could also display such a wealth of features as: a concern for the new sky-line and urban scenery (as can be seen in the Radovan apartment and business block by Slavko Löwy, Masarykova 22, 1933–34, or the high-rise building of the Cooperative Bank "Napretkova zadruga" by Stjepan Planić, Bogovićeva 1, 1936), a sophisticated use of vernacular elements (the Villa Deutsch of Frane Cota, Vončinina 20, 1937), large expressive gestures (two new secondary school buildings by Egon Steinmann at Križanićeva 4–4a, 1932–34, and Kušlanova 52, 1936), and the technical architectural aesthetic of the Machine Age (exemplified by the Kraus and Podvinec villas of Ernst Weismann at Nazorova 29 and Jabukovac 23, both from 1936–37).

As early as the mid 1930s, Alfred Albini had emphasized the diversity of Zagreb's architectural production and its ambition to distinguish itself typologically, stylistically, and regionally within modern functionalist architecture:

Present-day architecture is international, yet, examined more closely, we can find a national and an individual direction. Features such as the enjoyment of color, preference for rhythmic repetition, clarity and simplicity of arrangement, by which we ourselves are characterized, can be expressed in the architecture of today…. The economic upturn of the first post-war years focused the attention of the foreign building industry on our market, making continuous international contact possible and so allowing us to keep pace with the pivotal points of civilization…. However, outside trends should be reflected here, we will retain our individuality in all that we do.[7]

Albini, in his view of the situation, was certainly not mistaken. The new architecture of the 1920s and 1930s in Zagreb was to become a point of orientation and reference for subsequent generations. Its influence made it possible not only to escape the new course of Social Realism laid down under the specific social and political circumstances of the 1950s, but is still to be felt in Zagreb's architectural production today.

1 For the architecture of Zagreb during the inter-war years see *Arhitektura* [Architecture], Zagreb, vol. XXX, 1976, nos. 156–57. *Arhitektura*, Zagreb, vol. XL, 1987, nos. 1–4; pp. 200–203; Tomislav Prmerl, *Hrvatska moderna arhitektura između dva rata* [Modern Croatian Achitecture in the Inter-war Years], Zagreb, 1989; Aleksander Laslo, "Arhitektura modernog građanskog Zagreba" [The Architecture of the Modern Bourgeois in Zagreb], in *Život umjetnosti* [The Life of Art], Zagreb, vol. XXX, 1995, nos. 56–57, pp. 58–71.

2 N.S. [Nikola Smolčić], "Arhitektura i savremeni duh. Kod arhitekta Zlatka Neumanna" [Architecture and Zeigeist: A Visit with the Architect Zlatka Neumanna], in *Novesti* [The New], Zagreb, XXIV, 1930, no. 60, p. 5.

3 Architects from Croatia, Austria, France, Hungary, Germany, Spain, Romania, Finland, Switzerland, and other countries participated in the three competitions (new Jewish Hospital, new Polyclinic in Zagreb-Šalata, General Development Plan for the City of Zagreb). For more details see Bogdan Rajakovac, "Za modernu arhitekturu ili proti nej? Povodom izložbe projekata za Židovsku bolnicu a Zagrebu" [For or Against Modern Architecture? On the Occasion of the Exhibition of Projects for the Jewish Hospital in Zagreb], in *Merkurov vjesnik* [The Messenger Mercury], Zagreb, vol. XXVII, 1931, no. 5, pp. 103–04; ibid., "O savremenim arhitektima. Marginalija k izložbi projekata za novu Zakladnu i kliničku bolnicu u Zagreba" [About Contemporary Architects: Marginalia on the Exhibition of Projects for a new Polyclinic in Zagreb], in *Merkurov vjesnik*, Zagreb, vol. XXVII, 1931, nos. 7–8, pp. 187–88; Aleksander Laslo, "Internacionalni natječaj za generalnu regulatornu osnovu grada Zagreba 1930/1931" [The International Competition for the General Development Plan of the City of Zagreb 1930/1931], in *Čovjek i prostor* [Man and Space], Zagreb, vol. XXXI, 1984, no. 1/370, pp. 25–31.

4 See for example L. Ilitch [Ljubomir Ilić], "L'architecture en Yougoslavie" [Architecture in Yugoslavia], in *L'Architecture d'Aujourd'hui* [Architecture Today], Boulogne, vol. IV, 1933, no. 6, pp. 41–55.

5 For Novakova see Branko Siladin, "Novakova ulica, Zagreb. Primjer hrvatske moderne—Arheologija ili uzor?/Novak Street, Zagreb; A Sample of Croatian Modernism—Archaeology or Example?" in *Piranesi*, Ljubljana, vol. IV, 1995, nos. 5–6, pp. 6–34.

6 Instead of the original project several individual apartment and business blocks were later built (designed, among others, by Slavko Löwy, Otto Goldscheider, Stjepan Planić, Ulrich & Bahovec, 1932–38).

7 Alfred Albini, "Arhitektura sadašnjice" [The Architecture of the Present], in *Hrvatsko kolo* [The Croatian Round Dance], Zagreb, vol. XVI, 1935, p. 287.

Urbanism and Modernity in the New Zagreb

During the course of the 1920s, Zagreb increasingly took on the appearance of a modern capital. A generation of architects trained abroad returned at this time (among them Ernest Weissmann, who had studied with Le Corbusier; Drago Ibler and Zdenko Strižić, students of Hans Poelzig; and Antun Ulrich, a pupil of Josef Hoffmann). They rapidly assured a place for modernist thinking in city planning. The decision to develop a new plan for Zagreb through a competition sparked international interest, with Paul Bonatz and Ludwig Hilberseimer among those who submitted designs. The fundamental features of Zagreb architecture in the 1930s derived from a number of large modernist projects, such as the ensemble of villas along Novakova Street (1931–38) and the extensive use of commercial buildings right next to the city's center. Further inspiration from the international scene, and from Adolf Loos, appears in the Zagreb stock exchange, built between 1923 and 1927 after the designs of Viktor Kavačić.

Zagreb, East Side of Jelačićev trg with the Savings Bank by Ignjat Fischer (1926–30) and the Stern House (formerly "Elsa Fluid"), New Façade Design by Peter Behrens, 1927–28

Postcard, c. 1930
MKRH Zagreb

International Competition for the General Regulatory Plan for the City of Zagreb, 1930–31

Carl Christof Lörcher, Berlin, motto "Grad Hrvata", 4th prize
Rebuilding plan to scale 1 : 25,000 on the map of Zagreb and surroundings of 1929, sheet I
Colored print, mounted on card, 69.5 x 81.5 cm
HDA Zagreb

Carl Christof Lörcher, Berlin, motto "Grad Hrvata", 4th prize
Perspectival view of a city district, sheet X
Indian ink, wash on paper, mounted on card, 66 x 98 cm
HDA Zagreb

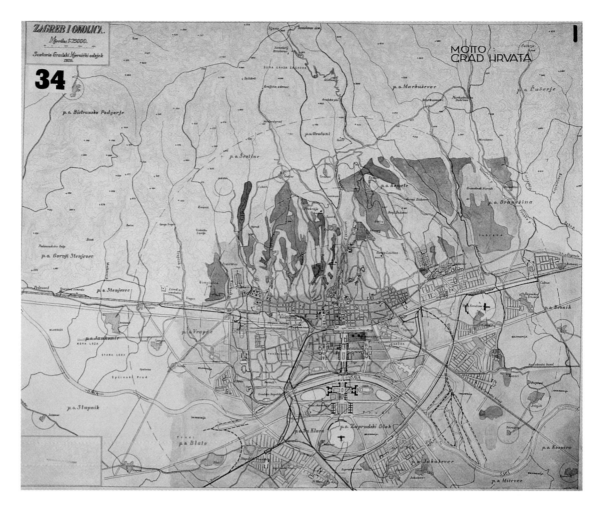

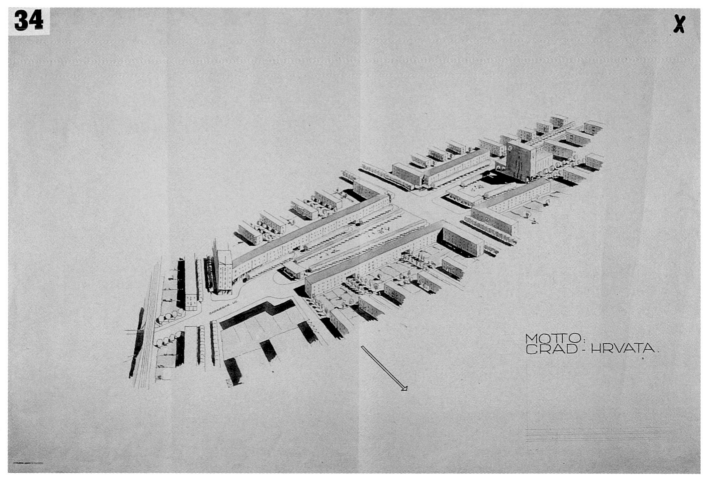

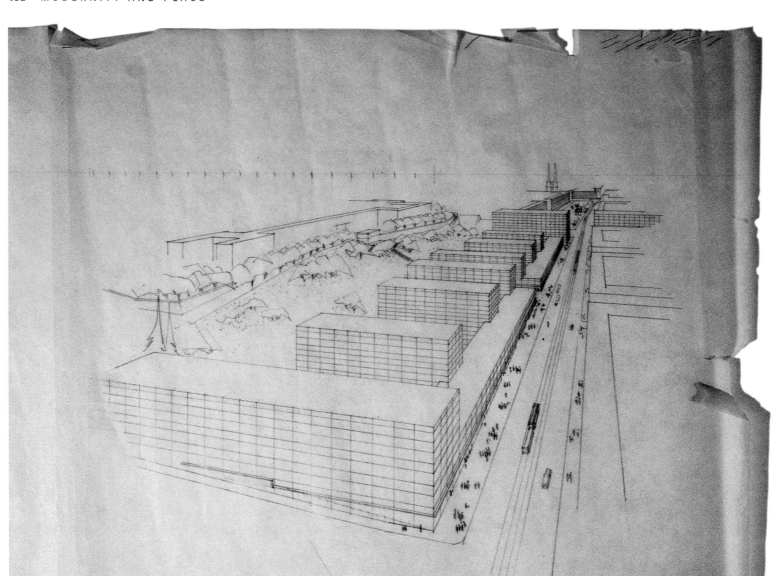

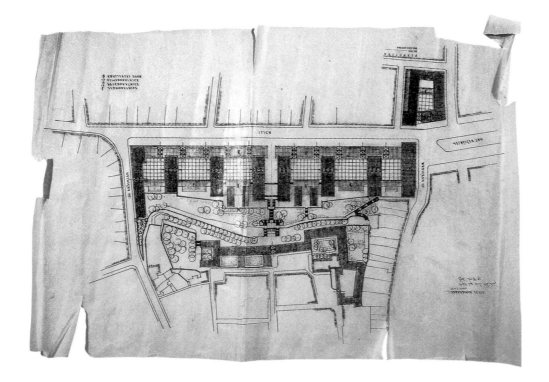

Zdenko Strižić, Study for the Development of the Ilica, Zagreb, 1931

Bird's eye view of of the square
Pencil on transparent paper, 38 x 50 cm
MKRH Zagreb

Plan, scale 1 : 1000
Pencil and indian ink on transparent paper,
46 x 69.5 cm
MKRH Zagreb

Ernest Weissmann, Competition Project for the Design of a Hospital, Zagreb, Na Šalati, 1930–31 (1st prize)

Bird's-eye view
Photomontage, 17.5 x 23 cm
Laslo collection, Zagreb

Antun Ulrich, Franjo Bahovec, competition sketch for offices and workers' accomodation in the Ciglana-Gründen, Zagreb, Ciglana, 1932–33

2nd round of competition, perspective
Charcoal on transparent paper,
47.5 x 90.5 cm
HMA Zagreb

Slavko Löwy, Radovan Residential and Business Premises, Zagreb, Masarykova 22, 1933–34

View at night
Photo: Donegani, Zagreb, from the
1930s, 23 x 16.5 cm
Levan collection, Zagreb

Slavko Löwy, Lebinec Residential and
Business Premises, Zagreb, Ribnjak 20,
1937–38

View after completion
Photo: c. 1933, 18 x 13 cm
Levan collection, Zagreb

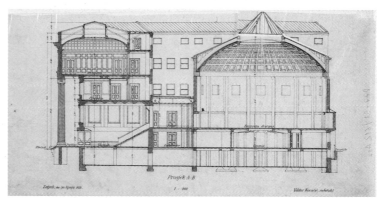

Viktor Kovačić, Stock Exchange,
Zagreb, Trg Burze 3, 1923–27

Section, scale 1 : 100, 1922
Indian ink on transparent paper,
30.5 x 62 cm
MKRH Zagreb

View
Postcard, c. 1928
Laslo collection, Zagreb

Ljubljana, 1895–1937

FROM PROVINCIAL TO NATIONAL CENTER: LJUBLJANA

Breda Mihelič

Ljubljana had, until the end of the nineteenth century, a very provincial character. Although the city had been connected to the rail network in the middle of the century, stimulating the development of industry and leading to a growth in the population and an expansion of the town, building activities were intensified only in the last quarter of the century resulting in the construction of new parts of the town between the old town center and the railway.

The earthquake which devastated the town in 1895 represented the turning point. More than ten percent of the buildings were destroyed and almost all the rest were severely damaged. Immediately after the earthquake, the municipal council began to prepare a general development plan which served as a basis for the rapid and effective reconstruction of the town and which provided general guidelines for the further development and expansion of the city.

Top experts in urban planning of the time were invited to participate in this task, including Camillo Sitte, proponent of a culturalist approach to urban planning, and Maks Fabiani, representing a progressivist urban planning model.[1] For the first time in history the future of the city of Ljubljana was discussed in a comprehensive way.

Sitte's concern was not so much with the growth of the town and its general functional organization.[2] He was more interested in individual details such as the layout of streets, the positioning, arrangement, and composition of the main square, the creation of urban prospects, etc. He concerned himself with only a small area of the town (about 250 hectares) where to a large extent he preserved the existing structure, changing only the courses and widths of some streets. For the new areas, however, he designed several streets and a monumental new square surrounded by representative public buildings.

Fabiani took a more scientific approach[3] and in 1895 published an explanatory report together with his plans[4] that addressed the entire range of urban problems—functional as well as aesthetic and architectural—at all levels simultaneously. Even more than Sitte he took the existing structures of the old town into account, carefully analyzing them, defining their basic features, and using them as the basis for his project. He repeated the motif of two roads winding themselves halfway around the castle hill on each bank of the river Ljubljanica. These form a new ring road which encircles the entire densely populated city area and its immediate surroundings. Though at the end of the century Ljubljana did not yet have to contend with the typical problems of the metropolis, as Vienna did, Fabiani was already then raising the question of its future urban development. He anticipated the expansion of the town beyond the railway line towards the north. In 1899 he prepared a plan for the reorganization, development, and incorporation of the northern part of the town, the present district of Bežigrad.[5]

Fabiani was also the first to base his urban plan on zoning and to foresee future traffic problems. The official development plan which the civil engineer Jan Duffé prepared by request of city council was based mainly on Fabiani's proposals. It was approved by the city in 1896.[6] Interestingly, this plan served as a basis for the development and reconstruction of the town center for more than fifty years and—what is truly astounding—some of the solutions that Fabiani proposed in the 1895 plan are still effective today.

In the first decade of the twentieth century the image of Ljubljana changed drastically. The number of houses and buildings tripled compared to 1890. Three-, four-, and five-story buildings were built in the former suburbs and the newly developing areas (Vodmat, Spodnja Šiška, Grajski hrib

Ljubljana, Slovenski trg (now
Miklošičev park)

The Law Courts on the left and on the
right, flanking them, the Krisper House
(Maks Fabiani, 1900–01), a model project
for the further development of the square
Postcard, before 1915
ZAL Ljubljana

Ljubljana, Slovenski trg
Laibach

[castle hill]) became districts of Ljubljana. Wide, paved streets were laid out and new squares and parks created. New types of building serving new activities sprang up, such as theaters, museums, hospitals, schools, hotels, department stores, banks, baths, industrial plants, etc. lending a newly modern look to the town. New residential areas with apartment blocks or single family houses also changed the town's overall appearance and an electric tram system connected the suburbs with the center.

The majority of buildings were constructed by local building contractors and masons. The most important building contractor was the Carniolan Building Company [Kranjska Stavbna Družba] established in 1873, which built almost all the important buildings in Ljubljana.[7]

In addition, there were a number of medium-sized family enterprises, for example those of the Faleschinis, Schupplers, and Tönnies, as well as the construction company of Filip Supančič.[8] Some these firms employed architects on a permanent basis or recruited them for special projects. Functional buildings, such as army barracks, hospitals, and railway stations, were built to standard plans, drawn up in planning offices chiefly in state departments in Vienna. Residential architecture was, with a few exceptions, designed by the local contractors themselves, while designs for the most important representative buildings were usually chosen by means of competitions. The participating architects were foreign, mostly from Vienna and other cities of the Monarchy, which contributed to the international character of Ljubljana's architecture at the end of the century.

When Ivan Hribar became Mayor of Ljubljana he insisted on establishing contacts with other Slavic, especially Czech, architects. He appointed the Czechs Jan Vladimír Hrásky and Jan Duffé as architects in charge of the municipal building office and employed Czech architects for important architectural works. He also succeeded in securing the expertise of Maks Fabiani for some important projects in Ljubljana. On his initiative, Fabiani was invited by the municipal council to develop the plan for the square in front of the Law Courts, Slovenski trg (1899, now Miklošičev Park), and to submit a new design for the façade of St. Jacob's Primary School for Girls (1900–01). Hribar also entrusted Fabiani with the design of his own house (Tavčarjeva ulica 2, 1902–03).

Around the turn of the century and later, architectural design here as elsewhere in the monarchy was dominated by historicism without any particular local or national features. Almost all public buildings were designed in a neo-Renaissance style. Jugendstil, which implicitly affirmed the notion of a national identity in architecture, did not come into fashion until the beginning of the twentieth century, and then only gradually. This was due, among other factors, to a certain provincial conservatism which was hostile to any change, and the municipal officials were particularly averse to modern ideas. The mentality of the civil servants is clearly revealed in the competition for the design of the so-called Country House [*Deželni dvorec*]. Although the competition was won by the young Joseph Maria Olbrich,[9] the contract was awarded to Jan Vladimír Hrásky and the building was later remodeled by the Viennese architect Josip Hudetz in a pure neo-Renaissance style. Jugendstil was adopted only by a small circle of wealthy citizens who wanted to keep pace with the latest trends and fashions, but it was not identified with an emerging national consciousness to the extent that it was in other Central European countries.

Jugendstil did not make its mark on the architecture of Ljubljana until the first decade of the twentieth century. Its main influence came from Vienna, but a few buildings

Friedrich Sigmundt, Urbanc Business Premises, Ljubljana, Prešernov trg/
Trubarjeva ulica 1, 1902–03

View of interior
Photo: Miran Kambič, 1997

The buildings designed by Jože Plečnik left a distinctive stamp on that part of the town center which is enclosed by the railway line. With the support of Matko Prelovšek, director of the city planning department, and France Stele, director of the Society for the Preservation of Monuments, Plečnik created from the mid-1920s several magnificent public squares and a series of important architectural monuments. His subtle urban design of the town center is quite impressive. The axis running from the square-like widening of the Eipprova ulica in Trnovo over the new Trnovo Bridge to the redesigned Emonska cesta, crossing the Trg francoske revolucije [Square of the French Revolution] to Vegova ulica and Kongresni trg [Congress Square], finally ending in a newly designed but never realised square to the north of the present-day Zvezda Park, connects the southern part of the town with the core of the old town. The footpath to the castle hill via the Tromostovje [The Three Bridges] to the covered market links the town on both sides of the Ljubljanica. In his designs for Ljubljana, Plečnik acted more as 'urban artist' rather than an urban planner, using traditional architectural elements such as monuments, obelisks, fences, various kinds of pavement, green areas, and elegant details, to reshape existing urban spaces and to combine them into a unified, but varied, whole. His architecture took as its model the forms of Antiquity employing Classical antique forms and composed of classical elements, transformed and adapted to new uses. His first important building in Ljubljana was the Church of St. Francis in Šiška and his last, the cemetery in Žale—considered to be the synthesis of his entire work.

The new, functionalist trends in architecture developed in the shadow of the great master and needed a longer time to unfold. The appeal to earlier national architectural styles which occurred in the successor states of the former monarchy strongly influenced the work of Ivan Vurnik, who designed two of his most significant buildings in a regional/Romanticist variant of Jugendstil: the Cooperative Bank and the Sokol Gymnastic Society Hall. After the academic year 1925–26 Vurnik divorced himself from Plečnik's ideas and devoted himself exclusively, in theory and in practice, to promoting modern architecture and modern urban planning.[10]

Functionalism/*Neues Bauen* did not assume a radical character in Ljubljana. In the period prior to World War II it spread only moderately finding application mainly in the area of residential building. The earliest collective housing estates in a modern style were built in the late twenties by the older generation of Slovenian architects (Vladimir Šubič, Vladimir Mušič, Ivo Spinčič, Josip Costaperaria among others) who took their cue largely from contemporary German and Austrian architecture.[11] The urban villas in the Levstikova ulica and surroundings, built in the late twenties, are reminiscent of the contemporary Weissenhof estate in Stuttgart built in 1927 for the Deutscher Werkbund exhibition *Die Wohnung* [The

demonstrated the influence of the Budapest and Prague varieties of Jugendstil and even of the more distant Belgian Art Nouveau architecture, as can be seen for example, in the Urbanc commercial building on the Trubarjeva ulica.

World War I brought about the ultimate break with the nineteenth century and the Habsburg dynasty. The union of the Slovenian territories to form a new state within the monarchy of the southern Slavs and the Ljubljana's new role as capital stimulated the development of the town. Several important new cultural institutions were established, including, among others, the National Gallery, the Municipal Museum, the Academy of Arts and Sciences, the National and University Library, a broadcasting station and—most importantly—the University of Slovenia. The foundation of a Department of Architecture within the Faculty of Science and Technology (1920–21) and the work and teaching activity of Jože Plečnik and Ivan Vurnik gave a fresh impetus to the architecture and urban character of Ljubljana during the post-war period. From that time on almost all architectural projects in Ljubljana were designed and carried out by Slovenian architects.

Ivan Vurnik, Sokol Building, Ljubljana,
Tabor 13, 1923–26
Photo: Miran Kambič, 1997

Apartment].[12] The so-called "Dukić apartments" to the south of the Ajdovščina Park (Jože Sivec, 1933) were the first examples of detached houses in a green area. New concepts for building tenement blocks were widely adopted especially after 1935, when the city council launched a major social housing program for which it hired a number of young architects.[13]

The town center shifted, from the old medieval core of the old town to the north. At the beginning of the 1930s a new business center was constructed on the western side of Slovenska cesta between Cankarjeva ulica and the present-day Ajdovščina Park. Six-story commercial buildings, mostly owned by banks and other financial institutions, began to tower above the city's otherwise low skyline. The thirteen-story "Skyscraper" [*Nebotičnik*], the first high-rise in Ljubljana, designed and built by Vladimir Šubic between 1930 and 1933, represented the crowning achievement for this center— a symbol of the new economic strength and the financial upturn of the city.

The expansion of the town and the swift development of the peripheral areas such as Bežigrad, Šiška, Moste, and Vič[14] made a new development plan seem necessary.[15] In this connection two interesting proposals are worth mentioning, of which (just like the two proposals made subsequent to the earthquake of 1895) one represents a culturalist, and the other a progressivist approach: Plečnik's master plan of 1928[16] and the design that was prepared as a dissertation in Vurnik's seminar in 1935.[17]

On the invitation of the municipal building office, Plečnik agreed to prepare a master plan for the city. As he explained in his report, he adopted existing plans and supplemented them with new detailed designs for particular areas within the Old City as well as with proposals for developing new districts outside the historic center. Plečnik also prepared the development plan for the northern parts of the town—the earlier Svetokriški okraj [Holy Cross area], now Bežigrad.

Like Fabiani thirty years earlier, he conceived his plan after Wagner's *Großstadt* (Vienna), designing a district equipped with all necessary services. Its streets, organized in a fan-like pattern, ran—unlike Fabiani's design—towards Dunajska cesta, over which they were then linked to the town center. Plečnik's plan, although at first sight very formalistic, was much better adapted than Fabiani's to the city structure, as it had evolved. Because of this, his plan had a marked influence on the urban development of Bežigrad not only prior but also subsequent to World War II.

Vurnik's contribution to the urban development of Ljubljana, as presented in the regulation study of his students in 1935, was also important, but more on a theoretical level than through completed buildings. Influenced by contemporary international trends, Vurnik was much more concerned with the functional organization of the town than with its formal structure. He elucidated his views on the problems of urban development in Ljubljana in his many papers and lectures, particularly in 1940, when he was chairman of the jury in the competition for a regulatory plan of Ljubljana.

This, the first open competition held in Yugoslavia, concluded the second phase of the development of modern Ljubljana. The competition results, however, had very little influence on the third phase, which, after World War II, took place against a completely different political, economic, and cultural background.

Vladimir Šubič, Complex of Business Premises with the 'Nebotišnik' [skyscraper], Ljubljana, Slovenska/Štefanova, 1930–33

Photograph from the 1930s
ZAL Ljubljana

6 Cf. *Zgodovinski arhiv Ljubljane (ZAL)* [Historical Archives Ljubljana (ZAL)], Cod. III / 45–1895, folio 326.

7 Cf. *Krainische Baugesellschaft in Laibach 1873–1898. Denkschrift über die Thätigkeit der Krainischen Baugesellschaft während des ersten Vierteljahrhundertes ihres Bestandes 1873–1898* [Carniolan Building Company in Ljubljana 1873–1898: A Memorandum on the Activities of the Company During the First 25 Years of Its Existence 1873–1898], Ljubljana, 1898.

8 Cf. Vlado Valenčič, "Gradbeni razvoj Ljubljane od dograditve južne železnice 1849 do potresa 1895" [The Architectural Development of Ljubljana from the Construction of the Southern Railway in 1849 to the Earthquake of 1895], in *Kronika* (Ljubljana), IX, 1961, no. 3, pp. 135–44.

9 Olbrich was awarded second prize; no first prize was awarded.

10 Cf. Ivan Vurnik, "Arhitekturni oddelek naše univerze" [The Department of Architecture of our University], in *Slovenec* [The Slovene] (Ljubljana), 1927, no. 269, p. 3.

11 The typology of the Viennese communal buildings ('Höfe' [courtyards]) in Vienna served as a model for the two most interesting housing complexes in Ljubljana: the 'Meksika' block of flats imitating the Sandleiten-Hof in Vienna (Njegoševa 6, Vladimir Šubič, 1926–27) and the so-called 'Red House' [Rdeča hiša] (Poljanska 13–15, Vladimir Mušič, 1928–29).

12 Josip Costaperaria built several houses on the Levstikova ulica, the house at no. 16 was built by Vladimir Šubič for himself (1929–30).

13 Cf. *Pet let dela za Ljubljano* [Five Years' Work for Ljubljana], Ljubljana 1940.

14 In 1935 Ljubljana was expanded by incorporating peripheral areas.

15 The new Yugoslav building legislation which was passed in 1931 contained a clause which obliged the city council of Ljubljana to prepare a new development plan (Cf. *Gradbeni zakon* [Building Legislation], Ljubljana 1932).

16 Jože Plečnik, "Študija regulacije Ljubljane in okolice" [Study for the Regulation of Ljubljana and its Surroundings], in *Dom in svet* [Home and World] (Ljubljana), XLI, 1928, suppl. 4, unpaginated.

17 Cf. Robert Tepež, Franc Hronek, Filip Kumbatovič, *Idejne rešitve k novi regulaciji Velike Ljubljane* [Conceptual Studies for the new Development Plan of Greater-Ljublana], 1935–36, now in the Archives of the Museum of Architecture in Ljubljana, UN, portfolio L–1. These studies were first discussed by Saša Sedlar, "Ivan Vurnik 1884–1971. Poskus orisa njegove vloge v sodobne urbanizmu" [Ivan Vurnik 1884–1971: An Attempt to Describe his Role in the Context of Contemporary Town Planning], in *Sinteza* (Ljubljana),1972, no. 23, pp. 25–27; Breda Mihelič, "Ivan Vurnik in Ljubljana / Vurnik and Ljubljana," in *Ivan Vurnik 1884–1971. Slovenski arhitekt / Ivan Vurnik 1884–1971. Slovenian Architect, Arhitektov bilten, posebna izdaja / Architect's bulletin*, special issue (Ljubljana), XXIV, 1994, nos. 119–24, pp. 79–90.

1 The idea of explaining the history of urbanism in terms of two basic models, culturalist and progressivist, first appeared in Françoise Choay, *L'urbanisme. Utopies et Réalités. Une anthologie*, Paris, 1965. Cf. also other works by the author in which she elaborates her views, e.g., *The Modern City: Planning in the 19th Century*, N.Y., 1965; *La règle et le modèle. Sur la théorie de l'architecture et de l'urbanisme*, Paris, 1980.

2 Cf. Boris Gaberščik, "Camillo Sittes Plan für Laibach. Ein Beitrag zur Aufgabenforschung des Städtebaus" [Camillo Sitte's Plan for Ljubljana: A Contribution to a Research Project in Urban Development], in *Berichte zur Raumforschung und Raumplanung* [Reports on Spatial Research and Planning] (Vienna), X, 1966, pp. 29–33. The plans remain with Sitte's estate in the Institute for Urban Development, Spatial Planning and Composition at the Institute of Science and Technology, Vienna.

3 The plan he presented contained the overall regulatory design to scale 1:5000, the main regulatory plan to scale 1:2880, in four parts, a view of St. Mary's Square (today Prešernov trg), as well as some detailed studies.

4 Cf. the report in German and in Slovenian: Max Fabiani, *Erläuterungs-Bericht zum Entwurfe eines General-Reguli[e]rungs-Planes der Stadt Laibach* [Exploratory Report on the Design of a General Development Plan for the Town of Ljubljana], Vienna 1895; Maks Fabiani, *Poročilo k načrtu občne regulacije stolnega mesta Ljubljane*, Dunaj (Vienna), 1895.

5 Maks Fabiani, "Pojasnilo k načrtu za osnovo in preosnovo severnega dela mesta Ljubljane" [Comments on the General Development Plan for the Northern Part of the City of Ljubljana], in Maks Fabiani, *Regulacija deželnega stolnega mesta Ljubljane* [Regulatory Plan for the Capital Ljubljana], Dunaj (Vienna), 1899, pp. 3–12 (facsimile reprint, Ljubljana, 1989).

The Persistence of Place: Plečnik's Ljubljana

Throughout the 1930s, Jože Plečnik's primary proposals and interventions in Ljubljana were geared to the restructuring of the city—physically, around its bridges, squares, castle, and riverbanks, and symbolically, around the recovery of its histories, real and imagined. Among these is a scheme for the conversion of Ljubljana's castle, which looks both to the founding myth of Illyria (in which the Slovenian nation serves as the repository of Roman culture) and to the courtly and folk traditions of the medieval city; a great riverside stoa (completed after World War II) to serve as a market hall; and proposals for monuments, bridges, municipal furniture, and riverside and castle walks. Opening a vista or a subtle axis here, adding a gate or monument or step there, Plečnik gradually cultivates the diverse fabric of this small-scale historic city into a unified promenade of national memory—a conception of modern architecture that adopts universal forms but remains particular to the geography and history of the site.

Jože Plečnik, Shoemakers' Bridge with a View of the Castle, Ljubljana 1931–32

Postcard
ZAL Ljubljana

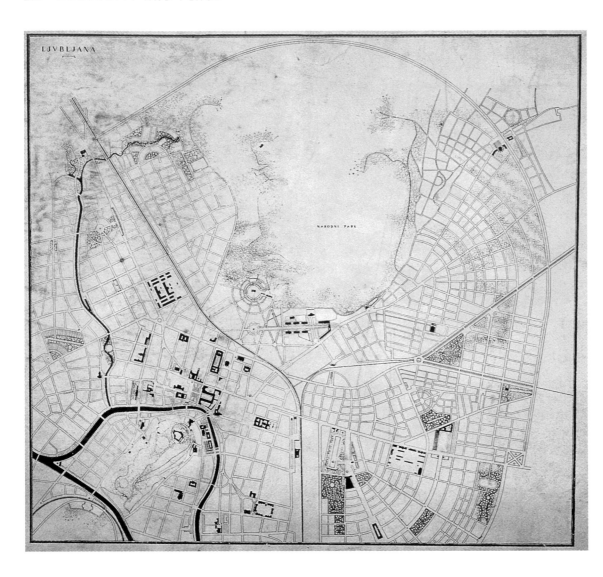

Jože Plečnik, A Study for the
Regulatory Plan of Ljubljana and
Surroundings, 1928

Print, 28.9 x 31 cm
Repr. from: Dom in svet, XLI, 1929
AM Ljubljana

Jože Plečnik, A Study for the
Regulatory Plan of the Ljubljanica,
Ljubljana, 1930

Colored print, 24 x 31 cm
AM Ljubljana

Jože Plečnik, Trnovo Bridge, Ljubljana,
1928–32

Postcard
ZAL Ljubljana

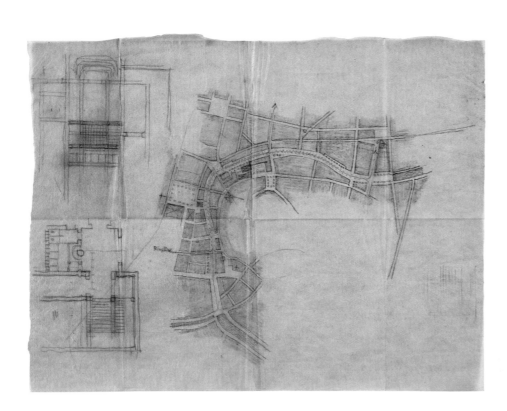

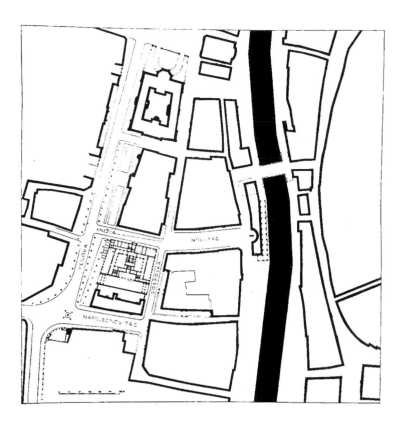

Jože Plečnik, Regulatory Plan for the
Vegova, Ljubljana, 1928–29

Print

Repr. from: Projekt Univerzitetne Biblioteke, Ljubljana,
Ljubljana, 1933
AM Ljubljana

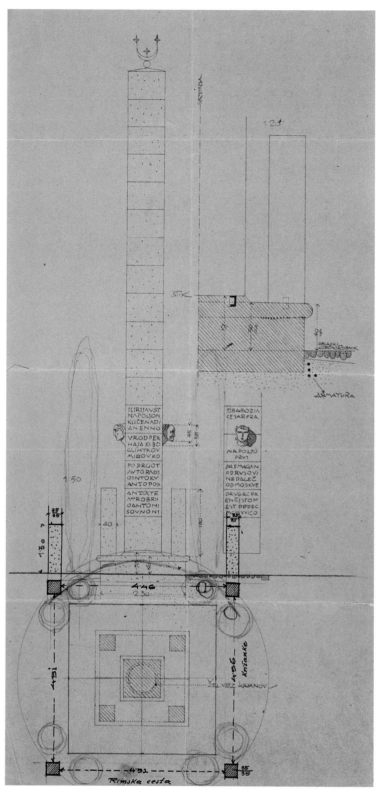

Jože Plečnik, The Spatial Arrangement
of Napoleonov trg (now Trg francoske
revolucije), Ljubljana, 1929

Napoleon Memorial
View
Processed print, 44.5 x 20.3 cm
AM Ljubljana

View of the square
Postcard
ZAL Ljubljana

LJUBLJANA - Napoleonov trg.

116a

Jože Plečnik, Tromostovje [The Three Bridges], Ljubljana, 1929

View at night
Postcard
ZAL Ljubljana

Several elevations and sections
Print, 68.1 x 94.8 cm
AM Ljubljana

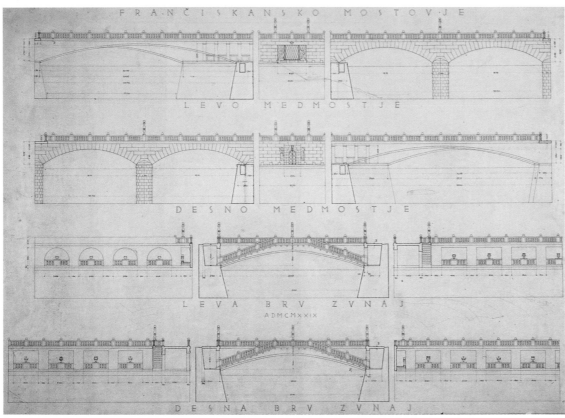

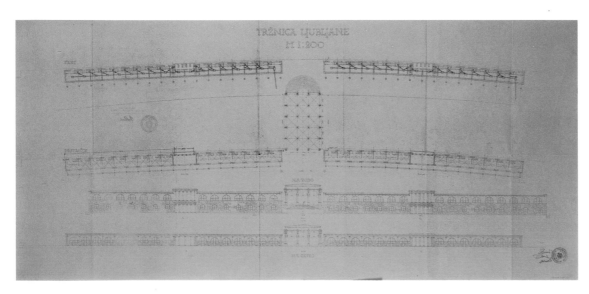

Jože Plečnik, Project for a Covered Market and Butchers' Bridge, Ljubljana, 1940–44

Plan, elevation
Print, 66.1 x 143 cm
AM Ljubljana

Vienna, 1919-34

GROßSTADT AND PROLETARIAT IN RED VIENNA

Eve Blau

A key episode in the history of modern European architecture, "Red Vienna" represents one of the most significant examples of large-scale urban intervention and political deployment of architecture in the inter-war period. For the Social Democrats who came to power in Vienna in 1919 and governed the Austrian capital until 1934, the building program—which involved the insertion of more than 400 new buildings known as *Gemeindebauten* into the existing fabric of Vienna—was the centerpiece of a wide-ranging program of reforms designed to reshape the social and economic infrastructure of Vienna along socialist lines. Architecturally, the *Gemeindebauten* represent the legacy of Otto Wagner's urban architectural vision as it was transmitted to his students: Karl Ehn, Hubert Gessner, Heinrich Schmid, Hermann Aichinger, and Rudolf Perco, among others, who received most of the large and important commissions, and whose work gave the architecture of Red Vienna its distinctive character.[1]

Learning to Dwell: The Garden Settlement Movement [Siedlerbewegung] in Vienna

A precursor and countermodel to the Social Democrat's program of municipal building was the radically independent settlement movement in Vienna that grew out of allotment gardening rather than Garden City ideas, and was a response to conditions of near famine in Vienna directly after the war. Beginning in 1915, as it became clear that neither the imperial bureaucracy nor the city administration was capable of providing shelter or enough food to sustain the two million inhabitants of the capital, private citizens took it upon themselves to provide their own makeshift dwellings and grow their own food on public land. This spontaneous self-help movement and wild settlement of public land soon evolved into a highly organized cooperative settlement movement that took an entirely different direction from the *Siedlungen* and garden suburb developments in Germany. It was shaped by architects and intellectuals—including Adolf Loos, Josef Frank, Margarete Schütte-Lihotzky, Gustav Scheu, Max Ermers, and Otto Neurath—who were sympathetic to garden city ideas but who also strongly supported the Social Democrats' social and economic policies for Vienna. As a consequence, the *Gartensiedlungen* they produced were very different from the ownership-oriented suburban settlements built in Central Europe before the war. Radically independent of bourgeois structures, they were cooperatively owned and run, anti-picturesque, urban, and inextricably bound to the cultivation of food.[2]

As chief architect of the *Siedlungsamt* from 1921–24, Adolf Loos played a significant part in determining the architectural and ideological character of Vienna's *Gartensiedlungen*; establishing design and planning guidelines, vetting designs, and drawing up an Allotment and Settlement Zoning plan for Vienna. The types developed by Loos were all row houses, whose organization, centered on the combined cooking and living area and kitchen garden [*Wohnküche und Nutzgarten*], emerged out of an analysis of the needs of the urban settler (employed for eight hours a day in a factory, workshop, or office) who undertook to grow his own food and participate in the construction of his house. Limited means, space, time, and skills were thus the determining factors in the design of house and garden, which had consequently to be not only economical but also simple—both to produce and to build. Loos's houses for the *Siedlung* Heuberg (Vienna XVII, in collaboration with Hugo Mayer, 1921–23) carried the logic of the *Gartensiedlung* further than any of his

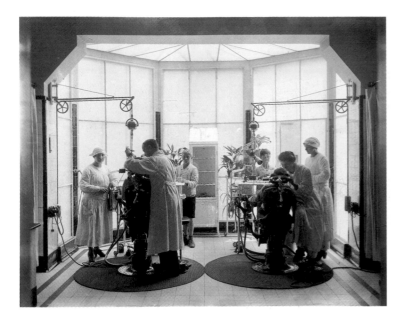

Adolf Stöckl, Julius-Tandler Hostel, Vienna IX, Lustkandlgasse 50, 1923–25
Dental clinic in the child adoption center
Photo: Gerlach, 1925
WSTLA Vienna

other designs. Built according to his patented construction "system Loos" in which adjacent houses share structural party walls from which the lateral walls are suspended, the Heuberg houses—each on its own plot of ground but part of a row of typified units, occupying little more than one-tenth of its long narrow lot, which was otherwise given over to productive gardening—were the most effective solution, in economic as well as social terms, to the post-war housing and food crisis in Vienna.[3]

Among the other architects who played a significant role in the *Siedlungsbewegung*, Margarete Schütte-Lihotzky made the most substantial contribution. Beginning in 1921 she undertook a thorough investigation of the optimal organization and equipment of the modern kitchen according to the

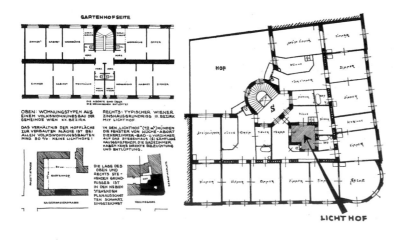

Juxtaposition of two ground plans: one of a typical Vienna tenement block with a light-well and another one of a social housing block of the city of Vienna with fenestration on both sides
Repr. from: Der Aufbau, I, 1926

"Taylor work method," a study that culminated in the *Frankfurter Küche*, the model kitchen she developed for the New Frankfurt in 1926. In 1922–23 Schütte-Lihotzky, under the auspices of the *Baubüro* [planning office] of the Österreichischer Verband für Siedlungs- und Kleingartenwesen [Austrian Association of Housing and Allotment Gardens], developed a new building concept, the *Siedlerhütte* [settlers' hut] and *Kernhaus* [core house], a simple, habitable structure in which the settler and family could live temporarily while the settlement house itself was under construction. According to *Siedlerhütte* type "B" for example, the hut would become the *Wohnküche* [kitchen and living area] of the full house.[4]

A response to the conditions of near famine in Vienna after World War I, the *Gartensiedlung* was abandoned as a housing form for the socialist municipality in the early 1920s when the worst of the economic crisis was over and the Social Democrats' priorities shifted from providing a starving urban population with provisional shelter and the means to supply its own food, to providing a newly enfranchised urban proletariat with permanent living space, social services, and employment.

The New Vienna

Inaugurated in 1923 with the introduction of a new "Housing Construction Tax" [*Wohnbausteuer*], the revenues of which (with other taxes) were to finance the new structures, the building program was carried out in less than 15 years. It involved the construction of 400 *Gemeindebauten* [communal buildings] throughout the city of Vienna, in which workers' housing was incorporated with a wide range of new social and cultural facilities: kindergartens, libraries, medical and dental clinics, laundries, workshops, theaters, cooperative stores, public gardens, sports facilities, and a wide range of other public facilities. Distributed throughout the city, the *Gemeindebauten* provided Vienna with not only a large amount of new living space—64,000 units in which one-tenth of the city's population was re-housed—but also a vast new infrastructure of social services and cultural institutions.[5]

The apartments in the new buildings, though modest compared to the Taylorized living environments of the New Frankfurt and Berlin, represented a significant improvement over existing tenement housing in Vienna: all rooms directly lit; toilets, running water, gas, and so forth contained within the apartment. But more significant than this, the new *Gemeinde-Wien-Type* apartments systematically erased all traces of the hated typological markers of the proletarian *Gangküchenhaus* [corridor kitchen tenement]—the long noxious corridor in which the shared water tap and toilet were located, and along which the dark one-room dwellings (themselves little more than passageways) were ranged— replacing it with a cluster of small, bright, interconnected

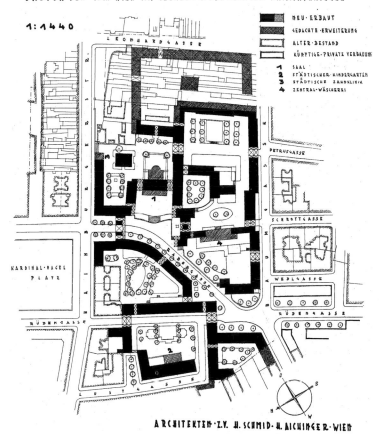

Heinrich Schmid, Hermann Aichinger, Rabenhof, Vienna III, Baumgasse 29-41, 1925–28

Site plan
Repr. from: Wohnhausanlage der Gemeinde Wien auf dem ehemaligen Gelände der Krimskykaserne im III. Bezirk, Vienna, 1928

View from the Rabengasse
Photo: Gerlach, 1930
WSTLA Vienna

rooms. Removing the corridor from the proletarian tenement also had urban implications. Since all rooms were directly lit and ventilated by windows facing onto either the street or a garden courtyard, the new buildings no longer had a privileged front and disadvantaged back, but rather two fronts. Furthermore, the façades, which for the first time in Vienna gave the full measure of the working class home, gave the proletariat itself a distinctive and privileged presence on the street.

Part public buildings, part dwellings, the new structures were monumental in scale—often occupying an entire city block and sometimes several—but were also intricately woven into the existing fabric of the city. Designed by 190 architects, a generation who had trained in Vienna before World War I (many with Otto Wagner) the new buildings represented the continuation of an architectural tradition rooted in the craft of building, the city, and a creative engagement with the facts of modern life. Typologically the *Gemeindebauten* differed radically from the widely spaced *Zeilenbau* [parallel row-block] favored by the modernist avant-garde and built in Germany during these years, which was oriented toward sun and grass and away from the street. Instead, the *Gemeindebauten*, which were densely built urban perimeter blocks, derived from a relatively new turn-of-the-century building type known in Austria as the *Arbeiterheim* [working

men's home], in which worker housing was spatially integrated with Social Democratic Party cultural and social institutions—a type first given shape by Hubert Gessner, a student of Otto Wagner and the designer of some of the most important *Gemeindebauten* of Red Vienna: the Metzleinstaler-Hof (Vienna V, 1919–25), the Reumann-Hof (Vienna V, 1924–26), and the Karl-Seitz-Hof (Vienna XXI, 1926–29). Of course the spatial organization around large open courtyards, from which the *Gemeindebauten* themselves were entered, has its origins in the traditional residential *Hofhaus* [courtyard building] types of Vienna, but it was assimilated through Gessner's earlier appropriation of the type in the *Arbeiterheim* Favoriten (Vienna X, 1901–12).[6]

But most important was the urban transformation effected by the new buildings. Defining squares and parks, they allocated not only private but also public space in the city to a social class that had previously had little access to either—and in the large interior courtyards created a new type of semi-public, communal space for the new form of socialized urban living envisioned by the Social Democrats. This is especially apparent in the group of buildings along the Margaretengürtel, designed by (among others) Gessner, Schmid, and Aichinger, Peter Behrens, and Josef Frank, known colloquially as the "Ringstrasse of the Proletariat." By replacing the analytical structure of streets, blocks, and open squares delineated by the *Regulierungsplan* (which enabled the speculative development of the turn-of-the-century city), the new socialist blocks created multiple-purpose, multiple-use spaces that destabilized while they seemed to reinforce

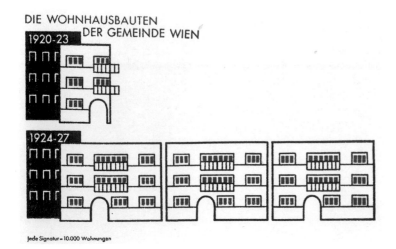

DIE WOHNHAUSBAUTEN DER GEMEINDE WIEN

1920–23

1924–27

Jede Signatur = 10.000 Wohnungen

Otto Neurath, Gerd Artz, *The New Housing Built for the Municipality of Vienna, c. 1928*

Exhibition panel showing distinctive proportions and features of new buildings against those of old tenements. Depicted according to the "Vienna method" of image statistics
Multicolor print, 21 x 30 cm
IC Reading

the existing order of the historical city by blurring the boundary between inside and out, public and private, insider and outsider.

It is the urban superblock that makes the significance of this kind of realignment of the urban terrain most clear. Inserted into the existing fabric of Vienna, the Karl-Marx-Hof (Vienna XIX, Karl Ehn, 1927–30), the Winarsky–Hof (Vienna XX, Peter Behrens, Joseph Frank, Oskar Strnad, Oskar Wlach, Josef Hoffmann, 1924–25), the Raben-Hof (Vienna III, Heinrich Schmid, Hermann Aichinger, 1925–28), and the Friedrich-Engels-Platz-Hof (Vienna XX, Rudolf Perco, 1930–33), and the other large building complexes that bridge streets to form superblocks, engage not only the topography but also the history of their urban sites, preserving what is there at the same time as introducing their own willfully aberrant scale and organization into the city. The political instrumentality of the new buildings lies in the Social Democrats' decision to allow the old order (of the *Regulierungsplan*) to coexist with the new order (of the socialist superblock) which, superimposed upon the old, engages it, enters into debate with it, and calls its authority into question.

There is also a discernible political dimension to the pluralistic forms of the *Gemeindebauten*, which are characterized by a play of standardization (of elements such as windows, doors, balconies, etc., that give the buildings a distinctive set of features and proportions) and highly individualized façade detailing. In terms of language, the *Gemeindebauten*, it can be argued, participate in the Social Democrats' wide-ranging program of public education and information; in particular, with the pictorial language of conventionalized type-forms developed by Otto Neurath and his associates to disseminate information about the building and social programs of Red Vienna at the Gesellschafts- und Wirtschaftsmuseum [Social and Economic Museum].[7] Like Neurath's type-forms (which he later called ISOTYPEs: International System Of TYpographic Picture Education), the *Gemeindebauten*, filled with historical allusion and local reference, communicated by means of conventionalized figures—portals, courtyards, arcades, balconies, standardized windows, communal facilities, and so on. It was through these typological markers of the new buildings that the *Gemeindebauten* became legible, communicating how each building was to be used and what its relationship was to the larger program of Red Vienna, as well as to the physical fabric of the historical city and the forces that had shaped it.

1 For a detailed list of the buildings and on the role of the Wagner school see Eve Blau, *The Architecture of Red Vienna 1919–1934*, Cambridge, Mass., and London, 1999.
2 Cf. ibid., pp. 90–133; Wilfried Posch, *Die Wiener Gartenstadtbewegung. Reformversuch zwischen erster und zweiter Gründerzeit* [The Garden City Movement in Vienna: An Attempt at Reform Between the First and Second *Gründerzeit*], Vienna, 1981; Klaus Novy, Wolfgang Förster, *Einfach bauen. Genossenschaftliche Selbsthilfe nach der Jahrhundertwende. Zur Rekonstruktion der Wiener Siedlerbewegung* [Building Simply: Cooperative Self-Help after the Turn of the Century—On the Reconstruction of the Viennese *Siedlerbewegung*], Vienna, 1985; as well as Hans Kampffmeyer's contemporary publication, *Siedlung und Kleingarten* [Housing Estate and Allotment], Vienna, 1926.
3 On Loos's designs for *Siedlungen* see Burkhardt Rukschcio, Roland Schachel, *Adolf Loos. Leben und Werk* [Adolf Loos: Life and Work], Vienna 1982, pp. 533–56.
4 On Schütte-Lihotzky see, for example, Peter Noever (ed.), *Margarete Schütte-Lihotzky. Soziale Architektur, Zeitzeugin eines Jahrhunderts* [Margarete Schütte-Lihotzky: Social Architecture, Witness to a Century], exh. cat., Österreichisches Museum für angewandte Kunst, Vienna, 1993.
5 Unable, for complicated legal/constitutional reasons, to expand beyond the existing boundaries of Greater Vienna, the Social Democrats determined to build in the city itself (cf. *Das Neue Wien* [The New Vienna], 4 vols., Vienna 1926–28). In the secondary literature detailed accounts of the financing and execution of the building program are given in Renate Schweitzer, *Der staatlich geförderte, der kommunale und der gemeinnützige Wohnungs- und Siedlungsbau in Österreich bis 1945* [The Publicly Funded, Communal, or Social Housing Programs in Austria Up to 1945], 2 vols., Phil.-Diss., Technische Universität Wien, 1972; Eve Blau, *The Architecture of Red Vienna 1919–1934*, pp. 136–51. The social and cultural programs are analyzed in Helmut Gruber, *Red Vienna. Experiment in Working-Class Culture, 1919–1934*, New York, 1991.
6 On Gessner's *Arbeiterheim* cf. the two essays by Markus Kristan, "Das Arbeiterheim Favoriten: Teil 1—Der Wettbewerb" [The Arbeiterheim Favoriten: Part 1—The Competition] and "Das Arbeiterheim Favoriten: Teil 2—Das vollendete Bauwerk" [The Arbeiterheim Favoriten: Part 2—The Completed Building], in *Wettbewerbe (Wien)* [Competitions (Vienna)], XVII, 1993, nos. 119–20, pp. 126–30 and XVII, 1993, nos. 121–22, pp. 109–12.
7 Otto Neurath, "Aufgaben des Gesellschafts- und Wirtschaftsmuseums in Wien" [Functions of the Social and Economic Museum in Vienna] in *Der Aufbau (Wien)* [Construction (Vienna)], I, 1926, pp. 169–74.

The Social Democratic City

The building program of Red Vienna provided the devastated capital of the former empire and new Republic of Austria with much-needed housing as well as a vast new infrastructure of social and cultural institutions and facilities. These components of the Social Democratic City, plotted on the map of the "New Vienna," show the extent of the program over the entire city region. In the immediate post-war years of near famine and political uncertainty, before major building operations could begin, the city supported the cooperative Garden Settlement [*Kleingartensiedlung*] Movement, in which urban settlers participated in the building of their own dwellings and the cultivation of their own food. Progressive architects, among them Adolf Loos and Margarete Schütte-Lihotzky, played a major role in designing these developments; others, including the Bauhaus-trained partners Friedl Dicker and Franz Singer, designed spaces for the city's new Montessori kindergartens. Most of the new buildings were so-called *Gemeindebauten*, many designed by students of Otto Wagner, which incorporated workers' housing with socialist institutional facilities, gardens, and parks, to appropriate urban space and amenities for the newly enfranchised proletariat. Thus the area along the Margaretengürtel became a "Ringstrasse of the Proletariat." In northern districts, the Karl-Marx-Hof, the apartment block at Friedrich-Engels-Platz, and Winarsky-Hof, which each housed more than a thousand people, were "superblocks" that introduced a new order and scale of urban building in Vienna.

Erich Leischner, The New Vienna, 1931

Multicolored print, 50 x 66 cm

Repr. from: Tourist Commission of the Federal States of Vienna and Lower Austria (ed.), Das neue Wien. Ein Album mit Plan, Vienna, 1931

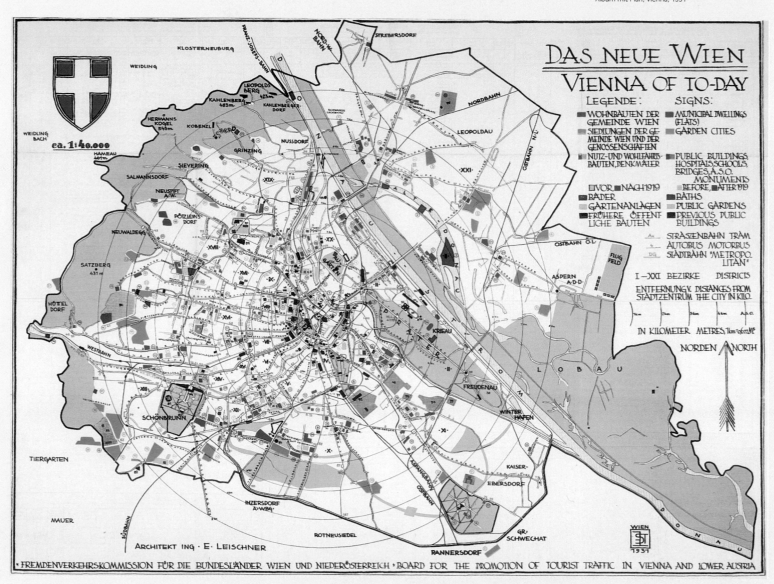

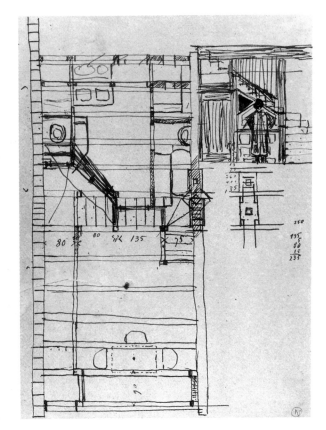

Adolf Loos, Projects for Settlement House Types, Vienna, 1921

5 m wide type
Blue ink on paper, 28 x 21 cm
Albertina Vienna
© VBK Vienna, 1999

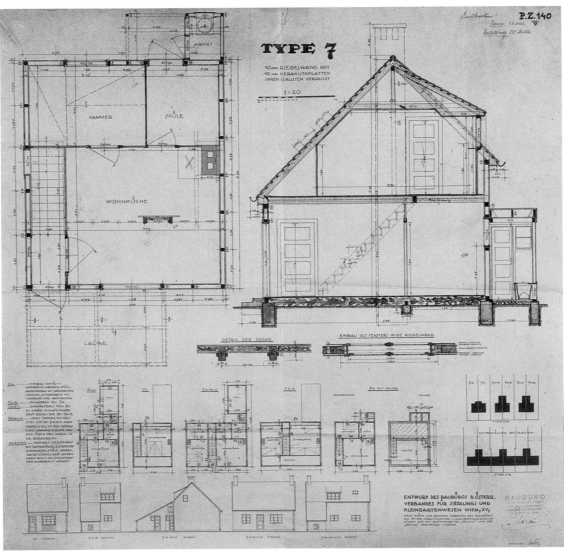

Margarete Schütte-Lihotzky, Core House, Type 7, 1923

Floor plans, section, elevations
Colored print, 74 x 71 cm
Schütte-Lihotzky collection, Vienna

Adolf Loos, Heuberg Model Estate,
"System Loos," Vienna XVII, Röntgen-
gasse 138, Plachygasse 1–13, 1921,
1923–24

Elevation, section, floor and garden plans
Print, 96 x 60 cm

Albertina Vienna
© VBK Vienna, 1999

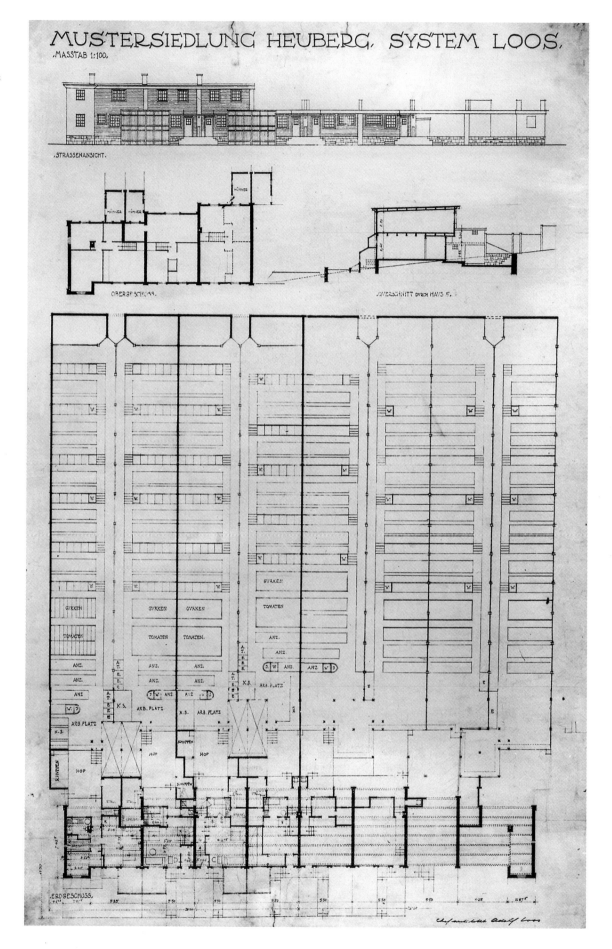

Hubert Gessner, Reumann-Hof, Vienna V, Margaretengürtel 100–110, 1924–26

View across Haydn-Park
Photo: Gerlach, c. 1925
WSTLA Vienna

Margarengürtel District General City Plan, Vienna, 1929

Sheet VIII, 5 showing new buildings
Print, 64 x 91 cm
WSTLA Vienna

Heinrich Schmid, Hermann Aichinger, Matteottihof, Vienna V, Siebenbrunnenfeldgasse 26–30, 1925–27

View across courtyard to the Fendigasse
Photo: Gerlach, c. 1928
WSTLA Vienna

Fritz Judtmann, Egon Riss, The People's House, Vienna V, Diehlgasse 20–26, 1928

Corner view
Photo: Gerlach, c. 1930
WSTLA Vienna

**Karl Ehn, Karl-Marx-Hof, Vienna XIX,
Heiligenstädterstraße 82–112, 1927–30**

View from forecourt
Photo: Gerlach, c. 1931
WSTLA Vienna

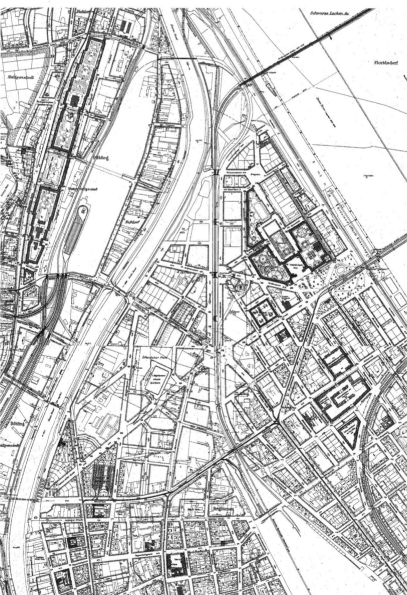

General City Plan, Vienna, 1942–46

Sheet III, 6, sheet IV, 6 showing ground
plan of Karl-Marx-Hof, Engelplatz-Hof,
Winarsky-Hof
Graphically processed
WSTLA Vienna

Rudolf Perco, Housing Complex at the Friedrich-Engels-Platz, Vienna XX, 1930–33

View of main façade
Photo: Gerlach, c. 1933
WSTLA Vienna

Oskar Strnad (in collaboration with Peter Behrens, Joseph Frank, Josef Hoffmann, Oskar Wlach), Winarsky-Hof, Wien XX, Stromstraße 74–76, Winarskystraße 17–19, Vorgartenstraße 44, Pasettistraße 44, Leystraße, 1924–25

Façade facing Winarskystraße
Photo: Gerlach, 1925
WSTLA Vienna

Prague, Brno, and Zlín, 1918-37

ARCHITECTURE AND SOCIETY

Rostislav Švácha

The Czechoslovakian Republic was founded on October 28, 1918, its territory situated in the most industrialized area of the disintegrated Danube monarchy. In contrast with its neighboring states it was, until 1938, based on a democratic form of government. In this liberal atmosphere, where the popular tendency was more towards the political left, the activities of the artistic avant-garde could flourish unimpeded: censorship or intervention by politicians was a rarity.

Domestically, the government could rely on the support of a strong middle class and pursued a course directed toward lessening the conflicts between capitalist entrepreneurs and the socially weaker classes. An important instrument in this undertaking was provided by modern architecture, whose democratic, even egalitarian character was emphasized by influential personalities of the Czech intelligentsia—foremost among these President Tomáš G. Masaryk—as well as by the architects themselves. They did, however, disagree on the question of whether the democratic character of architecture should first and foremost serve in a representational capacity for democracy, giving adequate expression to democratic institutions, or whether its predominant task lay rather in a fundamental democratization that would enable all layers of society to profit from its achievements and the new opportunities it offered.[1]

The beginning of a global economic crisis in 1929 proved to be a touchstone for both positions. The crisis undermined the upturn in the Czech economy, led to the impoverishment of large sections of the middle classes, and aroused in them a deep-rooted mistrust of capitalism. The government and the municipal authorities tried to maintain control by instituting social programs in which the construction of social housing played a not insignificant part. However, even during the periods when state and communal subsidies reached their

Jaromír Krejcar, Olympic Business Premises, Prague I, Spálená 16, 1925–28
Photo, c. 1927
AOV Prague 1

peak (1930–32 and 1936–38), social housing did not exceed more than 10 percent of the annual total volume of construction in Czechoslovakia.

Prague

After the founding of the new state, Prague became the seat of government and also the favored location for major banks and the head offices of leading companies and industries. Until the end of the 1920s the architectural scene in Prague was dominated by the conflict between those architects of the Otto Wagner school who wanted to give the new institutions a Neoclassical or national Rondo-Cubist appearance and the younger advocates of Purism and Functionalism. Gradually, however, almost all patrons became convinced that a modern, functionalist architecture was better suited to expressing the prosperity of the Czech economy, the scope of its democratic institutions, and the humanitarian ideals of the new republic. In 1924 Oldřich Tyl won the competition for the Prague Fairs Center with his functionalist project, and one year later construction work was begun in Prague's historic center on the first functionalist commercial buildings by Ludvík Kysela and Jaromír Krejcar.[2] The radical projects by Josef Štěpánek and Jaromír Krejcar received the two highest awards in the competition for a new government district in the Letná Plain of Prague, and finally the *Exhibition of Contemporary Culture in the Czechoslovakian Republic* in Brno (1928) symbolized the triumph of modern architecture on a national level.

Tyl and Kysela belonged to the circle around the architecture magazine *Stavba* [Construction], whose chief editor since 1923 was Karel Teige, the leading theoretician of the Prague avant-garde. Although many architects of the *Stavba* circle distanced themselves from Teige's Marxist and Soviet-ophile views, they agreed with him that, in the age of the industrial revolution, architecture would have to "liquidate" its artistic character and become a scientific discipline based on the findings of ergonomics, sociology, and standardization. Proceeding from these premises, Karel Teige launched a polemical attack on Le Corbusier's Mundaneum project in the forum of *Stavba*, accusing him of reactionary monumentalism.[3] Unlike their colleagues around *Stavba*, the architects of the avant-garde group Devětsil (1920–30), which had also been initiated by Teige, could not work up much enthusiasm for the idea of a scientific architecture. They tried rather to integrate the fascination of the modern metropolis, as celebrated by Baudelaire in literary form, into their architecture.[4]

From 1928 onward, Teige's writings show a growing interest in the sociology and typology of dwelling. He subsequently devoted numerous studies and papers to this vast subject, as he did for instance on the occasion of the third CIAM Congress in Brussels in a series of lectures at the Dessau Bauhaus, to which Hannes Meyer had invited him, or through his extensive publication *Nejmenší byt* [The Minimum-Sized Apartment] of 1932. Central to Teige's interest was the improvement of working-class living conditions, which he hoped to achieve through a collectivization of life-functions. This took shape in the collective residential building [*Koldům*], in which one-room sleeping cubicles without kitchen or double bed were to be supplemented by communal service facilities such as canteens, day nurseries, kindergartens, and clubs. His conception differed from similar Soviet projects for housing combines in that it accorded great importance to a meditative private life in the sleeping cubicles. Teige, moreover, attested to the active role his collective residence would play in the emancipation of women, an

Workers' Barracks with Baba Estate in the Background (Prague VI)
Photo: Ladislav Žák, c. 1932
Repr from: Světozor, XXXIV, 1934

important point on the agenda not only of the advocates of Marxism, but also of Czech anarchist circles.

An attempt to put Teige's vision into practice was undertaken in the L-project which was submitted to a competition for the City of Prague for apartment blocks with minimum-sized apartments in 1930. Entries were received from Jan Gillar, Josef Špalek, Augusta Müllerová, and Peer Bücking, all members of the architecture faction of the "Levá fronta" [Left Front]—a successor organization to the Devětsil group. The L-project, however, like the similarly-conceived KOLDOM project by Josef Havlíček and Karel Honzík, was rejected by the competition jury. Much to Teige's disappointment a similar scenario occurred a year later during the competition for residential buildings for the communist cooperative "Včela" [Bee]. Similar collective housing projects were submitted by, among others, Jiří Kroha, Havlíček and Honzík, Ladislav Žák, and Teige's then favorite architect Jan Gillar, whose French Schools in Prague (1932–34) can be regarded as the most precise practical application of Teige's conception of scientific functionalism.

Many architects were particularly frustrated by the fact that the new architecture benefitted the working classes less than it did the middle classes and affluent "individualistic" circles—as noted by Ladislav Žák, the architect of three residential buildings on the functionalist Baba housing estate in Prague-Dejvice, in a self-critical article of 1934 published in the magazine *Světozor* [A Look at the World].[5] In his discussion Žák takes up Vít Obrtel's trenchant thesis that Teige, with his theory of ergonomic minimal housing, had unintentionally accommodated capitalist entrepreneurial circles.[6] In 1934, Teige himself joined the Surrealist group in the Czech Republik. His interest in architecture began to wane though it was still sufficiently active for him to advance some

Bohuslav Fuchs, Municipal Baths, Brno, Zábrdovická 13, 1929–30,
Competition Project, 1929

Repr. from: Iloš Crhonek, Architekt Bohuslav Fuchs. Celoživotní dílo [The Architect Bohuslav Fuchs. His Life's Work],
Brno, 1995

Josef Polášek, Municipal Residences with Minimum-Sized Apartments, Brno,
Skácelova 23-69, 1931–32

Photo, c. 1932
PNP Prague, Karel Teige estate

Surrealist-psychoanalytical arguments in his critique of the newly built Neoclassical palaces in Moscow. In 1936 in his book *Sovětská architektura* [Soviet Architecture] he condemned their monumentalism—even more reactionary than that of the Mundaneum—calling it an instrument of intimidation directed against the Soviet people.

Brno

Brno, the second largest city in Czechoslovakia, had already developed into a center of the textile and engineering industry in the nineteenth century. Even today some areas of the city, like an unwitting open-air museum of industrial architecture and social housing, are still reminiscent of this era of early capitalism. The main objective of the Czech city council, in office since 1918, was to rid themselves of the Austrian *Altlasten* [baggage of the past] and to endeavor to raise living standards to a modern level. As in Prague, subsidies were first directed toward the middle-class housing cooperatives which built housing estates similar to garden cities that provided low-cost housing. At the same time the building of modern schools, public swimming pools, and, from 1930 onward, housing estates for the working classes, was promoted. In contrast to Prague, where conservative architects of the older generation had for a long time been in charge of municipal planning offices, town planning in Brno lay in the hands of young graduates of polytechnics and academies of architecture in Prague, Brno, and Vienna, among whom were Jindřich Kumpošt, Bohuslav Fuchs,[7] and Josef Polášek. Due to their efforts, modern architecture could be established in the mid 1920s, thus marginalizing conservative architectural trends. The number of functionalist buildings in Brno increased rapidly and reached a density comparable only to Frankfurt am Main, Rotterdam, or Tel Aviv.

Although ample opportunities and prospects for building in Brno did not offer any fertile ground for visionary ideologists of the Karel Teige variety, Jiří Kroha, professor at the Czech Technical College, nonetheless tried to take on Teige's role. With his cycle of collages and diagrams, *Sociologický fragment bydlení* [a sociological fragment of dwelling] (1930–32), he created a kind of visual analogy to Teige's book *Nejmenší byt*.[8] Together with Polášek and Fuchs he set up a branch of "Levá fronta" in Brno. Kroha was primarily concerned with collective housing projects and around 1937–38 he took up Teige's ideas, which revolved around a fusion of Functionalism and Surrealism.

The consistent lack of interest shown by the local cultural and architectural journals towards Mies van der Rohe's luxurious Tugendhat House (1928–30)—under the primacy of aesthetic guidelines—is testimony to the ideological stance prevalent in Brno in the early 1930s. The achievements of the architectural avant-garde in Brno were not, however, merely confined to ideological gestures, but are evident in the determination of its advocates to bring about clear and tangible improvements for the socially weaker classes.

Thus, from 1929 to 1932 Bohuslav Fuchs built large public baths with adjoining swimming-pool facilities for tenants living in older houses without bathrooms in the working-class quarter of Zábrdovice. At the same time Josef Polášek began the construction of cheap, but nonetheless architecturally satisfying residential buildings with minimal-sized apartments. The white prisms of Polášek's housing estates in the Vranovská and the Skácelova districts were intended to stand out in the immediate vicinity like visions of a better future.

František Lydie Gahura, Tomáš-Baťa Memorial, Zlín, Náměstí T. G. Masaryka 2570, 1933 (now Dům umění [The House of Art])

Photo, c.1933
ASG Zlín

Zlín

It might have seemed natural that the Czech avant-garde should adopt the town of Zlín—an almost exemplary rendering of Tony Garnier's *Cité industrielle* project—as the flesh-and-blood model of a modern, rationally functioning town. Yet, there was a decisive obstacle: because the client for the Zlín project, the shoe magnate Tomáš Baťa, was considered by the avant-garde to be a typical capitalist exploiter, Zlín was given limited coverage in the leftist-oriented architectural reviews. For all that, Baťa would have been in complete agreement with Karel Teige (who virtually ignored Zlín) on the economical non-viability and antisocial aspects of the architectural monumentality of "great palaces," against which Baťa himself had already warned in 1927.[9] The large buildings of Zlín—from schools, hotels, boarding schools, offices, and stores to Baťa's memorial, erected by the Kotěra pupil František Lydie Gahura[10] after the shoe magnate's death in an air crash in 1932—all had to conform to the formal language of the skeleton construction architecture of the Zlín industrial estate as laid down by Baťa.

Baťa had his shoe factory built along the lines of American models with which he had familiarized himself from 1904 during several study trips to the United States. Accommodations for his workers, however, were modeled on English Garden Cities. The employees of the shoe factory were not to live in apartment blocks, but were able to acquire cheaply their own houses and gardens—the different house types being designed by Jan Kotěra (from 1915), František Lydie Gahura (from 1924), Vladimír Karfík (from 1930), and other architects. In densely packed estates, these houses gradually filled the long Zlín valley. Baťa's famous slogan "Work collectively, live individually" became doctrine. Not even Le Corbusier succeeded in changing this: his 1935 project to expand Zlín in the spirit of the *ville radieuse* by erecting numerous high-rise apartment blocks found little favor with the Baťa company.

1 See Rostislav Švácha, "Czech Architecture in Plečnik's Time and the Ideal of Democracy" in *Josip Plečnik: An Architect of Prague Castle*, Prague, 1997, pp. 27–39.
2 See *Jaromír Krejcar 1895–1949*, exh. cat., Galerie Jaroslava Fragnera, Prague, 1995 (contributions by Klaus Spechtenhauser, Rostislav Švácha, Antonín Tenzer; Czech and English).
3 See George Baird, "Architecture and Politics: A Polemical Dispute—A Critical Introduction to Karel Teige's 'Mundaneum', 1929 and Le Corbusier's 'In Defense of Architecture,' 1933," in *Oppositions*, Cambridge, Mass., no. 4, 1974, pp. 80–82. For Karel Teige see *Rassegna*, Bologna, vol. XV, 1993, no. 53/1 ("Karel Teige, Architecture and Poetry"); Manuela Castagnara Codeluppi (ed.), *Karel Teige. Architettura. Poesia. Praga 1900–1951*, exh. cat., Scuderie del Castello di Miramare, Trieste, Milan, 1996.
4 See František Šmejkal and Rostislav Švácha (eds.), *Devětsil: Czech Avant-Garde Art Architecture and Design of the 1920s and 30s*, Museum of Modern Art, Oxford, and Design Museum, London, 1990.
5 Ladislav Žák, "Utopie bytové kultury?" [The Utopia of a Culture of Living?], in *Světozor* [A Look at the World], Prague, vol. XXXIV, 1934, no. 9, unpaginated.
6 See Vít Obrtel, "O architektuře a prostoru," in *Kvart*, Prague, 1930–31, pp. 23–26 (English translation: "On Architecture and Space," in Vladimír Šlapeta, *Czech Functionalism 1918–1938*, exh. cat., Architectural Association, London, 1987, pp. 164–45.)
7 See Zdeněk Kudělka, *Bohuslav Fuchs*, Prague, 1966; Iloš Crhonek, *Architekt Bohuslav Fuchs. Celoživotní dílo* [The Architect Bohuslav Fuchs: His Life's Work], Brno, 1995.
8 See *Jiří Kroha. Kubist Expressionist Funktionalist Realist* [Jiří Kroha: Cubist Expressionist Functionalist Realist], exh. cat., Architektur Zentrum Wien, 1998 (contributions by Monika Platzer, Klaus Spechtenhauser, Rostislav Švácha).
9 Tomáš Baťa, *Zámožnost všem* [Affluence for All], Zlín, 1927, p. 8.
10 See Ladislava Horňáková, *František Lydie Gahura. Zlínský architekt. urbanista a sochař* [František Lydie Gahura: Zlín Architect, Urbanist and Sculptor], exh. cat., Státní galerie ve Zlíně, Zlín, 1998.

Capitalism and Collectivism in the New Czechoslovak State

Three critical episodes in the architectural construction of the new Czechoslovak state focused on the city. All were concerned to enhance living and working conditions and to rationalize the relationship between work and domestic life.

In the early 1930s, the *Levá fronta* [Left Front] in Prague, building on Soviet models, concentrated on collective housing systems. Some of its members worked in anticipation of a new social order while others, like Jiří Kroha, pursued a radical restructuring of the historic city to accommodate the existing social realities of industrial society. In Brno, rebuilding in modern forms and materials exemplified the city's sense of itself as the center of a newly liberal-conservative democracy, dedicated to both free enterprise and advanced productivity.

At the company town of Zlín, the Baťa shoe company developed a model of collective work and individual living in which standardization and efficiency—exemplified by the use of concrete structural modules in building—formed the basis of an ideology of the universal and uniform. Tomáš Baťa's colonies could be implanted anywhere in the world, and his stores appeared in cities all over Central Europe as emblems of a forward-looking society. These Czech experiments in city-building drew worldwide attention. The Czechoslovak pavilion at the Paris World's Fair of 1937 by Jaromír Krejcar, with its sense of technological modernity, spoke eloquently for the confidence of a modern economy and a democratic state.

Jaromír Krejcar, Zdeněk Kejř, Ladislav Sutnar, Bohumil Soumar, Czechoslovak Pavilion at the Exposition Universelle in Paris, 1936–37

Perspective, 1936
Indian ink and watercolor on paper,
80 x 80 cm
NTM Prague

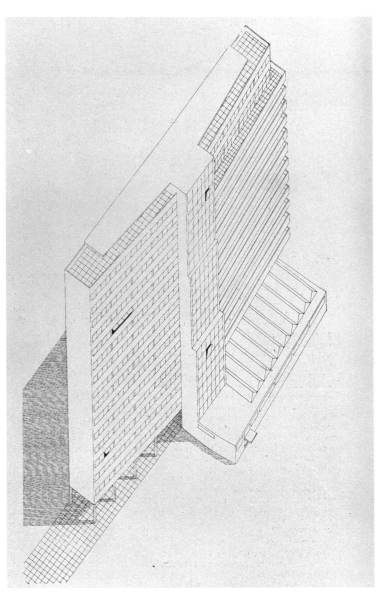

Jan Gillar, Josef Špalek, Peer Bücking,
Augusta Müllerová, Competition
Project for a Collective Housing Estate
("L-Project"), Prague, 1930

An apartment block
Indian ink on paper, 167 x 52 cm
NTM Prague

Plan of the entire complex
Repr. from: Stavba, IX, 1930–31

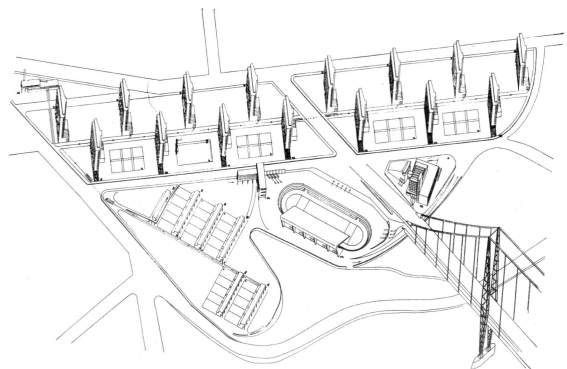

Jan Gillar, Competition Design for
Houses with minimal-sized apartments
for the VČELA Cooperative, Prague,
1930

Plans of Living Units
Indian ink and photos on card, 58 x 78 cm
NTM Prague

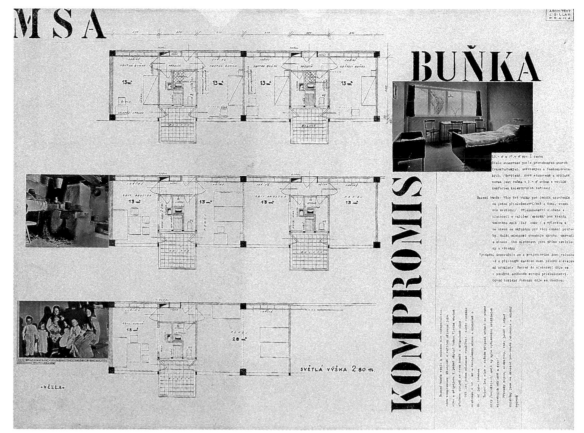

Jiří Kroha: A Sociological Fragment of
Dwelling, 1930–32

Plate 48: Illnesses and their Milieu II
Collage, 69 x 99 cm
MMB Brno
© Karel Šabata

Josef Kalous, Jaroslav Valenta, Central
Exhibition Pavilion, Exhibition of Con-
temporary Art ČSR, Brno, Exhibition
Grounds, 1926–28

2 pictures taken during construction
CCA Montréal

Ladislav Sutnar, Poster for the
"Exposition du commerce moderne",
Brno, 1929

Lithograph, 47 x 63 cm
UPM Prague

Bohuslav Fuchs, Avion Hotel, Brno, Česká 20, 1926–28

Interior view
Photo, 60 x 44 cm
NTM Prague

Exterior view
Photo, 59.5 x 27 cm
NTM Prague

Floor plans of café, hotel
Repr. from: Mihály Kubinszky, Bohuslav Fuchs,
Budapest – Berlin (East), 1986

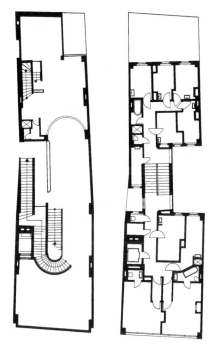

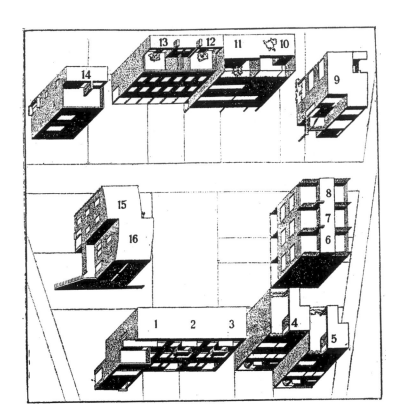

Model Estate Nový dům [The New House], Brno, 1927–28

Schematic overview
1–3: Bohuslav Fuchs; 4–5: Josef Štěpánek;
6–8: Jaroslav Grunt; 9: Jiří Kroha; 10: Hugo
Foltýn; 11: Miroslav Putna; 12–13: Jan
Víšek; 14: Jaroslav Syřiště; 15–16: Arnošt
Wiesner
Repr. from: Stavitel, X, 1929

Bohuslav Fuchs, houses 1–3;
Josef Štěpánek, houses 4–5
Photo, 59.5 x 84 cm
NTM Prague

Baťa's Shoe Town, Zlín

Postcard, from the 1930s
Private collection, Zurich

Josef Gočár, Zlín of the Future, 1927

Print
Repr. from: Sdělení zaměstnanců firmy
T. a A. Baťa ve Zlíně (Zlín), X, 1927
SOA Zlín

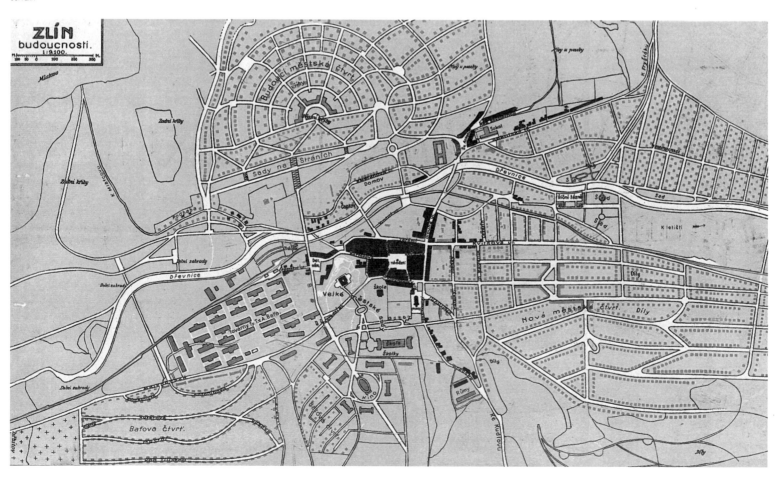

Vladimír Karfík, Baťa Department
Store, Liberec, 1930–31
Repr. from: Stavitel, XIV, 1933–34

Josef Gočár, Project for the Baťa
Department Store, Brno, 1929

Perspective, 1929
Indian ink with watercolor on paper,
170 x 128 cm
NTM Prague

Vladimír Karfík, Baťa Department
Store, Bratislava, 1930–31

Postcard, from the 1930s
Private collection Zurich

From CIAM to CIAM-Ost, 1928-37

CIAM AND CENTRAL EUROPE

Monika Platzer

In June 1928 the Congrès internationaux d'architecture moderne (CIAM) was founded at the castle of La Sarraz in west Switzerland. Its Foundation Charter was signed by twenty-four architects from eight countries, among whom were H.P. Berlage, Le Corbusier, Ernst May, Gerrit Rietveld, and Alberto Sartoris, as well as the future Secretary-General of CIAM, the Swiss art historian Sigfried Giedion. The basic guidelines as formulated in the charter referred to changes in the structure of society as well as the latest technological and economic conditions. The objectives which were set for participants at future congresses were to define the fundamental principles of contemporary architecture through systematic research and to communicate these results to the outside world. CIAM and its executive body, CIRPAC (Comité international pour la réalisation des problèmes d'architecture contemporaine), did not regard themselves merely as associations of proponents of a modern conception of architecture bound together by a common interest. Nor did CIAM ever become a homogeneous organization. Though its public statements give it the appearance of a group espousing a common point of view, the extensive correspondence among its members and the minutes that have been preserved from its meetings are testimony to the ideological breadth of a dialogue which was very often quite diverse. The following gives an overview of the common concerns, contacts, and active collaboration between the Central European states and the international association.[1]

The architectural avant-garde of the Central European countries very quickly made contact with CIAM. Gabriel Guevrékian, who was studying in Vienna, had presumably acted as the mediator, when, in 1928 he invited the Austrian Josef Frank and the Czech Karel Teige to participate in the La Sarraz congress.[2] After his return to Vienna, Frank formed a small local group consisting of Oswald Haerdtl, Ernst Plischke, and Walter Sobotka. When Plischke emigrated to the United States, Eugen Wachberger from Linz joined the group.[3] It is no coincidence that all the architects nominated by Frank are represented by buildings in the Vienna Werkbund housing estate. In 1929 Frank was involved in Basel with the preparations for the Second Congress, to be held in Frankfurt am Main on October 24–26, 1929 under the theme "Die Wohnung für das Existenzminimum" [The Minimum-Income Dwelling]. The confinement of the discussions to technical aspects and the consequent neglect of "architecture" were the decisive factors that led to Frank's resignation as the Austrian delegate in November 1929. He had already openly warned of a potential conflict between "rational and artistic" approaches to architecture during the conference in Basel:

> And then—regrettably this cannot be expressed in any other way—there is the German and the non-German approach, one being based on allegedly rational and the other on artistic principles and this, it seems to me, is something that will become more and more apparent. I, therefore, do not expect as positive an outcome of this congress as I would wish.[4]

After the congress Frank expressed to Sigfried Giedion his disbelief at how during the debates all questions of aesthetics had been ignored, stating that he considered it "dishonest" to make the ground plan the sole criterion of modern architecture.[5] The group representing Austria thereby ceased to exist.

Hungary was represented, for the first time at the meeting of delegates in Basel in 1929 by Marcel Breuer, who was then living in Berlin. A considerable Hungarian delegation participated in the 1929 Frankfurt congress.[6] The ideas of the congress were publicized at an exhibition organized in Frankfurt under the direction of Mart Stam with financial support from the *Hochbauamt* [city building authorities]. The aim was to

BUDAPEST

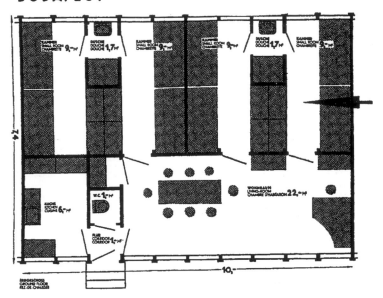

György Rácz, Ground plan of a single-story terraced house, 1929–30
Repr. from: Die Wohnung für das Existenzminimum, Frankfurt / Main, 1930

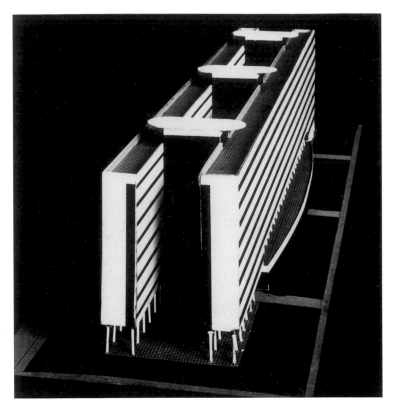

Josef Havlíček, Karel Honzík, KOLDOM Project, Prague, 1930
Model
Repr. from: Die Wohnung für das Existenzminimum , Frankfurt / Main, 1930

inform the general public about the fundamental principles of *Neues Bauen* through a series of ground plans prepared to a uniform scale, giving indications regarding furniture as well as the most important details about floor area, enclosed space, window areas, and number of beds per apartment.[7] The Austrians[8] exhibited one ground plan and the Hungarians three, all conceived for the small dwelling unit adapted to the new, communal style of living.[9] Farkas Molnár criticized the designs submitted by the western sections which in his opinion were "reduced and cheaper variants of the spacious middle class apartments suitable for purposes of entertainment."[10] In opposition to this, he proposed reducing the private living space to "living cells" and demanded a substantial spatial expansion of the areas used by all occupants. Already in this initial phase fundamental ideological differences came to light which were to be pursued further—particularly in contacts with the Czech delegation.[11]

A national group in Czechoslovakia was set up only after the Second Congress in Frankfurt. Giedion, in a letter to Frank, had already expressed his bewilderment that Czechoslovakia and Russia were the only countries with which it was difficult to establish real contacts.[12] Frank's reply was not very positive. He writes that in Czechoslovakia "modern architecture is carried out in a fairly disorganized way ... and what is completed looks anything but pleasing."[13]

Karel Teige informed Giedion in 1930 about the interest that several architects in Prague and Brno had expressed in working with CIAM.[14] They were Josef Chochol, Jaromír Krejcar, Josef Havlíček, and August Müllerová in Prague and Bohuslav Fuchs and Zdeněk Rossman in Brno. As a result, the Czech delegation participated in the Third Congress in

Brussels on the theme of "Rationelle Bebauungsweisen" [rational building methods] and submitted two designs. Its members came predominantly from the architectural faction of the Left Front [*Levá fronta*] and saw their architectural activities increasingly as an active form of social criticism. Two projects, KOLDOM and CIRPAC, were exhibited at the congress and later publicized in the catalogue. Josef Havlíček and Karel Honzík (KOLDOM, 1930) and Jan Gillar and Josef Špalek (CIRPAC) offered their models of collective housing as a possible solution to the existing housing shortage while at the same time demonstrating the potential for a radical societal change inherent in this type of building. The individual "living cell" was augmented by a wide variety of collective services such as refectories, recreational areas, laundries, nurseries, and libraries. Collectivization was meant to promote the emancipation of women, enabling them to use their newly won free time for the benefit of the community. These concepts and architectural designs bear a strong resemblance to Soviet models of architecture and society.

If the first congress had laid down the association's guidelines and dealt with the themes of the minimum-income dwelling and new building arrangements, all these innovative approaches now threatened to come to grief due to existing town extension plans and real estate conditions. The theme for the Fourth Congress, "The Functional City," was, therefore, an appropriate choice. This congress, originally planned to be held in Moscow in 1932, took place in 1933 in Athens

3rd CIAM Congress, Athens / Patris II, 1933
Alvar Aalto, Otto Neurath, and László Moholy-Nagy on board 'Patris II'
Photo: Welcher Moser
gta Zurich

aboard the *Patris II* on the Mediterranean. Beginning at the extraordinary congress held in Berlin in 1931 and continuing through the subsequent meetings held in Paris, Zurich, and Barcelona, a group of experts led by Cornelius van Eesteren set the parameters for a comparative city analysis.[15] As a result, the fundamental functions of a city—dwelling, work, recreation, and traffic—are set out here in three plans, two on a scale of 1:10,000 and one on a scale of 1:50,000.[16] The cartographic information is supplemented by photographs and explanatory reports on the individual cities.

Otto Neurath, who had already been suggested as a participant by Josef Frank in 1929, joined in 1933 as the first "specialist" and assumed an active role on the publications committee, on the committee for the preparation of statistics, and in preparing a list of demands to be sent to various official bodies.[17] In the end, reports, plans, and data on thirty-three cities—among them Prague, Budapest, and Zagreb[18]—had been assembled on board the *Patris*. The comparative analysis, prepared using a uniform method (identical scale, a standard set of symbols and colors for highlighting specific functions) was intended to be the first stage of a future scientific form of urban planning. The discussions were based neither on architectural nor on socio-political factors—here it was the universal demand of pure analysis which took center stage.

The evaluation of the material presented some difficulties, as it was structured in too varied a way to be conducive to a common solution. This was due partially to the peculiarities of the individual cities, but also to the diverging views of the members who, it was thought, by being assembled together, would arrive at a uniform solution.[19] Several drafts of the "Findings of the Congress" were prepared, but none of the publications originally planned materialized. It was not until 1943 that Le Corbusier published—on his own—the *Charte d'Athènes*.

The political and economic situation of the 1930s made the work of the delegates more difficult; they found themseves caught between fronts: "What we experience today is that the same movement of *Neues Bauen*—however with premises that run counter to those of a few years ago—is called the 'western bourgeois style' in Russia, 'cultural bolshevism' in Central Europe, and 'the true fascist style' in Italy."[20] Parallel with these findings an appeal went out to all members calling for active cooperation.[21] At the 1934 meeting in Amsterdam the German delegation was no longer present and contact with the Czech group had been severed because of ideological differences.

New impulses came from the Polish group (Szymon Syrkus and Jan Chmielewski), which exhibited its project "Warszawa Funkcjonalna" [Functional Warsaw] in London in 1934. Its call for a broadening of the discussion on urban planning to include regional planning was received with great interest and, at the next congress, "Logis et Loisirs" [Dwelling and Leisure] in Paris in 1937, the emphasis was on "the close interaction between town, region and country."[22] What emerged particularly clearly in Paris was the variety of viewpoints from which the subject of "town" could be considered, and how fundamentally present views differed from notions of urban architecture prior to World War I. It was no longer the "townscape" as the artistic construct of the architect which occupied planners' thoughts. What they were now concerned with was the question of how to break up the congested city and rearrange it according to its functions, as defined in 1933. The concept of the "urban landscape" emerged in opposition to that of the city/metropolis. This bringing-together of town and country carried on from the Garden City model—based on a socio-utopian vision—which had been developed by Ebenezer Howard and Raymond Unwin.

CIAM·Ost

In January 1936 Farkas Molnár, while being involved with preliminary work for the Fifth Congress in Paris, proposed to contact all states bordering the Danube for the purpose of preparing a joint study on the topic of "The Country on a Global Scale"—the planned overview of each country in relation to the world economy.[23] After the meeting of delegates in La Sarraz (in 1936) Sigfried Giedion suggested to František Kalivoda (who had, meanwhile, become the contact for the Czech group) that the CIRPAC groups of the "Balkan states" (Hungary, Czechoslovakia, Poland, Yugoslavia, and Greece) should form a group.[24] Immediately after his return to Brno, Kalivoda contacted Molnár who suggested Budapest as the first venue for a conference and insisted that the participation of Austria and Romania was essential.

The regional conference took place in Budapest from January 29 to February 3, 1937 and was attended by Czechs,

CIAM East Conference in Brno and Zlín, April 29–May 5, 1937

Standing from right: František Lydie Gahura, František Kalivoda, Pál Ligeti, Josef Polášek, Farkas Molnár, Bohuslav Fuchs, Roman Piotrowski, Jindřich Kumpošt, four unidentifiable persons. Seated from right: Eszter Pécsi, Szymon Syrkus, Helena Syrkus, Hélène de Mandrot and one unknown person
Photo, 1937
MEM Budapest

Poles, Yugoslavs, Austrians, and Hungarians. It was agreed that a joint organization of the eastern European national groups, the CIAM-Ost [CIAM-East], should be set up (with its head office in Budapest and under the direction of Molnár).[25] The recognition that the basic conditions for Neues Bauen in Central Europe differed fundamentally from those of Western Europe was an essential consideration in the amalgamation. Due to their similar structures, collaboration between these countries could prove extremely productive. In addition to this, the minutes record a request by Virgil Bierbauer, pointing out that problems similar to those facing the metropolis also existed for rural areas, and, in particular, for the village. It was part of the job of any modern-minded architect to seek solutions to the housing problems and living conditions of farmers and farm workers. In this connection Bierbauer took up the suggestion, made at the 1935 CIRPAC meeting in Amsterdam, of establishing scientific institutions which, while taking account of rural ways of building, geographic and climatic conditions, as well as local building material, would mobilize the forces and know-how of Neues Bauen.

The second CIAM-Ost meeting took place in Brno and Zlín from April 29 to May 5, 1937.[26] The complex urban solution presented by the shoe-manufacturing town of Baťa, with its location in the countryside, and its wide-ranging regional functions (including public administration, education, culture, and medical care) had a very productive influence on the meeting and caused Molnár to write a detailed report to Giedion.

The Fifth CIAM Congress in Paris (June 28 to July 2, 1937) was attended by the Hungarian delegates (Ligeti,

Bierbauer, and Forbát), who submitted statistical data and proposals for the restructuring of rural areas. The majority of Hungary's population lived in a rural environment where living conditions lagged far behind those of middle-sized towns like Kecskemét or Szeged. The farm worker was almost without exception a seasonal worker, commuting between his workplace (city) and home (village). The fluctuation between these two poles, it was argued, could only be checked by a systematic inner colonization. Bierbauer saw the solution in the establishment of regional centers which would concentrate the social, economic, cultural, and technical facilities for the rural population.[27] Bierbauer's initial investigations showed that approximately 347 of these centers would have to be established in Hungary. As an exemplary model he cited Jánoshalma, a community of 15,000 inhabitants, where a planned economy run according to statistical and business management methods had succeeded in raising the quality of life of the community to "Olympian" heights.[28] Whereas, at earlier meetings, the representation and interpretation of a "city" had generally been dominated by the critical analysis of its shortcomings, from this point on a connection was established between an architecturally ordered city and a well-ordered society (or local community). These first essays in the direction of an "organized city" were shortly afterward put into practice in the designs for the "Deutsche Volksgemeinschaft" [German People's Community].

The planning of further CIAM-Ost meetings did not proceed so smoothly: František Kalivoda suggested Bratislava as a venue for the conferences, while Walter Loos argued in favor of the triangle Vienna—Budapest—Bratislava.[29] For political reasons the next (and last) meeting eventually took place on Mykonos from June 5 to 6, 1938.[30] Once again, regional issues were foremost on the agenda: working methods for rural areas and health care for the rural population.

The political events of the late 1940s made continued collaboration impossible. CIAM-Ost's plan to launch its own newspaper—which was simultaneously intended to provide those countries which lacked such specialist journals (Austria, Yugoslavia, Bulgaria, and Rumania) with a forum in which they could present the "modern" architectural work being done in their respective countries—also failed.[31] Even so, the short-lived collaboration was significant in that it showed, for the first time, that the problems addressed by CIAM and the methods proposed for their solutions were not quite as universal as had been assumed by the leadership of the international organization.

1 In this connection I am indebted to András Ferkai, on whose research work the passages in this essay concerning the Hungarian CIAM group are based.

2 See the letter from Josef Frank to Gabriel Guevrékian of March 9, 1928; and the letter from Karel Teige to Gabriel Guevrékian of May 14, 1928, Archiv des Instituts für Geschichte und Theorie der Architektur [Archives of the Institute of History and Theory of Architecture] at the ETH Zurich (referred to subsequently as gta), CIAM Archives. Frank and Teige thank Guevrékian for the invitation to the congress and assure him of their participation. Unlike Frank, however, Teige did not go to La Sarraz. Josef Hoffmann and Oswald Haerdtl were also invited but declined (see letters from Hoffmann and Haerdtl to Guevrékian of June 20, 1928, gta, CIAM Archives).

3 Letters from Josef Frank to Sigfried Giedion of January 2, 1929 and of July 6, 1929, gta, CIAM Archives.

4 Letter from Josef Frank to Sigfried Giedion of May 25, 1929, gta, CIAM Archives.

5 "Like many others I take the view that form plays a very important role and should not be neglected alongside that of the, admittedly, more essential one of the ground plan, etc." (Letter of resignation from Josef Frank to Sigfried Giedion of November 5, 1929, gta, CIAM Archives). In the same letter Frank criticizes the papers presented by Walter Gropius and Hans Schmidt: "Papers of such superficiality as those of Gropius ["Low, medium, or High Buildings"— author's note] and Schmidt ["Building Regulations and Minimal Dwelling"— author's note] should not be presented—that is, papers in which the author has brought together a wealth of material, but is unable to put it to use, which is precisely the job of research."

6 Farkas Molnár, György Rácz, Pál Ligeti, György Masirevich, Tibor Weiner as delegates, Count I. Csáky as representative of the Budapest Municipal Council and Pál Virágh (see Oliver Arpad Istvan Botar, *Modernism in Hungarian Urban Planning: 1906–1938*, Ph.D. diss., University of Toronto, 1985, p. 123).

7 See Congress publication *Die Wohnung für das Existenzminimum* [The Minimum-Income Dwelling], Frankfurt am Main, 1930. This publication contains about 100 ground plans of model apartments and all the papers presented at the 2nd Congress.

8 Ibid., table 131: Block with Four Staircase-Access Dwelling Units per floor, by Anton Brenner.

9 Ibid., tables 1 and 16, György Rácz; table 110, Farkas Molnár.

10 Quoted from Botar, *Modernism in Hungarian Urban Planning*, p. 124.

11 See also the essay by Klaus Spechtenhauser and Daniel Weiss, "Karel Teige and the CIAM: The History of a Troubled Relationship," in Eric Dluhosch and Rostislav Švácha (eds.), *Karel Teige 1900–56. L'Enfant Terrible of the Czech Modernist Avant-Garde*, Cambridge, Mass. and London, 1999, pp. 217–55.

12 See letter from Sigfried Giedion to Josef Frank of July 30, 1929, gta, CIAM Archives.

13 Letter from Josef Frank to Sigfried Giedion of August 5, 1929, gta, CIAM Archives.

14 See letter from Karel Teige to Sigfried Giedion of 17 May 1930, gta, CIAM Archives.

15 See also Detailed Explanations and Data on Maps I and II, Amsterdam, 1931; Detailed Explanations and Data to Map III, Amsterdam, 1932, gta, CIAM Archives. Just how intensive this collaboration was emerges clearly from the correspondence with Western architects in the Soviet Union. So Alfréd Forbát reports to Walter Gropius about meetings which took place between himself and Hans Schmidt, Hans Blumenfeld, Peer Bücking, Otto Neurath, Eugen Kaufmann, and Margarete Schütte-Lihotzky at the Hotel Europa in Moscow (see letter from Alfréd Forbát to Walter Gropius of March 8, 1932, gta, CIAM Archives).

16 Map 1 contains: apartment (location, density of habitation, year of origin); recreation (green spaces, woods, sports fields, allotments); work (business district, industrial area, warehouses, indoor markets, municipal offices). Map II contains: traffic in the city (main traffic routes, means of transport, street cross-sections with approved subsequent development). Map III contains: city surroundings (number of people commuting to the city, long-distance traffic, suburban railway, arterial roads, agricultural provisions, industry, recreation areas, woods, cross-sections of the most important exit roads).

17 Already on August 22, 1929 Giedion had asked Frank for Neurath's address in Vienna. On August 4, 1933 Neurath gave a lecture about his Viennese method of *Bildstatistik* [image statistics] in the forecourt of the Institute of Science and Technology in Athens (see Martin Steinmann, *CIAM. Dokumente 1928–1939* [CIAM. Documents 1928–39], Basle, Boston, Stuttgart, 1979, p. 130, as well as the manuscript of Neurath's lecture, gta, CIAM Archives). He was also present on board the *Patris II*, where, on August 13, he was received as the first specialist. At the meeting of delegates in Barcelona from March 29 to 31 it was decided

to protest the results of the competition for the Palace of the Soviets. Apart from this, an official protest note was sent to the Zagreb authorities because of their rejection of the award-winning project by Ernest Weissman for a new hospital in Zagreb-Šalata (for all documents see gta, CIAM Archives).

18 Ernest Weissmann from Zagreb, then employed in the Paris studio of Le Corbusier, had been a member of CIAM since 1929. In 1932, together with Vlado Antolič and Josip Seissel, he formed the Yugoslavian regional group, which began its work for the Fourth Congress.

19 In this connection, see the response made by the Czech regional group to the Dutch concept of the "Functional City" (gta, CIAM Archives): "…all urban efforts to alleviate these elementary manifestations [traffic problems, city congestion, population explosion – author's note] must necessarily remain unproductive as long as only the symptoms are treated and the economic and social conditions are not seen as of prime concern. The 'synthetic' construction of new cities is equally determined by economic and social laws. Therefore, those cities which are created under the same capitalist conditions and with the same objectives as those already existing (Australia, America), will suffer from the same attendant symptoms (anarchy of growth, living space as a source of profit, etc.). We, therefore, are of the conviction that old or new towns under the existing conditions are totally incurable and that newly settled areas under socialist conditions will no longer be 'cities' in this sense."

20 Circular to regional delegates, April 1934, gta, CIAM Archives.

21 This letter had a "stimulating" effect on the Hungarian group. Farkas Molnár and József Fischer, in a letter to Giedion of July 7, 1934 (gta, CIAM Archives), report on the intensified activities of the delegates (press campaigns, planned exhibitions), emphasizing that the Hungarian group would increase its efforts toward their common goals.

22 Guidelines for the Fifth Congress, printed in Steinmann, *CIAM. Dokumente*, pp. 176–79.

23 "…Regrettably we do not have the Austrian and Romanian groups and I have not heard anything from Weissmann for quite some time now. It is crucial that our contacts with these countries should be extended. It would therefore be very good if they could hold at least one meeting of delegates in our area" (letter from Farkas Molnár to Sigfried Giedion on January 17, 1934, gta, CIAM Archives).

24 See letter from František Kalivoda to Farkas Molnár of October 20, 1936, gta, CIAM Archives.

25 Among others the following were present at the Budapest meeting: Sigfried Giedion, Vlado Antolič, Walter Loos, Helena and Szymon Syrkus, František Kalivoda, Josef Polášek and Ervin Katona (Prague), Farkas Molnár, József Fischer, Alfréd Forbát, Pál Ligeti, Zoltán Kósa, György Rácz, Béla Halmos and Virgil Bierbauer (see Resolutions of the Budapest Meetings, gta, CIAM Archives).

26 For the meetings in Zlín and Brno see *Magazin AKA*, (Brno), 1937, no. 1, p. 16; 1938, no. 2, p. 16 as well as the correspondence of František Kalivoda – Sigfried Giedion – Farkas Molnár, gta CIAM Archives. Apart from architects from Hungary, Poland, Austria, and Czechoslovakia, Helène Mandrot and Raoul Hausmann also participated in the Zlín meeting.

27 See Virgil Bierbauer, *Les bases de la reconstruction rurale en Hongrie*, gta, CIAM Archives.

28 Ibid.

29 See letter from František Kalivoda to Helena and Szymon Syrkus of November 10, 1937, gta, CIAM Archives.

30 See postcards to Werner M. Moser and Rudolf Steiger of June 6, 1938, gta, CIAM Archives.

31 See letter from František Kalivoda to Helena and Szymon Syrkus of November 10, 1937; letter from Farkas Molnár to Sigfried Giedion of February 21, 1938, gta, CIAM Archives. Molnár wanted to publish the first issue of the *CIAM-Ost Journal* instead of the minutes of the Budapest meeting; when this failed, Kalivoda tried to convert the journal *Forum* (Bratislava) into a CIAM journal.

The Functional City

The activities of Central European members of the Congrès internationaux d'architecture moderne (CIAM) and the founding of an Eastern European branch (CIAM-Ost) in 1937 is a little-known chapter in the history of the modern movement. CIAM's fourth congress, "The Functional City" of 1933, held in Athens and on board the *Patris II,* had been devoted to the social analysis and functional replanning of the city in connection with a newly expanded concept of zoning. Studies submitted to CIAM for Zagreb, Prague, and Budapest show the advanced scale of urban thinking that had already developed in Central Europe through the competitions, experiments, and inquiries of the 1920s. With the help of Otto Neurath's statistical methods, the utopia of a universal scientific concept of town planning became the declared goal of CIAM. At the same time, discussions in Athens encouraged Eastern European members to recognize fundamental differences between the urban conditions of their cities and those of the West. CIAM-Ost grew out of this conviction, generating a new sense of multinational identity only months before the Nazi annexations destroyed its hopes.

The dispersed, functionally zoned city envisaged by CIAM, with its emphasis on regional and neighbourhood planning, prefigures the anti-metropolitan dispersal of the postwar urban environment and the end of the "myth of the metropolis."

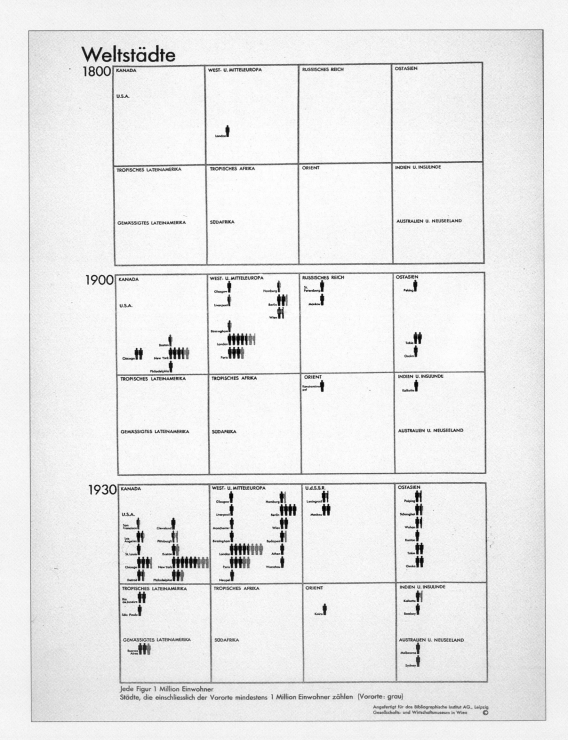

Otto Neurath, Gerd Artz, Large Cities of the World

Print, 30 x 46 cm

Repr. from: Gesellschaft und Wirtschaft. Bildstatistischen Mappenwerk der Gesellschafts- und Wirtschaftsmuseums in Wien, Leipzig, 1930
IISH Amsterdam

Tables for the 4th CIAM Congress, "The Functional City", Athens, 1933

Regulatory Plan of Budapest, plan 1 – contains: dwelling space (location, density of habitation, year of construction); recreation (green areas, woods, sports grounds, allotment gardens); work (city, industrial areas, warehouses, market halls, municipal services)
Print, mounted on wood, 4 parts, 120 x 120 cm each
gta Zurich

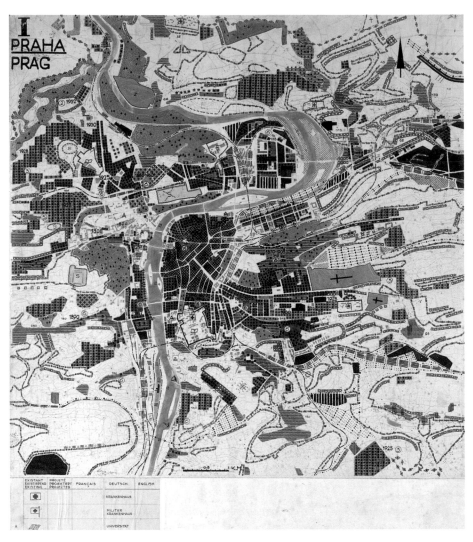

Table for the 4th CIAM Congress, "The Functional City", Athens, 1933

Regulatory plan of Prague, plan 1 – contains: apartment (location, density of habitation, year of construction); recreation (green areas, woods, sports grounds, allotment gardens); work (city, industrial areas, warehouses, market halls, municipal services)
Print, mounted on wood, 120 x 120 cm
gta Zurich

Otto Neurath, Gerd Artz, Large Cities of under 25 People each

Multicolor print, 30 x 46 cm
Rep. from: Gesellschaft und Wirtschaft. Bildstatistischen Mappenwerk der Gesellschaft- und Wirtschafts- museums in Wien, Leipzig, 1930
IISH Amsterdam

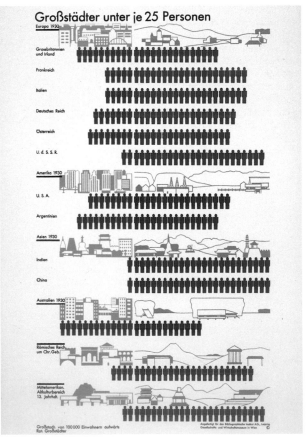

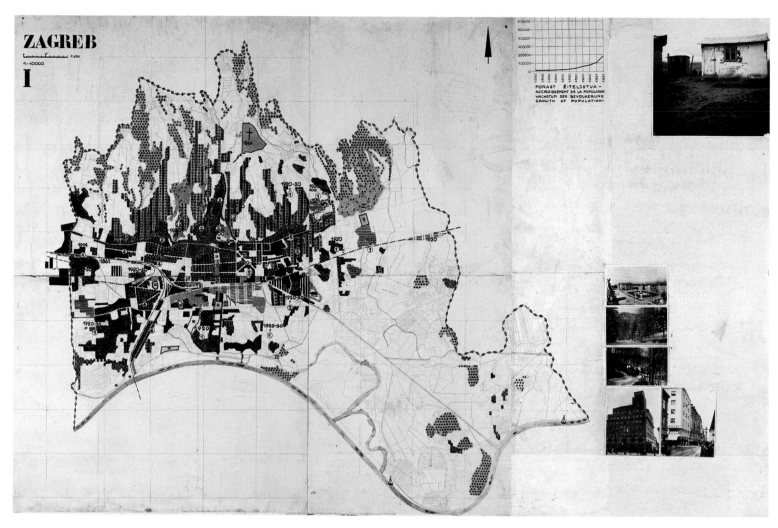

Tables for the 4th CIAM Congress, "The Functional City", Athens, 1933

Regulatory plan of Zagreb, plan 1 – contains: dwelling space (location, density of habitation, year of construction); recreation (green areas, woods, sports grounds, allotment gardens); work (city, industrial areas, warehouses, market halls, municipal services)
Print, mounted on wood, 2 parts, 120 x 120 cm, 66 x 120 cm
gta Zurich

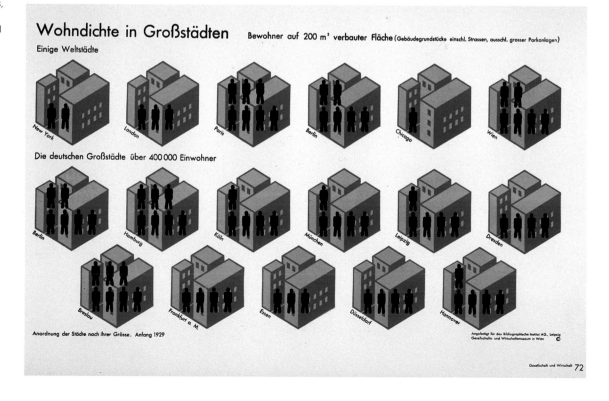

Otto Neurath, Gerd Artz, Population Density in Large Cities

Multicolor print, 30 x 46 cm
Repr. from: Gesellschaft und Wirtschaft. Bildstatistischen Mappenwerk der Gesellschaft- und Wirtschaftsmuseums in Wien, Leipzig, 1930
IISH Amsterdam

PUBLICATIONS AND PUBLIC REALMS: ARCHITECTURAL PERIODICALS IN THE HABSBURG EMPIRE AND ITS SUCCESSOR STATES

Andrew Herscher

The architectural periodical originated in Germany at the end of the eighteenth century as a means to establish and maintain communication among professionals, tradesmen, and lay people involved with architecture, people whose contiguity had previously been guaranteed by their shared affiliations to church, court, or guild.[1] The periodical constituted a new sort of public institution, an institution that complemented and increasingly supplanted those in which architecture had previously been practiced and discussed; originating along with the modern profession of architecture itself, the architectural periodical should be considered not only as a representation of that profession's activities and interests, but also as one of its constituent elements.

The tremendous increase in significance which the periodical assumed in the nineteenth century corresponded to the great changes that architecture itself underwent as it confronted the exigencies of capitalism, industrialization, and urbanization: the need to develop new building types, to utilize new building materials and construction technologies, and to re-assess the relevance of historically derived precedents for contemporary practice. The period-ical developed as the only format for dealing with the emerging profession's problems that could connect the various social settings, professional fields, and geographical territories which architecture's protagonists inhabited, and the only format that could provide up-to-date responses to the quickly developing issues that increasingly confronted the profession.

While this description characterizes the development of the nineteenth-century architec-tural periodical press in general, the press in the Habsburg lands was strongly influenced by conditions unique to the empire, the most important of which was the multinationality of its population. The ability of the press to constitute a community of readers was dependent on the possession of a common language; with its eleven linguistically defined nationalities (Ger-man, Hungarian, Czech, Slovak, Serbo-Croat, Polish, Ruthenian, Romanian, Slovene, and Italian), the empire possessed multiple "languages of the land" [*Landessprachen*] and "lan-guages customary in the land" [*landesüblichen Sprachen*], the two legal dimensions of lan-guage in the Habsburg Empire.[2] Even while German had been declared one of the "languages of the land" in almost all imperial provinces, in an atmosphere where political power was fre-quently contested over language rights—the prime minister Count Casimir Badeni, for exam-ple, lost his position as a result of the unpopularity of his language ordinances—the popula-tions of the provinces were concerned to publish books, periodicals, and newspapers in their own indigenous "languages customary to the land." The growth of the architectural press, then, occurred in parallel with the growth of national consciousness in the empire's provinces in the second half of the nineteenth century, and the latter acted as a friction on the former, a friction that was absent in neighboring countries such as Germany.[3]

Further problems prevailed in the Hungarian half of the empire, where Hungarian was far less familiar to non-Hungarians than was German to non-Germans in the Austrian provinces. Thus, as the Hungarian-language architectural press developed in Budapest at the end of the nineteenth century, some professional periodicals were published in parallel Hungarian and German editions, such as *Vállalkozók Lapja / Bauunternehmer und Lieferant* [Contractors'

Journal],[4] while others, such as *Ungarische Bauzeitung*,[5] were founded specifically as German-language counterparts to Hungarian publications which were inaccessible to significant portions of their intended audience. Because of the empire's multi-nationality, however, even the market for German-language periodicals was relatively circumscribed. As a result, Austrian publishing firms had to assume far more financial risk to produce periodicals than did firms in Germany, a fact which led the German periodical press, in art and architecture as in other fields, to develop far more intensively than its counterpart in the Habsburg Empire. In fact, the vastly greater publishing possibilities in Germany were often remarked upon by Viennese publishers and editors in the course of the nineteenth century; in the Habsburg Empire, the market for professional periodicals was simultaneously regarded as tantalizingly untapped and frustratingly difficult to cater to.[6]

As German remained the only common language throughout the empire, virtually all widely distributed architectural periodicals in the empire were published in Vienna. This concentration of publishing activity, with a concomitant concentration of editorial coverage of Vienna, asserted a relationship between the imperial capital and its provinces that was increasingly unacceptable to the empire's subject peoples. By the end of the century, both the state and the private sector founded architectural periodicals in Vienna that were specifically intended to constitute empire-wide, as opposed to Viennese, readerships; but by that time, periodicals which responded to and compensated for the general lack of attention from Vienna had already begun to develop in provincial capitals. However, as these periodicals were collected in the library of the Austrian Association of Engineers and Architects in Vienna and occasionally cited in the association's own periodical,[7] there was a certain reciprocity in the flow of information about architecture between Vienna and the provinces.

Until the last decades of the nineteenth century, there were two Viennese periodicals which dealt with architecture, one privately published, *Allgemeine Bauzeitung*, and one published by the Austrian Association of Engineers and Architects, *Zeitschrift des österreichischen Ingenieur- und Architekten-Vereines*. Each of these periodicals dealt with architecture as only one category within the field of building [*Bauwesen*], which encompassed the work of engineers, builders, craftsmen, and to some degree, archaeologists and artists, as well.

Allgemeine Bauzeitung (1836–1918),[8] the first architectural periodical founded in the Habsburg Empire, joined a group of German-language periodicals initiated at approximately the same time in Prussia and Bavaria.[9] Ludwig Förster, like many other founders of periodicals at this time, was both the publisher and editor of *Allgemeine Bauzeitung*; as the function of the periodical was conceived as simply reportage, no intervention was necessary between the collection and dissemination of newsworthy material.[10] In the case of *Allgemeine Bauzeitung*, this material was to pertain to all aspects of the field of building. As the magazine's subtitle states, its audience was "architects, engineers, decorators, builders, economists, and contractors," members of professions that represented all areas of building, from architecture [*Hochbau*] to engineering [*Zivil, Brücken-, Wasser- und Strassenbau*], and between all areas of practice, from design to construction.[11] Intended to simply report events to this audience, *Allgemeine Bauzeitung* avoided criticism in favor of a putatively objective treatment of building; works are not assessed, but described, and the contentious questions discussed in some contemporaneous German periodicals—"in welchem Styl sollen wir bauen?" [in what style should we build?] and so on—were, in *Allgemeine Bauzeitung*, studiously avoided.

Zeitschrift des österreichischen Ingenieur-Vereins, the periodical of the Austrian Association of Engineers, began to cover architecture in 1861, three years before the association expanded to include architects as members. In the following years, the professional associations of engineers in Prague, Budapest, and Zagreb similarly expanded, with their periodicals correspondingly devoting a certain amount of coverage to architecture.[12] The periodicals of these associations were intended, first and foremost, for the members of the associations which published them; they contained lectures and discussions from the associations' various subgroups, as well as association business. In each, architects were a distinct minority, a condition which was reflected in the relatively little attention given to architecture in the associations' periodicals, which typically consisted of reports on individual buildings or projects designed by association members. Only occasionally were potential synergies between engineers and architects exploited, as in discussions between the two groups in Vienna about the use of iron in architecture in 1865.[13]

As the interests of architects and engineers diverged in the course of the nineteenth century, the periodicals of the professional associations became increasingly inadequate venues for addressing issues of concern to the architectural field as a whole; even as these periodicals came to be issued more frequently, as, for example, when *Zeitschrift des österreichischen Ingenieur- und Architekten-Vereines* shifted from a monthly to a weekly in 1892, it dealt with too many disparate fields to be able to adequately encompass architecture. Only the Czech Association of Architects and Engineers responded to this problem by splitting its periodical, *Zprávy spolků architektů a inženýrů v království Českém* [Bulletin of the Association of Architects and Engineers in the Czech Crownland], into two separate publications, one dealing solely with architecture, *Architektonický obzor* [Architectural Horizon], and one exclusively with engineering, *Technický obzor* [Technical Horizon]; in the periodicals of other professional associations, architecture was simply marginalized.

In response to the generally held view that periodicals such as *Allgemeine Bauzeitung* and *Zeitschrift des österreichischen Ingenieur- und Architekten-Vereines* failed to deal adequately with architecture, in the last decades of the nineteenth century, a number of trade magazines were founded in both Vienna and Budapest. In Budapest, a publication founded in 1872 as a compilation of notices for renting and selling housing (*Pest-Ofner Wohnungs-Anzeiger*) expanded after 1873, when Buda, Pest, and Ó-Buda were unified, to include information on architectural projects and competitions, as well as advertisements by building material suppliers and tradesmen; the new periodical was re-named *Budapester Bau-Zeitung und Wohnungs-Anzeiger* (1874–75). In 1876, the periodical abandoned real-estate listings to become the first professional magazine for architects in Hungary, *Bauzeitung für Ungarn*,[14] and it was soon followed by Hungarian-language publications directed at architects and engineers, such as *Építő Ipar-Műszaki Hetilap* [Construction Industry-Technological Weekly] (1877–86) and *Építészeti Szemle* [Architectural Review] (1892).

In the same period, a similar kind of periodical was founded in Vienna, *Die Bauhalle* (1873), focused on building types such as factories, market halls, and military barracks, but also including a *Bau-Anzeiger* with various sorts of notices and advertisements of interest to architects. In 1883, another, longer-lasting professional magazine was founded in Vienna, *Wiener Bauindustrie-Zeitung*.[15] As the editors stated in the inaugural issue, *Wiener Bauindustrie-Zeitung* was intended to "take note of all professional and business-oriented knowledge from the standpoint of building activity … inclining exclusively towards a practical tendency."[16] Published bi-weekly, and thus more frequently than any other periodical dealing with architecture, taking advantage of the new availability of chromolithography to publish an annual *Wiener Bauten-Album* accompanying the periodical itself,[17] and including a wide selection of advertisements and job placement notices, *Wiener Bauindustrie-Zeitung* provided the most up-to-date and comprehensive information in late nineteenth-century Vienna about technical, industrial, and economic developments affecting architecture.

Architectural periodicals published privately in Vienna such as *Allgemeine Bauzeitung* and *Wiener Bauindustrie Zeitung* were focused on the city in which they originated; dealing with architecture, as well as news about architecture as a commodity, the editorial scope of these periodicals was defined by the commercial territory their readers tended to occupy. Two factors, however, prompted other periodicals to establish a wider editorial focus. First, beginning in 1891, an economic downturn slowed building activity in Vienna, while, in the meantime, the development of other cities such as Budapest, Prague, and Zagreb continued unabated. The fate of periodicals like *Allgemeine Bauzeitung* and *Wiener Bauindustrie Zeitung* was, to some degree, tied to the fate of Vienna itself; as a German critic noted with regard to *Allgemeine Bauzeitung*:

Allgemeine Bauzeitung served as a radiant diary of the great architectural renovation of Vienna; the first renaissance of the Austrian capital found in Förster's magazine an eloquent chronicle. The magazine, however, gradually became so intertwined with the architectural development of Vienna that as that development came to an end, and with it, building activity and artistic culture in Vienna, *Allgemeine Bauzeitung*, too, had to necessarily suffer a setback.[18]

Neubauten und Concurrenzen (1895–1903), founded by Oskar Marmorek, can be seen as a response to this problem.[19] *Neubauten und Concurrenzen* addressed and expanded coverage of two specialized aspects of architectural discourse: modern architecture [*Neubauten*] and (usually unexecuted) architectural designs produced for design competitions [*Concurrenzen*]. Each of these topics had recently been addressed by separate German periodicals;[20] combining these topics, Marmorek established a single periodical which concentrated on the most current Austrian architectural designs, an idea taken up a few years later by the Hungarian periodical *Magyar Pályázatok* [Hungarian Competitions] (1903–06).[21] Further, Marmorek, who had immigrated to Vienna from Galicia, was concerned to focus *Neubauten und Concurrenzen* not on Vienna, but on the empire's provinces, as he wrote in the first issue:

> The longing for and appreciation of buildings has certainly decreased in Vienna in the last years, but all the more intensive has been building activity in Budapest and in other county and provincial cities, cities upon which our attention must be focused in order to reveal the first signs of the most recent improvements.... We have thus given ourselves the task ... to publish the characteristic new building from all parts of Austria and Hungary.[22]

Another factor prompting broader geographical coverage, at least in state-sponsored publications, was the growth of nationalist consciousness in the empire's provinces, a development acknowledged on a multitude of cultural as well as political levels. The founding of *Österreichische Monatsschrift für den öffentlichen Baudienst*[23] in 1895 by the imperial Ministry of the Interior's Department of Architecture (then newly directed by Emil Ritter von Förster, son of the founder of *Allgemeine Bauzeitung*) can be seen as one of these acknowledgments.[24] In its inaugural issue, *Österreichische Monatsschrift für den öffentlichen Baudienst* declared itself to be a periodical devoted to "state building" [*Staatsbaudienst*], a category which was to include "the planning and execution of architecture, waterworks, street layouts, and bridge building ... (as well as) railroads, machine fabrication, technology, electrical technology, hygiene ... the field of public building as a whole."[25]

While this was more or less a typical mix of topics, *Österreichische Monatsschrift für den öffentlichen Baudienst* devoted only ten to twenty percent of its contents to buildings in Vienna, far less than in comparable publications. This shift of coverage from Vienna to the provinces was even more dramatic in the case of *Allgemeine Bauzeitung*, which the Ministry of Interior took over in 1895. While at least half of the buildings covered in *Allgemeine Bauzeitung* in the early 1890s were located in Vienna, in the next five years under the Ministry's editorship, only one Viennese building was published, with the vast majority of the periodical's contents devoted to buildings in other cities in the empire, most notably Budapest, Graz, L'viv, Podgorica, and Prague. With the founding of *Österreichische Monatsschrift für den öffentlichen Baudienst* and the take-over of *Allgemeine Bauzeitung* in 1895, then, the Austrian Ministry of the Interior attempted to shift coverage of architecture away from Vienna and towards the empire's more quickly developing—and restive—provincial cities.

Der Architekt, founded in 1895, continued the project of architectural periodicals such as *Allgemeine Bauzeitung* to provide a putatively neutral and comprehensive overview of contemporary architectural production;[26] this project, however, ignored the growing fragmentation of architectural practice into smaller, more specialized areas. Thus, in the decades before and after 1900, new periodicals were founded that reflected the diversity and complexity of the new tasks facing architects. In Vienna, for example, new periodicals were founded that focused on historic preservation (*Der Denkmalpflege*, 1899–1922), interior architecture (*Das Interieur*, 1900–15), new construction materials (*Beton und Eisen*, 1902), urbanism (*Der Städtebau*, 1904–29), and housing (*Wohnungsfürsorge*, 1911–31).

The most significant development in periodical literature and architectural culture generally at the turn of the century was the increasing importance and independence of architecture's aesthetic dimension, a development that removed architecture from the discursive field of engineering to that of art. Around 1900, periodicals published by Secessionist organizations in Vienna, Prague, and Zagreb included architectural designs from or influenced by Otto Wagner and the Wagner School along with Secessionist painting, sculpture, and graphic art. In these Secessionist periodicals, the emphasis on practice and production that characterized the professional or trade journals was replaced by a preoccupation with aesthetic program; if trade journals dealt with aesthetics as but one dimension of architecture, Secessionist periodicals dealt with aesthetics as the central architectural problematic. These periodicals were published by associations of artists and architects—Spolek Mánes, founded in Prague in 1896, the Wiener Secession, founded in 1897, and (though they did not publish their own periodical) Klub hrvatskih arhitektu, founded in Zagreb in 1905—that developed as counterparts to professional associations. The organs of self-constituted cultural associations independent of direct government control and sponsorship, the Secessionist periodicals gave artists and architects a higher degree of control over the public dissemination of their work than had hitherto been available to them. Although the editors of Secessionist periodicals described their objectives in much the same way that the editors of contemporaneous art and architecture periodicals described theirs—to provide a comprehensive overview of a field—the contents of their periodicals actually represented quite specialized versions of contemporary artistic practice.[27]

Ver Sacrum (1898–1903), the magazine of the Viennese Secession, of which the architects Otto Wagner, Josef Hoffmann, and Josef Olbrich were members, published the projects and buildings of various students and collaborators of Wagner.[28] In Zagreb, Viktor Kovačić, who had studied with Wagner, allied himself with the local Secessionist group, and promoted Wagner's ideas in the first issue of the group's periodical, *Život*.[29] In Prague, Jan Kotěra, another of Wagner's students, similarly argued for the validity of Wagner's principles in the Czech Secessionist periodical *Volné směry* [Free Directions].[30] When Kotěra became an editor of *Volné směry* in 1900, he published numerous examples of the work of Wagner and his students in the journal.[31]

In Vienna, some of the work featured in *Ver Sacrum* could also be found in the annual supplement to *Der Architekt* which appeared as "Aus der Wagnerschule" (1895–1900). In Prague, however, the work of Czech Secessionist architects and their Viennese counterparts that was published in *Volné směry* contrasted markedly with the work presented in the official organ of the Bohemian Association of Architects, *Architektonický obzor*. According to its editors, the objectives of *Architektonický obzor* were "to serve domestic fine art. To cultivate its specificity. To guard the treasures of our past. To be an honorable tribune of thoughtful struggles and a faithful mirror of Czech architectural creation on the threshold of the twentieth century."[32] Focused on buildings and projects primarily in Prague, and secondarily in other Bohemian cities, *Architektonický obzor* attempted to define a way in which "Slavic Prague, the center of a newly-awakened historic nation," could develop without compromising or destroying its specific identity. This attempt yielded historicist architecture and policies of historic preservation, as well as sustained criticism of just the sort of program of cultural modernity which was promoted in *Volné směry*.[33]

In 1907, a group of architects in the Mánes Association formed an architectural sub-group, Sdružení architektů Mánes [Mánes Association of Architects], and began to publish the periodical *Styl* [Style], in the following year. In *Styl*, a nationalist concern for historic Prague was balanced with a more cosmopolitan concern for architectural developments outside of Bohemia. As the editors wrote in the inaugural issue: "We will chiefly take notice of that which is closest to us, and we will strive for a beautiful Prague and a beautiful Czech countryside . . . but with the slogan of domestic art we do not want to be apostles of mediocrity or to be blind to foreign art. We will always acquire a high standard for Czech work by acquainting readers with the best foreign names and opening a window to the fresh European air."[34]

Accordingly, *Styl* published the latest work of Viennese Secessionist architects such as Hoffmann, Olbrich, and Wagner, and texts by Deutsche Werkbund members like Herman Muthesius, Karl Scheffler, Werner Sombart, and Henry Van de Velde; but it juxtaposed these with articles about, and illustrations of, Czech folk art and small provincial towns.

In 1911, the architects involved with *Styl* left the Mánes Association for the newly formed Skupina výtvarných umělců [Association of Fine Artists], a smaller and more progressive organization, and became involved with the periodical *Umělecký měsíčník* [Artistic Monthly]. In its variety of topics covered (poetry, literature, theater, painting, sculpture, architecture, industrial art, music, and aesthetics), small print-run (200 copies of each issue), and manifesto-like content (programmatic texts on Cubist architecture by Hofman and Janák, for example), *Umělecký měsíčník* anticipated some of the periodicals published by avant-garde groups in Central Europe just before and after World War I.

In the inter-war period, periodicals emerged as the main or even only public venue for Central European avant-garde groups.[35] An important link existed between avant-garde ideologies and the medium in which they were expressed: the modern design and typography of the periodical and the international provenance of its contents were primary representations of the type of culture which the avant-gardes were attempting to foster; as Fernand Divoire wrote in *L'Esprit Nouveau*: "It is in periodicals where one finds the clearest declarations, the premier signs, and the premier creations, in theory and example, of the new forms of the aesthetic."[36]

Avant-garde periodicals often changed their title, place of publication, editorial staff, and even ideological orientation because of government censorship, internal dissension, new international contacts, and changes in group membership; continuity was most often provided by an editor who published a succession of different periodicals for an artistic organization. Central European cities, their diverse citizenry a legacy of pre- and post-war population shifts, were particularly suitable places in which to produce avant-garde periodicals. These cities were the sites of meetings between the protagonists of Western European and Soviet avant-gardes; with their various émigré communities, they offered havens to Central European editors fleeing censorship or persecution; and these same communities provided editors with new audiences for their periodicals. Moreover, Central European editors of avant-garde periodicals could utilize wide networks of émigré correspondents, who could report on events which would otherwise be known only to small circles of locals.

Thus, the avant-garde periodical, at least until the middle or late 1920s, flourished in cities such as Berlin, Vienna, and Prague, as itineraries of some of the major periodicals suggest. For example, Lajos Kassák, a leader of the Hungarian Activists, edited *A Tett* [The Deed] in Budapest from 1915 to 1916, and after that journal was suppressed, he published *MA* [Today] from 1916 to 1919. After Kassák declared his opposition to Béla Kun's socialist regime, *MA* was banned, and Kassák moved to Vienna, where *MA* was published until 1926. At the end of 1926 Kassák returned to Budapest and founded *Dokumentum*, published until 1927, succeeded in 1928 by *Munka* [Work]. Similarly, the Yugoslavian *Zenit* [Zenith], founded and edited by Ljubomir Mičić, was published in Zagreb from 1921 to 1923, and then moved to the more congenial environment of Belgrade from 1923 to 1926. After *Zenit* was banned in 1926, two issues of a successor periodical, *Tank*, were published in Ljubljana in 1927 by Ferdo Delak and Avgust Černogoj, two of Mičić's collaborators. The Czech group Devětsil, founded in 1920, produced a series of different periodicals in Prague and Brno—they published one issue of the *Revoluční sborník Devětsil* [Devětsil Revolutionary Collection], guest-edited the second volume of *Život* [Life] in 1922, then published *Disk* in 1923 and *Pásmo* [Zone] from 1924 to 1926. In 1925, however, Devětsil was able to arrange for a private company, Odeon, to publish its periodicals and books, an arrangement that continued until 1931 and under which the longest-lasting of the group's periodicals, *ReD* (an acronym for Devětsil Revolutionary Edition), was published between 1927 and 1931.

Architecture was initially dealt with in avant-garde periodicals in the frame of engagements with Constructivism and other movements seen as complementary to it. Constructivist work was first publicized in the west through the activities of Konstantin Umanskij in Vienna and El Lissitzky and Il'ya Erenburg in Berlin. Umanskij, Constructivist artist, author of *Neue Kunst in Russland 1914–1919* (1920), and Viennese correspondent of the Soviet journal, *Tass*, met Béla Uitz, the co-editor of *MA*, in Vienna in October 1920, initiating a series of articles on Soviet avant-garde art in *MA* and, later, one of its off-shoot periodicals, *Egység* [Unity].[37] Umanskij's book was also reviewed in the Czech *Musaion*,[38] the review constituting the first account of what would become a decisive influence on the Czech avant-garde.

In 1922, Il'ya Erenburg published his Constructivist manifesto, *A vse-taki ona vertitsya* [And Still the World Turns], in Berlin, as well as co-edited the periodical *Veshch-Gegenstand-Objet* [Object] with El Lissitzky.[39] While Erenburg's book and the majority of articles in *Veshch-Gegenstand-Objet* were in Russian, intended mainly to inform Russian émigrés in Western and Central Europe about recent artistic developments in Berlin, Paris, and Moscow, images and translations from these texts were published in the next few months in *MA*, *Revoluční sborník Devětsil*, *Život*, and *Zenit*. Moreover, the October 1922 issue of *Zenit* was guest-edited by Lissitzky and Erenburg, who Micić met in Berlin in the summer of 1921, and it consisted of material on Soviet Constructivism from the fourth, never-released issue of *Veshch-Gegenstand-Objet*.[40]

While Micić's Zenitism explicitly proposed "Moscow against Paris" and a rejection of "Western" culture, other Central European avant-garde movements apprehended Le Corbusier and Ozenfant's Purism as compatible to Soviet Constructivism, just as many Constructivists themselves did at the same time.[41] Thus, the issue of *MA* that contained Tatlin's Monument to the Third International and Lissitzky's *Proun* also included an article by Le Corbusier and Ozenfant on Purism,[42] and the same article appeared in *Život* along with another by the same authors on Purist architecture.[43] Karel Teige, the main theoretician of Devětsil, met Le Corbusier and Ozenfant in Paris in the summer of 1922, initiating a close relationship that would last until the end of the 1920s. Issues 8, 9, and 10 of *L'Esprit Nouveau* included a Purist manifesto translated into Czech; the only such translations that the magazine ever made, attesting to the importance of the Czech audience for Le Corbusier and Ozenfant.

While architecture was only one of the subjects dealt with by the avant-garde periodicals of the early 1920s, periodicals focused particularly on architecture were founded or taken over by editors with backgrounds in avant-garde movements later in the 1920s. Initially, these periodicals continued the project of identifying and documenting progressive tendencies in contemporary culture, focusing on architecture. *Stavba* [Building], founded by graduates of Prague's Technical University and published by the Klub architektů [Architects' Club] in Prague in 1922, was the first European periodical dedicated specifically to modern architecture. The first volume of the periodical contained a long article by Oldřich Starý on modern architecture in Europe, and when Karel Teige joined *Stavba*'s editorial board in 1923, he published a series of articles reviewing the development of modern architecture in France, Germany, and the Netherlands.[44] Other Czech architecture journals—*Styl* and *Stavitel* [*Builder*], run largely by Kotěra's former students—subsequently began to report on modern architecture, though in a far more eclectic context of coverage. In Hungary, *Tér és Forma* [Space and Form] was founded in 1926; Virgil Bierbauer, who became a co-editor in 1928, focused the journal's contents more tightly on modernism and published a series of articles on modern architecture in England, France, and Italy. Both Teige and Bierbauer also published periodicals which were explicitly intended as international reviews of architecture, periodicals which followed a series of attempts, made through the 1920s, to provide "world-wide" documentations of modern art.[45] In 1928, one issue of the *Devětsil* periodical, *ReD*, was published as such a review,[46] and in the following year, Teige founded an annual publication, *Mezinárodní soudobá architektura* [International Contemporary Architecture] as a collection of primary texts and images of modern architecture.[47] Similarly, utilizing contacts made at the 12th International Congress of Architects held in Budapest in 1930, Virgil Bierbauer transformed one issue of *Tér és Forma* into an *International Revue of Architecture*.[48]

The *International Revue of Architecture* is of special interest in that it was actually produced by an international collective organized by Bierbauer; editors from twelve countries each prepared their own selection of work to be published. As Bierbauer and János Komor, the editors of the periodical, explained:

> It remains a fact that any one periodical can, of course, give only one aspect of the whole: the personal taste of the editor and his accidental connections are responsible for a narrower or broader insight into the whole problem. A comprehensive picture, such as that presented by the International Exposition of Architectural Designs in Budapest, is lacking. For this very reason, under the influence of the exhibition, the members of the 12th International Congress of Architects accepted the project of an international revue of architecture with great interest.[49]

If the putative worldliness of avant-garde architecture was based on a shared morphology of abstract forms, then the worldliness of the architecture presented in the *International Revue of Architecture* was quite different; the periodical presented a picture of uneven development, ambivalent support of aesthetic diktats, and no single "international style" unifying modern architecture around the world.

Despite Bierbauer's plans, no other issue of the *International Revue of Architecture* was ever published. In any case, by the 1930s, architects in Central European countries were teaching and building in ways influenced by the avant-gardes of the 1920s, and newly founded or existing architectural periodicals concentrated more on domestic affairs. The Yugoslavian *Arhitektura*, for example, published between 1931 and 1933, included only three articles devoted to architecture abroad, in Czechoslovakia, Japan, and Sweden; the balance of *Arhitektura*'s articles dealt with the development of modern architecture in Yugoslavia.[50] The success of modern architecture was thought to imply a homogeneity from one country to the next; as the article on Czech architecture in *Arhitektura* claimed, "contemporary Czech architecture, like all other world architectures, has lost its national character. It develops a certain international character—logical, objective, constructive, and utilitarian."[51] When progressive Central European periodicals shifted their coverage from foreign to domestic architecture, then, this shift occurred only when both architectures appeared to be more or less identical.

1 On the origin of architectural periodicals in Germany at the end of the eighteenth century, see Rolf Fuhlrott, *Deutschsprachige Architektur-Zeitschriften*, Munich, 1975, pp. 235–39.

2 On language ordinances in the Habsburg Empire, see Hannelore Burger, *Sprachenrecht und Sprachgerechtigkeit im Österreichischen Unterrichtswesen*, Vienna, 1995.

3 Some aspects of the press in late nineteenth-century Austria-Hungary are discussed in Murray G. Hall, *Österreichische Verlagsgeschichte 1918–1938*, Vienna, 1985.

4 In the introduction to the first issue of the German-language version of *Vállalkozók Lapja* [Contractors' Journal], the editors wrote that "in order to provide a professional magazine to both domestic and foreign contractors, producers, industrialists, and suppliers of German origin in Hungary, Croatia, Slavonia, lands located on the Danube, as well as in Bosnia and Hercegovina, we have put together a German edition of our Hungarian periodical." See "Prospekt," *Der Bauuntnehmer und Lieferant*, vol. 1, no. 1, June 17, 1882, p. 1.

5 As the editor of *Ungarische Bauzeitung* wrote in the inaugural issue, "besides the many good Hungarian magazines on architecture, why should there not also exist a German periodical? The Hungarian language is only very little understood abroad, so our building and architecture finds no response and cannot spread." Josef Summer, "An unsere geehrten Leser," *Ungarische Bauzeitung*, vol. 1, no. 1, July 10, 1896, p. 3.

6 On the publishing of art and architectural periodicals in turn-of-the-century Germany and Austria-Hungary, see Maria Rennhofer, *Kunstschriften der Jahrhundertwende in Deutschland und Österreich 1895–1914*, Vienna, 1987.

7 On the collection of the library of the Austrian Association of Engineers and Architects, see the annual "Literaturblatt" in the *Beiblatt zur Zeitschrift des österreichischen Ingenieur- und Architektenvereins*.

8 *Allgemeine Bauzeitung*, Vienna 1836–1918, founded by Ludwig Förster, published privately until 1894, from 1894 to 1899 by the imperial Ministry of Interior, and thereafter by a consortium of ministries.

9 Among the most important of these were *Journal für die Baukunst* (1829–51), *Notizblatt des Architekten-Vereins zu Berlin* (1833–50), and *Architektonische Entwürfe* (1833–42); see Fuhlrott, *Deutschsprachige Architektur-Zeitschriften*, pp. 240–44.

10 On the history and significance of the press's shift from a reportorial to an editorial function, see Jürgen Habermas, *Strukturwandel der Öffentlichkeit* (Darmstadt, 1962), trans. Thomas Burger, *The Structural Transformation of the Public Sphere*, Cambridge, Mass., 1989, pp. 181–88.

11 See Ludwig Förster, "Plan der Bauzeitung," *Allgemeine Bauzeitung*, vol. 1, no. 1, 1836, p. 1.

12 *Zeitschrift des österreichischen Ingenieur- und Architekten-Vereines*, Vienna, founded 1865, after 1892 published as *Wochenschrift des österreichischen Ingenieur- und Architekten-Vereines; Mitteilungen des Architekten- und Ingenieur-*

Vereines für das Königreich Böhmen, Prague, founded 1866, after 1892 published as *Zprávy spolků architektů a inženýrů v království Českém*; *A Magyar Mérnök- és Építész-egylet közlönye* [Hungarian Engineer- and Architects' Association Bulletin], Budapest, founded 1867; *Vijesti Društva Inžinira i Architekta u Hrvatskoj i Slavoniji*, Zagreb, founded 1880.

13 See *Der österreichische Ingenieur- und Architekten-Verein MDCCCIIL bis MDCCCIIC*, Vienna, 1898, pp. 22–23.

14 *Bauzeitung für Ungarn* (Budapest, 1876–96), later renamed *Ungarische Bauzeitung* (1896–14).

15 *Wiener Bauindustrie-Zeitung* (Vienna, 1883–1919), later renamed *Österreichische Bauzeitung* (1919–25).

16 "An die geehrten Leser der 'Wiener Bauindustrie-Zeitung'," *Wiener Bauindustrie-Zeitung*, vol. 1, no. 1, February 15, 1883, p. 1.

17 As photolithography and chromolithography both developed in the last decades of the nineteenth century, they were quickly taken up by art and architecture periodicals, some of which, like *Wiener Bauindustrie-Zeitung*, published supplements of illustrations using new printing techniques. Much innovative work in printing technology took place in nineteenth-century Vienna, such as Pretsch's development of photo-mechanical printing in 1853 and Klíč's development of halftone photogravures in 1879.

18 Albert Hofmann, "Österreichische Zeitschriften deutscher Sprache für das Baufach," *Deutsche Bauzeitung*, vol. 30, April 18, 1896, p. 199.

19 *Neubauten und Concurrenzen* (Vienna, 1895–99) later renamed *Architektonische Monatshefte* (1900–03). On the founding of *Neubauten und Concurrenzen*, see Markus Kristan, *Oskar Marmorek: Architekt und Zionist 1863–1909*, Vienna, 1996, pp. 102–04.

20 *Deutsche Konkurrenzen* (1892–24), and *Neubauten* (1894–1903), both founded and originally edited by Albert Neumeister and Ernst Haeberle.

21 *Magyar Pályázatok* [Hungarian Competitions] (Budapest, 1903–06). In its first two years, the periodical published only competition entries, but in 1905 it added coverage of realized buildings.

22 Oskar Marmorek, "An unsere Leser," *Neubauten und Concurrenzen*, vol. 1, no. 1, January 1895, p. 1.

23 *Österreichische Monatsschrift für den öffentlichen Baudienst* (1895–1901), later renamed *Österreichische Wochenschrift für den öffentlichen Baudienst* (1901–20), later merged with *Bergbau und Hütte* to form *Österreichische Monatsschrift für den öffentlichen Baudienst und das Berg- und Hüttenwesen* (1920–24).

24 The German Ministry of the Interior published a quarterly periodical on all types of public construction, including architecture (*Centralblatt der Bauverwaltung*) and a bi-weekly periodical concentrating on architecture (*Zeitschrift für Bauwesen*); with the founding of *Österreichische Monatsschrift für den öffentlichen Baudienst* and the take-over of *Allgemeine Bauzeitung* in 1895, the Austro-Hungarian Ministry of Interior replicated this publishing format.

25 "Vorwort," *Österreichische Monatsschrift für den öffentlichen Baudienst*, vol. 1, no. 1, 1895, p. 1.

26 As Ferdinand von Feldegg, the founding editor of *Der Architekt* wrote, "the periodical ... must approach the phenomena of the day without prejudice and bias and must place attention on the public realm, free from sympathy and antipathy. The periodical must not judge opinions and matters of dispute and must indefatigably follow only one basic principle: to grant validity to talent, springing from whatever school or conviction." See Ferdinand von Feldegg, "Program der Zeitschrift 'Der Architekt'," *Der Architekt*, vol. 1, no. 1, 1895, p. 1.

27 As the editors of *Ver Sacrum* wrote, "the shameful fact that Austria possesses not a single illustrated art magazine in wide circulation which conforms to its own special needs has made it until now impossible for the artist to carry his artistic endeavours into a wider circle. This should be rectified through this magazine. *Ver Sacrum* will allow Austria to appear for the first time as an independent artistic factor." "Weshalb wir eine Zeitschrift herausgeben," *Ver Sacrum*, vol. 1, no. 1, 1895, p. 1.

28 On *Ver Sacrum*, see *Ver Sacrum: Die Zeitschrift der Wiener Secession 1898–1903*, Vienna, 1983.

29 Viktor Kovačić, "Moderna Arhitektura," in *Život*, vol. 1, no. 1, 1900, p. 28.

30 Jan Kotěra, "O novém umění," in *Volné směry*, vol. 4, 1899, pp. 189–95.

31 Architecture was mainly featured in issues 4 (1900) through 19 (1906) of *Volné směry*, with issue 4, the first which Kotěra co-edited, publishing modern architecture from outside the Austro-Hungarian empire. On Kotěra's co-editorship of *Volné směry*, see Zdeněk Wirth and Antonin Matějček, *Česká architektura 1800–1920* (Prague, 1922), pp. 73–76. On *Volné směry*, see Roman Prahl and Lenka Bydžovská (eds.), *Volné směry: časopis secese a moderny* (Prague, 1993).

32 Redakce Architektonického obzoru, "Náš Programm," in *Architektonický obzor*, vol. 1, no. 1, January 1902, p. 1.

33 In a typical article, for example, an architect argued that "a city like Prague, with such highly-praised artistic beauties, never needs to compete with the great metropolises, originating almost yesterday with the creation of something new, sensational, and stylish—intentionally, I do not say 'modern'." František Halas, "Moderna v pražských ulicích," in *Architektonický obzor*, vol. 3, no. 9, September 1904, p. 33.

34 "Úvodem," in *Styl*, vol. 1, no. 1, 1908, p. 1.

35 On avant-garde periodicals, see Annette Ciré and Haila Ochs, *Die Zeitschrift als Manifest*, Basel, 1991, and Antoine Baudin, "Centralità e periferia: il contributo dell'Europa Centrale," *Rassegna*, vol. 12, December 1982.

36 Fernand Divoire, "Dans les revues," *L'Esprit Nouveau*, no. 3, 1920, p. 355.

37 In the February 1, 1921 issue of *MA* [Today], Uitz reported on a lecture by Umanskij in Vienna on Soviet avant-garde art; see Béla Uitz, "Jegyzetek a *Ma* orosz estélyéhez" [Notes from the *MA* Russian evening meeting], *MA*, vol. 6, no. 4, February 1, 1921, p. 52, and subsequent issues before the van Diemen exhibition included work by Archipeniko and Puni. Uitz travelled to Moscow in January 1921 and published a series of Constructivist works and translations of two constructivist manifestos—Gabo and Pevsner's "Realistic Manifesto" and Gan's "Program of the First Working Group of constructivists"—in the June 22 and September 16, 1922 issues of the periodical *Egység* [Unity]. *Egység* was a rival journal to *MA*, which Uitz was then co-editing, and these issues constituted the most extensive survey of Soviet Constructivist work then available in the west. On the Hungarian assimilation of Soviet Constructivism, see Kristina Passuth, "Contacts between the Hungarian and Russian Avant-Garde in the 1920's," in *The First Russian Show*; on the periodical *Egység*, see Oliver A. I. Botar, "From the Avant-Garde to 'Proletarian Art': The Emigré Hungarian Journals *Egység* and *Akasztott Ember* [Hanging Man], 1922–1923," in *Art Journal*, vol. 52, no. 1, spring 1993.

38 Václav Nebeský, "Ruská revoluce v umění," in *Musaion*, vol. 2, 1921. On early contacts between Czech and Soviet avant-gardistes, see Rostislav Švácha, "Sovětský konstruktívismus a česká architektura," in *Umění*, vol. 36, 1988.

39 On the history of *Veshch-Gegenstand-Objet*, see Roland Nachtigäller and Hubertus Gassner, "3 x 1 = 1 *Veshch-Gegenstand-Objet*," in *Veshch-Gegenstand-Objet: Commentary and Translations*, Baden, 1994; on the "First Russian Art

Exhibition," see *The First Russian Show*, London, 1983; on the dissemination of Soviet Constructivism in 1922 Berlin, see Manfredo Tafuri, "U.S.S.R.—Berlin: From Populism to Constructivist International," in *The Sphere and the Labyrinth: Avant-Gardes and Architecture from Piranesi to the 1970s*, Cambridge, Mass., 1983.

40 *Zenit*, nos. 17-18, October 1922. On this issue, see Irina Subotić, "Zenit i avangarda dvadesetih godina," in *Zenit i avangarda dvadesetih godina*, Belgrade, 1983.

41 Erenburg was in Paris in 1921, became acquainted with Le Corbusier and Ozenfant, and the first issue of *Veshch-Gegenstand-Objet* included five translations of articles from *L'Esprit Nouveau*; subsequent correspondence between Le Corbusier and El Lissitzky suggests that Le Corbusier might not have known that this material was reprinted. See Nachtigäller and Gassner, "3 x 1 = 1 *Veshch-Gegenstand-Objet*," p. 31.

42 Le Corbusier and Ozenfant, "Purism," in *MA*, vol. 8, no. 4, May 1922.

43 Le Corbusier and Ozenfant, "Purisma" and "Architektura a Purisma," in *Život*, vol. 2, 1922.

44 On Teige's editorship of *Stavba*, see Otakar Máčel, "La critica e i suoi strumenti (Teige e *Stavba*, 1923–1927)," in Manuela Castagnara Codeluppi (ed.), *Karel Teige: Luoghi e pensieri del moderno, 1900–1951*, Milan, 1996.

45 See, for example, Lajos Kassák and László Moholy-Nagy's *Buch Neuer Kunstler*, published in Vienna in September 1922, *Zenit* no. 25, February 1924, which was a catalogue of the "Prva Zenitova međunarodna izložba nove umetnosti" (First Zenitist International Exhibition of New Art) held in Belgrade in April 1924, and *Fronta*, published in Brno in 1927 by the Brno branch of Devětsil, which, similar to the *Buch Neuer Künstler*, attempted to document the current state of modern art.

46 *ReD*, vol. 1, no. 5, February 1928.

47 The first issue of *Mezinárodní soudobá architektura*, published in 1929, collected modernist architectural projects and manifestos from Europe and the Soviet Union; the second issue, published in 1930, documented modernist architecture in Czechoslovakia; the third and last issue, published in 1931, was devoted to the work of the architectural partnership of Josef Havlíček and Karel Honzík.

48 *Tér és Forma*, vol. 4, no. 7, July 1931.

49 Virgil Bierbauer and János Komor, "Bevezetés," in *Tér és Forma*, vol. 4, no. 7, July 1931.

50 While *Arhitektura* was not officially associated with Zemlja, the most important group of politically-engaged artists and architects in inter-war Yugoslavia, the periodical republished various sections of the book *Problemi savremene arhitekture* by Stjepan Planić, an architect associated with the group. On the architectural section of Zemlja, see Željka Čorak, "Arhitektura," in *Kritička retrospektiva "Zemlja,"* Zagreb, 1971.

51 Rado Kregar, "Sodobna češkoslovaška arhitektura," in *Arhitektura*, vol. 3, no. 1/2, 1933.

APPENDICES

p. 248
**Map of the Austro-Hungarian
Monarchy, c. 1904 (scale 1:1,500,500)**

Heinrich Hanau's map shows the new
administrative organization of the Monarchy, as imposed in 1904 by the Archduke
Franz Ferdinand. Alongside Austria and
Hungary a south Slavonic administrative
unity was to be established.
Cartographic collection, Austrian National Library

p. 249
**Map of the Successor States to the
Austro-Hungarian Monarchy, 1919
(scale 1:3,500,000)**
Cartographic collection, Austrian National Library

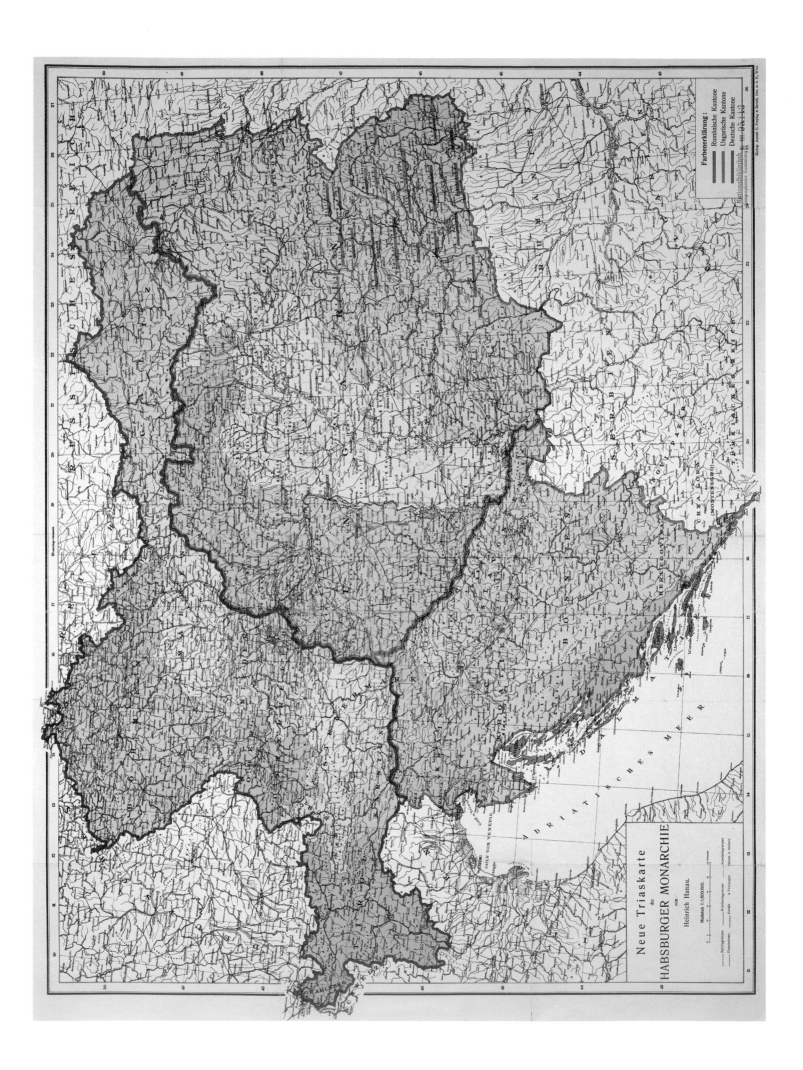

Neue Triaskarte
der
HABSBURGER MONARCHIE
von
Heinrich Hanau.

Maßstab 1:1,500.000.

Farbenerklärung:
Rumänische Kantone
Ungarische Kantone
Deutsche Kantone

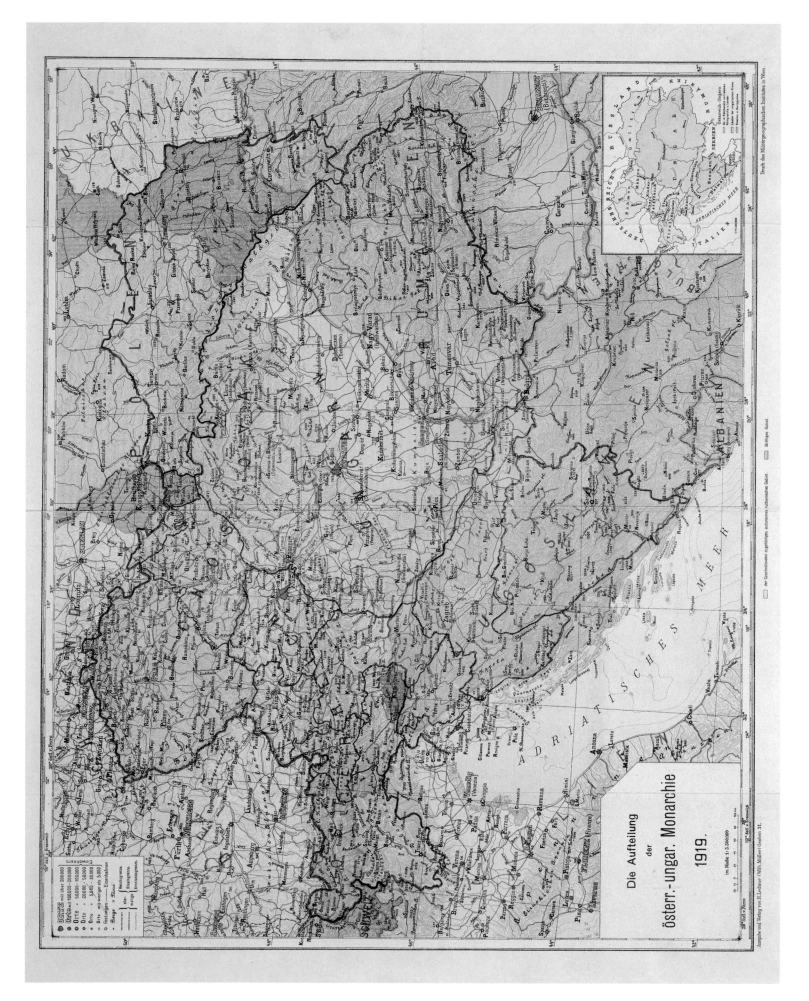

Die Aufteilung
der
Österr.-ungar. Monarchie
1919.

im Maße 1:3,500.000

Biographical Notes

Aladár Árkay

(Timişoara 1868–Budapest 1932)
1886–90 studied architecture and painting in Budapest; 1892 and 1900 at the École des Beaux-Arts in Paris; at the beginning of the 1890s building-site supervisor in the architect's office of Fellner & Helmer in Vienna, then worked with Alajos Hauszmann and, from 1894 onwards, worked in the office of Mór Kallina, Otto Wagner's Budapest partner.
Major buildings and projects: estate of villas for judges and lawyers, Budapest (1910–13); Protestant Church, Budapest VII (1911–13); Catholic Chapel, Budapest XII (1923); Catholic Church, Győr (1928); Sacred Heart Church, Budapest XII (1931–33, in collaboration with Bertalan Árkay).

Lit.: Balázs Dercsényi, *Árkay Aladár* [Aladár Árkay], Budapest, 1967.
Péter Farbaky, "A fasori református templom" [The Reformed Church in Városligeti Avenue], in *Ars Hungarica* (Budapest), XII, 1984, pp. 255–69.

Aladar Baranyai

(Szászvár 1879–Zagreb 1936)
1899 graduated from the National Crafts School in Zagreb, then external student at the College of Arts and Crafts in Vienna; 1902–05 practical training at the "Pilar-Mally-Bauda" studio in Zagreb; 1906–31 joint architects' office with Slavko Benedik (Benedik & Baranyai) and, from 1932 onwards, with his son Pavel.
Major buildings and projects in Zagreb: Tišov Villa and Studio (1900–01); Stern residential and business premises (1906–07); Harnisch House (1907); the Varžička-Prikril residential and business blocks (1907); Popović (1907–08); Švarc–Crnojević (1910); Ćuk (1910); Rubetić-Gollner House (1907–08); Croatian Real Estate Bank (1909–10);, Benedik villa estate, Baranyai, Paskiević, Segen and Lorković (1909–11); Grünwald House (1910–11); housing estate 'Mali Pantovčak (1911–12); Serbian Bank (1912–14 and 1930–31); Sochar commercial warehouse (1913); Villa Ilić (1918–20); Leon House (1920–21); Deutsch House (1924); building of the Association of Engineers and Architects (1927); Baranyai Villa (1930–31); Benedik-Baranyai House (1930–31).

Lit.: Aleksander Laslo, "Aladar Baranyai i građanski ideal" [Aladar Baranyai and the Middle-Class Ideal], in *Arhitektura* (Zagreb), XXXVI–XXXVII, 1983–84, no. 186–88, pp. 64–73.
Andreja Der Hazarijan-Vukić, "Arhitektura Aladara Baranyaia u Zagrebu" [The Architecture of Aladar Baranyai in Zagreb], in *Život umjetnosti* [The Life of Art] (Zagreb), XXX, 1995, nos. 56–57, pp. 28–43.
Aladar Vladimir Baranyai. Arhitektura in design 1899–34 [Aladar Vladimir Baranyai. Architecture and Design 1899–34], exh. cat., Pokrajinski muzej Celje-Muzej za umjetnost i obrt, Zagreb, 1997.

Vjekoslav Bastl

(Příbram 1872–Zagreb 1947)
1896 graduated from the National Crafts School in Zagreb; 1896–99 and 1903–05 worked at the Hönigsberg & Deutsch studio in Zagreb; 1899–02 studied architecture with Otto Wagner at the Academy of Fine Arts in Vienna; 1902, Gundel Prize; 1905 co-founder of the Club of Croatian Architects [Klub hrvatskih arhitekta]; 1906 set up own architect's office; from 1910 assistant lecturer, from 1919 Professor at the National Crafts School in Zagreb.
Major buildings and projects in Zagreb: Pečić House (1899); Chamber of Trade and Museum of Commerce and Trade (1902–03); "Elsa Fluid" House (1903); the Kallina residential and business blocks (1903–04); Rado (1904–05); Feller (1905–06); Goršak (1906); Kallina Villa (1905–06); Hodovsky House (1909–10); the National Croatian-Slavonic Central Savings Bank (1906–07); "Holy Ghost" Municipal Children's Orphanage (1910–13); Institute of Chemistry and Pharmacy (1913–14); project for the Bank of Commerce (1920) "Export–Import" residential and business blocks (1920–21); Bartu-lić (1929–30); the city's covered market Dolac 9 (1926–30); College of Trade and Economy (1927–28); Radošević Villa (1929–30).

Lit.: Zlatko Jurić, "Arhitekt Vjekoslav Bastl. Radovi 1901–10" [The Architect Vjekoslav Bastl: His Work 1901–10], in *Život umjetnosti* [The Life of Art] (Zagreb), XXX, 1995, nos. 56–57, pp. 44–57.
Aleksander Laslo, "Vjekoslav Bastl," in *Čovjek i prostor* [Man and Space] (Zagreb), XL, 1995, nos. 1–2, pp. 22–29.
Krešimir Galović, *Arhitekt Vjekoslav Bastl. Skice i crteži* [The Architect Vjekoslav Bastl: Sketches and Drawings], Zagreb, 1998.

Leopold Bauer

(Krnov 1872–Vienna 1938)
Studied at the National Crafts School in Brno; 1893–96 studied with Karl Hasenauer and Otto Wagner at the Academy of Fine Arts in Vienna; 1896 Prix de Rome and scholarship for Italy; 1913–19 succeeded Otto Wagner at the Academy of Fine Arts in Vienna.
Major buildings and projects: Reissig Villa, Brno (1901–02); Kurz Villa, Krnov (1902–03); Parish Church of Bielsko-Biała (1907); several villas, Vienna (from 1907); participated in the competition for the Imperial War Ministry, Vienna 1 (1907); club house for rifle club, Krnov (1907–08); Chamber of Trade, Opava (1908–10); Preißnitz Sanatorium, Jeseník (1908–10); Hecht Villa, Brno (1909 –11); project for the Austro-Hungarian Bank, Vienna IX (1911–18); printing works of the Austrian National Bank, Vienna IX (1913–26); Vogelweidhof, Vienna XV (1926–28); Breda & Weinstein Department Store, Opava (1927–28); participation in the Paul-Speiser Hof, Vienna XXI (1929–32).

Lit.: Leopold Bauer, *Verschiedene Skizzen, Entwürfe und Studien. Ein Beitrag zum Verständnis unserer modernen Bestrebungen in der Baukunst*, Vienna, 1899.
Ferdinand von Feldegg (ed.), *Leopold Bauer. Der Künstler und sein Werk*, Vienna, 1918.
Oberbaurat Professor Leopold Bauer. Seine Anschauung in Wort und Werk, Vienna - Leipzig, 1931.
Leopold Bauer zum 60. Geburtstage 1. September 1932. Widmungen seiner Freunde [Leopold Bauer. On the Anniversary of his 60th Birthday on 1 September 1932. Dedications from his Friends], Brno, 1932.
Jindřich Vybíral, "Hledáné kontinuity a řádu v díle Leopolda Bauera" [In Search of Continuity and Order in the Work of Leopold Bauer], in *Umění* [Art], Prague, XXXVII, 1989, pp. 438–53.

Lipót Baumhorn
(Kisbér 1860–Budapest 1932)
1878–83 studied architecture at the Institute of Science and Technology in Vienna; 1884–94 worked in the studio of Ödön Lechner and Gyula Pártos in Budapest; 1928 second place in the competition for a new synagogue in Slovak Žilina which was won by Peter Behrens, with Josef Hoffmann in third place.
Major buildings and projects: a number of synagogues and buildings for Jewish denominational communities, Hungary, Romania and Slovakia (1888–1930); New Synagogue, Timişoara-Fabric (1897–99); headquarters of the water supply and distribution company Timiş-Bega, Timişoara (1900–02); Gymnasium for Girls, Timişoara (1902–03 in collaboration with Jakob Klein); Lloyd Palace, Timişoara (1910–12); participated in the competition for a new synagogue, Žilina (1928).

Lit.: Peter A. Petri, *Biographisches Lexikon des Banater Deutschtums*, Marquartstein 1992, p. 100.
Mihai Opriş, *Timişoara. Mică monografie urbanistică* [Timişoara. A Short Monograph on the City], Bucureşti, 1987, p. 145.
János Gerle, Attila Kovács, Imre Makovecz, *A századforduló magyar építészete* [Hungarian Architecture around the Turn of the Century], Budapest, 1990, pp. 51–52.
Baumhorn Lipót, exh. cat., Magyar Zsidó Múzeum, Budapest, 1999.

Virgil Bierbauer
(Aiud 1893–1956)
1920 graduated in architecture after having studied with Theodor Fischer in Munich; 1922 set up his own architect's office and published a number of articles and specialist architecture journals; 1928–42 editor of journal of architecture *Tér és Forma* in Budapest; from 1931 honorary corresponding member of the Royal Institute of British Architects (RIBA).
Major buildings and projects: airport, Budapest XI, Kőérbereki út 36 (1936–37 in collaboration with László Králik); several projects and buildings for the municipal power station, Budapest (from 1925).

Lit.: Virgil Bierbauer, *Budapest városépítési problémái* [Problems with the Urban Development in Budapest], Budapest, 1933.
Nóra Pamer, *Magyar építészet a két világháború között* [Hungarian Architecture during the Years between the Wars], Budapest, 1986.

Josef Chochol
(Písek 1880–Prague 1956)
1898–04 studied architecture with Josef Schulz and Jan Koula at the Czech Institute of Science and Technology in Prague; 1907–09 studied with Otto Wagner at the Academy of Fine Arts in Vienna; member of the association of artists S.V.U. Mánes; 1911–12 member of Skupina výtvarných umělců [group of fine artists]; from 1920 member of the association of artists Devětsil, 1929 founder member of the Levá fronta [Left Front] and 1933 member of the Federation of Socialist Architects.

Major buildings and projects: three-family residence, Prague, Rašinovo nábřeží 6-10 (1912–13); Kovařovič Villa, Prague (1912–13); block of flats, Prague, Neklanova 30 (1913–14); project for the Osvobozené divadlo [Free Theater], Prague (1926–27).

Lit.: Josef Chochol, *K funkcí architektonického článku* [On the Functions of the Architectonic Element], in *Styl* [Style] (Prague), V, 1913, pp. 93–94.
Rostislav Švácha. "Josef Chochol 1880–80," in *Umění* [Art] (Prague), XXVIII, 1980, pp. 545–52.
Rostislav Švácha, "Josef Chochol. Pokus o intimnější portrét" [Josef Chochol: An Attempt to produce a more intimate Portrayal], in *Umění* [Art] (Prague), XLII, 1994, pp. 21–49.

Karl Ehn
(Vienna 1884–1957)
Studied at the National Crafts School in Vienna; 1904–07 studied architecture with Otto Wagner at the Academy of Fine Arts in Vienna; from 1908 worked at the municipal building and planning department; in the 1920s responsible for a number of buildings for the communal housing program in Vienna.
Major buildings and projects for the building and planning department in Vienna: Hermeswiese estate, Vienna XIII (1922–23); Linden-Hof, Vienna XVIII (1924–25); Bebel–Hof, Vienna XII (1925–27); Karl-Marx-Hof, Vienna XIX (1927–30); Adelheid-Popp-Hof, Vienna XVI (1932).

Lit.: Karl Ehn, personal files, Stadt- und Landesarchiv, Vienna

Maks Fabiani
(Kobdilj nr. Štanjel 1865–Gorizia 1962)
1883–89 studied architecture at the Institute of Science and Technology in Vienna; 1889–91 assistant at the Institute of Science and Technology in Graz; 1894–96 worked in the office of Otto Wagner and as an assistant to Carl König at the Institute of Science and Technology in Vienna; 1902 Ph.D. in Science and Technology; adviser to the Archduke Franz Ferdinand; 1910–18 Professor of Decorative Painting at the Institute of Science and Technology in Vienna; 1919 moved to Gorizia, Lecturer at the Institute of Technology in Gorizia.
Major buildings and projects: general development plans, Ljubljana (1895, 1898, partially developing them); Pavilion of the "Drei Commissionen" at the Kaiser's Anniversary Exhibition, Vienna II (1898); office and business premises Portois & Fix, Vienna III (1899–1900); office and business premises Artaria, Vienna I (1900–01); Urania, Vienna I (1905–09); project for the architectural design of the Slovenski trg, Ljubljana (1899, now Miklošičev Park); new design for the façade of the St Jacob's School for Girls, Ljubljana (1900); Krisper House, Ljubljana (1900–01); Hribar House, Ljubljana (1902–03); Bamberg House, Ljubljana (1906–07); Institute of Higher Education for Girls "Mladika," Ljubljana (1906–07).

Lit.: *Arhitekt Maks Fabiani 1865–62*, exh. cat., Narodna Galerija, Ljubljana 1966.
Marco Pozzetto, *Max Fabiani. Ein Architekt der Monarchie*, Vienna, 1983.
Marco Pozzetto (ed.), *Max Fabiani. Nuove Frontiere dell'Architettura*, exh. cat., Scuderie del Parco di Miramare, Trieste, Venice, 1988.
Marco Pozzetto, *Maks Fabiani. Vizije prostora* [Max Fabiani. Visions of Space], Kranj, 1997.

Roman Feliński
(L'viv 1886–Wrocław 1953)
Studied in L'viv and in Munich; continued his professional training in Paris and Vienna; worked as chief architect in the planning office of the Ulam company in L'viv, and later set up his own architect's office; in the 1920s: worked in Warsaw, then for the Polish Ministry of Public Works.

Major buildings and projects in Ľviv: Grüner House (1909–11 in collaboration with Ferdynand Kasler); Rohatyn House (1911–13); Liberman House (1911–12); department store, Špytaľna 2 (1911–13).

Lit.: Roman Feliński, *Budowa miast* [Urban Development], Ľviv, 1916.
Album inżynierów i techników polskich [Index of Polish Engineers and Technicians], Ľviv, 1932, p. 53.
Stanisław Łoza, *Architekci i budowniczowie w Polsce* [Architects and Builders in Poland], Warsaw, 1954, p. 74.

Alfréd Forbát

(Pécs 1897–Stockholm 1972)
1914 studied architecture at the Institute of Science and Technology in Budapest; 1920–22 worked in the office of Walter Gropius at the Bauhaus in Weimar; 1923 established the company "Neue Reklame-Gestaltung" [New Advertising Design]; practised as a freelance architect; 1925–28 chief architect at the Sommerfeld Company in Berlin; 1928 set up his own architect's office; 1930 taught at the Art School of Johannes Itten in Berlin; member of CIAM; 1932–33, sojourn in the USSR; after his return worked as an independent architect in Pécs; 1938 emigrated to Sweden; until 1942 involved with several projects of urban planning in Lund and Stockholm; 1959–60 Professor at the Institute of Science and Technology in Stockholm.
Major buildings and projects: project for the "Bauhaus Estate," Weimar (1922–23 in collaboration with Walter Gropius); numerous buildings and projects for the Sommerfeld company, Berlin (1925–29); participated in the competition for re-designing the Alexanderplatz, Berlin (1929); Mommsen Station, Berlin-Eichkamp (1929–30); participation in the major housing estates Siemensstadt and Haselhorst, Berlin (1930–31).

Lit.: *Fred Forbat. Architekt und Stadtplaner*, exh. cat., Ernst Ludwig House, Darmstadt, 1969.
"Ottó Mezei, Ungarische Architekten am Bauhaus," in Hubertus Gassner (ed.) *Wechselwirkungen. Ungarische Avantgarde in der Weimarer Republik*, exh. cat., New Gallery, Kassel-Bochum Museum, Marburg, 1986, pp. 339–46.

Josef Frank

(Baden nr. Vienna 1885–Stockholm 1968)
1903–08 studied architecture at the Institute of Science and Technology in Vienna; 1908–09 worked with Bruno Möhring in Berlin from 1910 Member of the German "Werkbund" and 1912 founding member of the Austrian "Werkbund" [association of avant-garde manufacturers and artists promoting the crafts and the quality of industrial design]; 1919–25 Professor of Civil Engineering at the College of Arts and Crafts in Vienna; 1925 founded furnishings company "Haus & Garten" [House and Garden] in collaboration with Oskar Wlach; 1928 only Austrian delegate participating in the inaugural congress of CIAM in La Sarraz in Switzerland; from 1929 initiator and head of the "Werkbund" estate in Vienna; 1934 emigrated to Sweden; 1934–66 worked with Svenskt Tenn; 1939 obtained Swedish citizenship; 1942–43 visiting lecturer at the New School for Social Research in New York.
Major buildings and projects in the 1920s and 1930s: Strauß House, Vienna XVIII (1913–14); workers housing estate, Ortmann nr. Pernitz (1919–21); two-apartment houses, Weißenhof Siedlung, Stuttgart (1926–27); participated in the Winarsky-Hof project, Vienna XX (1924–25); Villa Claëson, Falsterbo (1924–27); Villa Carlsten, Falsterbo (1927); block of community apartments, Wien XIV (1928, in collaboration with Oskar Wlach and Ernst Plischke); Villa Beer, Vienna XIII (1929, in collaboration with Oskar Wlach); two community estates, Vienna XI, Vienna XII (in collaboration with Oskar Wlach, 1931–32); plan for the development of Vienna Werkbund Estate, Vienna XIII (1930–32); family house,

"Werkbund" Estate, Vienna XIII (1930–32); Låftmann House, Seth House, Falsterbo (1934–35); Bunzl House, Vienna XVIII (1935–36, in collaboration with Oskar Wlach); Wehtje House, Falsterbo (1935–36).

Lit.: Josef Frank, *Architektur als Symbol. Elemente deutsches neuen Bauens*, Vienna, 1931, 2nd edition 1981.
Josef Frank (ed.), *Die internationale Werkbundsiedlung Wien 1932*, Vienna, 1932 (*New Forms of Building Worldwide*, vol. 6).
Josef Frank 1885–67, exh. cat., College of Applied Art, Vienna, 1981.
Mikael Bergquist, Olof Michélsen (eds.), *Josef Frank. Architektur*, Basle, Boston, Berlin, 1995.
Nina Stritzler-Levine (ed.), *Josef Frank. Architect and Designer—An Alternative Vision of the Modern Home*, exh. cat., The Bard Graduate Center for Studies in the Decorative Arts, New York, 1996.
Christopher A. Long, *Josef Frank and the Crisis of Modern Architecture*, Ph.D, University of Texas, Austin, 1993.
Maria Welzig, *Josef Frank (1885–1967). Das architektonische Werk*, Vienna, Cologne, Weimar, 1998.

Bohuslav Fuchs

(Všechovice 1895–Brno 1972)
1916–19 studied architecture with Jan Kotěra at the Academy of Fine Arts in Prague; worked until 1921 in the studio of Kotěra; 1923–29 employed at the city planning department in Brno; until 1972 worked as an independent architect in Brno; from 1925 member of the association of artists S.V.U. Mánes, from 1930 member of the Levá fronta [Left Front]; from 1933 member of the Association of Socialist Architects and 1936–48 member of the Czechoslovak CIAM Group.
Major buildings and projects in the 1920s and 1930s, in Brno: administrative building of the Meat Exchange (1924–25); Café Zeman (1925–26, demolished in 1964, rebuilt 1994–95); participated in the competition for the general development plan of the city of Brno (1926–27, in collaboration with Josef Peňaz and František Sklenář); own house (1927–28); a three-apartment residence, model estate Nový dům [The New House] (1927–28); Hotel Avion (1927–28); pavilion of the city of Brno, exhibition of contemporary culture in der ČSR (1928); "Vesna" vocational college for women (1928–30, in collaboration with Josef Polášek); Moravian Bank (1929–30, in collaboration with Arnošt Wiesner); Masaryk students' residences (1929–30); Eliška Machová Residence (1929–30); municipal baths, Zábrdovická 13 (1929–32); convalescent home "Morava," Tatranská Lomnica (1930–31); swimming pool "Zelená žába, Trenčanské Teplice (1935–36).

Lit.: Zdeněk Rossmann, *Architekt Bohuslav Fuchs*, Basel, 1930.
Zdeněk Kudělka, *Bohuslav Fuchs*, Prague, 1966.
František Kalivoda, *Architektonické dílo Bohuslava Fuchse v Brně* [The Architectural Works of Bohuslav Fuchs in Brno], Brno, 1970.
Mihály Kubinszky, *Bohuslav Fuchs*, Budapest, Berlin (East), 1986.
Iloš Crhonek, *Architekt Bohuslav Fuchs. Celoživotní dílo* [The Architect Bohuslav Fuchs. His Life's Work], Brno, 1995.
Architekt Bohuslav Fuchs 1895–1972, exh. cat., Dům umění města, Brna, Brno, 1995.

Hubert Gessner

(Valašské Klobouky 1871–Vienna 1943)
1885–89 studied at the National Crafts School in Brno, then worked as a technical draughtsman and construction supervisor; 1894–98 studied architecture with Otto Wagner at the Academy of Fine Arts in Vienna, and worked in Wagner's studio; from 1899 worked at the Moravian regional planning department in Brno, from 1904 own architect's office in Vienna.
Major buildings and projects: workers' home Favoriten, Vienna X (1901–12) regional health insurance building, Brno (1903–04); national asylum, Kroměříž (1905–08); premises for printing and publishing house "Vorwärts," Vienna V (1907–09); Hammerbrot

works, Vienna XXI (1918–21); Metzleinstaler-Hof, Vienna V (1919–25); Reumann-Hof, Vienna V (1924–26); Lasalle-Hof, Vienna II (1924–25); Karl-Seitz-Hof, Vienna, XXI (1926–29).

Lit.: *Hubert Gessner. Zivilarchitekt—Bauten und Entwürfe*, Vienna, Leipzig, 1931. Gemeinde Wien (ed.), *Metzleinstaler-Hof. Erbaut von der Gemeinde: Wien in den Jahren 1923–24*, Vienna, undated. Jan Tabor, "Hubert Gessner. Der Architekt des Herzens," in *Wien aktuell magazin* (Vienna), 1983, no. VI, pp. 29–31.

Jan Gillar

(Příbor na Moravě 1904–Prague 1967) 1921–22 studied architecture at the Czech Institute of Science and Technology in Prague; 1925–28 studied with Josef Gočár at the Prague Academy of Fine Arts; 1928–31 worked in the offices of Josef Kalous, Kamil Roškot and Jaromír Krejcar; 1931 set up his own architect's office in Prague; 1929 founder member of the Levá fronta [Left Front]; 1933 founder member of the association of socialist architects; from 1930 member of the Czechoslovak CIAM group. Major buildings and projects: participated in the competition for designing houses with minimal flats ("CIRPAC"), Prague (1930, in collaboration with Josef Špalek); participated in the competition for an estate of communal housing ("L-Projekt"), Prague (1930, in collaboration with Josef Špalek, Peer Bücking and Augusta Müllerová); French schools, Prague (1931–35).

Lit.: Alena Vondrová (ed.), *Český funkcionalismus 1920–40* [Czech Functionalism, 1920–40], vol. Architektura, Moravská Gallery v Brně-Uměleckoprůmyslové muzeum v Praze, Prague, Brno, 1978, reference "Jan Gillar." Rostislav Švácha, "Jan Gillar," in *Výtvarná kultura* [Applied Culture] (Prague), VIII, 1984, no 3, pp. 63–64.

Josef Gočár

(Semín nr. Pardubice 1880–Jičín, 1945) 1898–02 studied at the Crafts School in Prague; 1903–05 studied architecture with Jan Kotěra at Prague College of Arts and Crafts; worked until 1908 in the studio of Kotěra; 1908–11 and from 1917 member of the association of artists S.V.U. Mánes; 1911–13 member of the group of fine artists [Skupina výtvarných umělců]; 1912 co-founder of the Prague art workshops [a group of avant-garde architects and artists who, similar to the "Werkbund," wanted to create a national art] [Pražské umělecké dílny]; 1922–39 succeeded Jan Kotěra as Professor of Architecture at the Academy of Fine Arts in Prague. Major buildings and projects: participated in the competition for designing the new Town Hall for the old city of Prague (1910); business premises Wenke, Jaroměř (1910–11); department store Černé Matky Boží [To the Black Madonna], Prague (1912); Spa Hotel, Bohdaneč (1912–13); Bank of the Czechoslovak Legions, Prague (1921–23); general development plans and various buildings of the city infrastructure, Hradec Králové (1923–32, partially completed); projects for the new National Gallery, Prague (1923, 1929, 1934–40); St. Wenceslas Church [Kostel sv. Václava], Prague (1928–30); project for the department store Baťa, Brno (1929); Villa Maule, Baba estate, Prague (1931–32).

Lit.: Zdeněk Wirth, *Josef Gočár. Hradec Králové*, Vienna, Berlin, 1928 (Czech, German, French). Armand Weiser, "Professor Josef Gočár. Zu seinen Arbeiten," in *Die Bau und Werkkunst* (Vienna), VI, 1929–30, pp. 177–5, 192. Zdeněk Wirth, *Josef Gočár*, Geneva, 1930 (German and French). Marie Benešová, *Josef Gočár*, Prague, 1958.

Josef Hoffmann

(Brtnice 1870–Vienna 1956) 1887–91 studied architecture at the National Crafts School in Brno and later with Carl von Hasenauer and Otto Wagner at the Academy of Fine Arts in Vienna; 1897 co-founder of the Vienna Secession; worked until 1899 in the studio of Otto Wagner; from 1899 Professor at the College of Arts and Crafts in Vienna; 1903 joint co-founder of the Vienna "Werkstätte" [a group of avant-garde architects and artists who, similar to the "Werkbund," wanted to create a national art]; in 1905 Hoffmann, as a member of the Klimt Group, left the Secession; 1912 co-founder of the Austrian "Werkbund" [association of avant-garde manufacturers and artists promoting the crafts and quality of industrial design]; from 1920 head of the planning department of the city of Vienna. Major buildings and projects: estate of villas, Vienna XIX, Hohe Warte (1900–03); sanatorium, Purkersdorf nr Vienna (1904–06); Stoclet Palace, Brussels (1906–11); Ast House, Vienna XIX (1909–11); estate of villas, Vienna XIX, Kaasgrabengasse (1912–14); Austrian pavilion at the "Werkbund" exhibition in Cologne (1913–14); Skywa-Primavesi House, Vienna XIII (1913–15); Villa Knips, Vienna XIX (1923–24); participated in the Winarsky-Hof project, Vienna XX (1924–25); Austrian pavilion at the "Exposition Internationale des Arts Décoratifs et Industriels Modernes" in Paris (1925); block of flats of the city of Vienna, Vienna X, Laxenburgerstraße 94 (1928–32); terraced houses, "Werkbund" estate, Vienna XIII (1930–32); pavilion at the Austrian Biennial Exhibition, Venice (1934).

Lit.: Leopold Kleiner, *Josef Hoffmann*, Berlin, 1927. Armand Weiser, *Josef Hoffmann*, Geneva, 1930. Ludwig W. Rochowanski, *J. Hoffmann. Eine Studie geschrieben zu seinem 80. Geburtstag*, Vienna, 1950. Eduard F. Sekler, *Josef Hoffmann. Das architektonische Werk*, Salzburg, Vienna, 1982, second edition 1986.

Vlastislav Hofman

(Jičín 1884–Prague 1964) 1902–07 studied architecture at the Czech Institute of Science and Technology in Prague; 1911–12 member of the Group of Fine Artists [Skupina výtvarných umělců]; from 1912 member of the association of artists S.V.U. Mánes and from 1918 member of Tvrdošíjní [The Stubborn Ones]. Major buildings and projects: in Prague: cemetery, Prague-Ďáblice (1912–14, partially completed); project for the new design of the Palackého náměstí (1913); development project for the Vyšehrad (1914–15).

Lit.: François Burkhardt (ed.), *Vlastislav Hofman. Architektur des böhmischen Kubismus*, exh. cat., International Design Centre, Berlin, 1982. Rostislav Švácha, "Hofmanův Vyšehrad," in *Výtvarná kultúra* [Fine Culture] (Prague), VIII, 1984, no. 6, pp. 30–33.

Hönigsberg & Deutsch

Leo Hönigsberg

(Zagreb 1861–1911), 1879–83 studied architecture with Heinrich von Ferstel and Carl König at the Institute of Science and Technology in Vienna; worked from 1887 as an architect in Zagreb; from 1889 joint architects' office and building company (Hönigsberg & Deutsch); 1896 received an award at the Millennium Exhibition in Budapest; 1898 appointed builder and architect to the Court; 1905 Counsellor to the Court.

Julio Deutsch

(Linhartovy, 1859–Zagreb 1922), studied architecture with Heinrich von Ferstel and Carl König at the Institute of Science and Technology in Vienna; from 1889 joint architect's office and building company (Hönigsberg & Deutsch) in Zagreb; after 1898 the work emerging from the studio was mainly that completed independently by younger colleagues such as: Vjekoslav Bastl, Ivan Štefan and Otto Goldscheider.

Major buildings and projects: in Zagreb: the houses Schlesinger (1891); Priester-Schillinger (1891–93); Bukovac (1895–96); L. Hönigsberg (1898); Zagreb paper mill (1892–94); residential and business premises M. Hönigsberg (1894); Farkaš (1898); Spitzer (1899); Dreher Brewery (1895–96); District Court (1897–98); teacher training seminary (1899).

As a building company: in Zagreb: National Theatre (Fellner & Helmer, 1894–95); Arts Pavilion (Fellner & Helmer, 1897–98); Croat Discount Bank (Fellner & Helmer, 1898–99) and numerous other buildings commissioned by architect's offices in Zagreb.

Lit.: Lelja Dobronić, *Zagrebački arhitekti Hönigsberg i Deutsch* [The Zagreb Architects Hönigsberg and Deutsch], Zagreb, 1965.

Pavel Janák
(Prague 1882–1956)

1899–1905 studied architecture at the Czech Institute of Science and Technology and with Josef Schulz and Josef Zítek at the German Polytechnic in Prague; 1906–08 with Otto Wagner at the Vienna Academy of Fine Arts; 1908–09 worked in the architect's studio of Jan Kotěra; 1908–11 and from 1917 member of the association of artists S.V.U. Mánes; 1911–14 member of the Group of Fine Artists [Skupina výtvarných umělců]; 1912 co-founder of the Prague "Kunstwerkstätten" [a group of avant-garde architects and artists who, similar to the "Werkbund," wanted to create a national art] [Pražské umělecké dílny] and 1914 member of the Czechoslovak "Werkbund" (Chairman 1924–39); 1921–42 Professor of Architecture at the Prague College of Arts and Crafts; from 1923 member of the National Commission for a General Development plan for Prague; 1936 succeeded Jože Plečnik as chief architect for the design of Prague Castle.

Major buildings and projects: Hlávka Bridge, Prague (1909–12); Fára House, Pelhřimov (1913–14, conversions); reservoir, Přeměřice nad Labem (1913–15); crematorium, Pardubice (1921–23); office and business premises Riunione Adriatica, Prague (1922–24, in collaboration with Josef Zasche); double residence Filla / Krejčí, Prague (1923–24); overall planning of the Baba Estate, Prague (1929–31); own private house, Baba Estate, Prague (1931–32); Hus Church [Husův sbor], Prague (1930–33).

Lit.: Pavel Janák, "Hranol a pyramida" [Prism and Pyramid], in *Umělecký měsíčník* [Artists' Monthly] (Prague), I, 1911–12, pp. 162–70.
Pavel Janák, "Obnova průčelí" [A New Design for the Façade], in *Umělecký měsíčník* [Artists' Monthly] (Prague), II, 1912–13, pp. 136–38.
Marie Benešová, *Pavel Janák*, Prague, 1959.
Olga Herbenová, Vladimír Šlapeta, *Pavel Janák 1882–56. Architektur und Kunstgewerbe Pavel Janák 1882–56*, exh. cat., Prague, Vienna 1984.

Lajos Kassák
(Nové Zámky 1887–Budapest 1967)

Trained as a plumber; 1899–1907 worked variously as a metal worker; produced first autodidactic drawings and painting; 1909 sojourn in Paris, contacts with Apollinaire, Delaunay, Picasso and Modigliani; worked as an author; 1915–16 edited the newspaper *A Tett* [The Deed] in Budapest; founded the *MA* Group [Today] in 1916 after the newspaper was banned; 1916–25 edited the newspaper *MA* in Budapest and Vienna; 1919 emigrated to Vienna after the collapse of the republic of councils; 1921 first one-man show in Gallery Würtel in Vienna; 1922 edited the *Buch neuer Künstler* ["Book of New Artists"] in collaboration with Moholy-Nagy; 1926 returned to Budapest; 1926–27 edited the newspaper *Dokumentum*

in Budapest; 1927 co-founder of "Ring Neuer Werbegestalter" [Circle of new Advertising Designers]; 1928–38 edited the newspaper *Munka* [Work].

Lit.: Ludwig [Lajos] Kassák, Laszlo [László] Moholy-Nagy, *Buch neuer Künstler*, Vienna 1922 (Facsimile reprint, Budapest, 1977).
Kassák Lajos 1887–67, exh. cat., Magyar Nemzeti Galéria-Petőfi Irodalmi Múzeum, Budapest, 1987.
József Vadas (ed.), *Lajos Kassák: Laßt uns leben in unserer Zeit. Gedichte, Bilder und Schriften zur Kunst*, Budapest, 1989.
Lajos Kassák. Ein Protagonist der ungarischen Avantgarde [Lajos *Kassák. A Protagonist of the Hungarian Avant-Garde*, exh. cat., Upper Gallery in the House at Lützowplatz, Berlin, 1991.

Carl König
(Vienna 1841–1915)

Attended the Imperial Polytechnic Institute in Vienna; from 1861 studied architecture with Friedrich von Schmidt at the Vienna Academy of Fine Arts; worked from 1866 at the construction company of J. Hlávka in Vienna, then as an assistant to Heinrich von Ferstel at the Polytechnic; study trips to Italy, France, Belgium and Germany; from 1882 Professor at the Technical University in Vienna; 1884–88 Head of Faculty; 1901 Head of the University.

Major buildings and projects: Philipp-Hof, Vienna I (1883–84); agricultural exchange, Vienna II (1886–90); Rothenturm-Hof, Vienna I (1889–90); Villa Taußig, Vienna XIII (1893–95); Villa Kuffner, Vienna XIX (1905–08); House of Industry, Vienna I (1906–09); extension of the Technical University, Vienna IV (1907–10).

Lit.: *Bauten und Entwürfe von Carl König*, ed. by his pupils, Vienna, 1910.
Marcus Kristan, *Carl König 1841–1915. Ein neobarocker Großstadtarchitekt in Wien*, Vienna, 1999.

Károly Kós
(Timişoara 1883–Cluj-Napoca 1977)

1902–07 studied architecture at the Budapest Institute of Science and Technology; founder member of the Fiatalok group of architects and craftsmen [The Young Ones], initially influenced by the art historian John Ruskin as well as by William Morris and the Arts and Crafts movement; from 1908 own architect's office in Budapest; 1917–18 scholarship in Istanbul, 1918 moved to Transylvania; 1920–28 involved with various Hungarian parties and cultural institutions in Transylvania; 1940–53 Professor of Architecture at the College of Agriculture in Cluj-Napoca.

Major buildings and projects: Vicarage and House of Prayer of the Reformed Church, Budapest III (1908–09, in collaboration with Dezső Zrumeczky); Catholic Church, Zebegény (1908–09, in collaboration with Béla Jánszky); zoo pavilions, Budapest (1909–10, in collaboration with Dezső Zrumeczky); school and nursery school, Budapest XII (1910–11, in collaboration with Györgyi Dénes); Székely National Museum, Sfintu Gheorghe (1911–12); central square of the Wekerle Estate, Budapest XIX (1912–13, in collaboration with Dezső Zrumeczky); Reformed Church, Cluj-Napoca (1912–13).

Lit.: Károly Kós: *Erdélyország népének építése* [Buildings of the Transylvanian People], Budapest 1907 (manuscript), Budapest, 1997 (facsimile reprint).
Balázs Pál, *Kós Károly* [Károly Kós], Budapest, 1971, 1983.
Elemér Nagy, *Az építő Kós Károly* [The Architect Károly Kós], Budapest, 1995.
Anthony Gall, "Itinerario / Itinerary 145 – Kós a Budapest e in Transilvania / Kós in Budapest and Transylvania," in *Domus* (Milan), 1998, no. 804, pp. 117–124.

Jan Kotěra
(Brno 1871–Prague 1923)
1887–90 studied at the German School of Trade in Plzeň; 1894–97 studied architecture with Otto Wagner at the Vienna Academy of Fine Arts; 1897 Prix de Rome and a scholarship in Italy; 1898–1910 Professor of Architecture at the Prague College of Arts and Crafts (as a successor to Friedrich Ohmann) and 1910–23 at the Academy of Fine Arts in Prague; study trips to the USA (a. o. World Fair in St. Louis), to the Netherlands and Great Britain; member of the association of artists S.V.U. Mánes and founder member of the architecture journal *Styl*.
Major buildings and projects: Volkshaus, Prostajov (1905–07); own villa, Prague (1908–09); Laichter House, Prague (1908–09); City Museum, Hradec Králové (1909–13); Urbánek House (so-called Mozarteum), Prague (1911–13); Faculty of Law, Prague (1923–27, in collaboration with Ladislav Machoň).

Lit.: Jan Kotěra, "O novém umění" [On New Art], in *Volné směry* [Free Directions] (Prague), IV, 1900, pp. 189–5.
Karl B. Mádl, *Jan Kotěra*, Prague, 1922.
Otakar Novotný, *Jan Kotěra a jeho doba* [Jan Kotěra and his Time], Prague, 1958.

Viktor Kovačić
(Ločendol 1874–Zagreb 1924)
1889–91 studied at the School of Trade in Graz; 1891–96 work experience with Kuno Waidmann, Gjuro Camelutti and Hermann Bollé in Zagreb; 1896–99 studied architecture with Otto Wagner at the Academy of Fine Arts in Vienna, then worked as a freelance architect in Zagreb; 1904–06 architects' office Kovačić & Marković; 1910–15 Kovačić & Ehrlich; 1905 co-founder of the Club of Croatian Architects [Klub hrvatskih arhitekta]; from 1920 Lecturer and from 1923 Professor at the Faculty of Architecture of the Institute of Science and Technology in Zagreb.
Major buildings and projects in Zagreb: Kornitzer House (1902), Winkler House (1903); Ivančan House (1903–04); Villa F. Auer (1903); Villa and Studio R. Auer (1904–06); Villa Perok-Kavić (1905–06); residential and business premises Oršić & Divković (1906–07); Villa Frangeš (1910–11); Lustig House (1910–11); Croatian Real Estate Bank (1911–12); Villas Vrbanić (1911), Rado (1913), Čepulić (1913–14); Zagreb Stock Exchange (1923–27).

Lit.: Edo Šen, "Arhitekt Viktor Kovačić," Zagreb, 1927 (annotated reprint in *Čovjek i prostor* [Man and Space] (Zagreb), XXI, 1974, nos. 10–11 / 259–260, pp. 3–46).
Aleksander Laslo, "Arhitekt Viktor Kovačić 1874–1924," in *Čovjek i prostor* [Man and Space] (Zagreb), XXXI, 1984, no. 10 / 379, pp. 6–7.
Aleksander Laslo, "Die Loos-Schule in Kroatien," in *Adolf Loos*, exh. cat., Albertina Graphics Collection-History Museum of the City of Vienna, Vienna, 1989, pp. 307–323.
Aleksander Laslo, "Adolf Loos in hrvatska arhitektura," in *Arhitektov bilten* [Architect's bulletin] (Ljubljana), XXI, 1991, nos. 107–108, pp. 52–80.
Tihomil Stahuljak, "Ein Klatsch über den Architekten Adolf Loos," in *Peristil* (Zagreb), XXXIV, 1991, pp. 115–126.
Darja Radović Mahečić, Aleksander Laslo, "Viktor Kovačić—Promotor hrvatske moderne arhitekture" [Viktor Kovačić—Precursor of Modern Croatian Architecture], in *Radovi Instituta za povijest umjetnosti* [Reports of the Institute of History of Art] (Zagreb), XXI, 1997, pp. 143–165.
Krešimir Galović, *Arhitekt Viktor Kovačić. Skice i crteži* [The Architect Viktor Kovačić. Sketches and Drawings], Zagreb, 1997.

Lajos Kozma
(Kiskorpád 1884–Budapest 1948)
1903–06 studied architecture at the Institute of Science and Technology in Budapest; member of the Fiatalok Group [The Young Ones]; 1910–13 worked in the office of Béla Lajta; 1913 founder of the Budapesti-Műhely [Budapest *Werkstätte* (a group of avant-garde architects and artists who, similar to the *Werkbund*, wanted to improve the crafts and to create a national art style)];

1919 politically involved with the short-lived *Tanácsköztársaság* [republic of councils] which resulted later in a loss of commissions. Major buildings and projects: apartment block, Budapest II, Bimbó út 39 (1933); Villa Klinger, Budapest II, Hermann Ottó utca 10 (1933–34); Átrium residential block and Cinema, Budapest II, Margit körút 55 (1935–36); residential and business premises, Budapest V, Régiposta utca 13 (1937).

Lit.: Ludwig [Lajos] Kozma, *Das neue Haus*, Zurich, 1941.
László Beke, Zsuzsa Varga, *Kozma Lajos*, Budapest, 1968.
Judit Koós, *Kozma Lajos munkássága. Grafika, iparművészet, építészet* [Lajos Kozma and his Work. Graphics, Arts and Crafts, Architecture], Budapest, 1975.
Kozma Lajos 1884–1948. Építész, iparművész, műveiből [Lajos Kozma 1884–1948: Architect, Craftsman—a Selection of his Work], exh. cat., Országos Műemléki Felügyelőség, Magyar Építészeti Múzeum, Székesfehérvár, 1984–85.
Kozma Lajos, az iparművész / Lajos Kozma, the Designer (1884–1948), exh. cat., Iparművészeti Múzeum, Budapest, 1994.

Jaromír Krejcar
(Hundsheim 1895–London 1949)
1917–21 studied architecture with Jan Kotěra at the Prague Adademy of Fine Arts; 1921–23 worked in the office of Josef Gočár; from 1922 member of the association of artists Devětsil; 1929 founding member of the Levá fronta [Left Front]; 1933 member of the Association of Socialist Architects; from 1930 member of the Czechoslovak CIAM Group; 1934–35 sojourn in the USSR.
Major buildings and projects: Villa Vančura project, Prague (1924–26); Olympic Department Store, Prague (1925–28); project for the competition for a new government complex on the Letná Plain, Prague (1928); club house of the Association of Independent Civil Servants, Prague (1928–31); Machnáč Sanatorium, Trenčanské Teplice (1929–32); participated in a competition for devising a general traffic concept for the greater Prague area (1930–31, in collaboration with Josef Špalek); Czechoslovak pavilion at the World Fair in Paris (1936–37, in collaboration with Zdeněk Kejř, Ladislav Sutnar, Bohumil Soumar).

Lit.: Karel Teige, *Práce Jaromíra Krejcara* [The Work of Jaromír Krejcar], ESMA, vol. 2, Prague, 1933.
Jaromír Krejcar 1895–1949, exh. cat., Jaroslava Fragnera Gallery, Prague, 1995 (contributions by Klaus Spechtenhauser, Rostislav Švácha, Antonín Tenzer; Czech-English).

Jiří Kroha
(Prague 1893–Brno 1974)
1911–16 studied architecture with Jan Koula, Josef Fanta und Antonín Balšánekat the Czech Institute of Science and Technology in Prague; from 1918 member of the association of artists S.V.U. Mánes; from 1925 Professor of Architecture at the Czech Institute of Science and Technology in Brno; 1927–31 editor of the newspaper *Horizont* [Horizon]; 1929 founder member of the Levá fronta [Left Front]; 1933 first chairman of the Association of Socialist Architects.
Major buildings and projects until the 1930s: Montmartre-Bar, Prague (destroyed 1918); participated in the competition for designing a crematorium, Pardubice (1919–20); several buildings for the city infrastructure, Mladá Boleslav (1922–28); residence, model estate Nový dům [The New House], Brno (1927–28); own villa, Brno (1928–31); participated in the competition for apartment buildings with minimal flats for the VČELA cooperative, Prague (1930); exhibition project, a sociological fragment for living (1930–32); Villa Patočka, Brno (1935–36).

Lit.: Jaroslav B. Svrček, *Jiří Kroha*, Ženeva / Geneva 1930 (Czech and German).
Jiří Kroha, *Bytová otázka v SSSR* [The Housing Problem in the USSR], Prague, 1935.
Josef Císařovský, *Jiří Kroha a meziválečná avantgarda* [Jiří Kroha and the Avant-Garde during the Years between the Wars], Prague, 1967.

Jiří Kroha, *Sociologický fragment bydlení* [A Sociological Fragment for Living], Brno, 1973.
Jiří Kroha. Kubist Expressionist Funktionalist Realist [Jiří Kroha: Cubist Expressionist Functionalist Realist], Architektur Zentrum Wien, 1998 (contributions by Monika Platzer, Klaus Spechtenhauser, Rostislav Švácha).

Ludvík Kysela
(Kouřím 1883–Prague 1960)
1904–09 studied architecture and civil engineering at the Czech Institute of Science and Technology in Prague; 1913 founder member of the Club of Architects; 1909–14 and 1919–48 worked at the City Planning Department in Prague.
Major buildings and projects: Lindt business premises, Prague (1926–27); Baťa Department Store, Prag (1928–30, in collaboration with the building company Baťa); Alfa business premises with arcade, Prague (1927–29, in collaboration with Jan Jarolím).

Lit.: Alena Vondrová (ed.), *Český funkcionalismus 1920–40* [Czech Functionalism 1920–40], vol. *Architektura*, Moravská Gallerie v Brně-Uměleckoprůmyslové Muzeum v Praze, Prague, Brno, 1978, reference "Ludvík Kysela."

Béla Lajta
(Pest 1873–Vienna 1920)
1892–96 studied architecture at the Institute of Science and Technology in Budapest; worked in the office of Alajos Hauszmann; around 1897 worked with Alfred Messel in Berlin, later with Richard Norman Shaw in London; study trips to France, Spain, and Marocco.
Major buildings and projects: Villa Malonyay, Budapest XIV (1905–06); Jewish Institute for the Blind, Budapest XIV (1905–08); Jewish Nursing Home, Budapest XIV (1906–07); Parisiana Cabaret, Budapest VI (1908–09); City School of Commerce, Budapest VIII (1909–12); residential and business block Rózsavölgyi, Budapest V (1910–11); residential and bank building, Budapest VII (1911–12); own villa, Budapest XIV (1912).

Lit.: Ferenc Vámos, *Lajta Béla* [Béla Lajta], Budapest, 1970.
A Parisiana újjáépítése [The Reconstruction of the Parisiana], exh. cat., Országos Műemlékvédelmi Hivatal Építészeti Múzeuma [Architectural Museum of the Hungarian Society for the Preservation of Monuments], Budapest, 1991.
Marco Biraghi, "Béla Lajta e i suoi angeli. Il restauro del cabaret Parisiana a Budapest," in *Casabella* (Milan), XL, 1996, no. 632, pp. 50–59.
Marco Biraghi, *Béla Lajta. Ornamento e modernita*, Milan, 1999.

Ödön Lechner
(Pest 1845–Budapest 1914)
1865 studied architecture at the Budapest Institute of Science and Technology; 1866–68 studied at the Berlin Academy of Architecture; from 1869 joint architects' office with Gyula Pártos in Budapest; 1875–78 worked with Clement Parent in Paris; 1889 sojourn in London, research work in the oriental collections of the South Kensington Museum.
Major buildings and projects: tenement block for the Pensions Institute of the Hungarian National Railways, Budapest VI (1881–84); business premises Thonet, Budapest V (1888–89); town hall, Kecskemét (1890–97); Museum and College of Arts and Crafts, Budapest (1891–96); Szent László Church [St. László Church], Budapest X (1893–98); Geological Institute, Budapest XIV (1896–99); Post Office Savings Bank, Budapest V (1899–1901); Villa Sipeky, Budapest XIV (1905–06); Queen Elizabeth Church, Bratislava (1907–13).

Lit.: Jenő Kismarty-Lechner, *Lechner Ödön*, Budapest, 1961.
Tibor Bakonyi, Mihály Kubinszky, *Lechner Ödön*, Budapest, 1981.
Lechner Ödön 1845–1914, exh. cat., OMF Magyar Építészeti Múzeum, Budapest, 1985.
Ödön Lechner 1845–1914, exh. cat., The Hungarian Museum of Architecture, Budapest, 1988 (abridged English version of the Budapest Catalogue of 1985 for the exhibition in London).
Ilona Sármány, "Sorspárhuzamok a századfordulón (Otto Wagner és Lechner Ödön pályarajza)" [Parallel Lives around the Turn of the Century (The Careers of Otto Wagner and Ödön Lechner)], in Éva Somogyi (ed.), *Polgárosodás Közép-Európában. Tanulmányok Hanák Péter 70. születésnapjára / Proliferation of Middle-Class Values in Central Europe. On the occasion of Péter Hanák's 70th birthday*, Budapest 1991, pp. 341–56.
Ödön Lechner 1845–1914, exh. cat., College of Applied Art Vienna, Heiligenkreuzerhof, Budapest, 1991 (abridged German version of the Budapest catalogue of 1985).

Erich Leischner
(Vienna 1887–1970)
1906–12 studied architecture at the Technological University in Vienna; worked from 1911 as a trainee in the City Planning Department in Vienna; from 1913 comprehensive responsibilities within the Planning Department, initially in the Education Department of School Buildings, later in the Architecture Department; 1924 city planning officer; 1937 head of city planning; 1938 officer with "special responsibilities" in the Regulatory Department; 1945 appointed head of the re-established Municipal Architecture Department and Building Advisory Department; 1947 Council of the Senate; 1949 retired but continued to work as a freelance architect.
Major buildings and projects: for the Vienna City Planning Department: Robert-Blum-Hof, Vienna XX (1923); Franz-Kurz-Hof, Vienna XIV (1923); Congress swimming pool, children's swimming pool, Kongreßplatz, Vienna XVI (1927–28); Sandleiten Nursery School, Vienna XVI (1928–29); Alois-Appel–Hof, Vienna XXI (1931–32); Wiener Höhenstraße, Vienna XVII–XIX (1934–38); children's swimming pool, Raxstraße, Vienna X (1937); Aspern Bridge, Vienna I–II (1949–51).
As a freelance architect: WBW allotment garden complex, Vienna-Schafberg (1920, in collaboration with Adolf Stöckl); cinema, Vienna XXII, Wagramer Straße 108 (1935); residence, Vienna VIII, Josefstädter Straße 3 (1935–36); Laaer Mountain Spa, Vienna X (1957–59); Salztor Bridge, Vienna I–II (1960–61).

Lit.: *Amt Macht Stadt. Erich Leischner und das Wiener Stadtbauamt*, exh. cat., Architektur Zentrum Wien, Salzburg, 1999.

Ivan Levyns'kyj
(Dolyna 1851–Ľviv 1919)
1869–74 studied at the Academy of Technology Ľviv; 1881 set up his own planning and building company; 1885 established the (soon to become) largest building supply company in Galicia and the most prestigious contracting business in Ľviv; from 1901 Professor at the Polytechnic in Ľviv.
Major buildings and projects in Ľviv: development plan for Ľviv-Kastelivka (1880s, in collaboration with Julian Zachariewicz); Mikolasz Arcade (1899–1901, in collaboration with Alfred Zachariewicz); several tenement blocks and buildings in the city center (1900–10, in collaboration with other architects in the Levyns'kyj office); "Dnister" Insurance Company (1905–06, in collaboration with Tadeusz Obmiński).

Lit.: Franciszek Mączyński, "Najnowszy Lwow" [The Latest Ľviv], in *Architekt* [Architect] (Cracow), IX, 1908, pp. 91–97.
Ivan Levyns'kyj, joho žyttja ta pracja [Ivan Levyns'kyj, his Life and Work], Ľviv, 1934.
Ihor Žuk, "Ivan Levyns'kyj, architektor-budivnyčyj L'vova" [Ivan Levyns'kyj: Architect and Builder in Ľviv], in *Architektura Ukraïny* [The Architecture of the Ukraine], (Kiev), 1992, no. 2, pp. 20–28.

Adolf Loos

(Brno 1870–Kalksburg nr. Vienna 1933)
1885–88 attended the National College of Commerce in Liberec; apprenticeship in Brno as a bricklayer; 1892–93 studied at the Institute of Science and Technology in Dresden; 1893–96 sojourn in the USA, returned to Vienna and worked with Carl Mayreder; from 1897 published critical essays in the *Neue Freie Presse* about the cultural life in Vienna, 1903 launched the newspaper *Das andere–ein blatt zur einführung abendländischer kultur in Österreich* which had two issues only; 1912 opened his own School of Architecture; 1920–22 Chief Architect of the Vienna Settlement / Housing Office; 1922–32 alternate sojourns in France, Austria and Czechoslovakia.

Major buildings and projects: alterations of the Café Museum, Vienna I (1899); Villa Karma, Clarens nr. Montreux (1903–06); Kärntner Bar, Vienna I (1908); Goldman & Salatsch Department Store, Vienna I (1909–11); Steiner House, Vienna XIII (1910); gentlemen's outfitters Kniže, Vienna I (1910–13); project for a general development plan of the city, Vienna I (around 1912); Horner House, Vienna XIII (1912); Scheu House, Vienna XIII (1912–13); Heuberg Estate, Vienna XVII (1921–23, in collaboration with Hugo Mayer); Rufer House, Vienna XIII (1922); Tristan Tzara House, Paris
(1925–26); Moller House, Vienna XVIII (1927–28); Müller House, Prague (1928–30).

Lit.: Karl Marilaun, *Adolf Loos*, Vienna, 1922 (in Czech, Brno, 1929).
Adolf Loos zum 60. Geburtstag am 10.12.1930. Festschrift, Vienna, 1930.
Franz Glück, *Adolphe Loos*, Paris, 1931.
Heinrich Kulka, *Adolf Loos. Das Werk des Architekten, Wien 1931 (Neues Bauen in der Welt*, vol. 4; reprinted, Vienna, 1979).
Zdeněk Kudělka, "Činnost Adolfa Loose v Československu" [The Work of Adolf Loos in Czechoslovakia] I / II, in *Sborník prací filosofické fakulty Brněnské university, řada uměnovědná* [An Anthology compiled by the Faculty of Philosophy of the University of Brno, History of Art Series], XXII, 1973, fo. 17, pp. 141–55 / XXIII, 1974, fo. 18, pp. 7–32.
Hermann Czech, Wolfgang Mistelbauer, *Das Looshaus*, Vienna, 1977.
Burkhardt Rukschcio, Roland Schachel, *Adolf Loos. Leben und Werk*, Vienna, 1982, 1987.
Adolf Loos, exh. cat., Albertina Graphics Collection-History Museum of the City of Vienna, Vienna, 1989.
Aleksander Laslo, "Die Loos-Schule in Kroatien," in *Adolf Loos*, exh. cat., Albertina Graphics Collection-History Museum of the City of Vienna, Vienna, 1989, pp. 307–23.
Aleksander Laslo, "Adolf Loos in hrvatska arhitektura / Adolf Loos and Croatian Architecture," in *Arhitektov bilten / Architect's bulletin* (Ljubljana), XXI, 1991, no. 107–08, pp. 52–80.
Tihomil Stahuljak, "Ein Klatsch über den Architekten Adolf Loos," in *Peristil* (Zagreb), XXXIV, 1991, pp. 115–126.

Slavko Löwy

(Koprivnica 1904–Zagreb 1996)
1926–28 studied at the Technical University in Vienna; 1928 in Zagreb; 1928–30 studied with Martin Dülfe in Dresden; 1931 worked with Ignjat Fischer and 1931–32 with Stanko Kliska in Zagreb; 1932–42 set up his own architect's office in Zagreb.

Major buildings and projects in Zagreb in the 1920s and 1930s: Villa Hirschler (1932–33); residential and business premises Günsberg (1932–33); Schlenger I (1932–33); Radovan (1933–34); Schlenger II (1936–37); Villas Federbuš (1936–37); Beck (1937); participated in the competition for the Zagreb exhibition complex (1936); residence and business premises Lebinec (1936–38).

Lit.: Darja Radović–Mahečić, "Slavko Löwy. Elegancija jednostavnosti" [Slavko Löwy. The Elegance of Simplicity], in *Čovjek i prostor* [Man and Space] (Zagreb), XLI, 1994, no. 11–12, pp. 14–19.
Darja Radović–Mahečić, "Slavko Löwy. Humano mjerilo stanovanja i rada. Uz 90. rođendan" [Slavko Löwy. Living and Working in a Manner Appropriate for the Human Condition. For his 90th Birthday], in *Život umjetnosti* [The Life of Art] (Zagreb), XXX, 1995, no. 56–57, pp. 72–83 (incl. an English summary).

Darja Radović–Mahečić, "Tri susreta arhitekta Slavka Löwyja i Drage Iblera" [The Three Clashes of the Architects Slavka Löwy and Drago Ibler], in *Peristil* (Zagreb), XXXIX, 1996, pp. 157–166.

Franciszek Mączyński

(Wadowice 1874–Kraków 1947)
1888–92 studied at the School of Trade in Kraków, then worked in the studio of Sławomir Odrzywolski; 1897 joined the architect's office of Tadeusz Stryjcński where, but for a few breaks, he worked until 1906; 1899 study trip to Paris; 1901 graduated from the Polytechnic in L'viv as a master (qualified) builder; from 1902 member of the society of "Polsa Szutka Stosowana" [Polish Applied Art]; from 1906 member of the team editing the Kraków Newspaper *Architekt*; 1914–26 worked at the "Warszaty Krakowskie" [Kraków "Werkstätten" (group of architects and artists wanting to improve the crafts and to create a National style)] .

Major buildings and projects: pavilion of the Society of Fine Arts, Kraków (1898–1901; reconstruction of the Old Theater, Kraków (1903–06, together with Tadeusz Stryjeński); Chamber of Commerce and Industry, Kraków (1904–06, together with Tadeusz Stryjeński).

Lit.: L Kontkowski, "O. Franciszek Mączyński dokladniej" [More about Franciszek Mączyński], in *Tygodnik Powszechny* [Weekly General] XXIX, 1975, no. 5.

István Medgyaszay

(Budapest 1877–1959)
1896 studied at the Budapest School of Trade; 1900–03 studied at the Technical University in Vienna and in Otto Wagner's master class; 1904 studied at the Budapest Institute of Science and Technology; 1904–06 did research work for the first two volumes of the publication *A magyar nép művészete* [Hungarian Folk Art] by Dezső Malonyay; 1906–08 sojourn in Paris; 1907 worked in the architect's office of François Hennebique; 1908 presented a paper about the artistic aspects of reinforced concrete architecture at the VIII. International Congress of Architects in Vienna; 1911 study trip to the Near East and in 1932 to India.

Major buildings and projects: studio houses for the artists' commune, Gödöllő (1904–06); theatre, Veszprém (1907–08); church and mausoleum, Muľa (1908–10); theater, Sopron (1909); residence, Budapest XI, Elek utca 14 (1910); Catholic church, Ógyalla (1912–13); tenement block, Budapest V, Dorottya utca 8 (1914); pavilions at the war exhibition, L'viv (1916); church, Püspökladány (1921); municipal housing estate, Budapest XI, Budaörsi út 2-18 (1925–26); theatre, Nagykanizsa (1926); sports hotel, Mátraháza (1927); Baár–Madas Reformed Church gymnasium, Budapest II (1929).

Lit.: István Medgyaszay, "Über die künstlerische Lösung des Eisenbetonbaues" [On the Artistic Solution of Building with Reinforced Concrete], in *Report of the VIII. International Congress of Architects in Vienna*, Vienna, 1908, Vienna, 1909, pp. 538–54 (Hungarian: A vasbeton művészi formájáról, in *Művészet* [Art] (Budapest), VIII, 1909, pp. 30–37).
István Medgyaszay, "Népünk Építőművészetéről" [The Architecture of our People], in *Magyar Építőművészet* [Hungarian Architecture] (Budapest), VII, 1909, no. 5, pp. 1–2.
Imre Kathy, *Medgyaszay István*, Budapest, 1979.
A soproni színház [The Theatre in Sopron], exh. cat., Országos Műemlékvédelmi Hivatal Építészeti Múzeuma [Museum of Architecture of the Hungarian Society for the Preservation of Monuments], Budapest, 1993.
Keletre Magyar! [Hungary, let's go East!], exh. cat., István Magyar Építészeti Múzeum, Budapest, 1997.

Farkas Molnár

(Pécs 1897–Budapest 1945)
1921–25 studied at the Bauhaus in Weimar; participated in a course given by Johannes Itten, then worked with Walter Gropius; 1925 returned to Budapest, worked with Pál Ligeti, then as a freelance architect; 1929 participated in the 2nd CIAM Congress in Frankfurt; from 1930 active member of CIAM and CIPRAC; 1937 co-initiator of CIAM-Ost.
Major buildings and projects: "Der Rote Würfel" (1923); a number of villas and residences in Budapest (1928–38); Villa Hevesy, Budapest II, Cserje utca 4a (1931–32); Villa Dálnoki–Kovács, Budapest XII, Lejtő utca 2a (1932); Villa Balla, Budapest II, Hankóczy utca 3a (1932); residential complex for the National Institute of Social Security (OTI), Budapest, Köztársaság tér 14-16 (1933–34, in collaboration with other architects); administrative building for the hospital for OTI employees, Budapest (1936, in collaboration with József Fischer); apartment block Pekanovich, Budapest II, Pasaréti út 7 (1936); residence and Villa Baja, Budapest II, Trombitás út 32, Pasaráti út 7 (1936–37).

Lit.: *Molnár Farkas munkái / Arbeiten des Architekten F. Molnár 1923–33*, Budapest, 1933 (An Introduction by László Moholy-Nagy).
Ottó Mezei, "Ungarische Architekten am Bauhaus," in Hubertus Gassner (ed.), *Wechselwirkungen. Ungarische Avantgarde in der Weimarer Republik*, exh. cat., New Gallery, Kassel, Bochum Museum, Marburg, 1986, pp. 339–346.
Ottó Mezei, *Molnár Farkas*, Budapest, 1987.
András Ferkai, "Farkas Molnár 1897–1945. Der Klassiker des ungarischen Funktionalismus," in *Archithese* (Niederteufen, Switzerland), XVIII, 1988, no. 1, pp. 29–32.
Molnár Farkas. Festő, grafikus, építész [Farkas Molnár: Painter, Graphic Artist, Architect], exh. cat. Kassák, Museum, Budapest, 1997.

Tadeusz Obmiński

(Ľviv 1874–1932)
1893–98 studied architecture at the Polytechnic in Ľviv; 1898–1900 in Berlin-Charlottenburg; later taught at the Polytechnic in Ľviv; worked in the offices of the building contractors Levyns'kyj and Ulam.
Major buildings and projects, in Ľviv: Segal House (1904–05); "Dnister" Insurance Company (1905–06, in collaboration with Ivan Levyns'kyj); Chamber of Commerce and Trade (1907–11, in collaboration with Alfred Zachariewicz).

Lit.: Tadeusz Obmiński, *Budownictwo ogólne* [Building in General], Ľviv, 1925.

Vít Obrtel

(Olomouc 1901–Prag 1988)
1918–25 studied architecture at the Czech Institute of Science and Technology in Prague; from 1923 member of the association of artists Devětsil and of its architectural branch ARDEV; 1929 founder member of the Levá fronta [The Left Front], and 1933 of the Association of Socialist Architects; between 1931 and 1948 working as an independent architect in Prague; 1930–35 and 1945–48 edited the newspaper *Kvart* with a focus on art, science and poetry.
Major buildings and projects in the 1920s and 1930s: several villa projects (1920–23); project for a competition for the House of Art, Ostrava (1923); project for a competition for Industrial Accident Insurance Building, Prag (1924, in collaboration with Evžen Linhart and Alois Mikuškovic); project for a villa built after classical motifs (1931–34); project for a functional villa (1931–34).

Lit.: Rostislav Švácha, "Vít Obrtel a teorie architektury" [Vít Obrtel and Architectural Theory], in *Umění a řemesla* [Art and Craft] (Prague), 1981, no. 2, pp. 56–59.
Rudolf Matys, Rostislav Švácha (eds.), *Vít Obrtel. Vlaštovka, která ma geometrické hnízdo* [Of the Swallow and its Geometric Nest], Prague, 1985.
Vít Obrtel (1901–88). Architektura, typografie, nábytek [Vít Obrtel (1901–88). Architecture, Typography, Furnishings], exh. cat., Galerie hlavního města Prahy, Prague 1992.

Rudolf Perco

(Gorizia 1884–Vienna 1942)
Attended the National School of Trade in Vienna; 1906–10 studied architecture with Otto Wagner at the Vienna Academy of Fine Arts; 1908 Pein Prize; 1910 government travel scholarship, travels to Paris and Rome; 1906–11 worked in the architect's office of Hubert Gessner; 1911–12 worked in the office of Friedrich Ohmann, then as an independent architect; 1919 returned to Vienna after his release as an Italian prisoner of war; 1920–23 studied architecture at the Technical University in Vienna; 1929–34 studied Law at the University of Vienna; from 1932 member of the "Verein christlicher Kunst;" 1938 sojourn in Berlin 1938–41 worked in the office of Franz Kaym; 1941 appointed by Hans Dunstmann to a post in the planning department; 1942 died under mysterious circumstances.
Major buildings and projects: Fürstenhof, Vienna II (1913); Jodl-Hof, Vienna XIX (1925–26, in collaboration with Rudolf Frass and Karl Dorfmeister); Holy-Hof, Vienna XVII (1928–29); several church projects (from 1930); residential estate at the Friedrich-Engels-Platz, Vienna XX (1930–33).

Lit.: "Einige neue Arbeiten von Rudolf Perco / Rudolf Perco, Auf dem Wege zur kommenden fünften Wiedergeburt der Antike. Programm einer wirklichen Architektur," in *Österreichische Kunst* (Vienna), III, 1932, no. 12, pp. 5–14.
Ursula Prokop, *Rudolf Perco 1884–1942. Architektur jenseits von Tradition und Moderne*, Ph.D. Dissertation, University of Vienna, Vienna, 1997.

Josip Pičman

(Lekenik 1904–Zagreb 1936)
1925–29 studied architecture with Hugo Ehrlich at the Institute of Science and Technology in Zagreb; 1929–30 worked in the office of Hans Poelzig in Berlin (and with others on projects for the IG Farben Industry in Frankfurt); 1932–35 member of the "Zagreb Working Party" and of the Yugosloav CIAM group.
Major buildings and projects in Zagreb: project for the so-called "Zakladni blok" [endowment block] (1932, in collaboration with Josip Seissel); residence and business premises Puk (1932–33, in collaboration with Stjepan Hribar and Ivan Velicogna); Institute of Agriculture and Dairy Production of the Faculty of Agriculture and Forestry (1933–34, in collaboration with the "Zagreb Working Party"); Villa Zimpermann (1936, completed posthumously by Ivan Velicogna).

Lit.: Josip Pičman, Josip Seissel, *Izložba projekta za izgradnju Zakladnog zemljišta na Jelačićevom trgu* [Exhibition of the Project for the Completion of the "Zakladni zemlište" at the Jelačićev trg], exh. cat., Salon Ulrich, Zagreb, 1932.
Andrija Mutnjaković, *Arhitekt Josip Pičman / Der Architekt Josip Pičman*, Zagreb, 1997.
Andrija Mutnjaković, *Josip Pičman*, exh. cat., Hrvatski muzej arhitekture, Zagreb, 1998.
Zvonimir Vrkljan, *Sjećanja* [Memories], Zagreb 1995, pp. 142–143.

Stjepan Planić

(Zagreb 1900–80)
1920 graduated from the Zagreb School of Trade; 1920–22 work experience with Rudolf Lubynski and 1923–27 with Ivančić & Wolkenfeld; from 1927 own architect's office in Zagreb; 1926–31 studied architecture with Drago Ibler at the Academy of Fine Arts in Zagreb; 1930–35 member of the association of artists "Zemlja."
Major buildings and projects in Zagreb: participated in competitions for the Polyclinic and the Jewish hospital (1930); tenement block for the Zagreb Ice Factory (1930–31); own house and studio (1931–32); residential and business premises Mokrović (1932); Villas Vurdelja (1931–32); Fuhrmann (1935); Veble (1936); Čuvaj (1937); multi-story building for the Cooperative Bank "Napretkova zadruga" (1936); residential and business premises Šepetanc (1936–37). Planić completed approximately 600 projects.

Lit.: Stjepan Planić, *Problemi savremene arhitekture* [Problems of Contemporary Architecture], Zagreb, 1932 (annotated new edition: Zagreb 1996).
Stjepan Planić, "50 godine arhitekture u Hrvatskoj" [50 Years of Architecture in Croatia], in *Knjiæevnik* [The Author] (Zagreb), XII, 1939, no. 2, pp. 49–64.
Tomislav Premerl, "Stjepan Planić. Graditelj Zagreba" [Stjepan Planić: A 'Builder' of Zagreb], in *Iz starog i novog Zagreba* [From the Old and the New Zagreb] (Zagreb), VI, 1984, 253–274.
Radovan Ivančević, "Stjepan Planić i avangarda moderne hrvatske arhitekture" [Stjepan Planić and the Avant-Garde of modern Croatian Architecture], in *Stjepan Planić: Problemi savremene arhitekture*, Zagreb, 1996, pp. VII–LIV (see above).

Joæe Plečnik
(Ljubljana 1872–1957)
1888–92 trained as a carpenter at the School of Trade in Graz, then worked as a draughtsman in a furniture manufacturing company in Vienna; 1894 accepted at the Academy of Fine Arts in Vienna, 1895–99 studied in Otto Wagner's master class; until 1911 worked as an independent architect in Vienna; 1911–21 taught at the College of Arts and Crafts in Prague; 1920–34 architect of Prague Castle under the direction of Tomáš G. Masaryk; after 1921 Professor at the newly established Faculty of Technology in Ljubljana.
Major buildings and projects: Zacherl House, Vienna (1903–05); Church of the Holy Ghost, Vienna (1910–13); several conversions at Prague Castle (1920–34); general development plan for the northern part of Ljubljana (1928–29, partially completed); "Vzajemna" insurance building, Ljubljana (1928–30, in collaboration with France Tomažič); Sacred Heart Church, Prague (1928–31); bridge design for Tromostovje [The Three Bridges], Ljubljana (1929–31); St. Francis Church, Ljubljana (1930–31); Schuster Bridge, Ljubljana (1931–32); lock installation on the Ljubljanica, Ljubljana (1933–44); cemetery, Žale (1938–40); National and University Library, Ljubljana (1939–41); covered market, Ljubljana (1940–44); conversion of the former Convent of the German Order of Knights [Kriæanke], Ljubljana (1950–56).

Lit.: Damjan Prelovšek, *Josef Plečnik. Wiener Arbeiten von 1896 bis 1914* [Josef Plečnik. The Works in Vienna from 1896 to 1914], Vienna, 1979.
Marjan Mušič, *Joæe Plečnik*, Ljubljana, 1980.
François Burkhardt, Claude Eveno, Boris Bodrecca (ed.), *Joæe Plečnik. Architect 1872–1957*, Cambridge, Mass., London, 1989.
Peter Krečič, *Joæe Plečnik*, Ljubljana, 1992.
Damjan Prelovšek, *Josef Plečnik 1872–1957. Architectura perennis*, Salzburg, Vienna, 1992.
Peter Krečič, *Plečnik. The Complete Works*, London, 1993.
Josip Plečnik, An Architect of Prague Castle, Prague, 1997.
Jürgen Stabenow, *Joæe Plečnik. Städtebau im Schatten der Moderne*, Brunswick, Wiesbaden, 1996.
Andrej Hrausky, Janez Koæelj, Damjan Prelovšek, *Plečnik's Ljubljana: An Architectural Guide*, Ljubljana, 1997.
Marco Pozzetto, *Joæe Plečnik e la Scuola di Otto Wagner*, Turin, 1968.

Margarete Schütte–Lihotzky
(Vienna 1897–)
1915–19 studied architecture with Oskar Strnad and Heinrich Tessenow at the College of Arts and Crafts in Vienna; 1918 worked with Oskar Strnad; 1919 with Robert Örley; 1921 collaboration with Adolf Loos; 1921–22 worked in the office of Ernst Egli; 1926 appointment in the Building Standards Department of the city of Frankfurt, development of a rational kitchen system ("Frankfurter Küche") and designs of different types of terraced houses; 1926–30 busy publishing and lecturing schedule; 1930–33 sojourn in Moscow as a member of the May group; 1934–36 worked at the Academy of Architecture in Moskau; 1938 emigrated to Istanbul, member of the anti-fascist resistance group around the architect Herbert Eichholzer; 1940 arrested and imprisoned by the Gestapo during a short visit to Vienna; 1945 released from the Aichach Prison in Bavaria, returned to Vienna; 1946 worked for the city planning department in Sofia. The architect lives and works in Vienna.
Major buildings and projects in Vienna and Frankfurt: participated in the Eden Estate, Vienna XIV (1921–22); participated in the Winarsky Hof project, Vienna XX (1924–25); various types of terraced houses, Praunheim estate, Frankfurt (1926); standardised kitchen for the estates at Bruchfeldstraße, Praunheim and Ginnheim, Frankfurt (1926); nursery school project for the Ginnheim and Praunheim estates, Frankfurt (1928); two houses, "Werkbund" estate [group of artists and manufacturers trying jointly to improve the crafts and industrial design], Vienna XIII (1930–32).

Lit.: Peter Noever (ed.), *Margarete Schütte-Lihotzky. Soziale Architektur, Zeitzeugin eines Jahrhunderts* [Social Architecture, A Contemporary Witness of the Century], exh. cat., Austrian Museum of Applied Art, Vienna 1993.
Irene Nierhaus (ed.), *Margarete Schütte-Lihotzky. Erinnerungen aus dem Widerstand. Das kämpferische Leben einer Architektin von 1938–45*, Vienna, 1994.

Josip Seissel
(Krapina 1904–Zagreb 1987)
1923–28 studied architecture with Hugo Ehrlich at the Institute of Science and Technology in Zagreb; 1927–37 employed at the Zagreb City Planning Department (from 1932 –36 working on the new regulations for the urban development of Zagreb in collaboration with Vlado Antolić, Stjepan Hribar and Antun Ulrich); 1932–35 member of the "Zagreb Working Party;" member of the Yugoslav CIAM group; from 1939 Head of the School of Trade in Zagreb.
Major buildings and projects in Zagreb: project of the so-called "Zakladni blok" [endowment block] (1932, in collaboration with Josip Pičman); Institute of Agriculture and Dairy Production of the Faculty of Agriculture and Forestry (1933–34, in collaboration with the "Zagreb Working Party"); Yugoslav pavilion at the World Fair in Paris (1937).

Lit.: Josip Pičman, Josip Seissel, *Izloæba projekta za izgradnju Zakladnog zemljišta na Jelačićevom trgu* [Exhibition of the project for the completion of the "Zakladni zemlište" at the Jelačićev trg], exh. cat., Salon Ulrich, Zagreb, 1932.
Josip Seissel, *Jugoslavenski paviljon na Pariškoj izloæbi 1937* [The Yugoslav Pavilion at the Paris Fair 1937], Zagreb, 1937.
Drago Galić (ed.), *Arhitekti članovi JAZU* [Members of the Yugoslav Academy of Arts and Sciences: Architects], Zagreb, 1991, pp. 56–61.
Zvonimir Vrkljan, *Sjećanje* [Reminiscences], Zagreb, 1995, pp. 145–146.

Camillo Sitte
(Vienna 1843–1903)
1863–68 studied architecture with Heinrich von Ferstel at the Technical University in Vienna; 1863–69 studied history of art with Eitelberger at the University of Vienna and, at the same time, mathematics and philosophy; while studying he worked in the architect's office of his father Franz Sitte; 1874 appointed by the Imperial Ministry of Culture and Education to a post in Salzburg; 1875–83 founder and Director of the Imperial School of Trade in Salzburg; 1883 returned to Vienna; until his death in 1903 Director and Head of the Imperial School of Trade in Vienna.
Major buildings and projects: Mechitarist Church, Vienna II (1873–94; 1900: interior design); St Mary's Church, town hall and vicarage, Přívoz (1896–99); general development plans for Ostrava-Přívoz (1893–95), Olomouc (1894–95), Ljubljana (1900–01), Liberec (1900–01), Ostrava-Mariánské Hory (1903–09 in collaboration with Siegfried Sitte).

Lit.: Heinrich Sitte, "Camillo Sitte," in *Neue Österreichische Biographie*, vol. 4, Vienna, 1929.
Camillo Sitte, *Der Städte–Bau nach seinen künstlerischen Grundsätzen*, Vienna 1889, 2nd ed. 1889, 3rd ed. 1900, 4th ed. 1909 (reprinted: Brunswick, Wiesbaden 1983).

Daniel Wieczorek, *Camillo Sitte et les début de l'urbanisme moderne*, Brussels, 1981.
George R. Collins, Christiane Crasemann Collins, *Camillo Sitte: The Birth of Modern City Planning*, New York, 1986.
Rudolf Wurzer, "Franz, Camillo und Siegfried Sitte. Ein langer Weg von der Architektur zur Stadtplanung," in *Berichte zur Raumforschung und Raumplanung*, (Vienna), XXXIII, 1989, pp. 9–34.
Zucconi Guido, *Camillo Sitte e is suoi interpreti*, Milan, 1992.
Mönninger Michael, *Vom Ornament zum Nationalkunstwerk: Zur Kunst und Architekturtheorie Camillo Sittes*, Brunswick, 1998.

Josef Špalek

(Plzeň 1902–Moscow 1942)
1923–26 studied architecture with Josef Gočár at the Prague Academy of Fine Arts; from 1926 member of the association of artists "Devětsil;" member of the Union of Architects and the Association of Academic Architects; 1929 founder member of the Levá fronta [Left Front]; 1930 member of the Czechoslovak CIAM group and from 1933 of the Association of Socialist Architects; 1929–33 worked in the office of Jaromír Krejcar; from 1933 sojourn in the USSR, worked in the offices of the Vesnin Bros. and of Moisej Ginzburg; 1937 acquired Soviet citizenship.
Major buildings and projects: participated in the competition for blocks of residences with minimal-sized apartments ("CIRPAC"), Prague (1930, in collaboration with Jan Gillar); participated in the competition for an estate of collective houses ("L-Project"), Prague (1930, in collaboration with Jan Gillar, Peer Bücking and Augusta Müllerová); participated in the competition for an overall traffic plan for Prague and suburbs (1930–31, in collaboration with Jaromír Krejcar).

Lit.: Josef Špalek, Oldřich Stibor, *Utopie technokracie* [The Utopia of Technology], Prague, 1933.
Alena Vondrová (ed.), *Český funkcionalismus 1920–40* [Czech Functionalism 1920–40], vol. *Architektura*, Moravská Galerie v Brně-Uměleckoprůmyslové Muzeum v Praze, Prague, Brno 1978, reference "Josef Špalek."

Josef Štěpánek

(Mořice 1889–Prague 1964)
1913–16 studied architecture with Jože Plečnik at the Prague College of Arts and Crafts; 1916–19 with Jan Kotěra at the Prague Academy of Fine Arts; 1921–49 worked as an independent architect in Prague; from 1924 regular editorial work for the newspaper *Stavitel*, member of several professional bodies.
Major buildings and projects: residence for two families, model estate Nový dům [The New House], Brno (1927–28); participated in the competition for a new government complex in the Letná Plain Prague (1928); participated in the competititon for designing a sports stadium, Prague-Braník (1929).

Lit.: Alena Vondrová (ed.), *Český funkcionalismus 1920–40* [Czech Functionalism 1920–40], vol. *Architektura*, Moravská Galerie v Brně – Uměleckoprůmyslové Muzeum v Praze, Prague, Brno 1978, reference "Josef Štěpánek."

Zdenko Strižić

(Bjelovar 1902–Hanover 1990)
1921–23 studied architecture at the Institute of Science and Technology in Dresden and 1924–26 with Hans Poelzig in Berlin–Charlottenburg; 1926–31 qualification and work experience with Hans Poelzig in Berlin (including projects for the Büllowplatz and the Babylon Cinema in Berlin as well as for the Casino of the IG Farben Industry in Frankfurt); 1931–33 architect's office Strižić & Holzbauer in Berlin; from 1933 own architect's office in Zagreb.
Major buildings and projects: in Zagreb: participated in the competition for the so-called "Zakladni blok" [endowment block] (1930); participated in the competition for a general development plan for

the city of Zagreb (1930–31); a study for the reconstruction of Ilica (1931); participated in the competition for the Ukrainian National Theatre in Charkiv (1931); housing estate for the First Croatian Savings Bank (1934–35); housing for bachelors, Turković (1937–38).

Lit.: H. J. Z., "Der Wettbewerb um das ukrainische Staatstheater für musikalische Massenaufführungen," in *Baukunst und Städtebau* (Berlin), XVI, 1932, no. 2, pp. 68–72.
Zvonomir Vrkljan, *Sjećanje* [Reminiscences], Zagreb, 1995, pp. 139–142.

Oskar Strnad

(Vienna 1879–1935)
1903 graduated in architecture from the Technical University in Vienna; 1903–06 worked in the studio of Friedrich Ohmann; from 1909 taught at the Vienna College of Arts and Crafts; from 1918 took over the course taught by Heinrich Tessenow; from 1919 worked as an architect, stage designer, author, draughtsman, and sculptor.
Major buildings and projects: residence, Vienna XIX, Kobenzlgasse (1910, in collaboration with Oskar Wlach); Wassermann House, Vienna XIX (1914, in collaboration with Josef Frank and Oskar Wlach); theater project, Vienna VIII (1921); participated in the Winarsky-Hof project, Vienna XX (1924–25); project for a theater in the castle of Leopoldskron, Salzburg (1930); residence for two families, "Werkbund" estate, Vienna XIII (1930–32).

Lit.: Max Eisler, *Oskar Strnad*, Vienna, 1936.
Joseph Gregor, *Rede auf Oskar Strnad*, Vienna, 1936.
Otto Niedermoser, *Oskar Strnad 1879–35*, Vienna, 1965.
Johannes Spalt, *Der Architekt Oskar Strnad. Zum hundertsten Geburtstag am 26. Oktober 1979*, Vienna, 1979 (College of Applied Art in Vienna, Report 20).

Tadeusz Stryjeński

(Carouge 1849–Kraków 1943)
1866–67 studied mathematics at the Polish University in Paris; 1867–68 attended the School of Decorative Arts in Geneva; 1868–72 studied architecture with Gottfried Semper at the Eidgenössisches Polytechnikum in Zurich; 1872–73 worked at the Vienna construction company L. Tischler; 1873–77 sojourn in Peru working for the government; 1878 studied at the Paris École des Beaux-Arts and worked for P. Ginain then moved to Kraków; 1889 appointed community architect; 1894 appointed to a post in the Planning Department; 1895–10 Keeper of Monuments; 1906–10 director of the Museum of Arts and Crafts in Kraków.
Major buildings and projects: main Post Office, Kraków (1885–87, in collaboration with K. Knaus), reconstruction of the Old Theater, Kraków (1903–06, in collaboration with Franciszek Mączyński); staircase in the Museum of Arts and Crafts, Kraków (1908–14).

Lit.: A. Woltanowski, "Tadeusz Stryjeński (1849–1943). Materiały spuścizny rękopiśmiennej w Archivum Polskiej Akademii Nauk w Warsawie" [Tadeusz Stryjeński (1849–1943). Manuscripts from the Literary Estate in the Archives of the Polish Academy of Sciences in Warsaw], in *Kwartalnik architektury i urbanistyki* [Architecture and Urbanism Quarterly] (Warsaw), XVI, 1971.
L. Lameński, *Tadeusz Stryjeński in Znak* [Sign], XXXII, 1980, pp. 1694–1703.
L. Lameński, "Z dziejów środowiska architektonicznego Krakowa w latach 1879–1932. Tadeusz Stryjeński i jego współ" [From the History of Architectural Activities in Cracow during the Years 1897–1932. Tadeusz Stryjeński and his Circle], in T. Gygiel (ed.), *Architektura 19. i początku 20. wieku* [The Architecture at the end of the 19th and the beginning of the 20th Century] Wrocław, 1991, pp. 23–28.

Vladimir Šubic

(Ljubljana 1894–Lukavac 1946)
1913–15 studied shipbuilding at the Institute of Science and Technology in Graz; 1919–22 studied architecture at the German Institute of Science and Technology in Prague; in Ljubljana first

employment in the construction company Obnova, run by the Tönnies family; until 1926 taught at the Institute of Science and Technology in Ljubljana and was employed later in the city planning department of Ljubljana; from1930 chief architect and then head of the planning department at the Pension Insurance Company for Wage Earners in Ljubljana.

Major buildings and projects: in Ljubljana: municipal block of flats "Meksika" (1926–27); Board of Wage Earners (1927); "Grafika" palace (1929–31); residential and business complex with the "Nebotičnik" [skyscraper], Slovenska/Štefanova (1930–33); Academy of Commerce and Trade (1930–34).

Lit.: "Arhitekt Vladimir Šubič / Architect Vladimir Šubič," in *Arhitektov bilten, posebna izdaja / Architect's Bulletin special issue* (Ljubljana), XXII, 1992, nos. 111–114.

László Székely

(Salonta 1877–Timişoara 1934)
1895–1900 studied at the Budapest Polytechnic; from 1903 own architect's studio; 1903–22 city planner in Timişoara.
Major buildings and projects in Timişoara: a number of buildings of the town infrastructure (1904–22); abattoir (1904–05); hydroelectric plant at the Bega (1907–10); gymnasium for the Piarists [members of a Catholic teaching order] (1907–09); Dauerbach residence, Hilt residence, Neuhausz residence, Széchenyi residence (1910–12); Villa Blăjan, Villa Rieger, Villa Lindner (1911–14); Hungaria baths (1913–14); headquarters of the chamber of commerce (1925).

Lit.: Peter A. Petri, *Biographisches Lexikon des Banater Deutschtums*, Marquartstein, 1992, pp. 1912–13
Mihai Opriş, Timişoara. *Mică monografie urbanistică* [Timişoara. A brief City Monograph], Bucureşti 1987, pp. 145, 211.
János Gerle, Attila Kovács, Imre Makovecz, *A századfordul magyar építészete* [Hungarian Architecture around the Turn of the Century], Budapest, 1990, p.186.
Ileana Pintilie, "Documente din arhive particulare contribuind la cunoaşterea unui architect timişorean de la începutul secolului XX—László Székely" [Documents from the Literary Estate of an Architect at the Beginning of the 20th Century in Timişoara—László Székely], in *Studii şi comunicări* [Studies and Communications] (Muzuel judiţan Arad), III, 1996, pp. 202–224.

Karel Teige

(Prague 1900–51)
Leading personality of the Czech avant-garde in the years between the wars; initiator of the avant-garde groups Devětsil (1920), the Levá fronta [Left Front] (1929), as well as of a group of surrealists in the ČSSR (1934). Teige's influence as a critic, theoretician, typographer and editor (1923–29 of *Stavba*, 1927–31 of *ReD*) was crucial for the development of Czech cultural and creative forces after 1920. In the mid-1920s he developed his contrary model of constructivism and poeticism; from 1928 the main focus of his theoretical concepts was directed towards architecture which, following Hannes Meyer's concepts, he saw as a scientific-utilitarian discipline. At the beginning of the 1930s Teige was actively involved with the cultural Left, and from 1934 he chose surrealism as an area for experimenting with his theories.

Lit.: Karel Teige, *Stavba a báseň* [Architecture and the Poem], Prague, 1927.
Karel Teige, *Moderní architektura v Československu* [Modern Architecture in Czechoslovakia, MSA, vol. 2, Prague, 1930.
Karel Teige, *Nejmenší byt* [The Minimal Flat], ESMA, vol.1, Prague, 1932.
Karel Teige, *L'architecture moderne en Tchécoslovaquie*, Prague, 1947 (also published in English.: Modern Architecture in Czechoslovakia).
Karel Teige, *Svět stavby a básně. Výbor z díla I* [The World of Architecture and of the Poem. Selected Work I], Prague, 1966.
Karel Teige, *Liquidierung der 'Kunst'*, Frankfurt / Main, 1968.
Karel Teige, *Zápasy o smysl moderní tvorby. Výbor z díla II* [The Debate about the Meaning of Modern Design. Selected Work II], Prague, 1969.

Rassegna (Bologna), XV, 1993, no. 53 / 1 (Karel Teige: Architecture and Poetry).
Karel Teige, *Osvobozování života a poezie. Výbor z díla III* [The Liberation of Life and of Poetry. Selected Work III], Prague, 1994.
Karel Teige 1900–51, exh. cat., Galerie hlavního města Prahy, Dům u kameného zvonu, Prague, 1994.
Manuela Castagnara Codeluppi (ed.), *Karel Teige. Architettura, Poesia. Praga 1900–51*, exh. cat., Scuderie del Castello di Miramare, Trieste, Milan, 1996.
Eric Dluhosch, Rotislav Švácha (eds.), *Karel Teige 1900–1951. L'Enfant Terrible of the Czech Modernist Avant-garde*, Cambridge, Mass./London, 1999.

Antun Ulrich

(Zagreb 1902–98)
1917–21 vocational training at the School of Trade in Zagreb; 1923–27 studied architecture with Josef Hoffmann at the Vienna College of Arts and Crafts; 1927–28 worked in the planning department of the Faculty of Medicine in Zagreb; from 1928 employed in the Zagreb city planning department (1932–36, in collaboration with Vlado Antolić, Stjepan Hribar and Josip Seissel, compilation of new guidelines for the urban development of Zagreb).
Major buildings and projects in Zagreb: Villa Matica (1932); residential and business premises for the endowment trust commissioning the new hospital (1932–33, in collaboration with Franjo Bahovec); residential and business premises for the community of the Orthodox Church (1932–40, with Stanko Kliska); Rebro Polyclinic (1936–41, in collaboration with Franjo Gabrić, Ivan Juranović and Stanko Kliska).

Lit.: Vesna Mikić-Brodnjak, "Antun Ulrich. Uz 90. obljetnicu života arhitekta" [Antun Ulrich: On the Anniversary of the Architect's 90th Birthday], in *Život umjetnosti* [The Life of Art] (Zagreb), XXVIII, 1993, nos. 52–53, pp. 22–29

Ivan Vurnik

(Radovljica 1884–1971)
1911 graduated after having studied architecture with Carl König and Karl Meyreder in the Department of Civil and Construction Engineering at the Technical University in Vienna, then worked in the office of Ludwig Baumann; 1915 moved to Radovljica; 1919 to Ljubljana; guest lecturer at the newly established university.
Major buildings and projects: Cooperative Bank, Ljubljana (1921–22); Sokol building, Ljubljana (1923–26); housing estate, Maribor (1927); projects for regulatory plans for Bled, Grosuplje, Hrastnik, Trbovlje (1930–31); swimming pool Obla Gorica, Radovljica (1932–33); project for an overall regulatory plan for Ljubljana (1935, in collaboration with students of the Faculty of Architecture in Ljubljana).

Lit.: "Ivan Vurnik 1884–1971. Slovenski arhitekt" [Ivan Vurnik 1884–1971: A Slovenian Architect], in *Arhitektov bilten, posebna izdaja* [Architect's bulletin special issue], (Ljubljana), XXIV, 1994, no. 119–124 (also catalogue of the exhibition of the same name in the Cankarjev Cathedral, Ljubljana, 1995).
Saša Sedlar, "Ivan Vurnik 1884–1971. Poskus orisa njegove vloge v sodobne urbanizmu" [Ivan Vurnik 1884–1971: An Attempt to define his Position in Contemporary Urban Building], in *Sinteza* (Ljubljana),1972, no. 23, pp. 25–27.

Otto Wagner

(Vienna 1841–1918)
1857–59 studied construction at the Technical University in Vienna; 1860–61 studied at the Berlin Academy of Architecture; 1861–62 studied with August Siccard von Siccardsburg and Eduard van der Nüll at the Vienna Academy of Fine Arts; 1894–1913 Professor at the Vienna Academy of Fine Arts; Oberbaurat [senior architect], head of the "Meisterschule;" 1899–1905 member of the Vienna Secession.
Major buildings and projects: National Bank, Vienna I (1882–84); project for an overall development plan, Vienna (1892–93); buildings

for the Vienna Metropolitan Railway (1894–1901); "Anker" residential and commercial block, Vienna I (1894–95); apartment blocks, Vienna VI, Linke Wienzeile 38–40 (1898–99); Post Office Savings Bank, Vienna I (1904–06, 1910–12); Church at the Steinhof, Vienna XIV (1902–04); apartment block, Vienna VII, Neustiftgasse 40 (1909–10).

Lit.: Otto Wagner, *Einige Skizzen, Projekte und ausgeführte Bauwerke*, 4 vols., Vienna, 1889–1922 (reprinted Tübingen, 1987).
Otto Wagner, *Moderne Architektur*, Vienna, 1896 (enlarged: 2nd ed. 1898, 3rd ed. 1902, Czech: *Moderní architektura*, Prague, 1910).
Otto Wagner, *Die Baukunst unserer Zeit*, Vienna, 1914 (also published as: 4th ed.1914 by *Moderne Architektur*).
Otto Wagner, *Die Groszstadt. Eine Studie über diese*, Vienna, 1911.
Josef A. Lux, *Otto Wagner. Eine Monographie*, Munich, 1914.
Hans Tietze, *Otto Wagner*, Vienna, Berlin, Munich, Leipzig, 1922.
Heinz Geretsegger, Max Peintner, *Otto Wagner (1841–1918). Ungegrenzte Großstadt, Beginn der modernen Architektur*, Salzburg, Vienna, 1964, 2nd ed. 1983.
Otto Antonia Graf, *Otto Wagner. Das Werk des Architekten*, 2 vols., Vienna, Cologne, Graz, 1985, 2nd ed. 1994.
Harry Francis Malgrave (ed.), *Otto Wagner. Reflections on the Raiment of Modernity*, Santa Monica, 1993 (*Issues & Debates*, vol. 3).

Ernest Weissmann
(Đakovo 1903–Haarlem 1985)
1922–26 studied architecture with Hugo Ehrlich und Viktor Kovačić at the Institute of Science and Technology in Zagreb; 1926–27 worked with Adolf Loos, and 1927–30 with Le Corbusier in Paris; until 1935 regular collaboration with Le Corbusier; 1932–35 member of the "Zagreb Working Party" of the Yugoslav National CIAM group, and from 1938 member of the CIRPAC; 1937 moved to Paris; 1938 to the USA; employed later at the UNO.
Major buildings and projects in Zagreb: participated in the competition for the Stiftungskrankenhaus (Polyclinic) and the Jewish hospital (1930); Institute of Agriculture and Dairy Production of the Faculty of Agriculture and Forestry (1933–34, in collaboration with the "Zagreb Working Party"); Villas Kraus and Podvinec (1936–37).

Lit.: Aleksander Laslo, "Raumplan, plan libre ili…" [Space Design, plan libre or …], in *Arhitektura* (Zagreb), XL, 1987, no. 1–4 / 200–03, pp. 35–40.
Neven Šegević, "Haarlemski egzodus Ernesta Weissmana" [Ernest Weissmann's Exodus to Haarlem], in *Čovjek i prostor* [Man and Space] (Zagreb), XXXVIII, 1991, nos.1-2 / 454–55, pp. 16–19.
Bogdan Rajakovac, "Iz sjećanja na Ernesta Weissmana" [Remembering Ernest Weissmann], in *Čovjek i prostor* [Man and Space] (Zagreb), XXXVIII, 1991, nos. 1–2 / 454–455, pp. 20–21.
Ariana Štulhofer, Andrej Uchytil, *Arhitekt Ernest Weissmann — monografija radova* [The Architekt Ernest Weissmann–A Monograph of his Work], Zagreb, 1993.

Alfred Zachariewicz
(Ľviv 1871–Warsaw 1937)
1890–95 studied architecture at the Ľviv Polytechnic; 1895–98 studied at the Technical University in Vienna; 1899–1903 worked in the architect's office of the Levyns'kyj company; 1903 established own design office and the company Sosnowski-Zachariewicz (with Józef Sosnowski), which undertook the construction of many bridges and buildings in the Austro-Hungarian monarchy after the Hennebique system (sole patent rights for Galicia), i.e. using steel reinforced concrete (also in main station in Ľviv).
Major buildings and projects: In Ľviv: Mikolasz Arcade (1899–1901, in collaboration with Ivan Levyns'kyj); Chamber of Commerce and Trade (1907–11, in collaboration with Tadeusz Obmiński); Bałaban House (1908–10); Insurance Company "Assicurazioni Generali" (1908–10); Land Credit Bank (1912–13); numerous buildings in Ľviv, including exhibition pavilions, students' residences for the Polytechnic (in the 1920s, mostly in collaboration with Eugeniusz Czerwiński).

Lit.: Jerzy Nechay, "Pierwsze kroki żelbetu w Polsce" [The Beginnings of Steel Reinforced Concrete in Poland], in *Cement* (Warsaw), 1937, no. 8, pp. 113–115.
Ihor Žuk, "Das Gebäude der Handels- und Gewerbekammer in Lemberg," in Hanns Haas, Hannes Stekl (eds.), *Bürgerliche Selbstdarstellung. Städtebau, Architektur, Denkmäler*, Vienna, Cologne, Weimar, 1995, pp. 145–151.
Ihor Žuk, *Julian Zachariewicz 1837–98, Alfred Zachariewicz 1871–37. Wystawa Twórzości, Katalog* [Julian Zachariewicz 1837–98, Alfred Zachariewicz 1871–37: Exhibition of Works, Catalogue], exh. cat., Warsaw, 1996.
Ihor Žuk, *Torhovo-promyslova palata* [The Chamber of Commerce and Trade], Ľviv 1998 (Istoryko–architekturnyj Atlas Ľvova [Atlas of the History of Architecture of Ľviv], series 2, issue no. 3).

Jan Zawiejski
(Kraków 1854–1922)
1892 studied engineering at the Institute of Science and Technology in Munich; from 1873 continued his studies in Vienna; 1874–78 studied architecture with Carl König and Heinrich von Ferstel at the Technical University in Vienna; from 1880 work experience with Heinrich von Ferstel; 1882 sojourn in Berlin; 1884–89 architectural work in Ľviv and Krynica; 1889 moved to Kraków; 1890–94 taught at the School of Trade in Kraków; 1900 appointed city architect in Kraków; 1900–04 member of the editorial board of the Kraków newspaper *Architect*.
Major buildings and projects: Spa Hotel, Krynica (1884–89); City Theater, Kraków (1888–93); Austrian restaurant pavilion and "Chateau d'Eau" for the World Fair in Paris (1897–1900); Academy of Commerce, Kraków (1904–06); participated in the competition for designing the Palace of Peace in the Hague (1905–06); Ohrenstein House, Kraków (1911–13).

Lit.: Jacek Purchla, *Jan Zawiejski. Architekt przełomu XIX i XX wieku* [Jan Zawiejski. An Architect at the Transition from the 19th to the 20th Century], Warsaw, 1986.

Selected Bibliography

General Bibliography

Friedrich Achleitner, *Regio, ein Konstrukt? Regionalismus, eine Pleite?*, Basel, Boston, Berlin, 1997.

Gerhard Brunn, Jürgen Reulecke (eds.), *Metropolis Berlin. Berlin als deutsche Hauptstadt im Vergleich europäischer Hauptstädte 1871–1939*, Bonn, Berlin, 1992.

Annette Ciré, Haila Ochs (eds.), *Die Zeitschrift als Manifest. Aufsätze zu architektonischen Strömungen im 20. Jahrhundert*, Basel, Berlin, Boston, 1991.

Andrei Corbea-Hoisie, Jacques Le Rider (eds.), *Metropole und Provinzen in Alt-österreich (1880–1918)*, Vienna, Cologne, Weimar, Iaşi (Romania), 1996.

Otto Antonia Graf, *Die vergessene Wagnerschule*, Vienna, 1969 (*Schriften des Museums des 20. Jahrhunderts*, Vienna, vol. 3).

Rudolf Haller (ed.), *Nach Kakanien. Annäherung an die Moderne*, Vienna, Cologne, Weimar, 1996.

Andreas Lehne, Tamás K. Pintér, *Jugendstil in Vienna und Budapest*, Vienna, 1990.

Jacques Le Rider, *Mitteleuropa. Auf den Spuren eines Begriffes*, Vienna, 1994.

Wojciech Leśnikowski (ed.), *East European Modernism. Architecture in Czechoslovakia, Hungary, and Poland between the Wars 1919–1939*, New York, 1996.

Gerhard Melinz, Susan Zimmermann (eds.), *Vienna—Prag—Budapest. Blütezeit der Habsburgermetropolen. Urbanisierung, Kommunalpolitik, gesellschaftliche Konflikte (1867–1918)*, Vienna. 1996.

Ákos Moravánszky, *Die Architektur der Donaumonarchie 1867–1918*, Budapest, Berlin, 1988.

Ákos Moravánszky, *Die Erneuerung der Baukunst. Wege zur Moderne in Mitteleuropa 1900–1940*, Salzburg, Vienna, 1988.

Ákos Moravánszky, *Competing Visions. Aesthetic Invention and Social Imagination in Central European Architecture 1867–1918*, Cambridge, Mass., London, 1998.

Neubauten in Vienna, Prag, Budapest, Vienna, 1904.

Monika Oberhammer (et al., eds.), *25 Jahre Institut für Kunstgeschichte der Universität Salzburg, Vorträge zum Thema, Nationale und übernationale Kunstströmungen in der Habsburger-Monarchie*, Salzburg, 1989 (contributions by Ilona Sármány-Parsons, Marco Pozzetto, Damjan Prelovšek, Pavel Zatloukal).

Werner Oechslin, *Stilhülse und Kern. Otto Wagner, Adolf Loos und der evolutionäre Weg zur modernen Architektur*, Zürich, Berlin, 1994.

Marco Pozzetto, *Die Schule Otto Wagners 1894–1912*, Vienna, Munich, 1980.

Rassegna (Bologna), IV, 1982, no. 12 (*Architettura nelle riviste d'avantguardia*).

Martin Steinmann, *CIAM. Dokumente 1928–1939*, Basel, Boston, Stuttgart, 1979.

Heidemarie Uhl (ed.), *Kultur—Urbanität—Moderne. Differenzierungen der Moderne in Zentraleuropa um 1900*, Vienna 1999 (*Studien zur Moderne*, vol. 4)

Wagnerschule 1902/1903 und 1903/1904. Projekte, Studien und Skizzen aus der Spezialschule für Architektur des Oberbaurat Otto Wagner, Professor an der k. k. Akademie der bildenden Künste in Vienna, Leipzig, 1905.

Wagnerschule. Arbeiten aus den Jahren 1905/06 und 1906/07. With an appendix, Leipzig, 1910.

Exhibition Catalogues

Koos Bosma, Helma Hellinga (eds.), *Mastering the City. North-European City Planning 1900–2000*, 2 vols., Netherlands Architecture Institute, Rotterdam, The Hague, 1997.

Gerhard M. Dienes (ed.), *"transLOKAL." 9 Städte im Netz (1848–1918): Bratislava/Preßburg, Brno/Brünn, Graz/Kraków/Krakau, Ljubljana/Laibach, München, Pécs/Fünfkirchen, Trieste/Triest, Zagreb/Agram*, Graz City Museum, Graz, 1996.

Europa, Europa. Das Jahrhundert der Avantgarde in Mittel- und Osteuropa, Kunst- und Ausstellungshalle der Bundesrepublik Deutschland, Bonn, Ostfildern-Ruit, 1994.

Hermann Filitz (ed.), *Der Traum vom Glück. Die Kunst des Historismus in Europa*, Künstlerhaus, Akademie der bildenden Künste Vienna, Vienna, Munich, 1996.

Budapest

Archithese (Niederteufen, Switzerland), XVII, 1987, no. 3 (Ungarn. Seele und Form).

András Ferkai, *Buda építészete a két világháború között* [The Architecture of Budapest in the Inter-war Years], Budapest, 1995.

Eszter Gábor, *A CIAM magyar csoportja (1928–1938)* [The Hungarian CIAM Group (1928–1938)], Budapest, 1972.

János Gerle, *A pénz palotái*, Budapest [English version: *Palaces of Money*], Budapest, 1994.

János Gerle, Attila Kovács, Imre Makovecz, *A századforduló magyar építészete* [Hungarian Architecture of the Turn of the Century] (including German and English summaries), Budapest, 1990.

Andreas Lehne, Tamás K. Pintér, *Jugendstil in Wien und Budapest*, Vienna, 1990.

Zsuzsa Lőrinczi, Mihály Vargha (eds.), *Építészeti kalauz. Budapest építészete a századfordulótól napjainkig / Architectural Guide: Architecture in Budapest from the Turn-of-the-Century to the Present*, Budapest, 1997.

Gyula Kabdebó, *Budapest székesfőváros kislakás és iskola építkezései* [Small Residential and School Buildings in Budapest], Budapest, 1913.

John Lukacs, *Budapest 1900. A Historical Portrait of a City and Its Culture*, New York, 1988.

Dezső Malonyay, *A magyar nép művészete* [The Art of the Hungarian People], 5 vols., Budapest, 1907–22.

Ferenc Merényi, *A magyar építészet 1867–1967* [Hungarian Architecture 1867–1967], Budapest, 1970.

Nóra Pamer, *Magyar építészet a két világháború között* [Hungarian Architecture between the Wars], Budapest, 1986.

Tamás K. Pintér, *Budapest Architectura 1900*, Budapest, 1990 (German, English and revised 2nd edition, 1999).

Dora Wiebenson, József Sisa (eds.), *The Architecture of Historic Hungary*, Cambridge, Mass., London, 1998.

Exhibition Catalogues

Hubertus Gassner (ed.), *Wechselwirkungen. Ungarische Avantgarde in der Weimarer Republik*, Neue Galerie, Kassel / Museum Bochum, Marburg, 1986.

Lélek és forma. Magyar művészet 1896–1914 [Soul and Form: Hungarian Art 1896–1914], Magyar Nemzeti Galéria, Budapest, 1986.

Panorama, Architecture and Applied Arts in Hungary 1896–1916, Museum of Contemporary Art Sapporo, Kyoto, 1995.

Contemporary Journals and Periodicals

Bauzeitung für Ungarn (Budapest), I, 1876 to XXI, 1896.
Dokumentum (Budapest), I, 1926 to 1927.
A Ház [The House] (Budapest), I, 1908 to IV, 1911.
100% (Vienna), 1927 to 1929.
MA [Today] (Budapest, Vienna), I, 1916 to X, 1925.
Magyar Építőművészet [Hungarian Architecture] (Budapest), V, 1907 to LXXXVII, 1996.
Magyar Mérnök- és Építészegylet Közlönye [Proceedings of the Hungarian Engineers' and Architects' Union] (Budapest), I, 1867 to LXXVIII, 1944.
Magyar Művészet [Hungarian Art] (Budapest), I, 1925 to XIV, 1938.
Magyar Pályázatok [Hungarian Competitions] (Budapest), I, 1903 to V, 1907 (*Magyar Építőművészet*).
Munka [Work] (Budapest), I, 1928 to XII, 1939.
Művészet [Art] (Budapest), I, 1902 to XVII, 1918.
Tér és Forma [Space and Form] (Budapest), 1926–28; I, 1928 to XXI, 1948.
A Tett [The Deed] (Budapest), 1915, no. 1 to 1916, no. 17.

Kraków

Zbigniew Beiersdorf, Jacek Purchla, *The Globe House—the Former Headquarters of the Chamber of Commerce and Industry*, Kraków, 1997.
Janina Bieniarzówna, Jan Małecki, *Dzieje Krakowa* [The History of Kraków], vol. 3, Kraków, 1979.
Janusz Bogdanowski, *Warownie i zieleń twierdzy Kraków* [The Fortifications and the Green Spaces of Kraków Castle], Kraków, 1979.
Juliusz Demel, "Podstawy rozwoju nowoczesnego Krakowa w latach 1846–1956" [The Principles of the Development of Modern Kraków in the Years 1846–1956], in J. Dabrowski (ed.), *Kraków—jego dzieje i sztuka* [Kraków—its History and Art], Warsaw, 1965, pp. 439–98.
Adam Miłobędzki, *Architektura ziem Polski / The Architecture of Poland*, Kraków, 1994.
Andrzej K. Olszewski, *Nowa forma w architekturze polskiej 1900–1925* [New Form in Polish Architecture, 1900–1925], Wrocław, Warsaw, Kraków, 1967.
Krzysztof K. Pawłowski, "Początki polskiej nowoczesnej myśli urbanistycznej" [The Beginnings of Modern Urban Thought in Poland], in *Sztuka około 1900* [Art c. 1900], Warsaw, 1969, pp. 67–81.
Jacek Purchla, *Jak powstał nowoczesny Kraków* [The Emergence of Modern Kraków], Kraków, 2nd edition, 1990.
Jacek Purchla, *Krakau unter österreichischer Herrschaft, 1846–1918. Faktoren seiner Entwicklung*, Vienna, Cologne, Weimar, 1993.
Jacek Purchla, "Wiener Einflüsse auf die polnische Architektur der Jahrhundertwende—Forschungsstand," in *Österreichische Zeitschrift für Kunst und Denkmalpflege*, Vienna, XLV, 1991, nos. 1–2, pp. 66–73.
Jacek Purchla, "Krakau um die Jahrhundertwende und sein kreatives Milieu," in Emil Brix, Allan Janik (eds.), *Kreatives Milieu, Wien um 1900. Ergebnisse eines Forschungsgespräches der Arbeitsgemeinschaft Wien um 1900*, Vienna, Munich, 1993, pp. 54-84.
Jacek Purchla, "Kraków 1910. Greater Kraków Competition," in Koos Bosma, Helma Hellinga (eds.), *Mastering the City. North-European City Planning 1900–2000*, exh. cat., Netherlands Architecture Institute, Rotterdam, The Hague, 1997, vol. 2, pp. 168–75.
Jacek Purchla, "Cracow and its Architecture at the Turn of the Century," in Piotr Krakowski, Jacek Purchla (eds.), *Art around 1900 in Central Europe. Art Centres and Provinces*, Kraków, 1999, pp. 81–112.

Contemporary Journals and Periodicals

Architekt (Kraków), I, 1900–1901 to XXIII, 1930.
Blok (Warsaw), no. 1, 1924 to no. 11, 1926.
Praesens (Warsaw), no. 1, 1926 to no. 2, 1927–30.

Ljubljana

Ferdo Gestrin (ed.), *Zgodovina Ljubljane, Prispevki za monografijo* [The History of Ljubljana, Contributions to a Monograph], Ljubljana, 1984.
Andrej Hrausky, "Funkcionalizem v slovenski arhitekturi med obema vojnama / Functionalism in Slovene Architecture between the Wars," in *Arhitektov bilten / Architect's Bulletin*, XXIII, 1993, no. 117–18, pp. 22–43.

Branko Korošec, *Ljubljana skozi stoletja, Mesto na načrtih, projektih in v stvarnosti* [Ljubljana across the Centuries: the City in Plans, Projects, and in Reality], Ljubljana, 1991.
Breda Mihelič, *Urbanistični razvoj Ljubljane* [The Urban Development of Ljubljana], Ljubljana, 1983.
Breda Mihelič, *Ljubljana Stadtführer*, Ljubljana, 1994.
Darja Mihelič (ed.), *Dunaj in Slovenci* [Vienna and the Slovenes], Ljubljana, 1994.
Jelka Pirkovič, Breda Mihelič, *Art Nouveau Architecture in Slovenia*, Ljubljana, 1996.
Damjan Prelovšek, "Ljubljanska arhitektura Hribarjevega časa" [The Architecture of Ljubljana in the Era of Hribar], in Vincenc Reisp (ed.), *Grafenauerjev zbornik* [Grafenau Almanach], Ljubljana, 1996, pp. 597–606.
Borut Rovšnik, "Stilni razvoj ornamenta na fasadah v Sloveniji od 1895 do prve svetovne vojne" [The Stylistic Development of Façade Ornamentation in Slovenia from 1895 to World War I], in *Zbornik za umetnostno zgodovino / Archives d'Histoire de l'Art* (Ljubljana), XVI, 1980, no. 16, pp. 25–50.
Vlado Valenčič, "Gradbeni razvoj Ljubljane od dograditve južne železnice 1849 do potresa 1895" [The architectonic Development of Ljubljana from the Construction of the Southern Railway in 1849 to the Earthquake of 1895], in *Kronika* (Ljubljana), IX, 1961, no. 3, pp. 135–44.
Vlado Valenčič, "Ljubljansko stavbeništvo od srede 19. do začetka 20. stoletja" [Architecture in Ljubljana from the Mid-19th Century to the Beginning of the 20th Century], in *Kronika* (Ljubljana), XXVII, 1979, no. 3, pp. 135–47.

Exhibition Catalogues

Taja Čepič, Janja Rebolj (eds.), *Homo sum, Ivan Hribar in njegova Ljubljana* [Homo sum: Ivan Hribar and his Ljubljana], Mestni muzej, Ljubljana, 1997.
Slovenija in Dunaj / Slowenien und Wien, Cankarjev dom, Ljubljana—Österreichische Akademie der Wissenschaften, Vienna, 1995.
Nace Šumi, *Arhitektura secesijske dobe v Ljubljani* [Jugendstil Architecture in Ljubljana], Mestni muzej, Ljubljana, 1954.

Contemporary Journals and Periodicals

Arhitektura (Ljubljana), I, 1931 to IV, 1934.
Dom in svet [Home and World] (Ljubljana), I, 1888 to XLV, 1932; I (XLVI), 1933 to V (L), 1936; LI, 1939 to LVI, 1944.
Kronika slovenskih mest [Chronicle of Slovenian Cities] (Ljubljana), I, 1934 to VII, 1940.

Ľviv

Bohdan Čerkes, Martin Kubelik, Elisabeth Hofer (eds.), *Architektura Halyčyny XIX–XX stolit' / Architektura Galicji XIX–XX wjeków / Baukunst in Galizien XIX–XX Jahrhundert*, Ľviv, 1996 (with Ukrainian, Polish, and German contributions).
Jurij Birjul'ov, *Secesja we Lwowie* [Ľviv Jugendstil], Warsaw, 1996.
Peter Fässler, Thomas Held, Dirk Sawitzki (eds.), *Lemberg—Lwów—Lviv. Eine Stadt im Schnittpunkt europäischer Kulturen*, Cologne, Weimar, Vienna, 1995.
Stanisław Łoza, *Architekci i budowniczowie w Polsce* [Architects and Master Builders in Poland], Warsaw, 1954.
Franciszek Mączyński, "Najnowszy Lwow" [The latest Ľviv], in *Architekt* (Kraków), IX, 1908, pp. 91–97.
Mieczysław Orłowicz, *Ilustrowany przewodnik po Lwowie* [Illustrated Guide to Ľviv], Ľviv, Warsaw, 1925.
"Nowy dworzec kolei państwowej we Lwowie" [The New Station of the State Railway in Ľviv], in *Architekt* (Kraków), V, 1904, pp. 101–04.
Zbysław Popławski, *Dzieje Politechniki Lwowskiej 1844–1945* [The History of the Polytechnic in Ľviv, 1844–1945], Wrocław, Warsaw, Kraków, 1992.
Jacek Purchla (ed.), *Die Architektur Lembergs im 19. Jahrhundert*, Kraków, 1997.
Volodymyr Vujtsyk, *Deržavnyj istoryko-architekurnyj zapovidnyk u Ľvovi* [The Conservation of State Monuments in Ľviv], Ľviv, 1991.
Tetjana Trehubova, Roman Mych, *Ľviv. Architekturno-istoryčnyj narys* [Ľviv: An Architectural-Historical Sketch], Kyïv, 1989.
Ihor Žuk, "Architekci secesyjnego Lwowa" [The Jugendstil Architects in Ľviv], in, *Architektura XIX i początku XX wieku* [The Architecture of the Nineteenth and Early Twentieth Centuries], Wrocław, Warsaw, Kraków, 1991, pp. 181–83.

Exhibition Catalogues

Lemberg / Lviv 1772–1918. Wiederbegegnung mit einer Landeshauptstadt der Donaumonarchie, Peter Fässler, Thomas Held, and Dirk Sawitzki (eds.), Museum of History Vienna, Vienna, 1993.

Contemporary Journals and Periodicals

Czasopismo techniczne [Technical Journal] (Lviv), I, 1883, LVI, 1939.

Prague, Brno, and Zlín

L'Architecture d'Aujourd'hui (Boulogne), IV, 1933, no. 5 (L'Architecture moderne en Tchécoslovaquie).
Archithese (Niederteufen, Switzerland), X, 1980, no. 6 (Avantgarde zwischen West und Ost. Tschechoslowakei 1918–1939).
Bauforum (Vienna), XXXIII, 1990, no. 136 (Baťa. Architektur eines Unternehmens).
Ladislav Foltyn, *Slowakische Architektur und die tschechische Avantgarde 1918–1939*, Dresden, 1991.
Fronta [The Façade] (Brno), 1927.
Jan E. Koula, *Nová česká architektura a její vývoj ve XX. století* [New Czech Architecture and its Development in the Twentieth Century], Prague, 1940.
Das kubistische Prag 1909–1925. Ein Stadtführer, Prague, 1995.
Alena Kubova, *L'Avant-garde architecturale en Tchécoslovaquie 1918–1939*, Liège 1992.
Zdeněk Kudělka, *Brněnská architektura 1919–1928* [Architecture in Brno 1919–1928], Brno, 1970.
Pavel Novák, *Zlínská architektura 1900–1950* [Architecture in Zlín 1900–1950], Zlín 1993.
Roman Prahl, Lenka Bydžovská, *Freie Richtungen. Die Zeitschrift der Prager Secession und Moderne*, Prague, 1993.
Jan Sedlák, *Brno v době secese / Brünn in der Epoche der Sezession*, Brno, 1995.
Stavitel [Builder] (Prague), XIV, 1933–34, no. 10–12 (Baťa).
Rostislav Švácha, *The Architecture of New Prague 1895–1945*, Cambridge, Mass., London, 1995.
Karel Teige, *L'architecture moderne en Tchécoslovaquie*, Prague, 1947 (English edition, *Modern Architecture in Czechoslovakia*).
Stephan Templ, Michal Kohout, Vladimír Šlapeta (ed.), *Prag. Architektur des XX. Jahrhunderts*, Prague, Vienna, 1996.
Jindřich Vybíral, *Počátky moderní architektury na Moravě a ve Slezsku* [The Beginnings of Modern Architecture in Moravia and Silesia], Olomouc, 1981.
Zlínský funkcionalismus / Funktionalismus von Zlín, Zlín, 1993.

Exhibition Catalogues

Jaroslav Anděl, Carmen Alborch (eds.), *The Art of the Avant-Garde in Czechoslovakia 1918–1938*, IVAM Centre Julio González, Valencia, 1993.
Jaroslav Anděl, Emmanuel Starcky (eds.), *Prague 1900–1938. Capitale secrète des avant-gardes*, Musée des Beaux-Arts, Dijon, 1997.
Susanne Anna (ed.), *Das Bauhaus im Osten. Slowakische und Tschechische Avantgarde 1928–1939*, Ostfildern-Ruit, 1997.
Jiný dům. Německá a rakouská architektura v letech 1890–1938 na Moravě a ve Slezsku / Das andere Haus. Die Deutsche und die österreichische Architektur in Mähren und Schlesien in den Jahren 1890–1938, Národní galerie v Praze, Prague, 1993.
Zdenek Primus (ed.), *Tschechische Avantgarde 1922–1940. Reflexe europäischer Kunst und Fotografie in der Buchgestaltung*, Kunstverein Hamburg, 1990.
Vladimír Šlapeta, *Die Brünner Funktionalisten. Moderne Architektur in Brünn (Brno)*, Innsbruck, 1985.
Vladimír Šlapeta, *Czech Functionalism 1918–1938*, Architectural Association, London, 1987.
Vladimír Šlapeta, *Baťa. Architecture and Urbanism 1910–1950*, The State Gallery in Zlín, Zlín, 1992.
František Smejkal, Rostislav Švácha (eds.), *Devětsil. Czech Avant-Garde Art Architecture and Design of the 1920s and 30s*, Museum of Modern Art, Oxford, Design Museum, London, 1990.
Jiří Švestka, Tomáš Vlček (eds.), *1909–1925 Kubismus in Prag. Malerei, Skulptur, Kunstgewerbe, Architektur*, Kunstverein für die Rheinlande und Westfalen, Düsseldorf, Stuttgart, 1991.
Tschechische Kunst der 20er und 30er Jahre. Avantgarde und Tradition, Mathildenhöhe, Darmstadt, 1989.

Alexander von Vegesack (ed.), *Tschechischer Kubismus 1910–1925. Architektur und Design*, Vitra Design Museum, Weil am Rhein, 1991.
Alena Vondrová (ed.) *Český funkcionalismus 1920–1940* [Czech Functionalism 1920–1940], 3 vols., Moravská Galerie v Brně—Uměleckoprůmyslové muzeum v Praze, Prague, Brno, 1978.

Contemporary Journals and Periodicals

Architektoniký obzor [Architectural Horizon] (Prague), I, 1902 to XX, 1921.
Disk (Brno, Prague), 1923, no. 1 to 1925, no. 2.
Forum (Bratislava), I, 1931 to VIII, 1938.
Horizont (Brno), 1927, no. 1, 1931, nos. 37–38 [undated].
Index (Brno, Olomouc), I, 1929 to XI, 1939.
Levá fronta [The Left Façade] (Prague), I, 1930 to III, 1933.
Musaion (Prague), 1920–31.
Pásmo [Zone] (Brno), I, 1924 to II, 1926.
ReD (Revue Devětsilu [Devětsil Review]) (Prague), I, 1927–28 to III, 1929–31.
Stavba [The Building] (Prague), I, 1922 to XIV, 1937–38.
Stavitel [Builder] (Prague), I, 1919–20 to XVI, 1937–38.
Styl [Style] (Prague), I, 1908–09 to V, 1913; I (VI), 1920–21 to XVI (XXI), 1938.
Technický obzor [Technical Horizon] (Prague), I, 1893 to LVIII, 1958.
Umělecký měsíčník [Artistic Monthly] (Prague), I, 1911–12 to III, 1913.
Volné směry [Free Directions] (Prague), I, 1897 to XLVI, 1949.
Zprávy spolku architeků a inženýrů v Království Českém [Bulletin of the Association of Architects and Engineers in the Czech Crownland] (Prague), I, 1866 to XLIV, 1910 (XXXVI, 1902 to XLIV, 1910 equivalent to I–IX of *Architektonický obzor* [Architectural Horizon] and X to XVIII of *Technický obzor* [Technical Horizon]).
Život [Life] (Prague), I, 1921 to XXI, 1948.

Timişoara

Josef Geml, *Alt-Temesvar im letzten Halbjahrhundert. 1870–1920*, Timişoara, 1927.
Mihai Opriş, *Timişoara. Mică monografie urbanistică* [Timişoara: A Brief City Monograph], Bucharest, 1987.
Ileana Pintilie, "Vienna, Budapesta şi Timişoara—raportul dintre centru şi periferie în anii 'întemeierii,' premisă a răspândirii 'stilului 1900'" [Vienna, Budapest, and Timişoara—the Relationship between Center and Periphery in the Gründerzeit Years, a Premise for the Spread of the "1900 Style," in *Analele Banatului*, vol. *Arta* [Annals of the Banat, vol. Fine Arts] (Timişoara), II, 1997, pp. 33–49.
Hans H. Rieser, *Temesvar*, Sigmaringen, 1992.

Vienna

Friedrich Achleitner, *Wiener Architektur. Zwischen typologischem Fatalismus und semantischem Schlamassel*, Vienna, Cologne, Weimar, 1996.
Eve Blau, *The Architecture of Red Vienna 1919–1934*, Cambridge, Mass., London, 1999.
Ernst Bruckmüller, *Nation Österreich. Kulturelles Bewußtsein und gesellschaftlich-politische Prozesse*, Vienna, Cologne, Graz, 1996 (2nd edition).
Hermann Czech, *Zur Abwechslung. Ausgewählte Schriften zur Architektur*, Vienna, 1977 (new edition, 1996).
Franco Borsi, Ezio Godoli, *Wiener Bauten der Jahrhundertwende. Die Architektur der habsburgischen Metropole zwischen Historismus und Moderne*, Stuttgart, 1985.
Astrid Gmeiner, Gottfried Pirhofer, *Der Österreichische Werkbund*, Salzburg, Vienna, 1985 (among other contributions to the Czech and Hungarian Werkbund).
Helmut Gruber, *Red Vienna: Experiment in Working-Class Culture, 1919–1934*, New York, 1991.
William M. Johnston, *Österreichische Kultur- und Geistesgeschichte. Gesellschaft und Ideen im Donauraum 1948–1938*, Vienna, Cologne, Weimar, 1974.
Karl and Eva Mang (eds.) *Wiener Architektur 1860–1930 in Zeichnungen*, Stuttgart, 1979.
Maria Marchetti (ed.), *Vienna um 1900. Kunst und Kultur*, Vienna, Munich, 1985.
Neubauten in Vienna, Prag, Budapest, Vienna, 1904.
Das Neue Wien, 4 vols., Vienna, 1926–28.
Klaus Novy, Wolfgang Förster, *Einfach bauen. Genossenschaftliche Selbsthilfe nach der Jahrhundertwende. Zur Rekonstruktion der Wiener Siedlerbewegung*, Vienna, 1985.

Österreichischer Ingenieur- und Architekten-Verein (ed.) *Wien am Anfang des 20. Jahrhunderts. Ein Führer in technischer und künstlerischer Richtung*, 2 vols., Vienna, 1905–06.

Wilfried Posch, *Die Wiener Gartenstadtbewegung. Reformversuch zwischen erster und zweiter Gründerzeit*, Vienna, 1981.

Ursula Prokop, *Wien. Aufbruch zur Moderne, Geschäfts- und Wohnhäuser der Innenstadt 1910 bis 1914*, Vienna, Cologne, Weimar, 1994.

Maria Rennhofer, *Kunstzeitschriften der Jahrhundertwende in Deutschland und Österreich 1895–1914*, Vienna, Munich, 1987.

Carl E. Schorske, *Wien. Geist und Gesellschaft im Fin-de-siècle*, Frankfurt am Main. 1982.

Renate Schweitzer, *Der staatlich geförderte, der kommunale und der gemeinnützige Wohnungs- und Siedlungsbau in Österreich bis 1945*, 2 vols., Phil. Diss., Technische Universität Wien, Vienna, 1972.

Manfredo Tafuri, *Vienna Rossa. La politica residenziale nella Vienna socialista 1919–1933*, Milan, 1980, 2nd edition 1995.

Helmut Weihsmann, *Das Rote Wien. Sozialdemokratische Architektur und Kommunalpolitik 1919–1934*, Vienna, 1985.

Wiener Neubauten im Style der Secession, Vienna, 1902 (1st series), 1904 (2nd series).

Wiener Neubauten im Style der Secession und anderen modernen Stylarten, Vienna, 1906 (3rd series), 1908 (4th series), undated (5th series).

Exhibition Catalogues

Werner Hofmann (ed.) *Experiment Weltuntergang. Wien um 1900*, Kunsthalle Hamburg, 1981.

Traum und Wirklichkeit. Wien 1870–1930, Historisches Museum der Stadt Vienna, Künstlerhaus, Vienna, 1985.

Das Zeitalter Kaiser Franz Josephs, 2 vols., Schloß Grafenegg, 1987.

Contemporary Journals and Periodicals

Allgemeine Bauzeitung (Vienna), I, 1836, LXXXIII, 1918.

Der Architekt (Vienna), I, 1895, XXIV, 1921–22 (supplementary volumes 1–6, 1895–1901, *Aus der Wagner-Schule*).

Architektonische Monatshefte (Stuttgart), VI, 1900, IX, 1903.

Der Architektur des XX. Jahrhunderts (Berlin), I, 1901, XIV, 1914.

Der Aufbau (Vienna), I, 1926.

Die Bau- und Werkkunst (Vienna), IV, 1927–28, VIII, 1932 (see *Profil*).

Hohe Warte (Vienna, Leipzig), I, 1904–05, IV, 1908.

Kunst und Kunsthandwerk (Vienna), I, 1898, XXIV, 1924.

Neubauten und Concurrenzen (Vienna), IV, 1898, V, 1899 (see *Architektonische Monatshefte*).

Neubauten und Concurrenzen in Österreich und Ungarn (Vienna), I, 1895, III, 1897 (see *Neubauten und Concurrenzen*).

Österreichs Bau- und Werkkunst (Vienna), I, 1924–25, III, 1926–27 (see *Die Bau- und Werkkunst*).

Österreichische Bauzeitung (Vienna), I, 1925, XI, 1935, I (XII), 1936, III (XIV), 1938.

Profil (Vienna), I, 1933, IV, 1936.

Zeitschrift des Österreichischen Ingenieur- und Architekten-Vereines (Vienna), I, 1848, XC, 1938.

Zagreb

Alfred Albini, "Uslovi razvitka nove arhitekture" [Conditions for the Development of Modern Architecture], in *Narodna republika Hrvatska, Informativni priručnik* [The People's Republic of Yugoslavia: An Information Handbook], Zagreb 1953, pp. 300–08.

Arhitektura (Zagreb), XXX, 1976, nos. 156–57 [Inter-war Architecture in Zagreb, contributions by Tomislav Prmerl and others].

Arhitektura (Zagreb), XL, 1987, nos. 1–4 / 200–03 [Inter-war Architecture in Zagreb, contributions by Aleksander Laslo and others].

Damir Barbarić, Michael Benedikt (eds.), *Ambivalenz des fin de siècle: Wien–Zagreb*, Vienna, Cologne, Weimar, 1998.

Lelja Dobronić, *Graditelji i izgradnja Zagreba u doba historijskih stilova* [Architects and Building in Zagreb During the Historicist Period], Zagreb, 1983.

Stjepan Gomboš, "Moderna arhitektura u Hrvatskoj" [Modern Architecture in Croatia], in *Jugoslavija* (Belgrade), XI, 1955, pp. 102–07.

Stjepan Hribar, "Razvitak grada Zagreba 1919–1929" [The Development of Zagreb 1919–1929], in Rajko Kušević (ed.), *Jugoslavija na tehničkom polju 1919–1929* [Yugoslavia and Technology 1919–1929], Zagreb, 1930, pp. 239–45.

L. Ilitch [Ljubomir Ilić] "L'Architecture en Yougoslavie," in *L'Architecture d'Aujourd'hui* (Boulogne), IV, 1933, no. 6, pp. 41–55.

Snješka Knežević, *Zagrebačka zelena potkova* [The Green Horseshoe of Zagreb], Zagreb, 1996.

Aleksander Laslo, "Internacionalni natječaj za generalnu regulatornu osnovu grada Zagreba 1930/31" [The International Competition for the General Regulatory Plan of the City of Zagreb 1930/1931], in *Čovjek i prostor* [Man and Space] (Zagreb), XXXI, 1984, no. 1 / 370, pp. 25–31.

Aleksander Laslo, "Die Loos-Schule in Kroatien," in *Adolf Loos*, exh. cat. Graphische Sammlung Albertina, Historisches Museum der Stadt Wien, Vienna, 1989, pp. 307–27.

Aleksander Laslo, "Arhitektura modernog građanskog Zagreba" [The Architecture of the Modern Movement in Zagreb], in *Život umjetnosti* [The Life of Art] (Zagreb), XXX, 1995, nos. 56–57, pp. 58–71 (including a short English summary).

Darja Radović Mahečić, Sanja Štok, "Presedan zagrebačkog urbanizma. Međunarodni natječaj za generalnu regulatornu osnovu grada Zagreba 1930/31" [A Precedent of Zagreb Urbanism: The International Competition for the General Regulatory Plan of the City of Zagreb 1930/31], in *Život umjetnosti* [The Life of Art] (Zagreb), XXXII, 1997, no. 59, pp. 10–27 (including a short English summary).

Andre Mohorovičić, "Analiza historijsko-urbanističkog razvoja grada Zagreba" [Analysis of the Historical and Urbanistic Development of the City of Zagreb], in *Rad JAZU* [Work of the South Slav Academy of Arts and Sciences], vol. 287, Zagreb, 1952, pp. 27–51.

Stjepan Planić, *Problemi savremene arhitekture* [Problems in Contemporary Architecture], Zagreb, 1932 (annotated new edition, Zagreb, 1996).

Stjepan Planić, "50 godine arhitekture u Hrvatskoj" [50 Years of Architecture in Croatia], in *Književnik* [The Writer] (Zagreb), XII, 1939, no. 2, pp. 49–64.

Vladimir Potočnjak, "Arhitektura u Hrvatskoj 1888–1938" [Architecture in Croatia 1888–1938], in *Građevinski vjesnik* [Architectural Messenger] (Zagreb), VIII, 1939, no. 4-5, pp. 49-79.

Tomislav Prmerl, *Hrvatska moderna arhitektura između dva rata. Nova tradicija* [Modern Croatian Achitecture in the Inter-war Years: A New Tradition], Zagreb, 1989, 2nd edition, 1990 (with extensive bibliography).

Branko Siladin, "Novakova ulica, Zagreb. Primjer hrvatske moderne—Arheologija ili uzor? / Novak Street, Zagreb: A Sample of Croatian Modernism—Archaeology or Example?" in *Piranesi* (Ljubljana), IV, 1995, nos. 5–6, pp. 6–34.

Neven Šegvić, "Prilog razumijevanju razvitka moderne arhitekture" [A Contribution to the Understanding of the Development of Modern Architecture], in *Hrvatsko kolo* [The Croatian Round] (Zagreb), XXVII, 1946, pp. 294–310.

Neven Šegvić, "Arhitektonska 'Moderna' u Hrvatskoj" [The Architectonic Modern in Croatia], in *Republika* (Zagreb), VIII, 1952, no. 3, pp. 179-85.

Tomislav Timet, *Stambena izgradnja Zagreba do 1954. godine* [Apartment Building in Zagreb till 1954], Zagreb, 1961.

Zvonimir Vrkljan, *Sjećanja* [Memories], Zagreb, 1995.

Exhibition Catalogues

Arhitektura secesije u Rijeci. Arhitektura i urbanizam početka 20. stoljeća 1900–1925 / Secessional Architecture in Rijeka: Architecture and Town Planning at the Beginning of the 20th Century 1900–1925, 2 vols., Moderna galerija Rijeka, Rijeka, 1997 (contributions in Croatian and English).

Moderna arhitektura Rijeke. Arhitektura i urbanizam međuratne Rijeke 1918–1945 / L'Architettura e urbanistica a Fiume nel periodo fra le due guerre 1918–1945, Moderna galerija Rijeka, Rijeka, 1996 (contributions in Croatian and English).

Zagrebačka moderna arhitektura između dva [Modern Architecture in Zagreb Between the Wars], Muzej grada Zagreba, Zagreb, 1976.

Contemporary Journals and Periodicals

Arhitektura (Zagreb), I, 1931 to IV, 1934.

Građevinski vjesnik [Architectural Messenger] (Zagreb), I, 1932 to X, 1941

Svijet [The World] (Zagreb), I, 1926 to XIV, 1939.

Viesti Društva inžinira i arhiteka u Hrvatskoj i Slavoniji [Bulletin of the Engineers' and Architects' Union of Croatia and Slovenia] (Zagreb), I, 1880 to XXXIX, 1918 (numerous variations in title).

Zenit (Zagreb, Belgrade), I, 1921 to VI, 1926.

Život [Life] (Zagreb), I, 1900 to II, 1900.

List of Abbreviations

Albertina Vienna:	Graphische Sammlung der Albertina, Vienna
AM Ljubljana:	Arhitekturni muzej, Ljubljana – Architecture Museum, Ljubljana
AM Timişoara:	Arhiva municipiului, Timişoara – Archives of the City of Timişoara
AOV Prague 1:	Archív Odboru výstavby Obvodního úřadu Praha 1 – Archives of the Office of Public Works, Prague 1
AP Kraków:	Archiwum Państwowe w Krakowie – State Archives, Kraków
AUR Prague:	Archív Útvaru rozvoje hlavního města Prahy – Archives of the City Development Authorities, Prague
BKMÖL Kecskemét:	Bács-Kiskun Megyei Önkormányzat Levéltára, Kecskemét – Local Archives Bács-Kiskun, Kecskemét
Budapesti Történeti Múzeum:	Historical Museum of the City of Budapest (formerly Kiscelli-Museum)
CCA Montréal:	Canadian Centre for Architecture, Montréal
DA Zagreb:	Državni arhiv u Zagrebu, Zbirka građevinske dokumentacie – State Archives in Zagreb, Collection of Architectural Documentation
DALO Ľviv:	Deržavnyj archiv Ľvivs'koï oblasti – State Archives of the Region of Ľviv
DAM Frankfurt am Main:	Deutsches Architektur–Museum, Frankfurt am Main
Getty Los Angeles:	The Getty Research Institute, Los Angeles
gta Zürich:	Institut für Geschichte und Theorie der Architektur (gta) ETH Zürich
HMA Zagreb:	Hrvatski muzej arhitekture, Zagreb – Croatian Architecture Museum, Zagreb
HM Vienna:	Historisches Museum der Stadt Wien
IC Reading:	Isotype Collection, Department of Typography & Graphic Communication, The University of Reading, England
IISH Amsterdam:	Sammlung, Internationaal Instituut voor Sociale Geschiedenis, Amsterdam
JPM Pécs:	Janus Pannonius Múzeum, Pécs
Kunstbibliothek Berlin:	Kunstbibliothek Berlin, Staatliche Museen zu Berlin – Preußischer Kulturbesitz, Kulturforum
LIM Ľviv:	Ľvivs'kyj istoryčnyj muzej – Historical Museum, Ľviv
MA 37 Vienna:	MA 37, Baupolizei, Wien
MB Timişoara	Muzeul Banatului, Timişoara – Banat Museum, Timişoara
MEM Budapest:	Magyar Építészeti Múzeum, Budapest – Hungarian Architecture Museum, Budapest
MGZ Zagreb:	Muzej Grada Zagreba – Museum of the City of Zagreb
MH Kraków:	Muzeum Historyczne miasta Krakowa – Historical Museum of the City of Kraków
MKRH Zagreb:	Ministarstvo kulture Republike Hrvatske, Uprava za zaštitu kulturne baštine, Zagreb – Culture Ministry of the Republic of Croatia, Administration for the Preservation of Cultural Heritage, Zagreb
MMB Brno:	Muzeum města Brna – Museum of the City of Brno
MUJ Kraków:	Muzeum Uniwersytetu Jagiellońskiego, Kraków – Museum of the Jagiellonian University, Kraków
MVČ Hradec Králové:	Muzeum východních Čech, Hradec Králové – Museum of Eastern Bohemia, Hradec Králové
NG Prague:	Národní galerie v Praze – National Gallery, Prague
NTM Prague:	Národní technické muzeum v Praze, Archív architektury – National Technical Museum, Prague, Architectural Archives
OMVH Budapest:	Országos Műemlék Védelmi Hivatal, Budapest – State Offices for the Preservation of Monuments, Budapest
PNP Prague:	Památník národního písemnictví v Praze – National Literature Memorial, Prague
SOA Zlín:	Státní okresní archív, Zlín – State Archives, Zlín
TU Vienna:	Institut für Städtebau und Raumplanung, Technische Universität, Vienna
TU Vienna, Archives:	Archiv der Technischen Universität, Vienna
UAK Vienna:	Sammlung, Universität für angewandte Kunst, Vienna
ÚDU AVČR Prague:	Ústav dějin umění Akademie věd České republiky, Praha – Art Historical Institute of the Academy of Sciences of the Czech Republic, Prague
UPM Prague:	Uměleckoprůmyslové muzeum v Praze – Arts and Crafts Museum, Prague
WSTLA Vienna:	Wiener Stadt- und Landesarchiv
ZAL Ljubljana:	Zgodovinski arhiv Ljubljane – Historical Archives, Ljubljana

Index